Story by **KookHwa Huh**
Art by **SuJin Kim**

2

pig bride

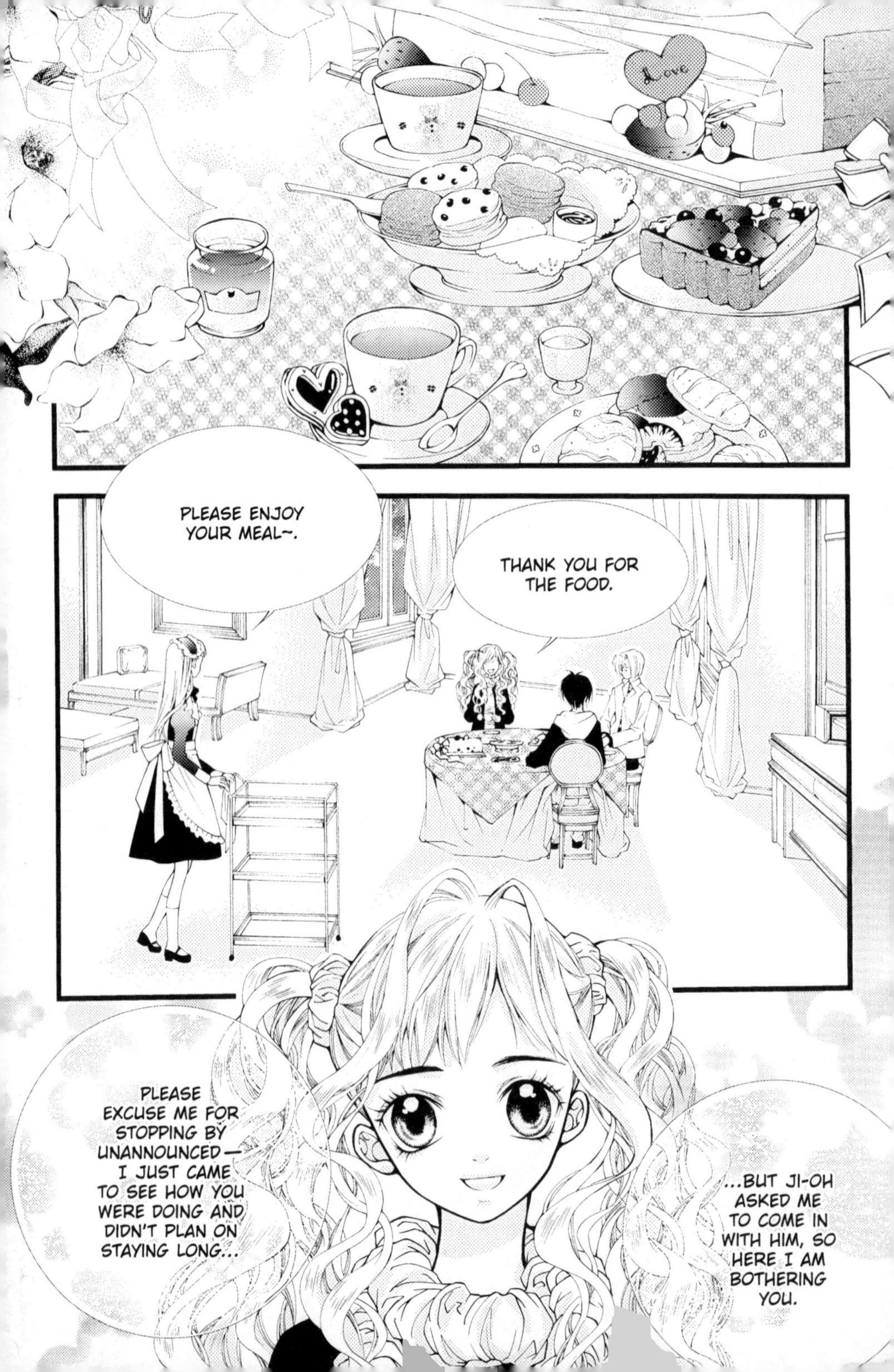
Love
PLEASE ENJOY YOUR MEAL~.
THANK YOU FOR THE FOOD.
PLEASE EXCUSE ME FOR STOPPING BY UNANNOUNCED—I JUST CAME TO SEE HOW YOU WERE DOING AND DIDN'T PLAN ON STAYING LONG...
...BUT JI-OH ASKED ME TO COME IN WITH HIM, SO HERE I AM BOTHERING YOU.

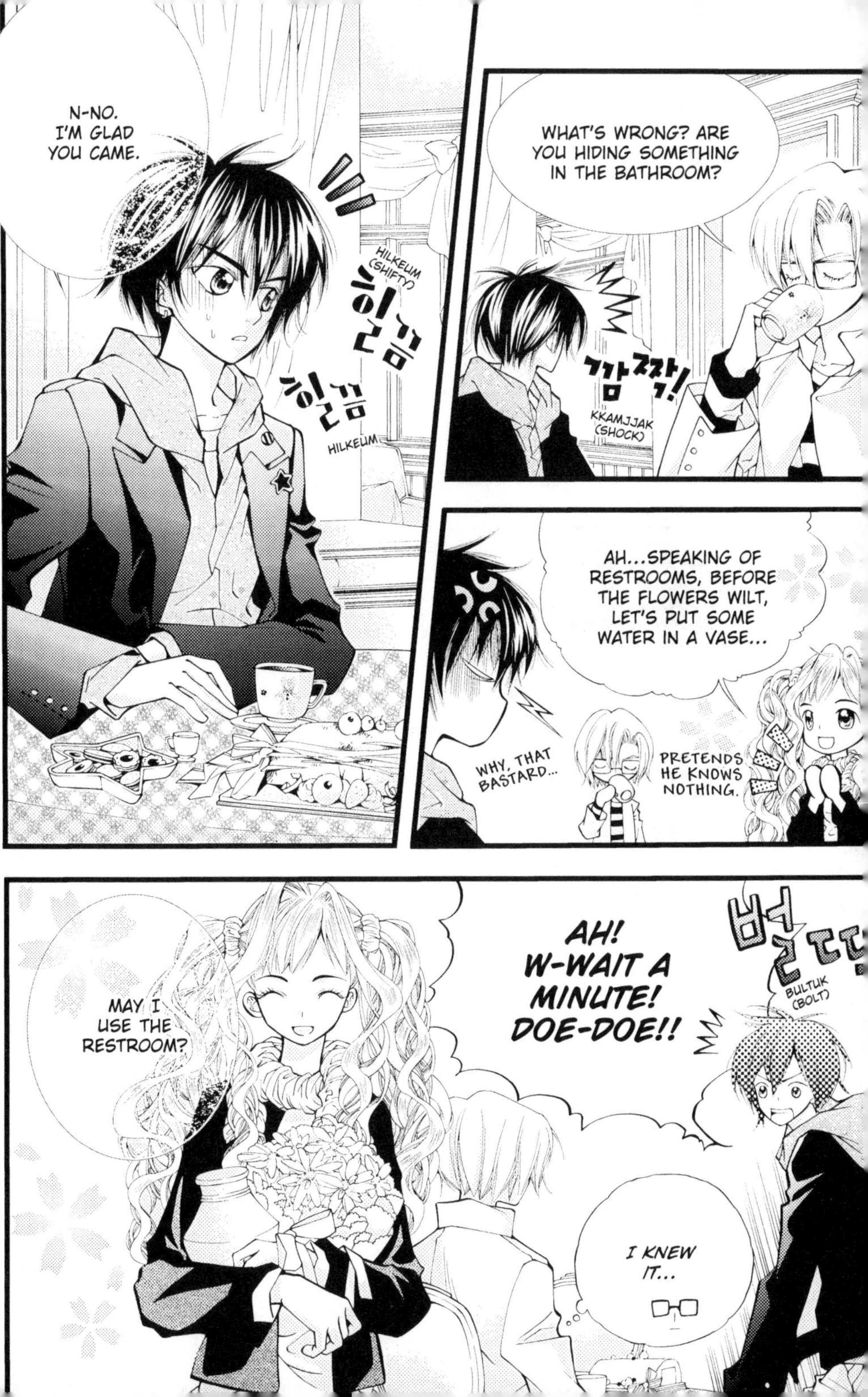
N-NO. I'M GLAD YOU CAME.
HILKEUM (SHIFTY)
힐끔
힐끔
HILKEUM
WHAT'S WRONG? ARE YOU HIDING SOMETHING IN THE BATHROOM?
깜짝!
KKAMJJAK (SHOCK)
AH...SPEAKING OF RESTROOMS, BEFORE THE FLOWERS WILT, LET'S PUT SOME WATER IN A VASE...
WHY, THAT BASTARD...
PRETENDS HE KNOWS NOTHING.
MAY I USE THE RESTROOM?
AH! W-WAIT A MINUTE! DOE-DOE!!
BULTUK (BOLT)
I KNEW IT...

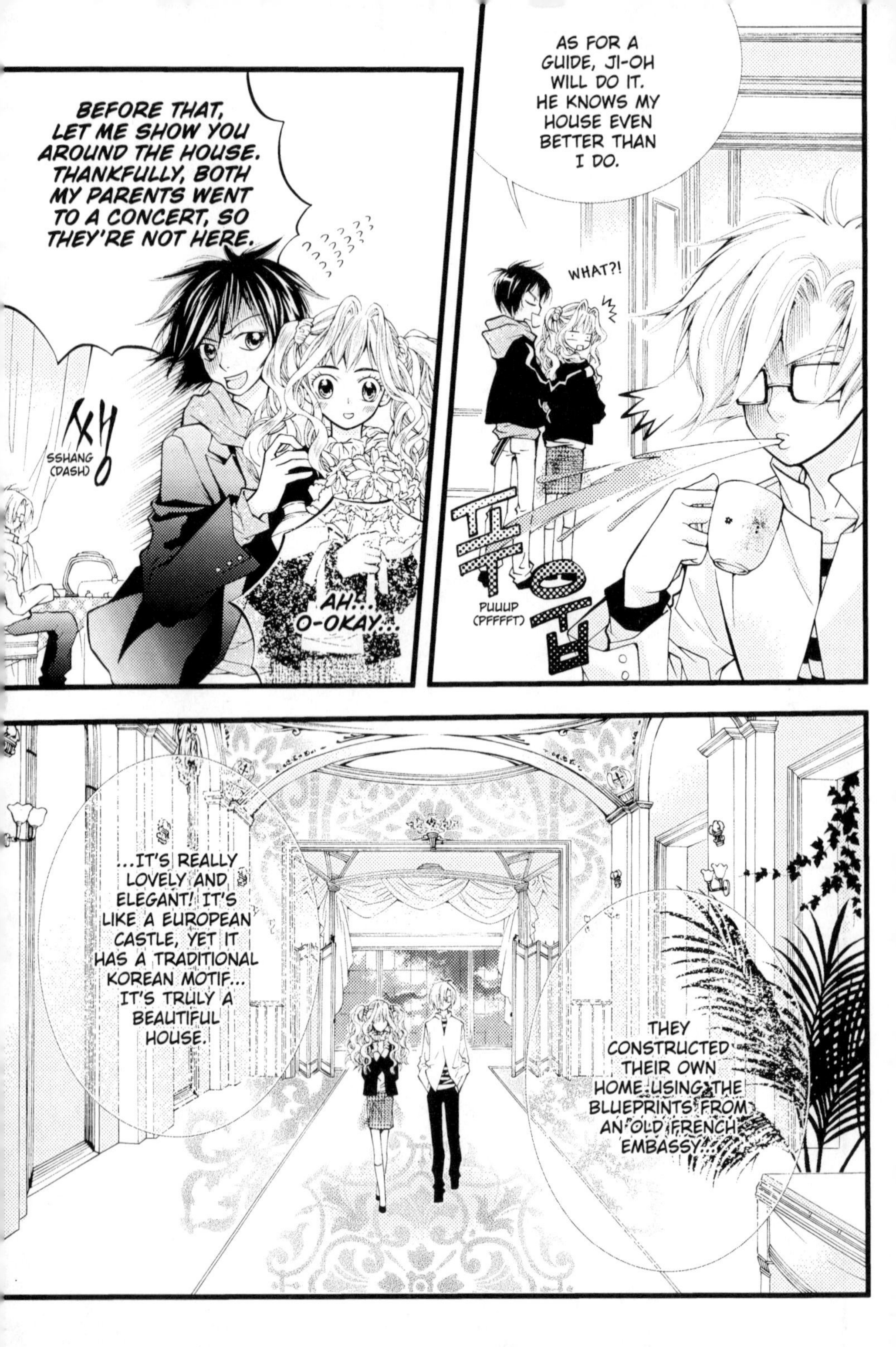
BEFORE THAT, LET ME SHOW YOU AROUND THE HOUSE. THANKFULLY, BOTH MY PARENTS WENT TO A CONCERT, SO THEY'RE NOT HERE.
SSHANG (DASH)
AH... O-OKAY...
AS FOR A GUIDE, JI-OH WILL DO IT. HE KNOWS MY HOUSE EVEN BETTER THAN I DO.
WHAT?!
PUUUP (PFFFFT)
...IT'S REALLY LOVELY AND ELEGANT! IT'S LIKE A EUROPEAN CASTLE, YET IT HAS A TRADITIONAL KOREAN MOTIF... IT'S TRULY A BEAUTIFUL HOUSE.
THEY CONSTRUCTED THEIR OWN HOME USING THE BLUEPRINTS FROM AN OLD FRENCH EMBASSY.

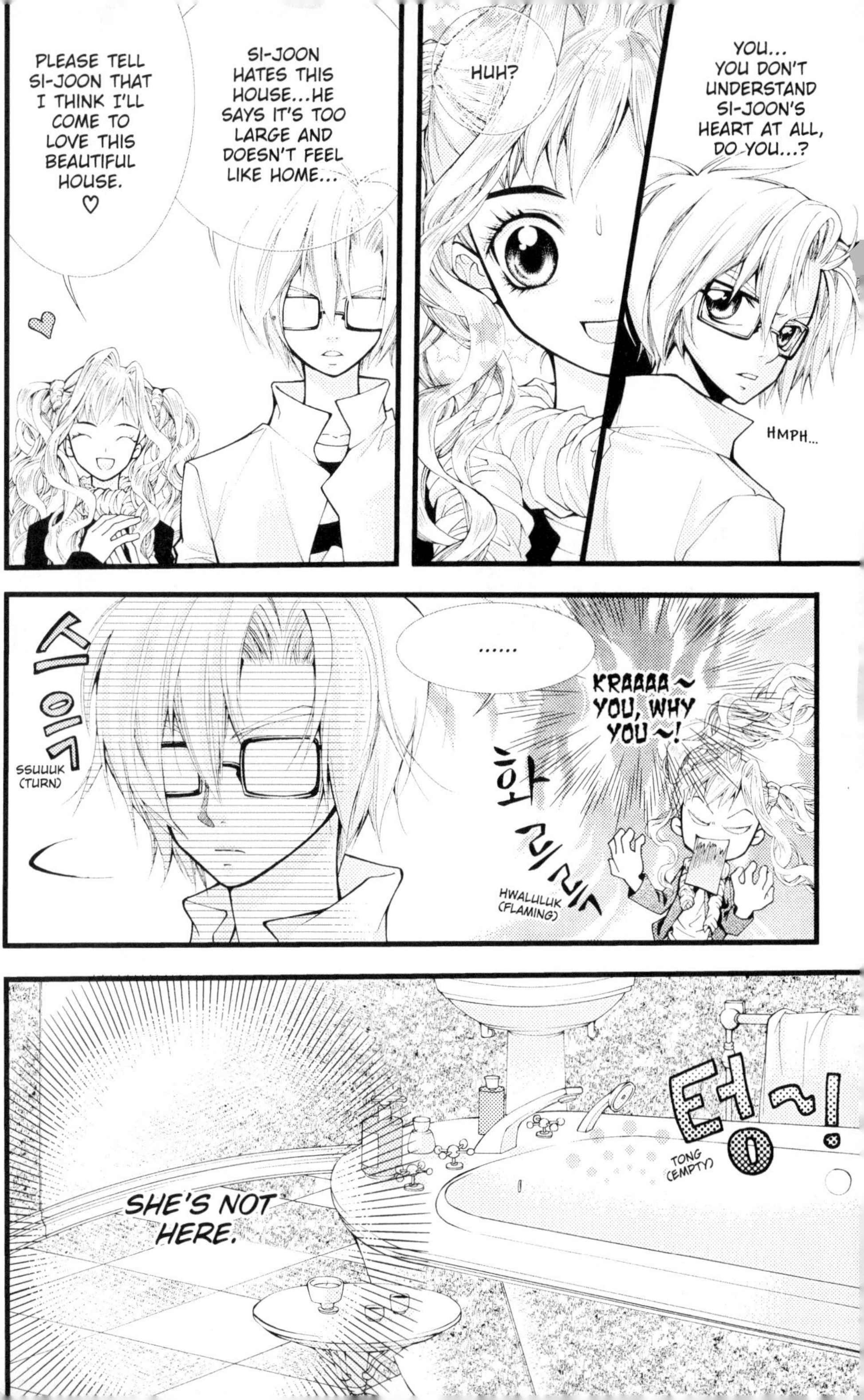
PLEASE TELL SI-JOON THAT I THINK I'LL COME TO LOVE THIS BEAUTIFUL HOUSE. ♡
SI-JOON HATES THIS HOUSE...HE SAYS IT'S TOO LARGE AND DOESN'T FEEL LIKE HOME...
HUH?
YOU... YOU DON'T UNDERSTAND SI-JOON'S HEART AT ALL, DO YOU...?
HMPH...
스으윽
SSUUUK (TURN)
......
KRAAAA~ YOU, WHY YOU~!
화르르르
HWALULUK (FLAMING)
SHE'S NOT HERE.
텅~!
TONG (EMPTY)

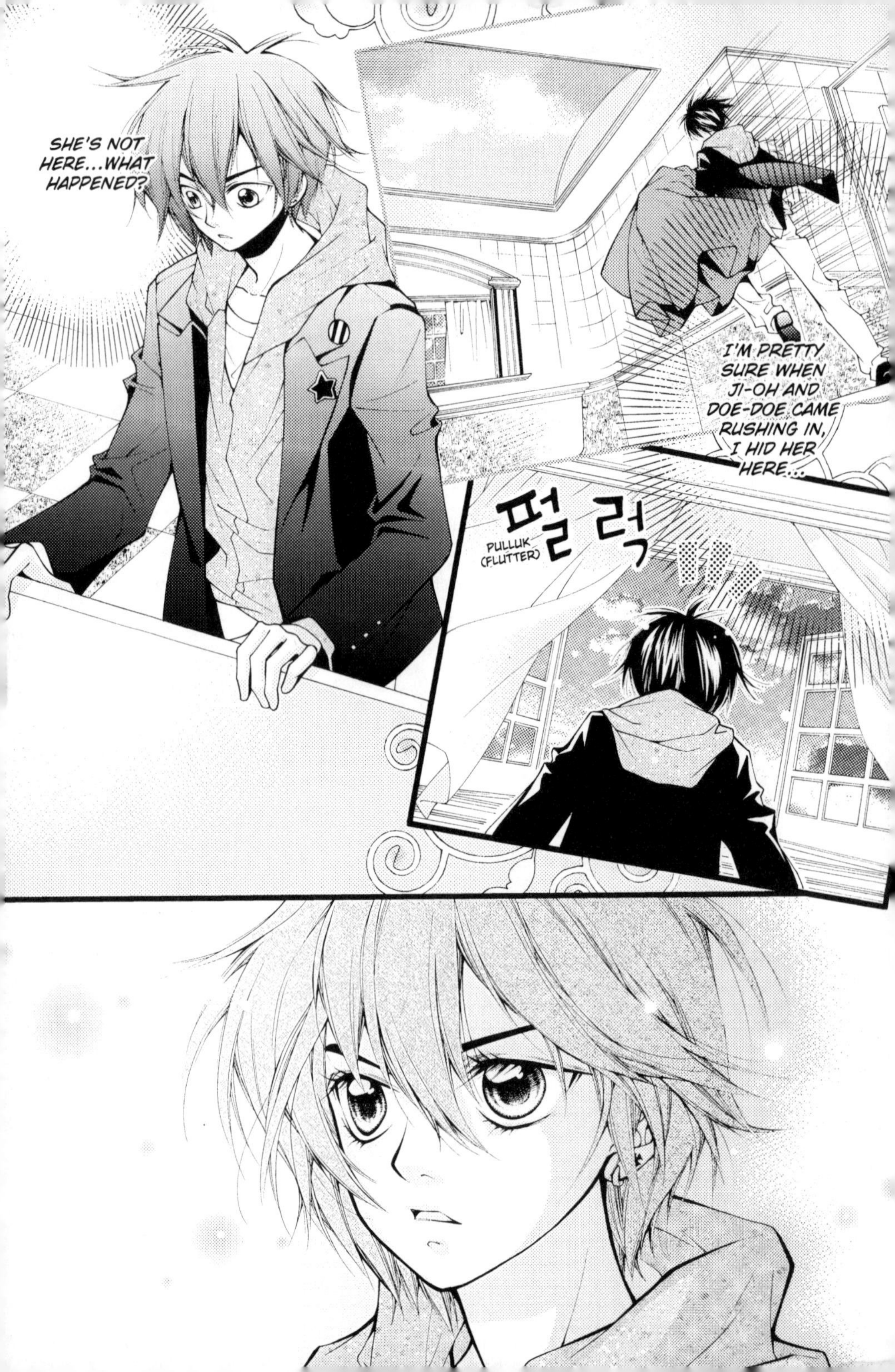
SHE'S NOT HERE...WHAT HAPPENED?
I'M PRETTY SURE WHEN JI-OH AND DOE-DOE CAME RUSHING IN, I HID HER HERE...
펄럭
PULLUK (FLUTTER)

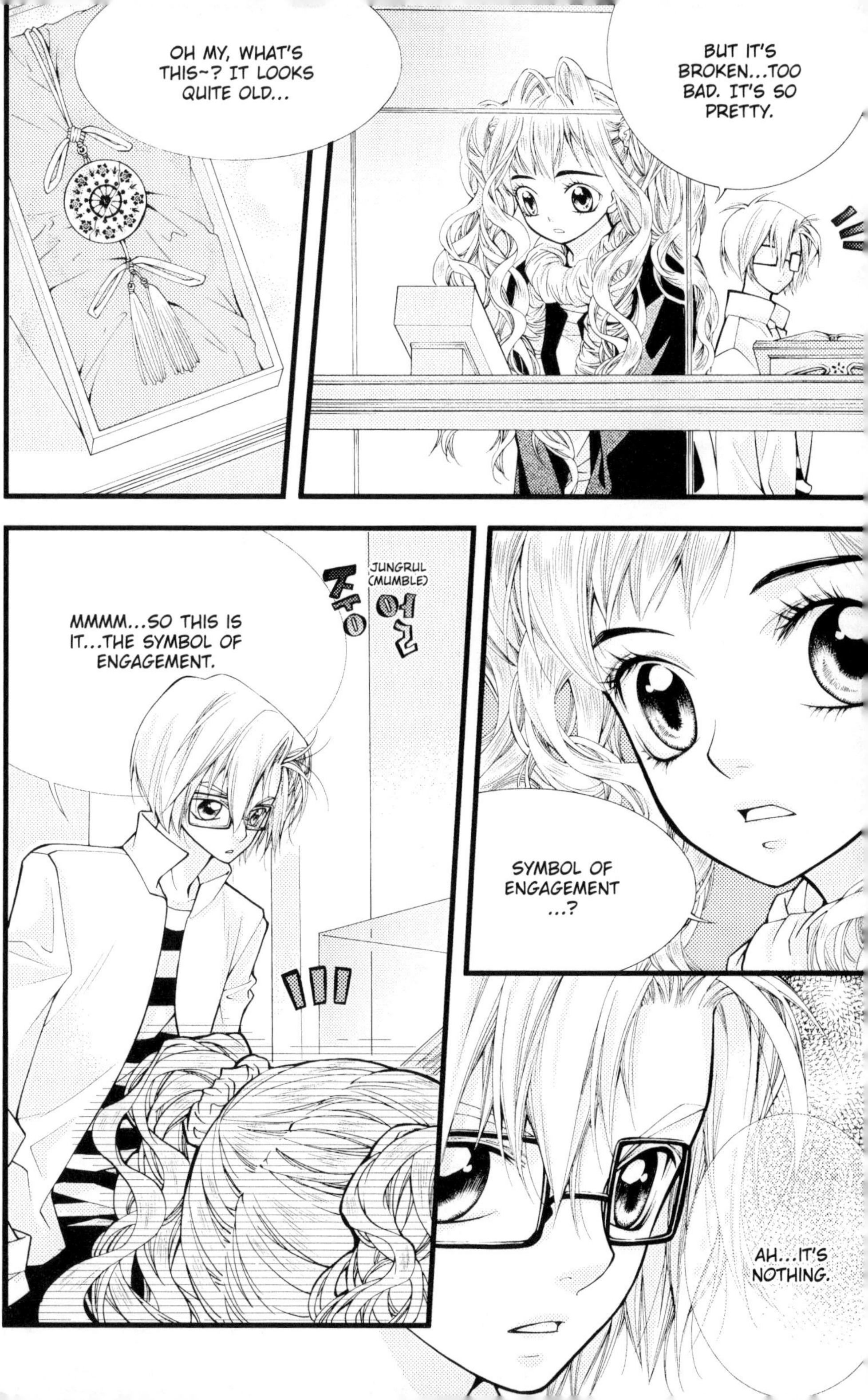
OH MY, WHAT'S THIS~? IT LOOKS QUITE OLD...
BUT IT'S BROKEN...TOO BAD. IT'S SO PRETTY.
MMMM...SO THIS IS IT...THE SYMBOL OF ENGAGEMENT.
JUNGRUL (MUMBLE)
SYMBOL OF ENGAGEMENT ...?
AH...IT'S NOTHING.

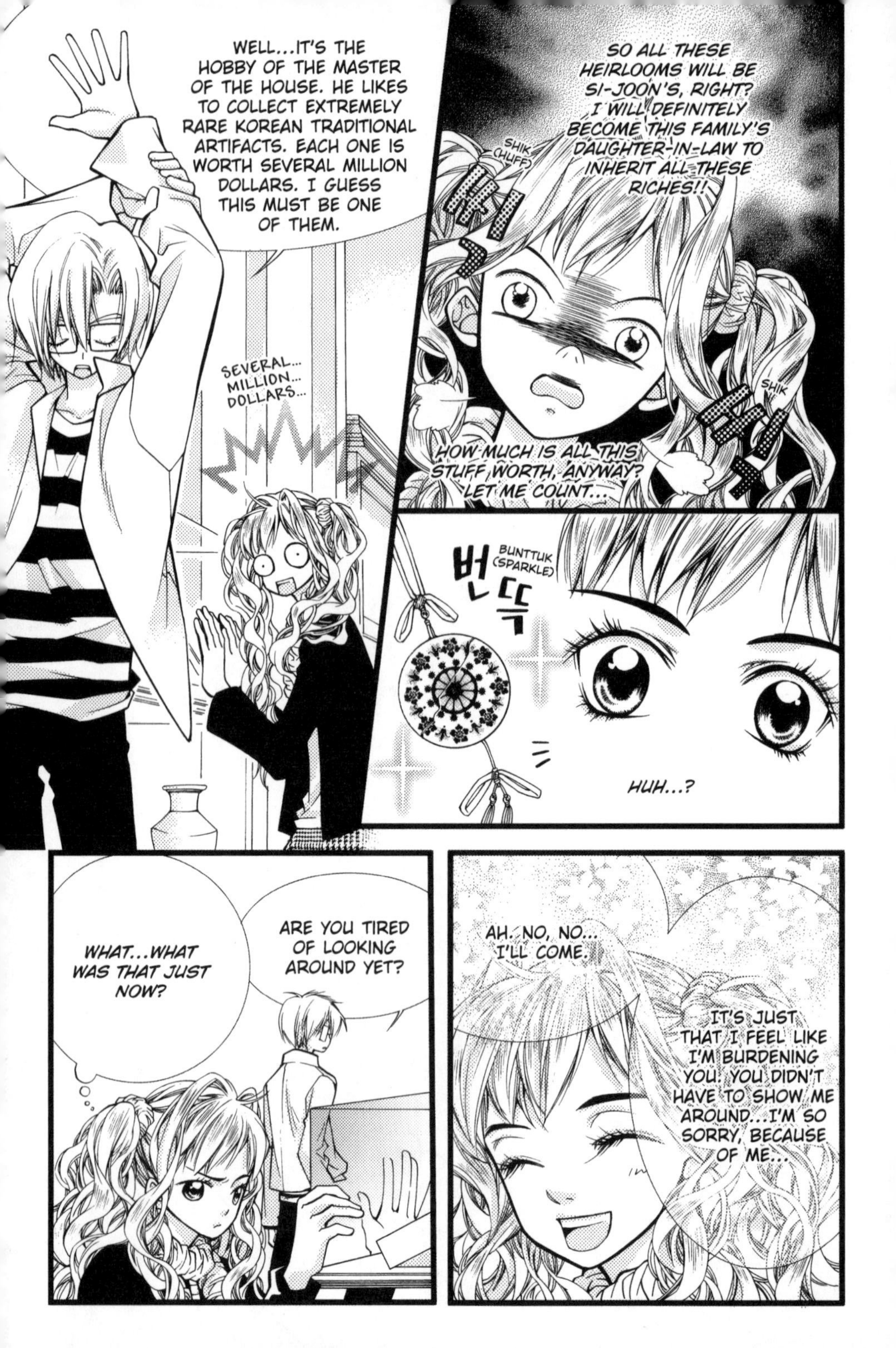
WELL...IT'S THE HOBBY OF THE MASTER OF THE HOUSE. HE LIKES TO COLLECT EXTREMELY RARE KOREAN TRADITIONAL ARTIFACTS. EACH ONE IS WORTH SEVERAL MILLION DOLLARS. I GUESS THIS MUST BE ONE OF THEM.
SEVERAL... MILLION... DOLLARS...
SO ALL THESE HEIRLOOMS WILL BE SI-JOON'S, RIGHT? I WILL DEFINITELY BECOME THIS FAMILY'S DAUGHTER-IN-LAW TO INHERIT ALL THESE RICHES!!
SHIK (HUFF)
씩
SHIK
씩
HOW MUCH IS ALL THIS STUFF WORTH, ANYWAY? LET ME COUNT...
번뜩
BUNTTUK (SPARKLE)
HUH...?
WHAT...WHAT WAS THAT JUST NOW?
ARE YOU TIRED OF LOOKING AROUND YET?
AH. NO, NO... I'LL COME.
IT'S JUST THAT I FEEL LIKE I'M BURDENING YOU. YOU DIDN'T HAVE TO SHOW ME AROUND...I'M SO SORRY, BECAUSE OF ME...

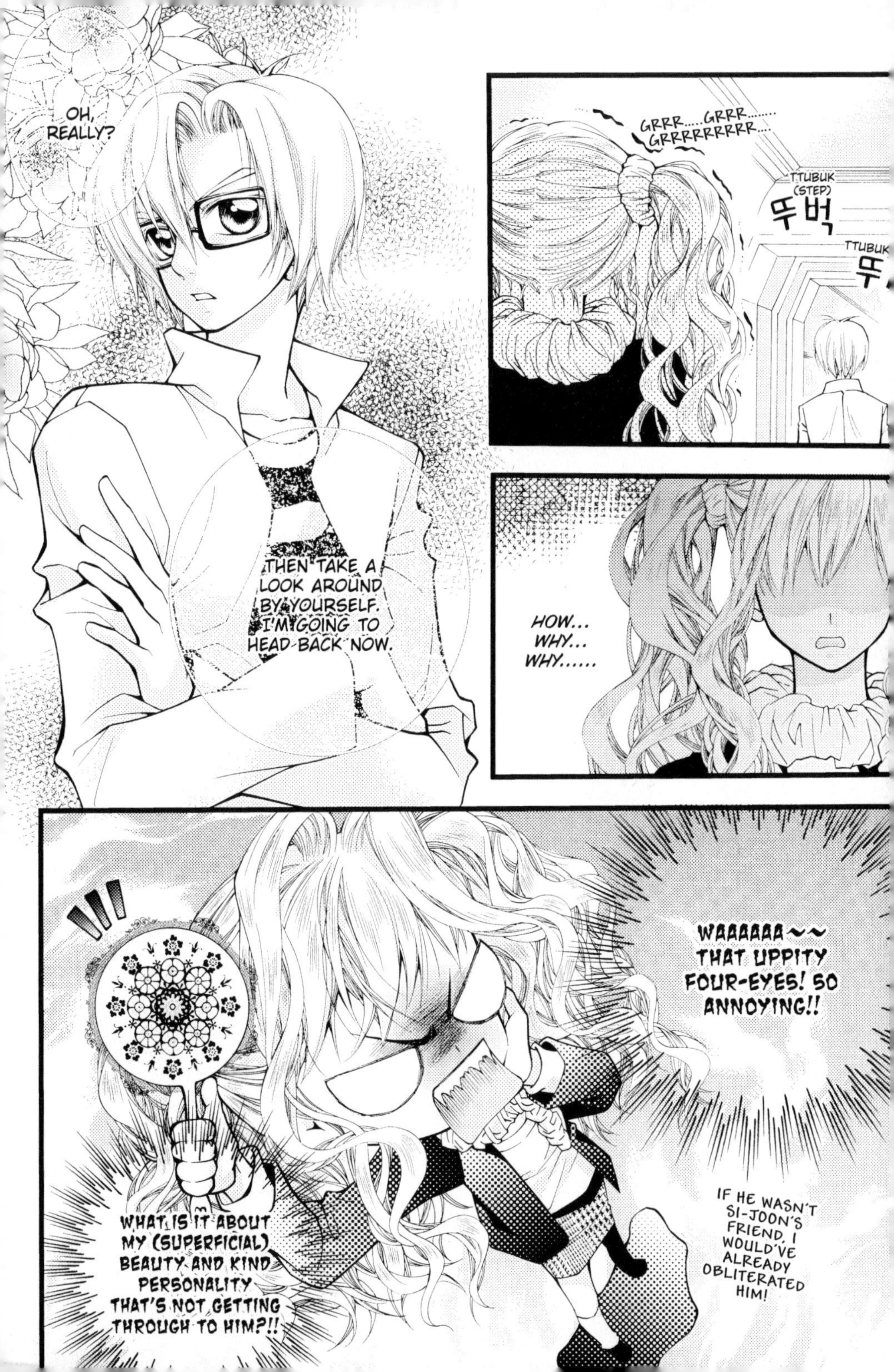
OH, REALLY?
THEN TAKE A LOOK AROUND BY YOURSELF. I'M GOING TO HEAD BACK NOW.
GRRR..... GRRR....... GRRRRRRRRR....
TTUBUK (STEP)
뚜벅
TTUBUK
뚜
HOW... WHY... WHY......
!!!
WAAAAAA~~ THAT UPPITY FOUR-EYES! SO ANNOYING!!
WHAT IS IT ABOUT MY (SUPERFICIAL) BEAUTY AND KIND PERSONALITY THAT'S NOT GETTING THROUGH TO HIM?!!
IF HE WASN'T SI-JOON'S FRIEND, I WOULD'VE ALREADY OBLITERATED HIM!

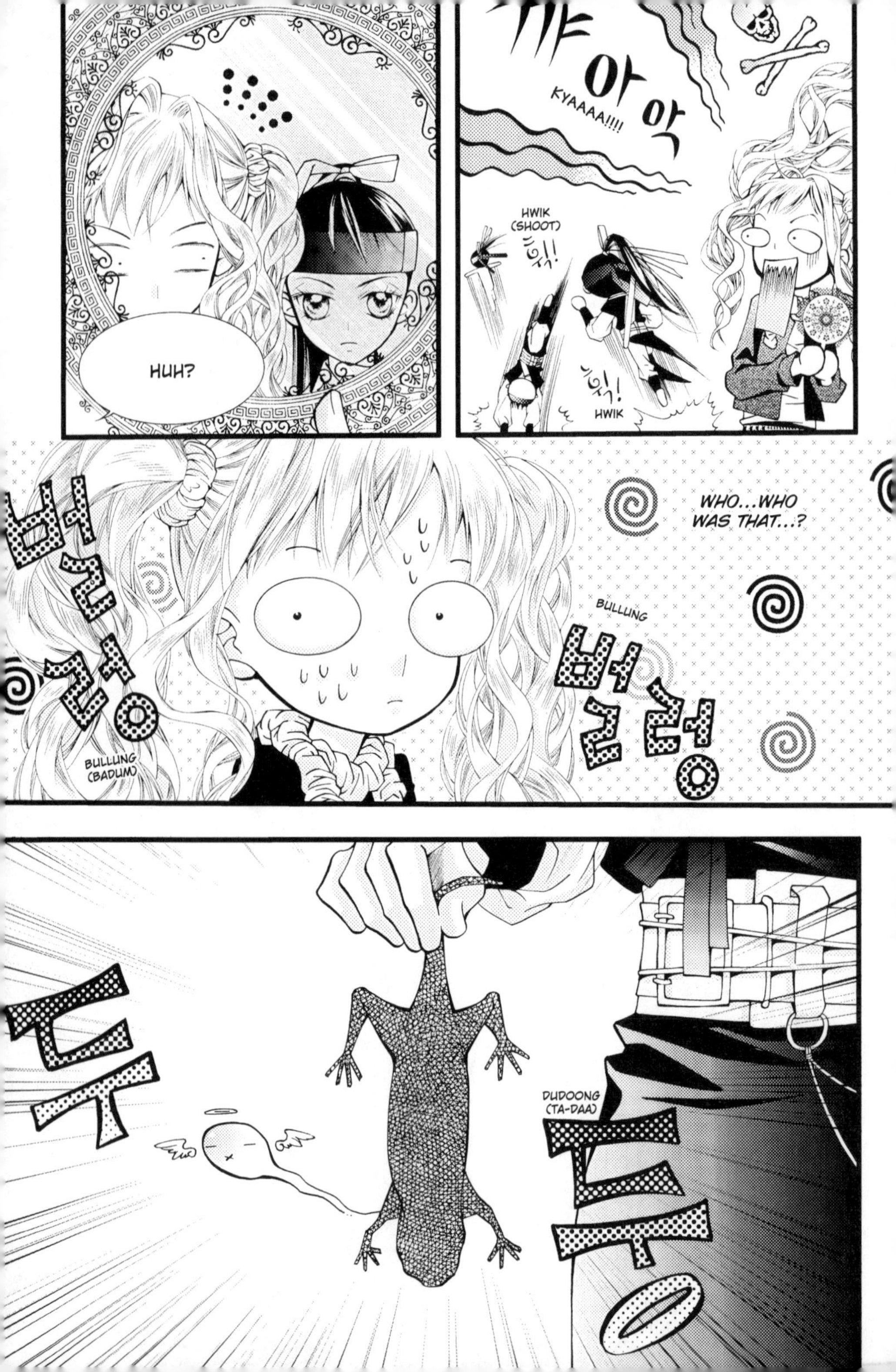
HUH?
꺄아악
KYAAAA!!!!
HWIK (SHOOT)
휘익!!
휘익!
HWIK
벌렁
BULLUNG (BADUM)
WHO...WHO WAS THAT...?
BULLUNG
벌렁
두
DUDOONG (TA-DAA)
둥

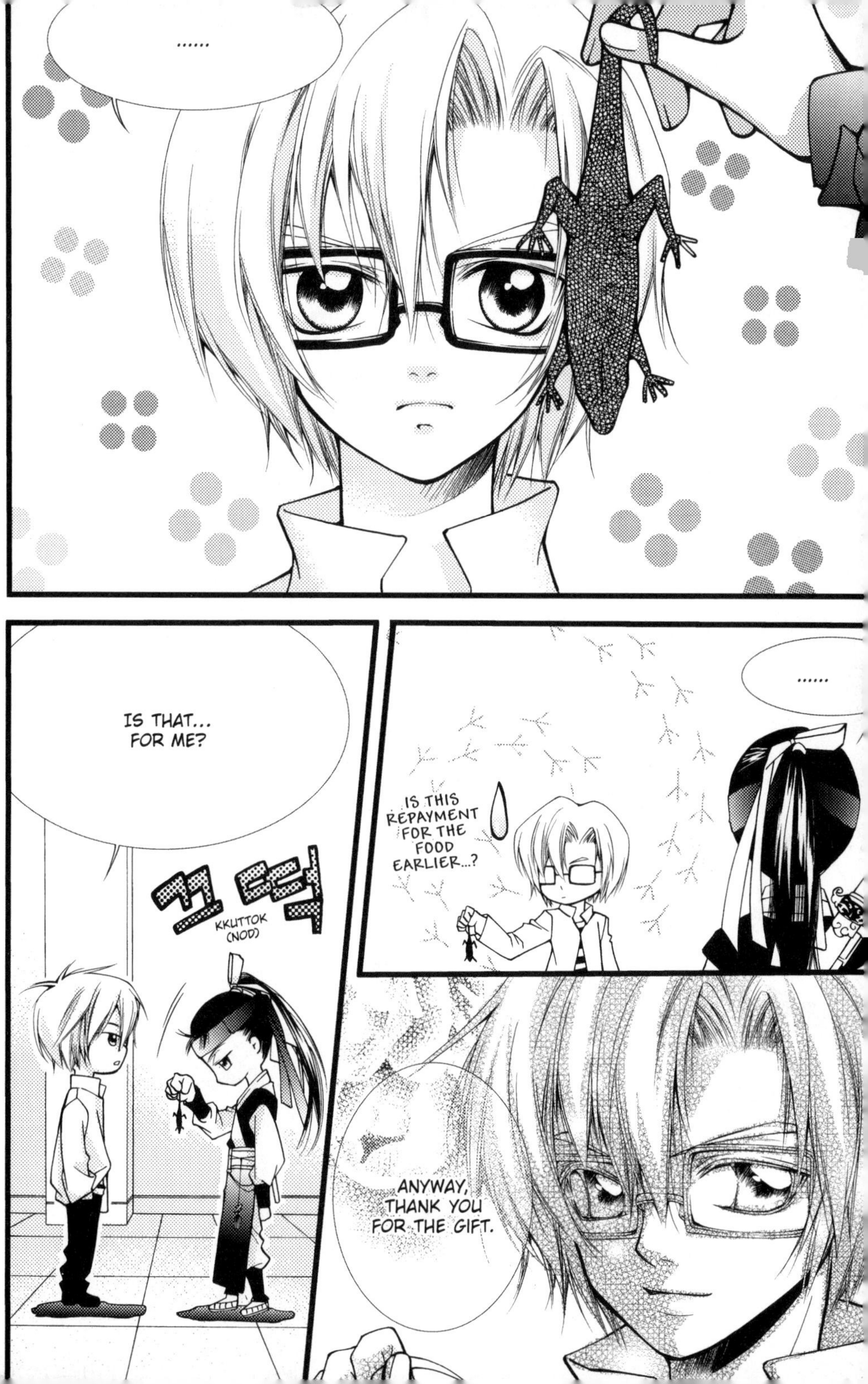
......
IS THAT... FOR ME?
끄덕
KKUTTOK (NOD)
......
IS THIS REPAYMENT FOR THE FOOD EARLIER...?
ANYWAY, THANK YOU FOR THE GIFT.

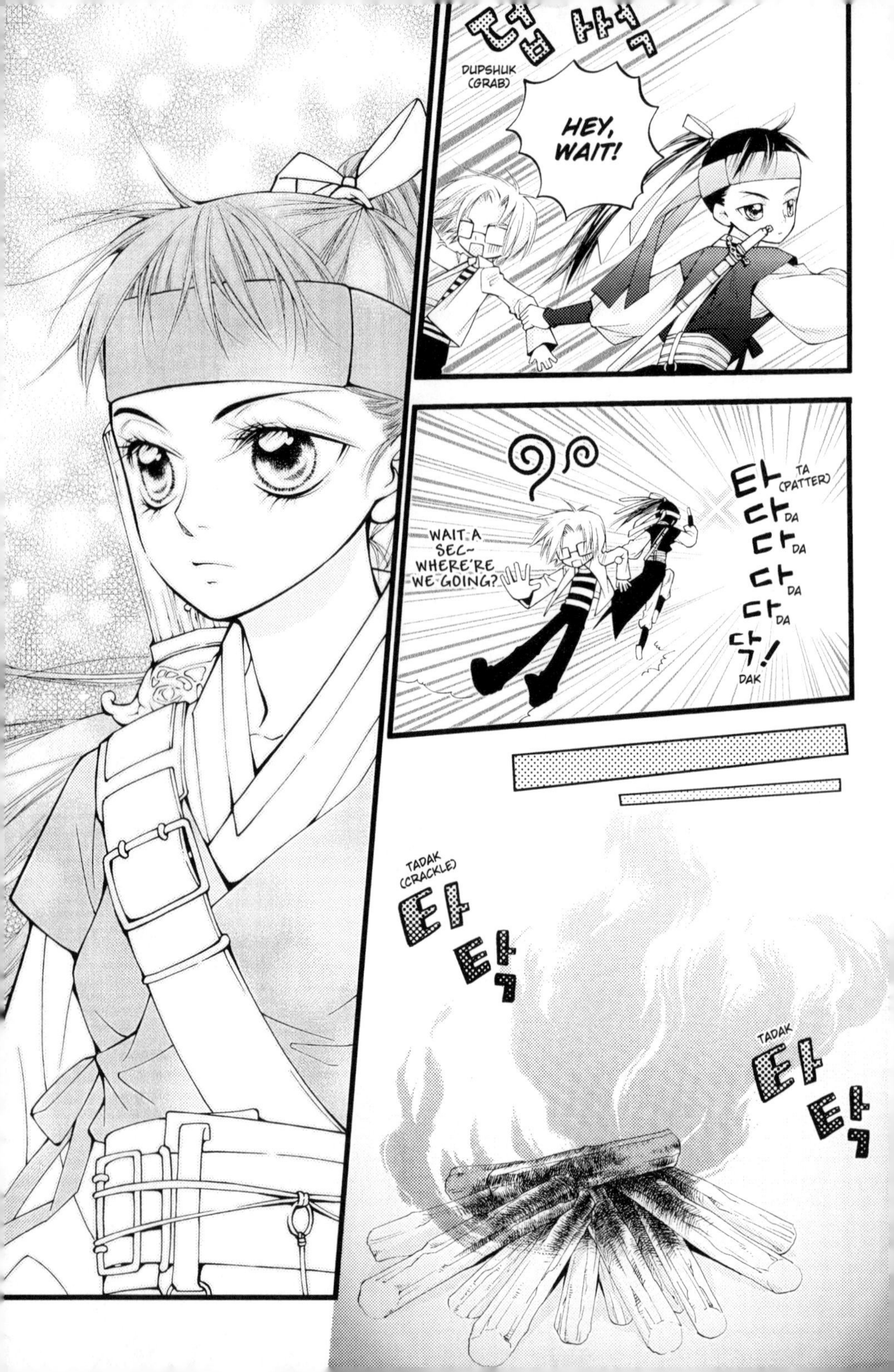
덥썩
DUPSHUK (GRAB)
HEY, WAIT!
타다다다다닥!
TA (PATTER) DA DA DA DA DAK
WAIT A SEC-WHERE'RE WE GOING?
TADAK (CRACKLE)
타닥
TADAK
타닥

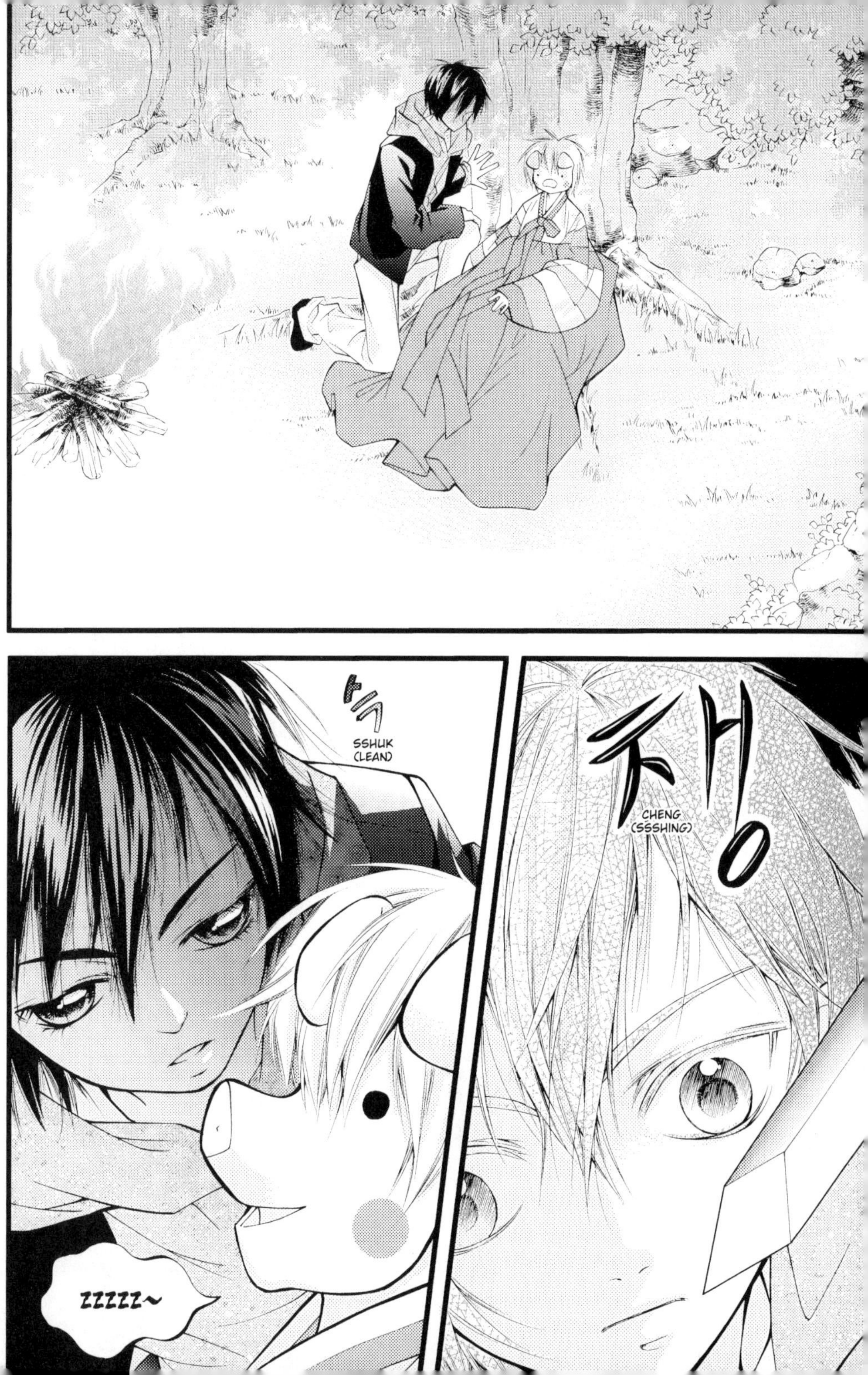
SSHUK (LEAN)
ZZZZZ~
CHENG (SSSHING)

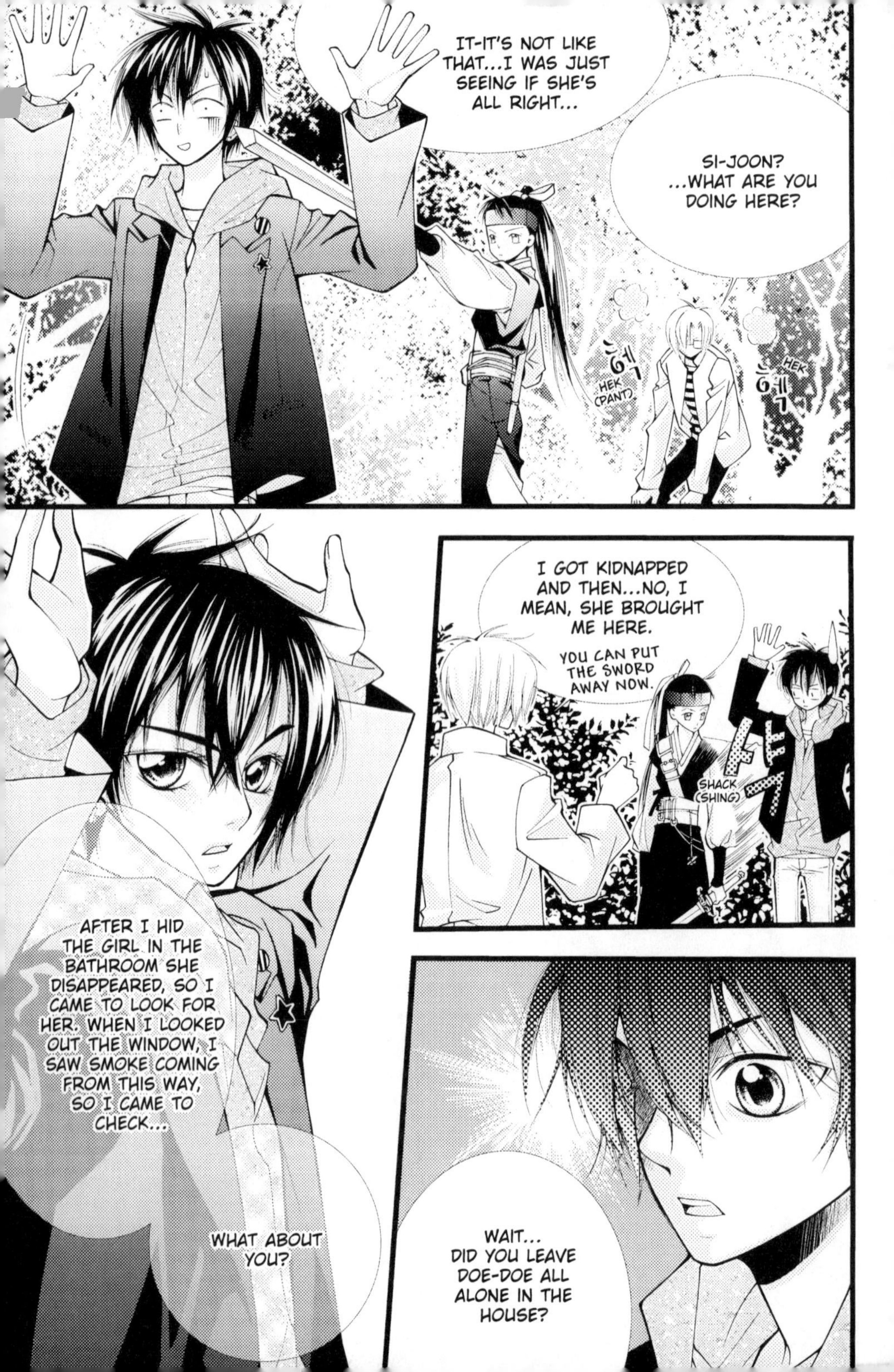
IT-IT'S NOT LIKE THAT...I WAS JUST SEEING IF SHE'S ALL RIGHT...
SI-JOON? ...WHAT ARE YOU DOING HERE?
헉
HEK (PANT)
헉
HEK
I GOT KIDNAPPED AND THEN...NO, I MEAN, SHE BROUGHT ME HERE.
YOU CAN PUT THE SWORD AWAY NOW.
SHACK (SHING)
AFTER I HID THE GIRL IN THE BATHROOM SHE DISAPPEARED, SO I CAME TO LOOK FOR HER. WHEN I LOOKED OUT THE WINDOW, I SAW SMOKE COMING FROM THIS WAY, SO I CAME TO CHECK...
WHAT ABOUT YOU?
WAIT... DID YOU LEAVE DOE-DOE ALL ALONE IN THE HOUSE?

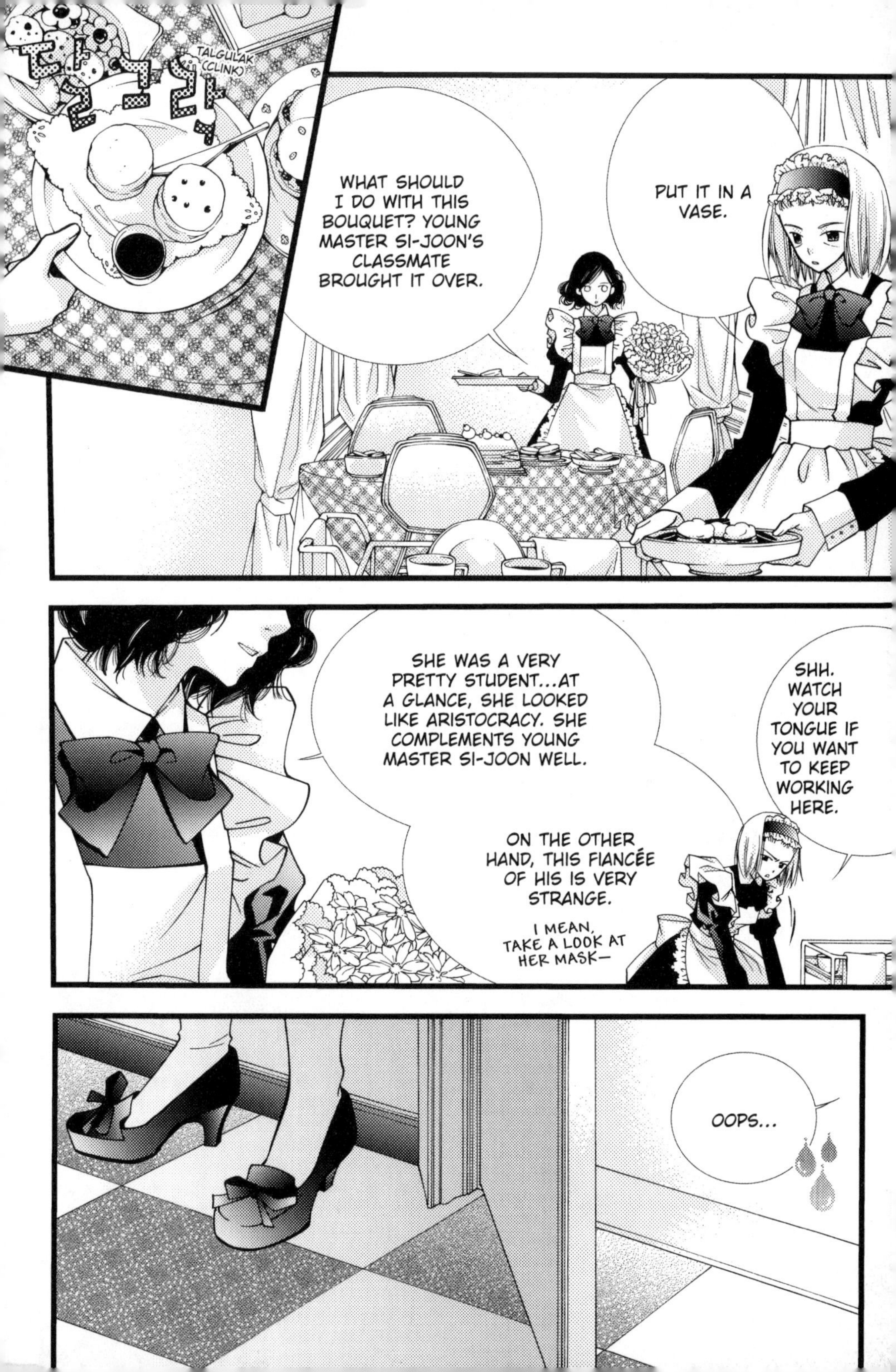
딸그락
TALGULAK (CLINK)
WHAT SHOULD I DO WITH THIS BOUQUET? YOUNG MASTER SI-JOON'S CLASSMATE BROUGHT IT OVER.
PUT IT IN A VASE.
SHE WAS A VERY PRETTY STUDENT...AT A GLANCE, SHE LOOKED LIKE ARISTOCRACY. SHE COMPLEMENTS YOUNG MASTER SI-JOON WELL.
ON THE OTHER HAND, THIS FIANCÉE OF HIS IS VERY STRANGE.
I MEAN, TAKE A LOOK AT HER MASK—
SHH. WATCH YOUR TONGUE IF YOU WANT TO KEEP WORKING HERE.
OOPS...

FIANCÉE?!!!

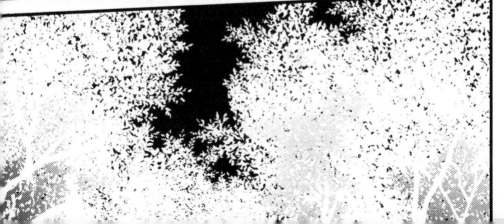

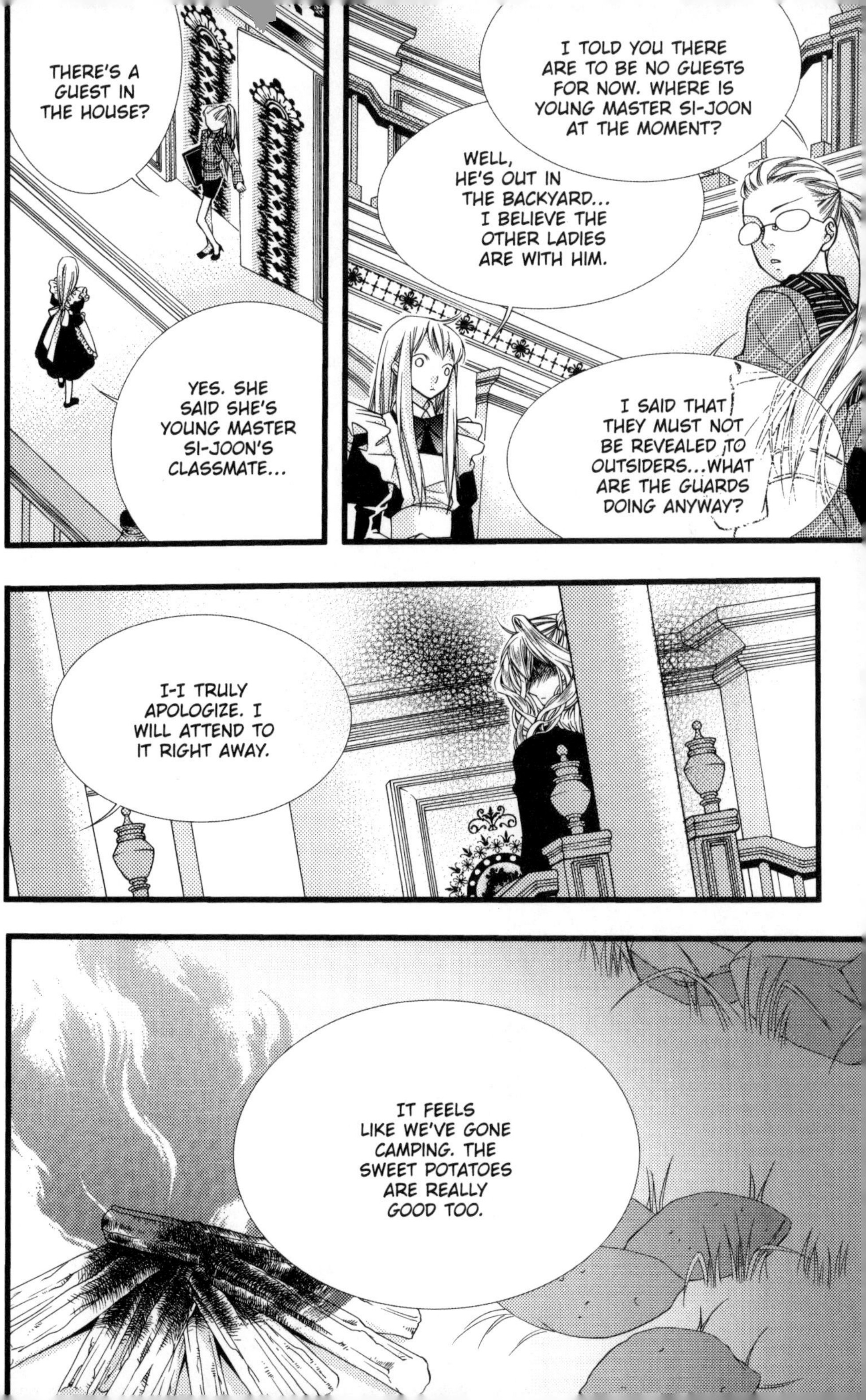
THERE'S A GUEST IN THE HOUSE?
YES. SHE SAID SHE'S YOUNG MASTER SI-JOON'S CLASSMATE...
I TOLD YOU THERE ARE TO BE NO GUESTS FOR NOW. WHERE IS YOUNG MASTER SI-JOON AT THE MOMENT?
WELL, HE'S OUT IN THE BACKYARD... I BELIEVE THE OTHER LADIES ARE WITH HIM.
I SAID THAT THEY MUST NOT BE REVEALED TO OUTSIDERS...WHAT ARE THE GUARDS DOING ANYWAY?
I-I TRULY APOLOGIZE. I WILL ATTEND TO IT RIGHT AWAY.
IT FEELS LIKE WE'VE GONE CAMPING. THE SWEET POTATOES ARE REALLY GOOD TOO.

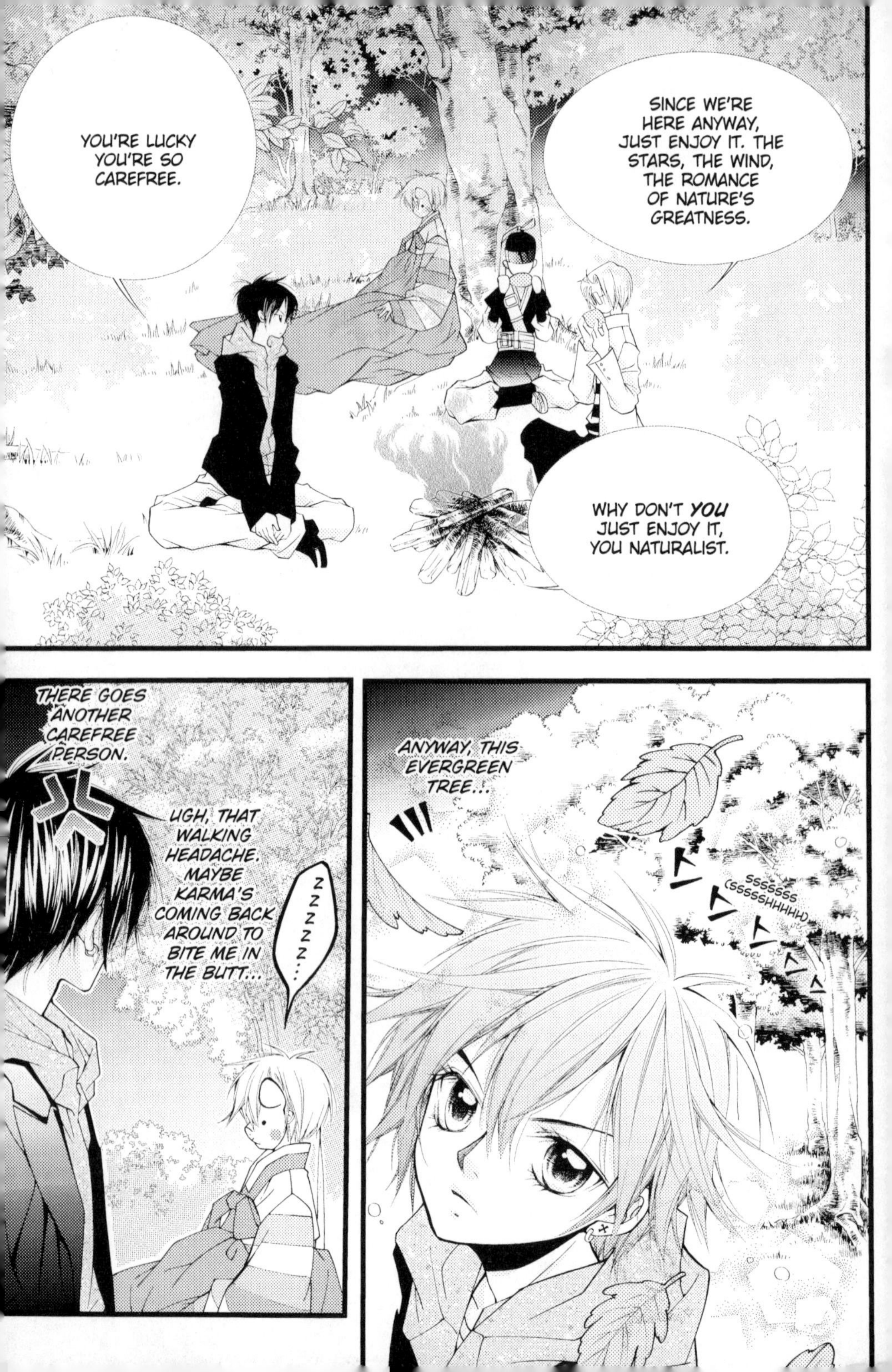
YOU'RE LUCKY YOU'RE SO CAREFREE.
SINCE WE'RE HERE ANYWAY, JUST ENJOY IT. THE STARS, THE WIND, THE ROMANCE OF NATURE'S GREATNESS.
WHY DON'T *YOU* JUST ENJOY IT, YOU NATURALIST.
THERE GOES ANOTHER CAREFREE PERSON.
UGH, THAT WALKING HEADACHE. MAYBE KARMA'S COMING BACK AROUND TO BITE ME IN THE BUTT...
ZZZZZ...
ANYWAY, THIS EVERGREEN TREE...
SSSSSSS (SSSSSHHHHH)

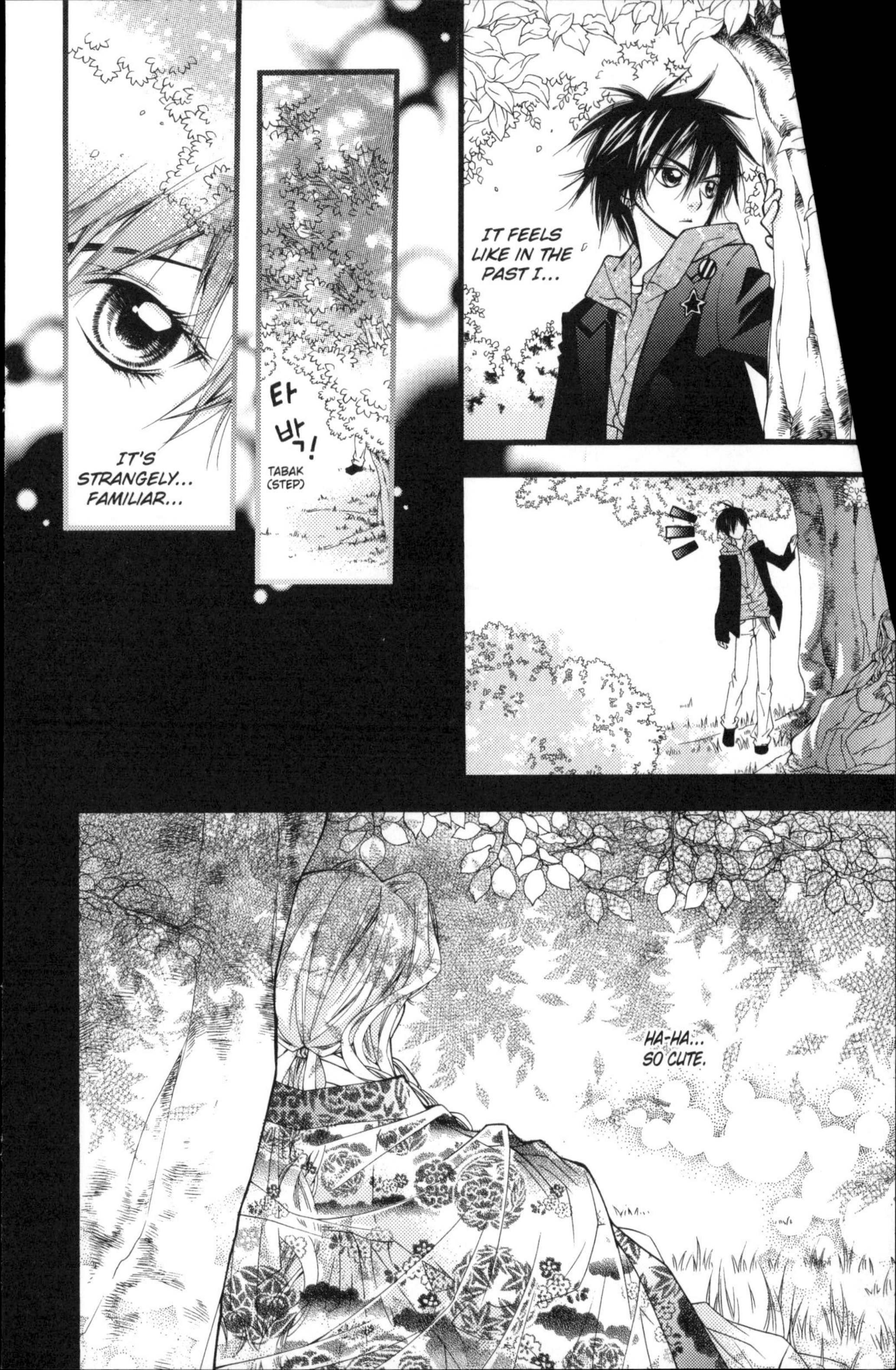
IT'S STRANGELY... FAMILIAR...
타박!
TABAK (STEP)
IT FEELS LIKE IN THE PAST I...
HA-HA... SO CUTE.

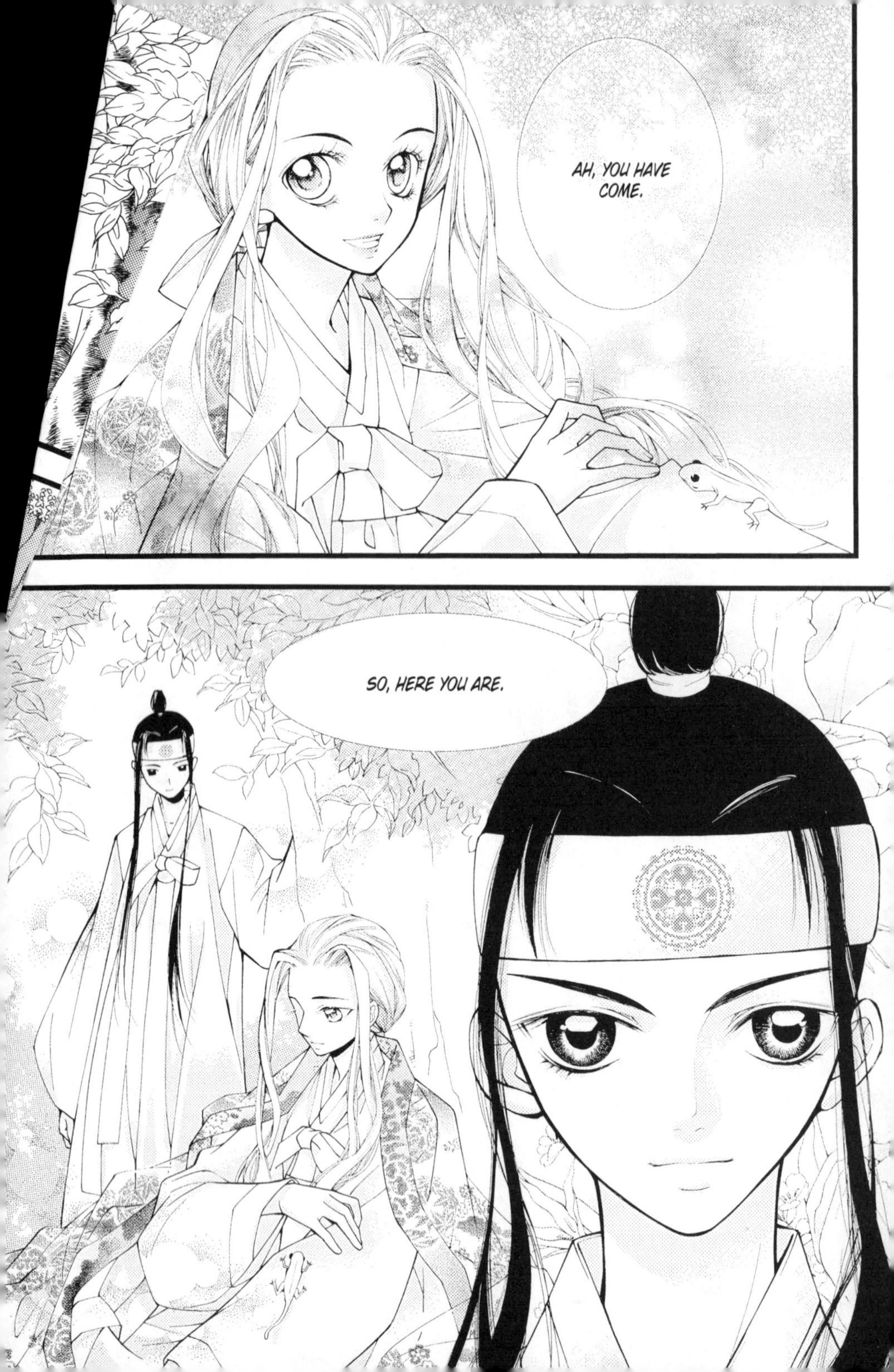
AH, YOU HAVE COME.
SO, HERE YOU ARE.

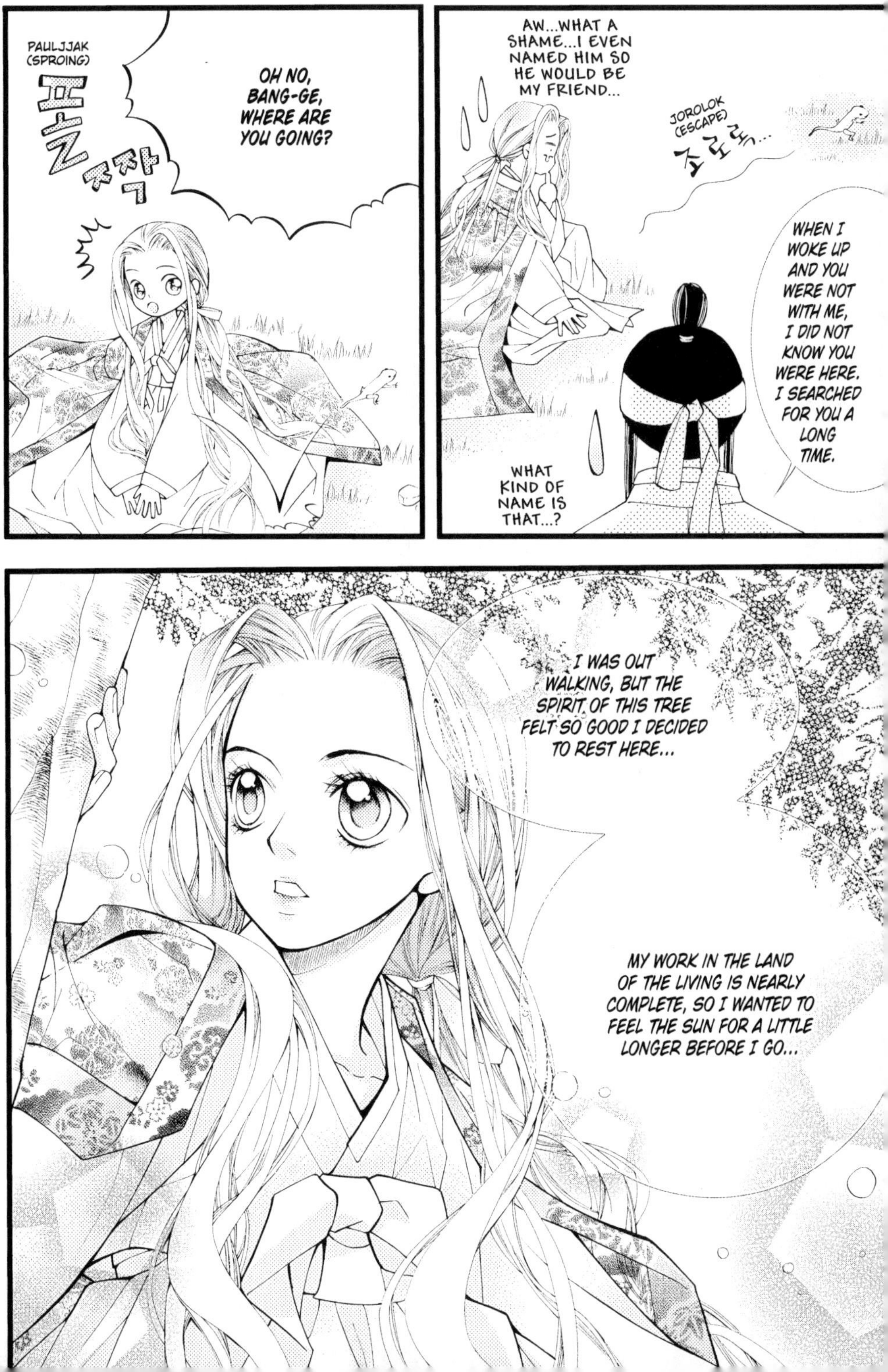
PAULJJAK (SPROING)
OH NO, BANG-GE, WHERE ARE YOU GOING?
AW...WHAT A SHAME...I EVEN NAMED HIM SO HE WOULD BE MY FRIEND...
JOROLOK (ESCAPE)
WHEN I WOKE UP AND YOU WERE NOT WITH ME, I DID NOT KNOW YOU WERE HERE. I SEARCHED FOR YOU A LONG TIME.
WHAT KIND OF NAME IS THAT...?
I WAS OUT WALKING, BUT THE SPIRIT OF THIS TREE FELT SO GOOD I DECIDED TO REST HERE...
MY WORK IN THE LAND OF THE LIVING IS NEARLY COMPLETE, SO I WANTED TO FEEL THE SUN FOR A LITTLE LONGER BEFORE I GO...

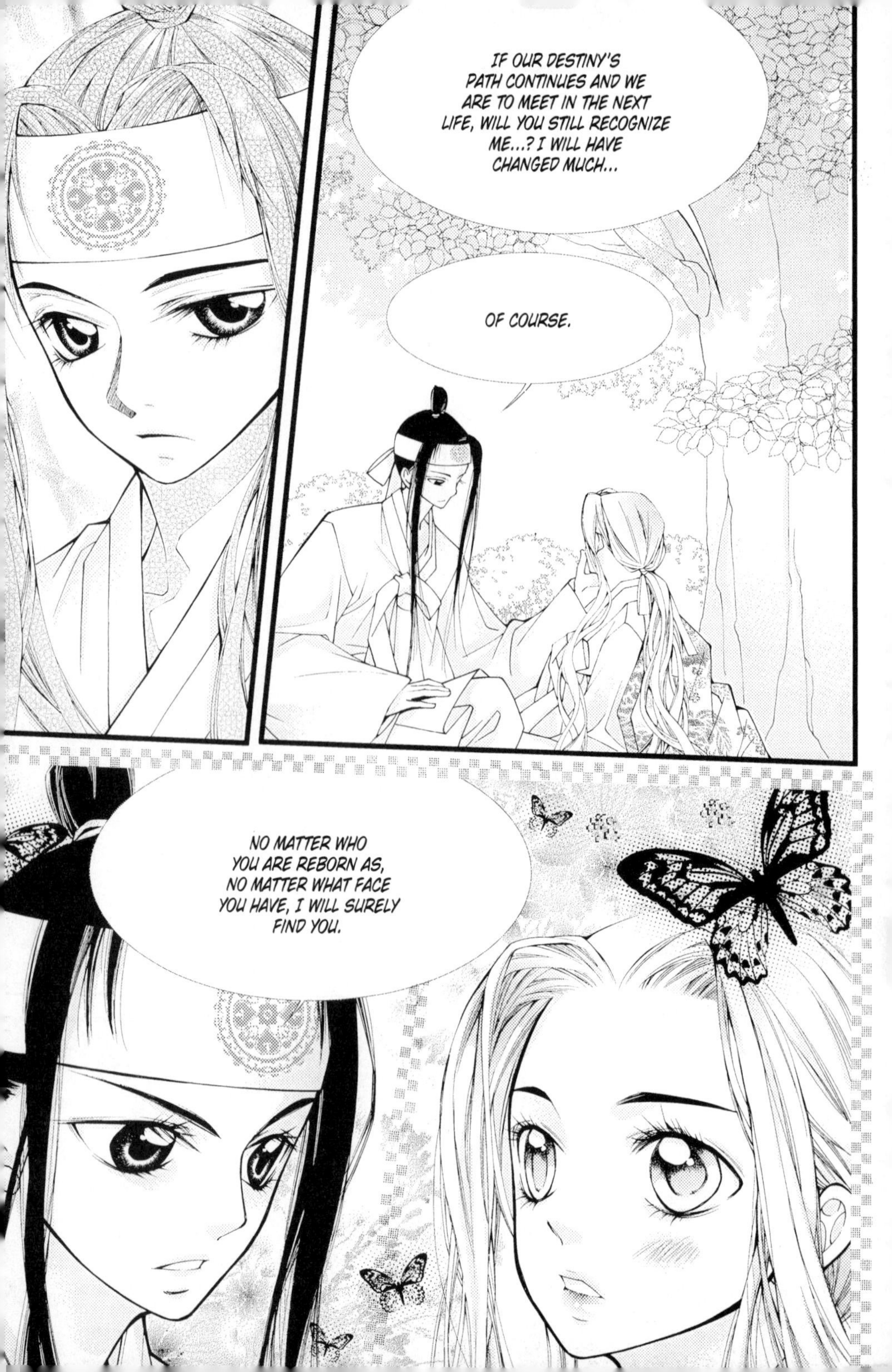
IF OUR DESTINY'S PATH CONTINUES AND WE ARE TO MEET IN THE NEXT LIFE, WILL YOU STILL RECOGNIZE ME...? I WILL HAVE CHANGED MUCH...
OF COURSE.
NO MATTER WHO YOU ARE REBORN AS, NO MATTER WHAT FACE YOU HAVE, I WILL SURELY FIND YOU.

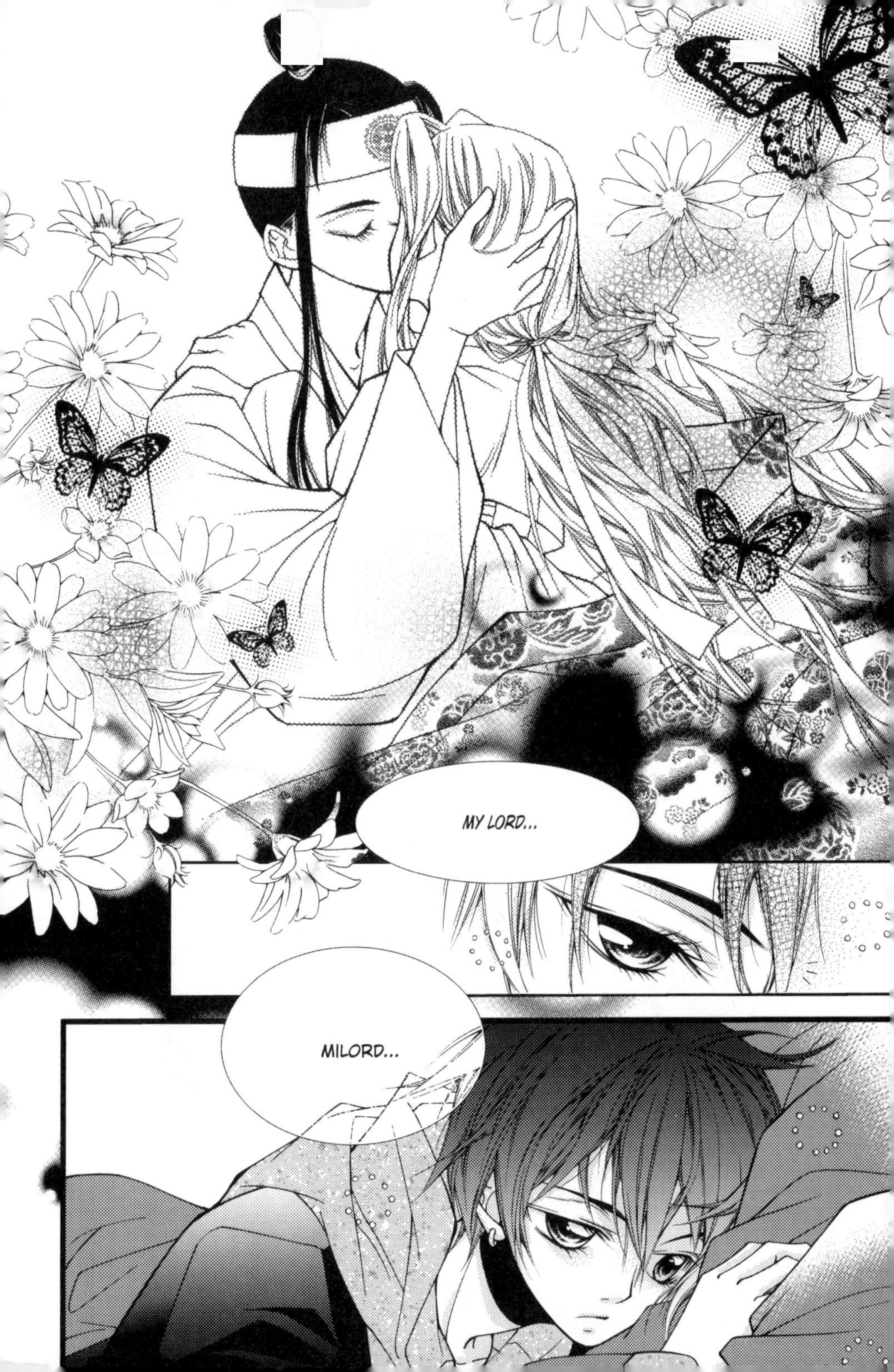
MY LORD...
MILORD...

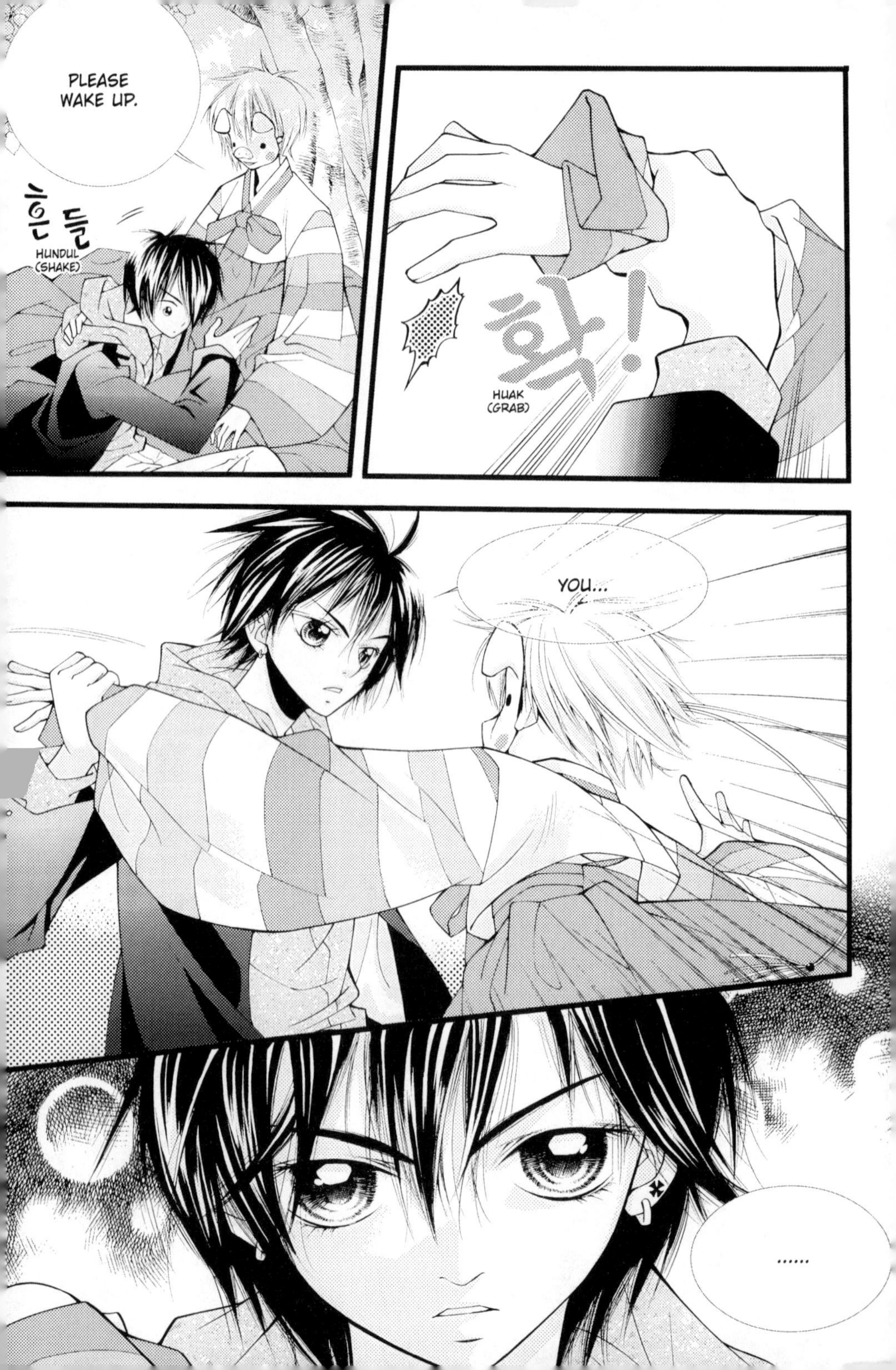
PLEASE WAKE UP.
흔들
HUNDUL (SHAKE)
확!
HUAK (GRAB)
YOU...
......

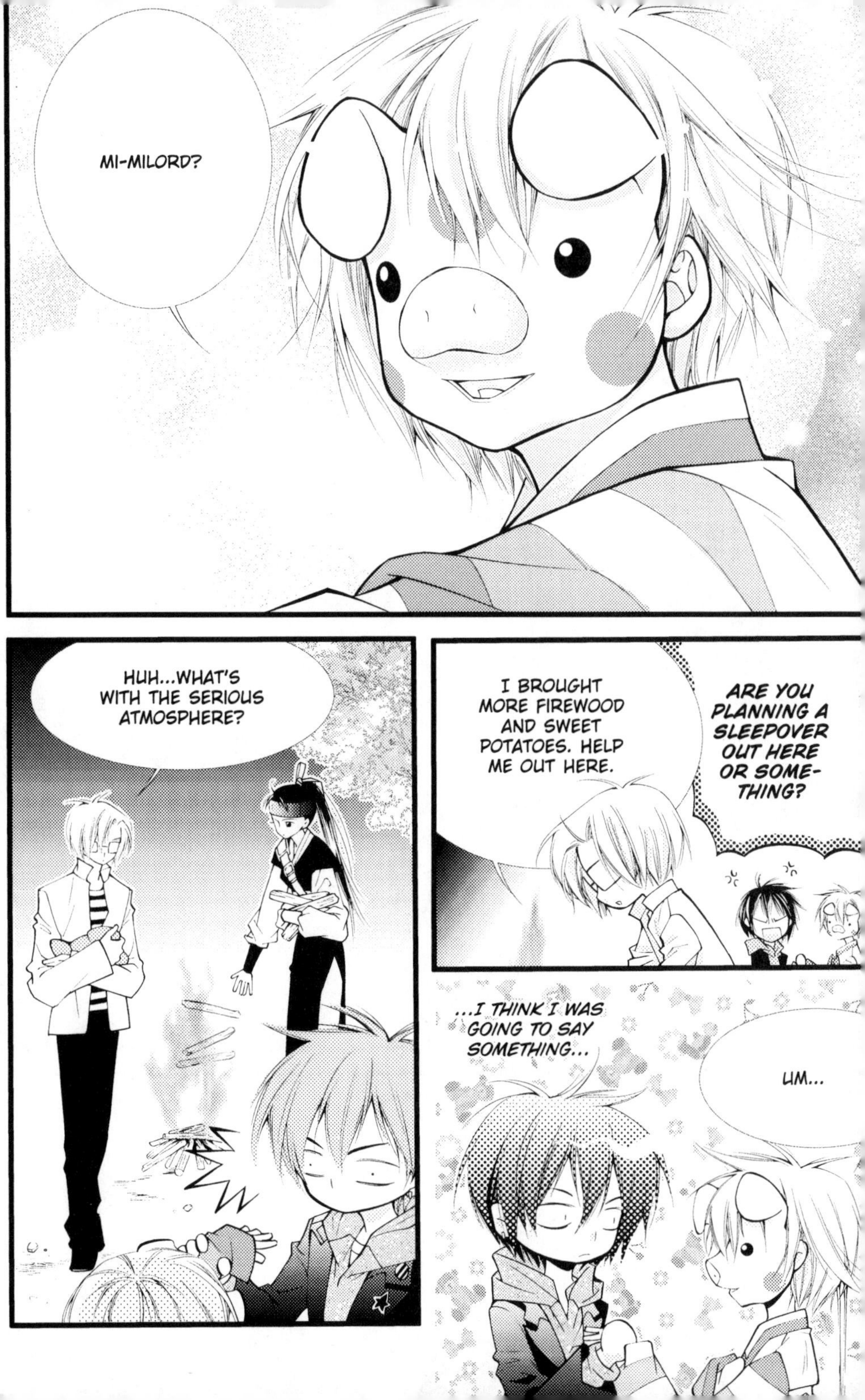
MI-MILORD?
HUH...WHAT'S WITH THE SERIOUS ATMOSPHERE?
I BROUGHT MORE FIREWOOD AND SWEET POTATOES. HELP ME OUT HERE.
ARE YOU PLANNING A SLEEPOVER OUT HERE OR SOMETHING?
...I THINK I WAS GOING TO SAY SOMETHING...
UM...

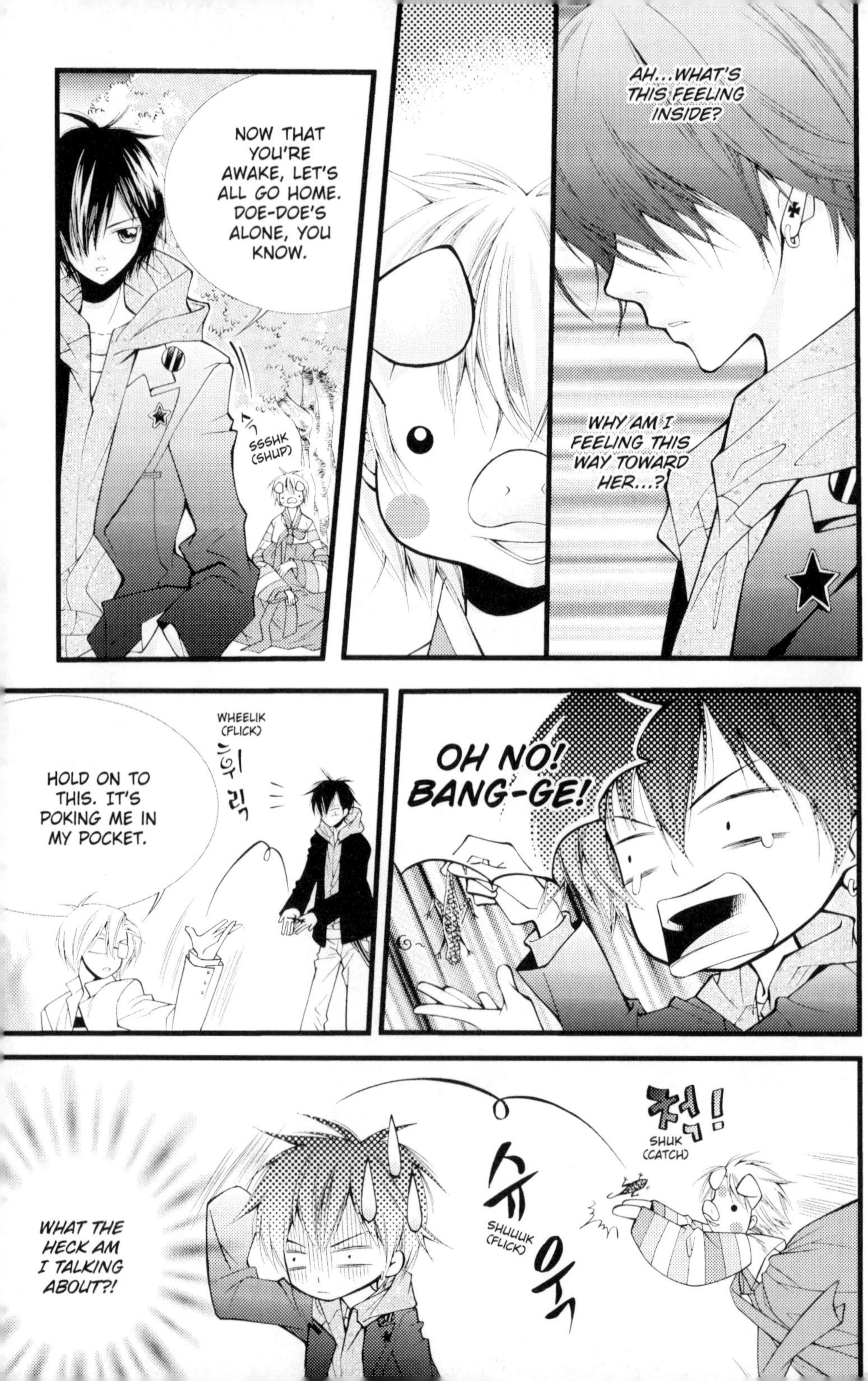

NOW THAT YOU'RE AWAKE, LET'S ALL GO HOME. DOE-DOE'S ALONE, YOU KNOW.
SSSHK (SHUP)
AH...WHAT'S THIS FEELING INSIDE?
WHY AM I FEELING THIS WAY TOWARD HER...?
HOLD ON TO THIS. IT'S POKING ME IN MY POCKET.
WHEELIK (FLICK)
OH NO! BANG-GE!
WHAT THE HECK AM I TALKING ABOUT?!
SHUUUK (FLICK)
척!
SHUK (CATCH)

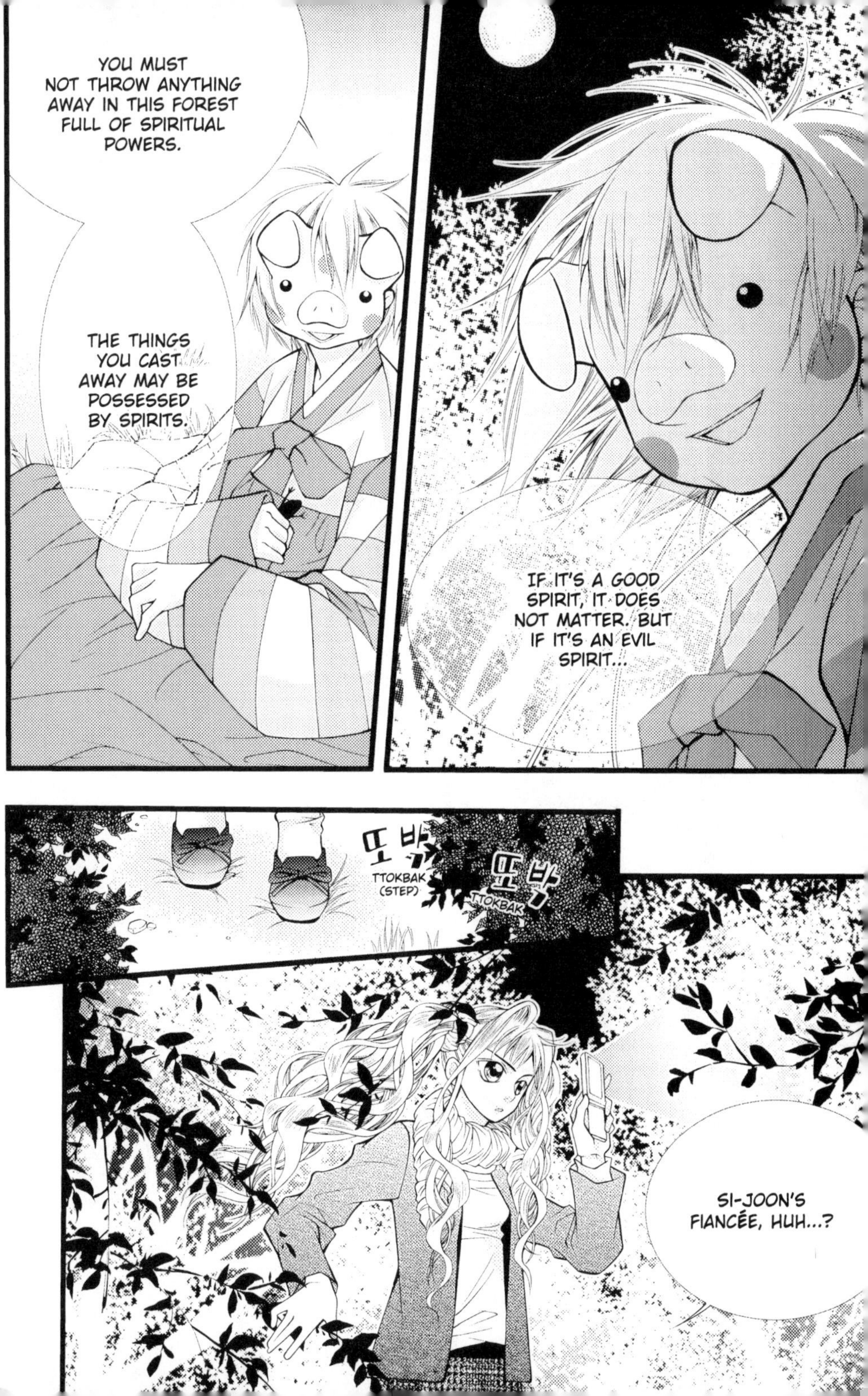
YOU MUST NOT THROW ANYTHING AWAY IN THIS FOREST FULL OF SPIRITUAL POWERS.
THE THINGS YOU CAST AWAY MAY BE POSSESSED BY SPIRITS.
IF IT'S A GOOD SPIRIT, IT DOES NOT MATTER. BUT IF IT'S AN EVIL SPIRIT...
또박
TTOKBAK (STEP)
또박
TTOKBAK
SI-JOON'S FIANCÉE, HUH...?

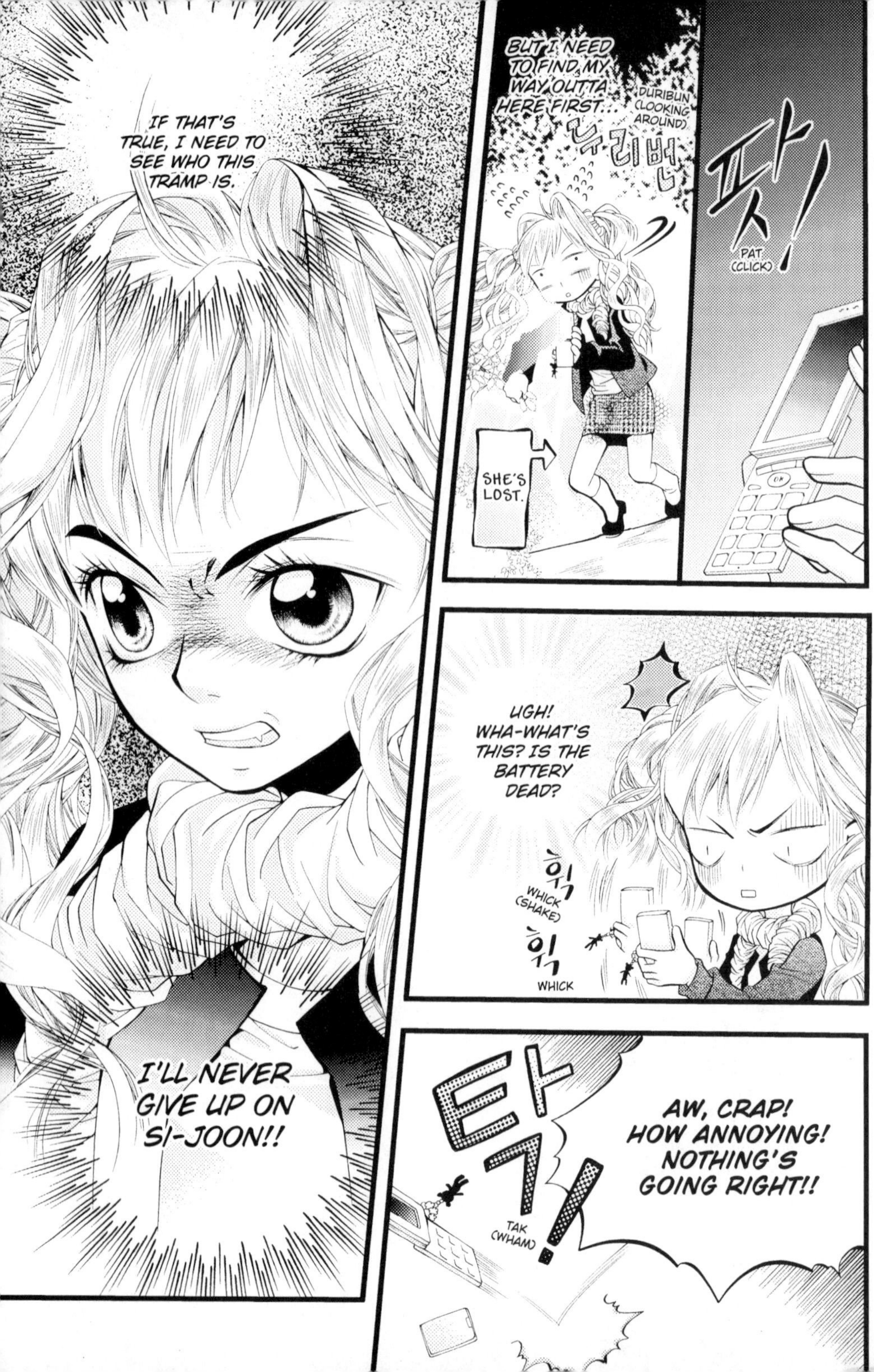
IF THAT'S TRUE, I NEED TO SEE WHO THIS TRAMP IS.
I'LL NEVER GIVE UP ON SI-JOON!!
BUT I NEED TO FIND MY WAY OUTTA HERE FIRST.
두리번
DURIBUN (LOOKING AROUND)
SHE'S LOST.
팟!
PAT (CLICK)
UGH! WHA-WHAT'S THIS? IS THE BATTERY DEAD?
휘익
WHICK (SHAKE)
휘익
WHICK
탁!
TAK (WHAM)
AW, CRAP! HOW ANNOYING! NOTHING'S GOING RIGHT!!

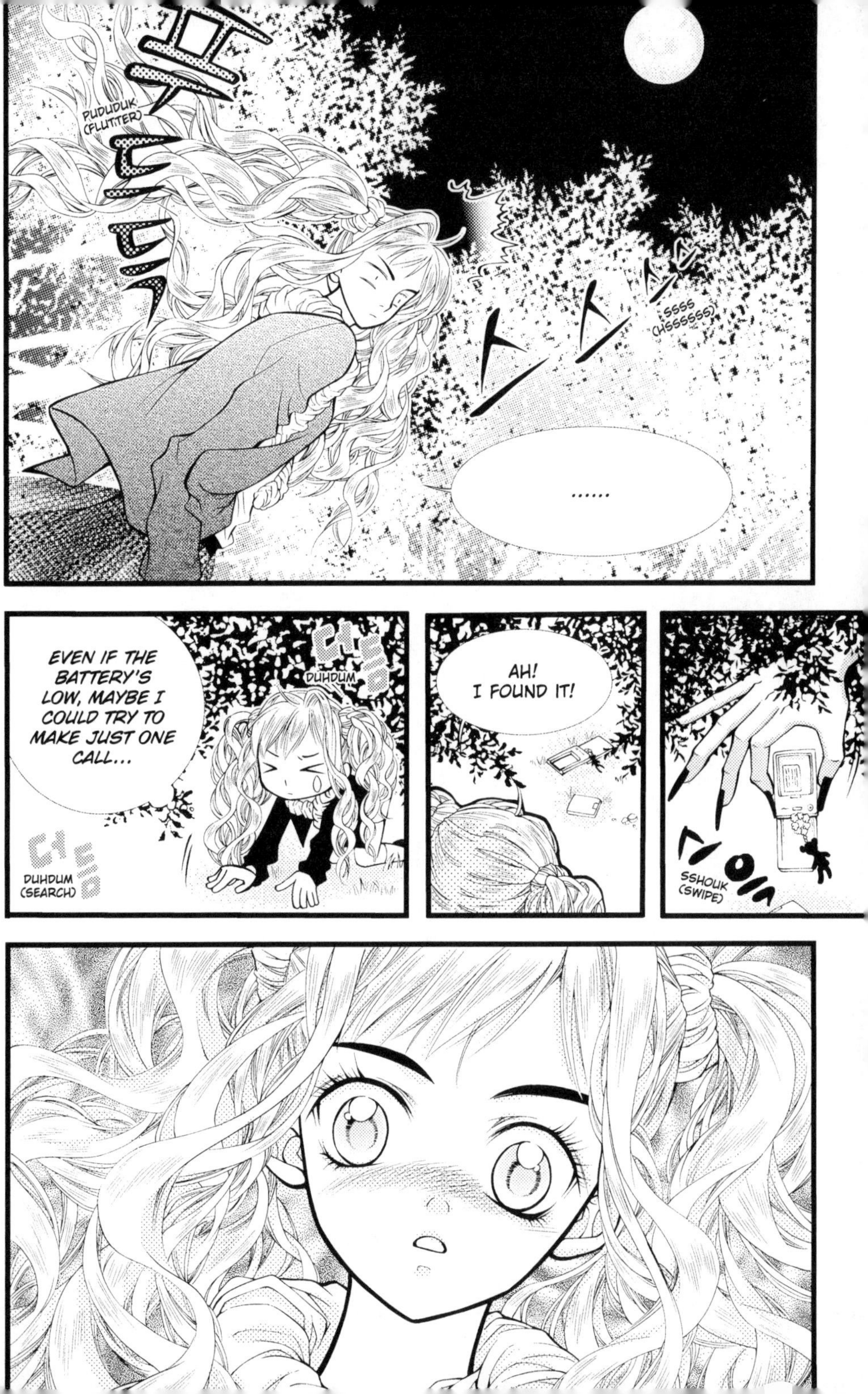
PUDUDUK (FLUTTER)
SSSS (HSSSSSS)
......
EVEN IF THE BATTERY'S LOW, MAYBE I COULD TRY TO MAKE JUST ONE CALL...
DUHDUM
DUHDUM (SEARCH)
AH! I FOUND IT!
SSHOUK (SWIPE)

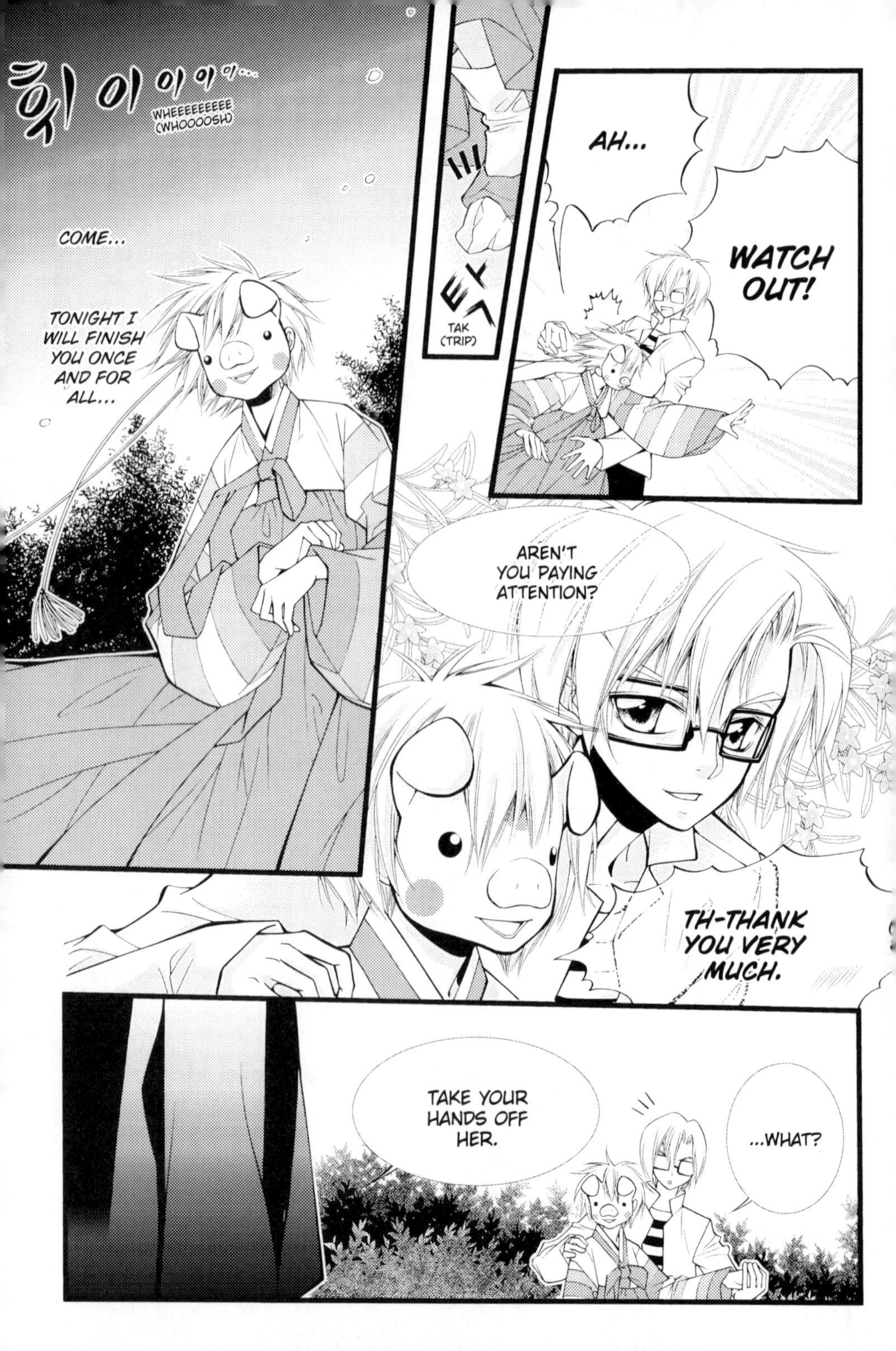
휘이이이이···
WHEEEEEEEE (WHOOOOSH)
COME...
TONIGHT I WILL FINISH YOU ONCE AND FOR ALL...
TAK (TRIP)
AH...
WATCH OUT!
AREN'T YOU PAYING ATTENTION?
TH-THANK YOU VERY MUCH.
TAKE YOUR HANDS OFF HER.
...WHAT?

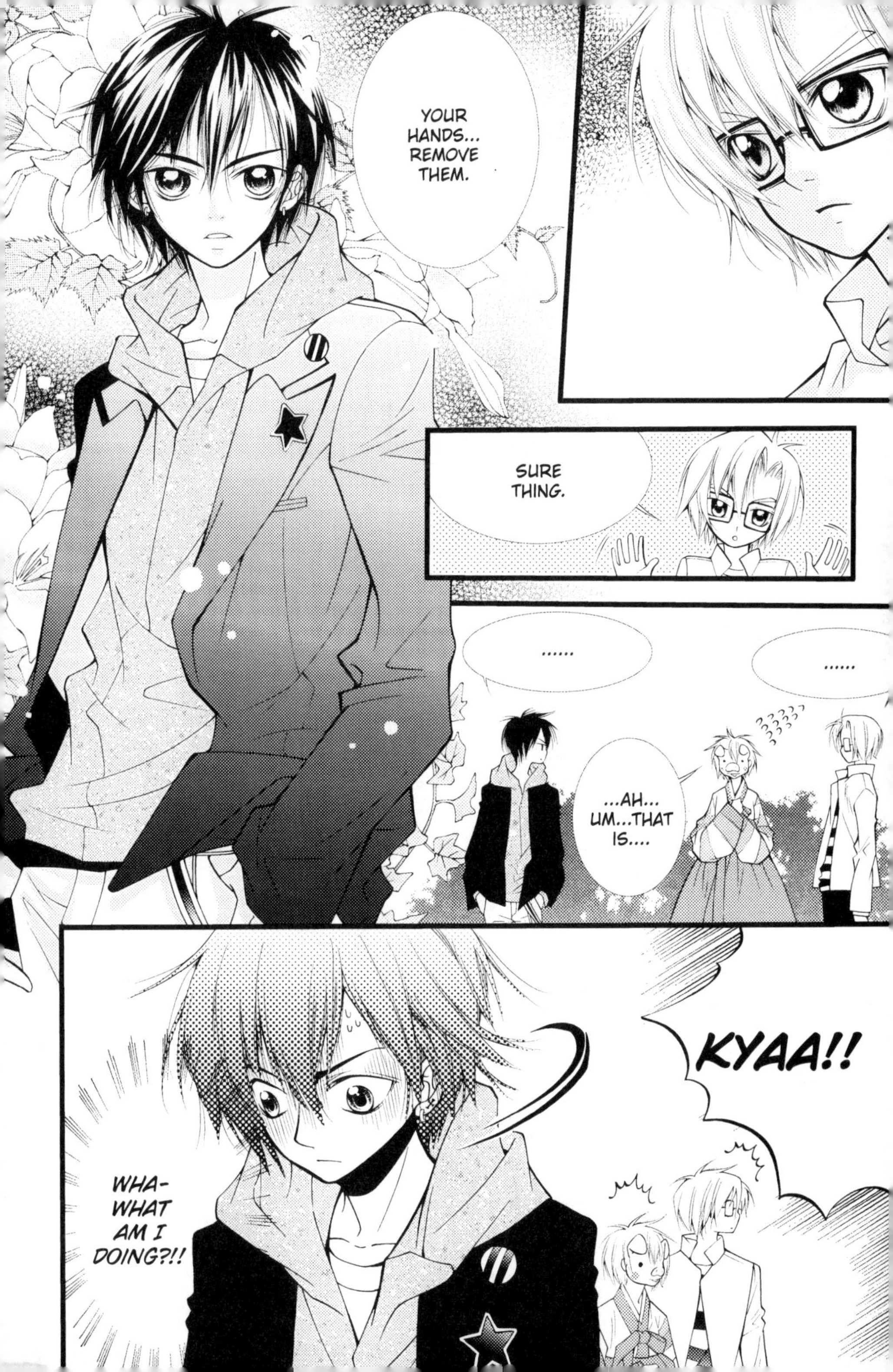
YOUR HANDS... REMOVE THEM.
SURE THING.
......
......
...AH... UM...THAT IS....
WHA-WHAT AM I DOING?!!
KYAA!!

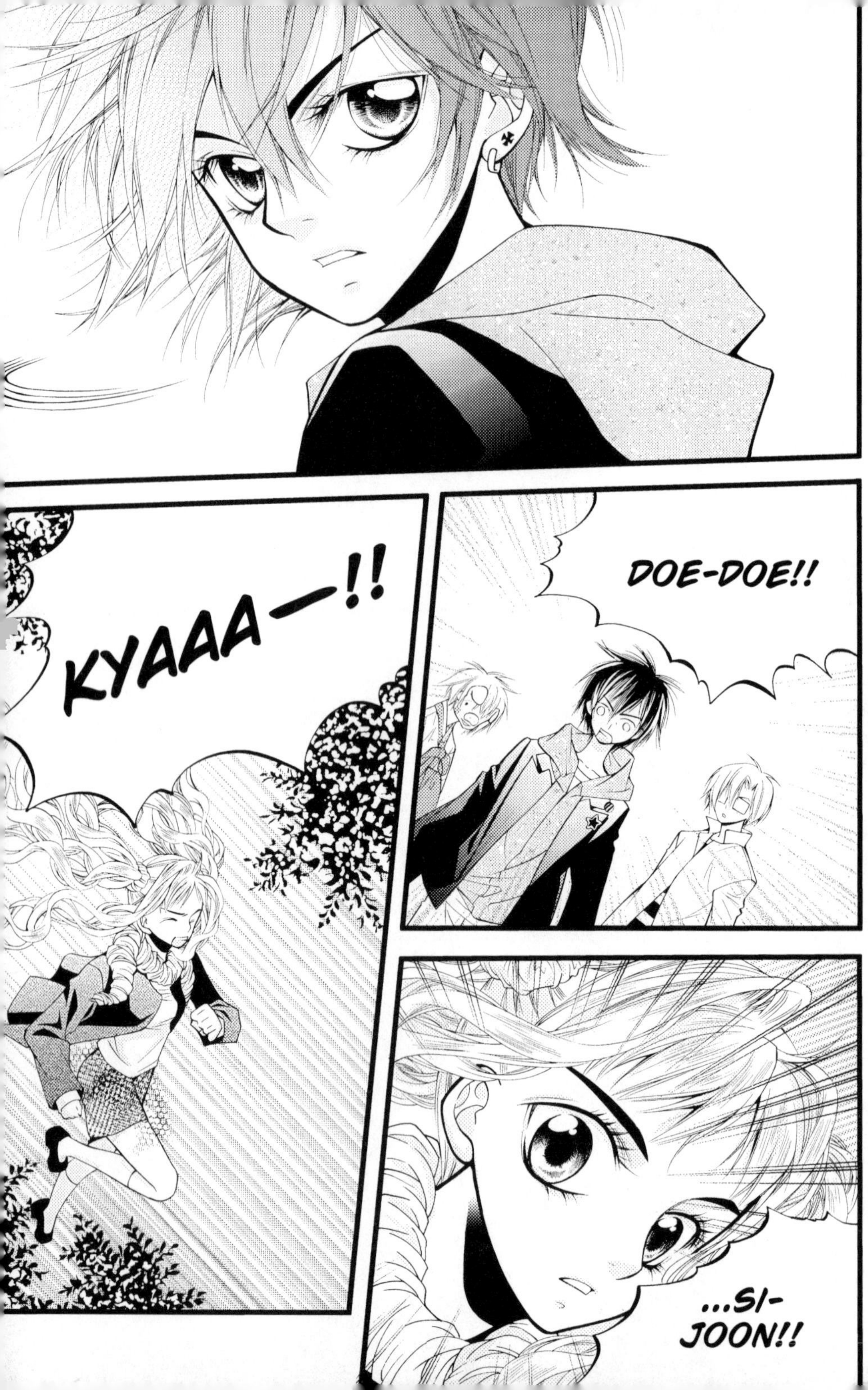
KYAAA—!!
DOE-DOE!!
...SI-JOON!!

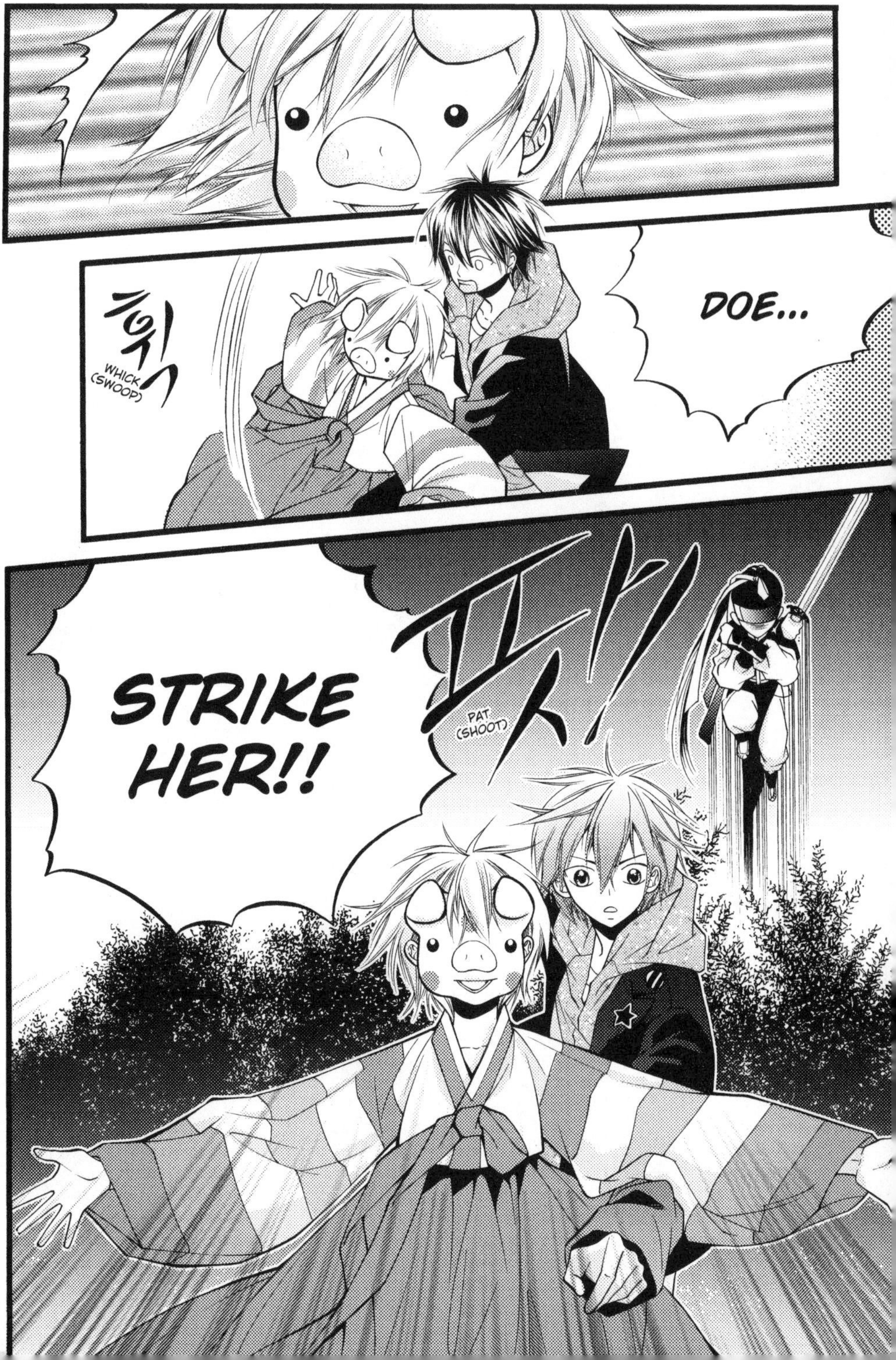
WHICK (SWOOP)
DOE...
STRIKE HER!!
PAT (SHOOT)

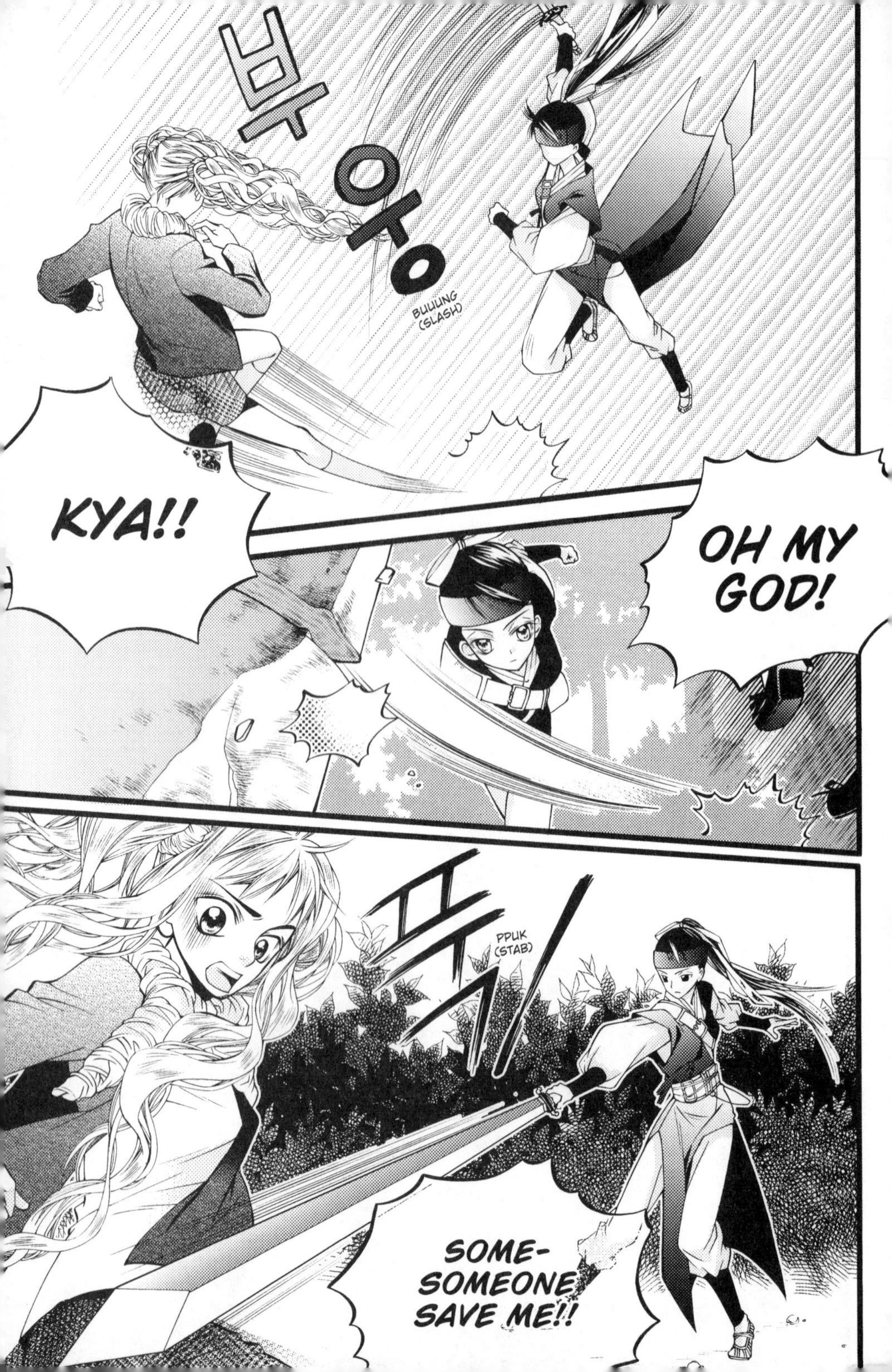
BUUUNG (SLASH)
KYA!!
OH MY GOD!
PPUK (STAB)
SOME- SOMEONE SAVE ME!!

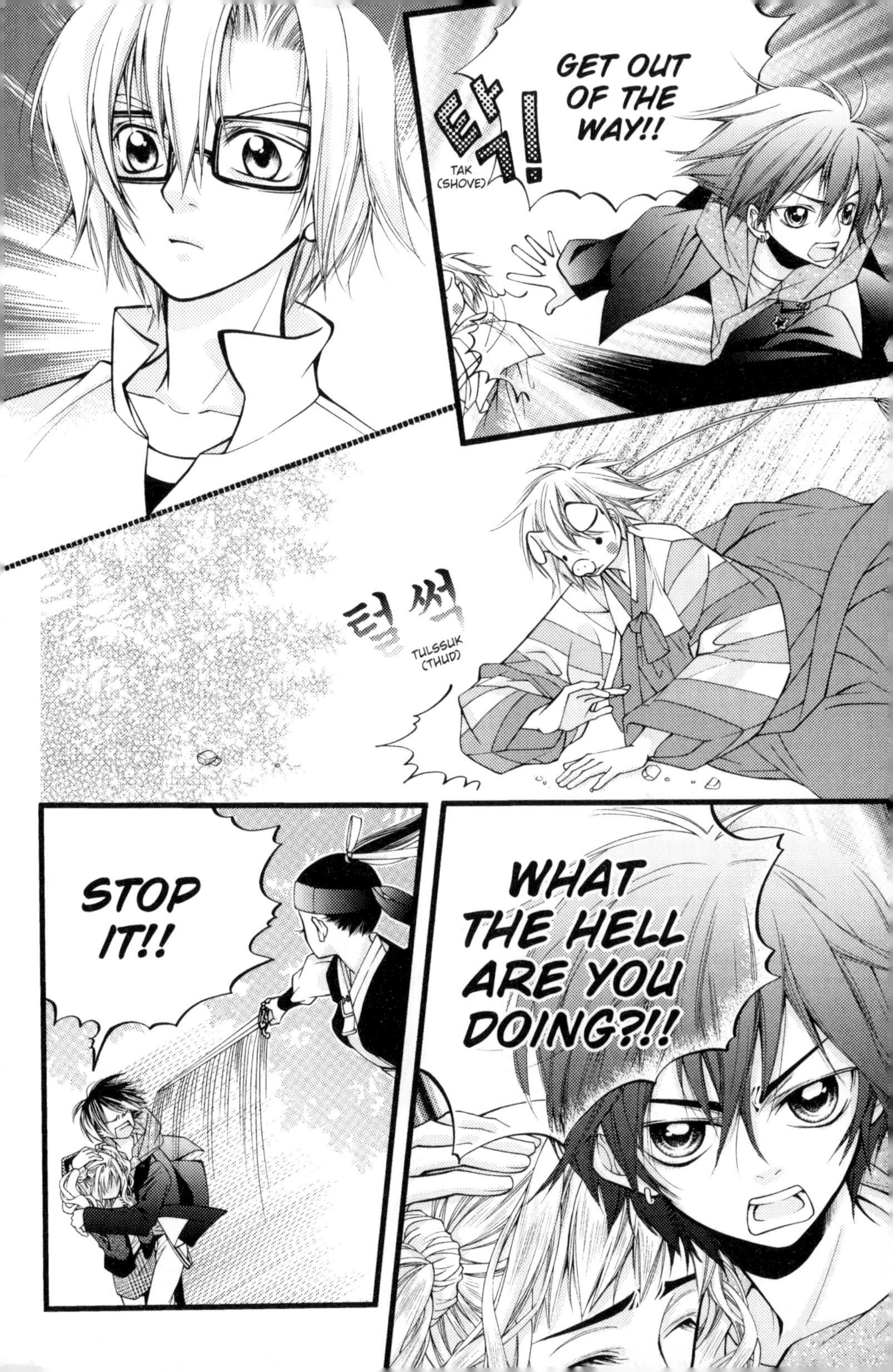
탁!
TAK (SHOVE)
GET OUT OF THE WAY!!
털썩
TULSSUK (THUD)
STOP IT!!
WHAT THE HELL ARE YOU DOING?!!

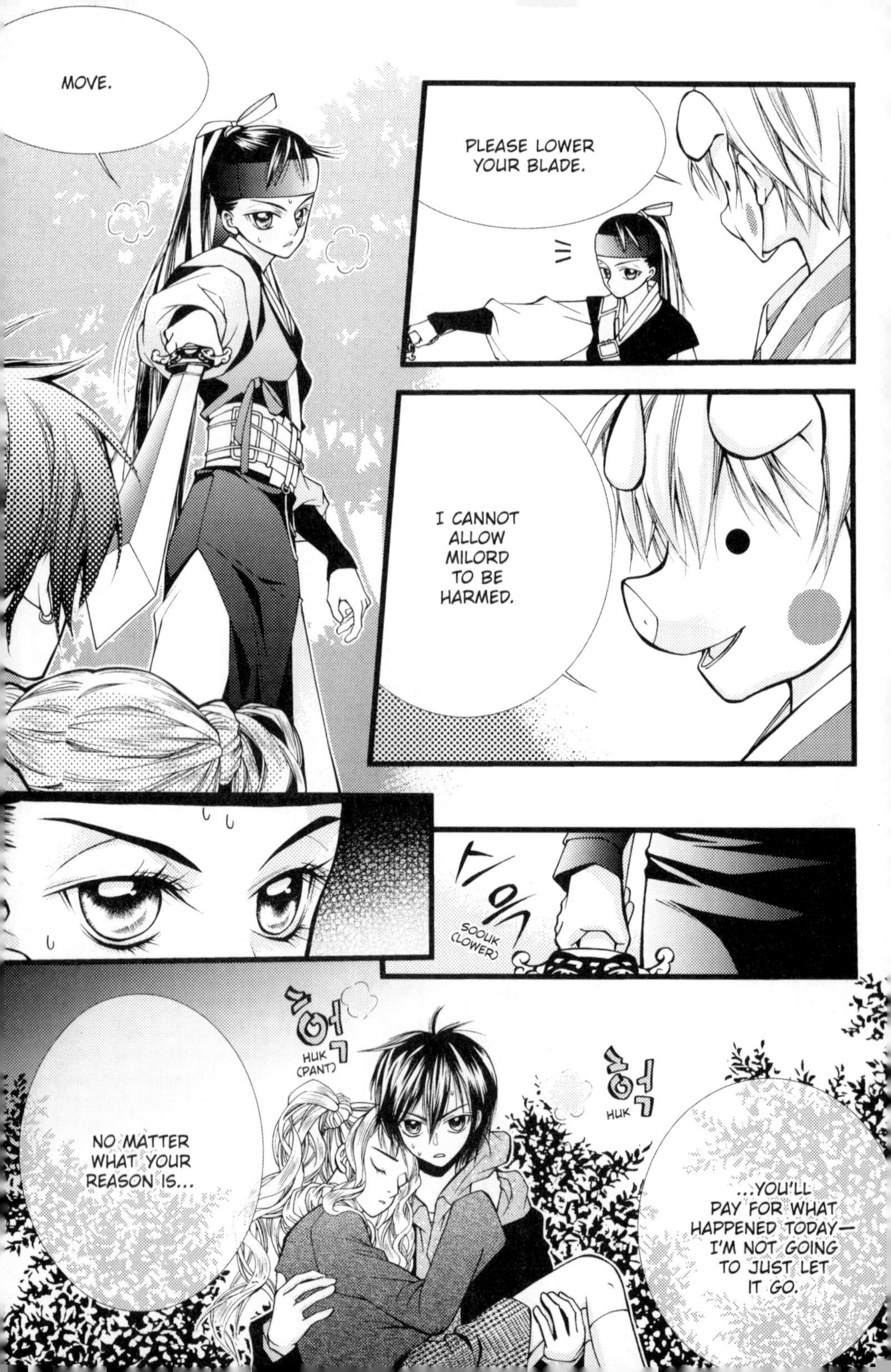
MOVE.
PLEASE LOWER YOUR BLADE.
I CANNOT ALLOW MILORD TO BE HARMED.
스윽
SOOUK (LOWER)
헉
HUK (PANT)
헉
HUK
NO MATTER WHAT YOUR REASON IS...
...YOU'LL PAY FOR WHAT HAPPENED TODAY— I'M NOT GOING TO JUST LET IT GO.

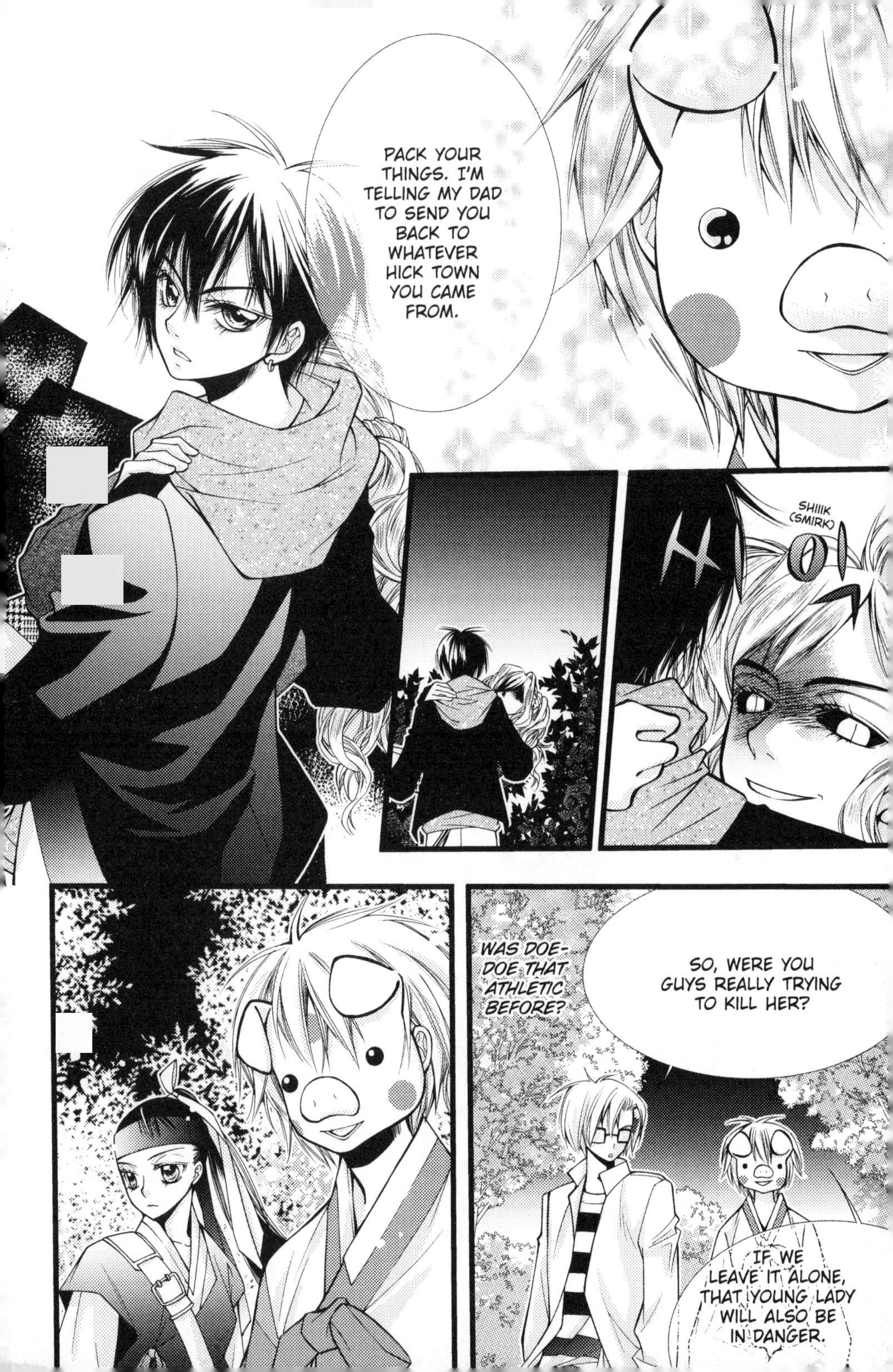
PACK YOUR THINGS. I'M TELLING MY DAD TO SEND YOU BACK TO WHATEVER HICK TOWN YOU CAME FROM.
SHIIIK (SMIRK)
WAS DOE-DOE THAT ATHLETIC BEFORE?
SO, WERE YOU GUYS REALLY TRYING TO KILL HER?
IF WE LEAVE IT ALONE, THAT YOUNG LADY WILL ALSO BE IN DANGER.

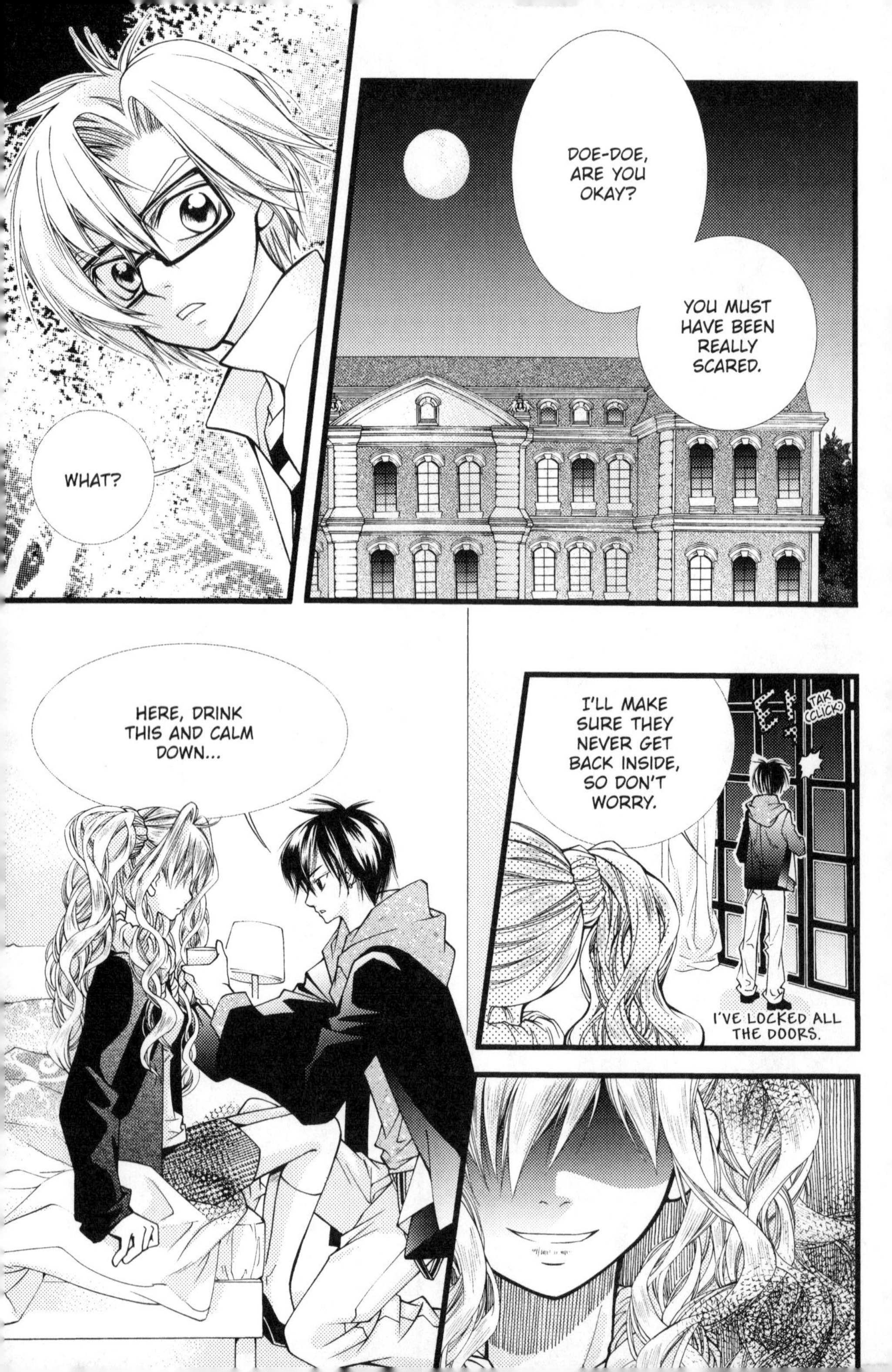
WHAT?
DOE-DOE, ARE YOU OKAY?
YOU MUST HAVE BEEN REALLY SCARED.
HERE, DRINK THIS AND CALM DOWN...
I'LL MAKE SURE THEY NEVER GET BACK INSIDE, SO DON'T WORRY.
TAK (CLICK)
I'VE LOCKED ALL THE DOORS.

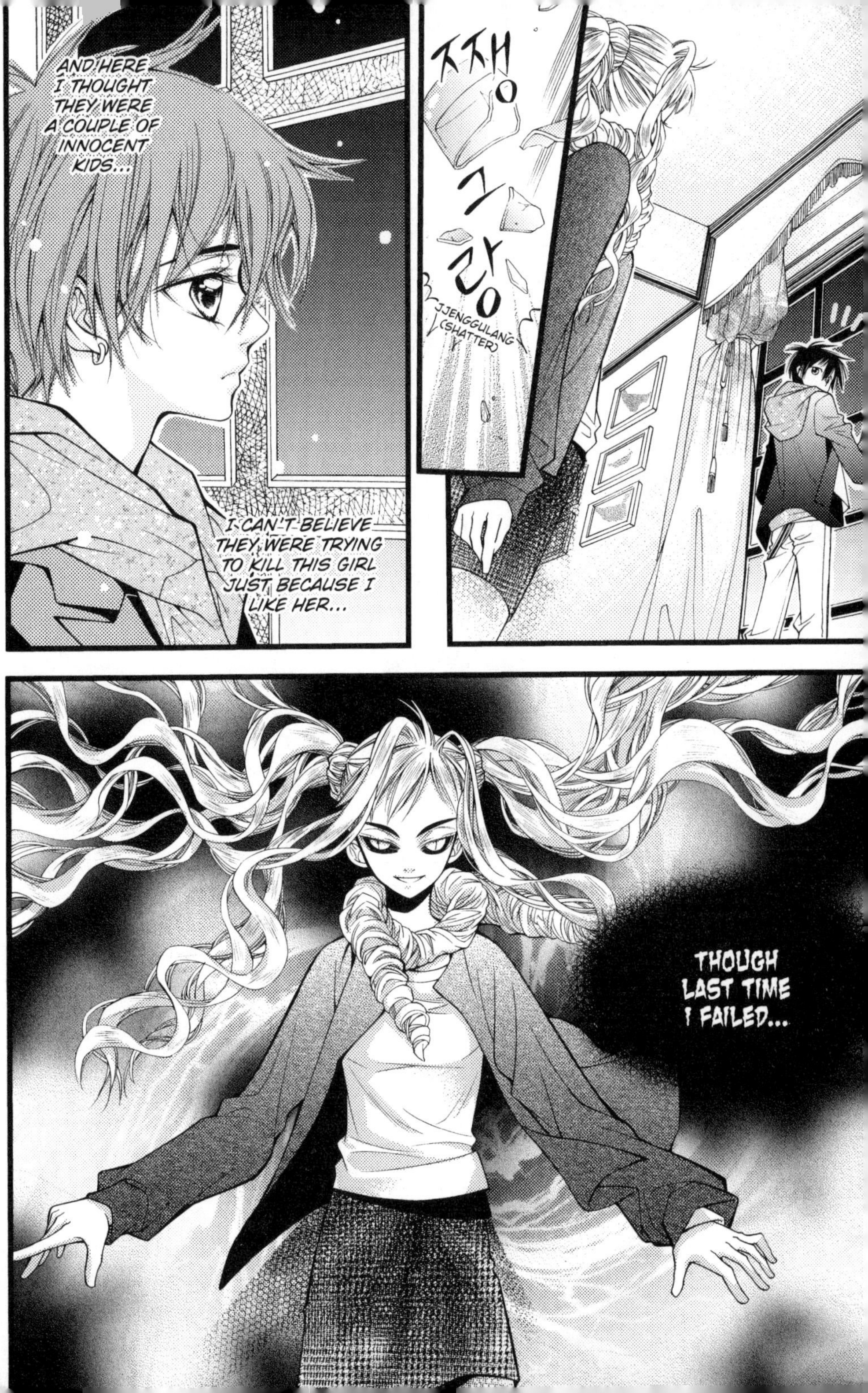
AND HERE I THOUGHT THEY WERE A COUPLE OF INNOCENT KIDS...
I CAN'T BELIEVE THEY WERE TRYING TO KILL THIS GIRL JUST BECAUSE I LIKE HER...
쨍그랑
JJENGGULANG (SHATTER)
THOUGH LAST TIME I FAILED...

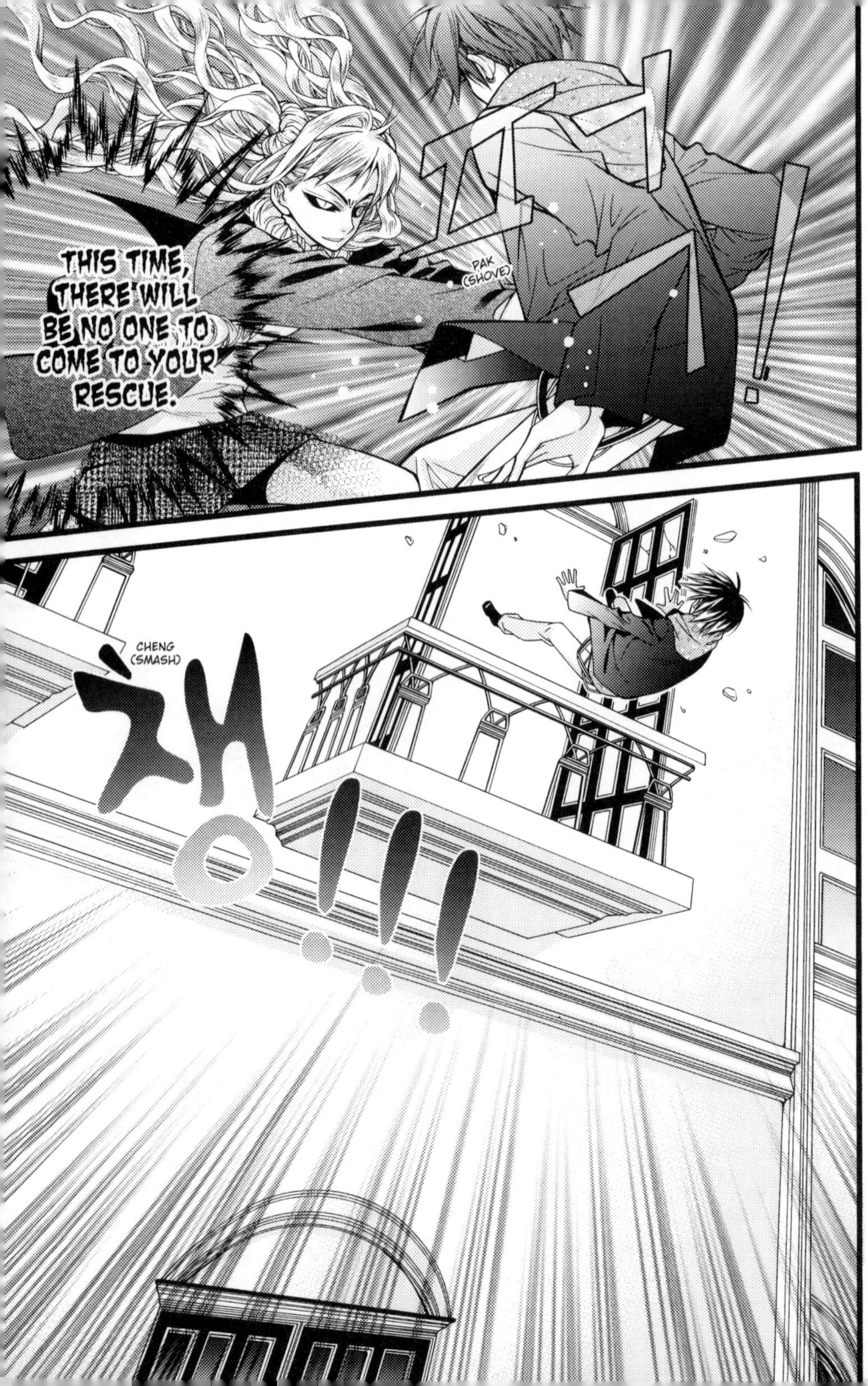
THIS TIME, THERE WILL BE NO ONE TO COME TO YOUR RESCUE.
PAK (SHOVE)
CHENG (SMASH)

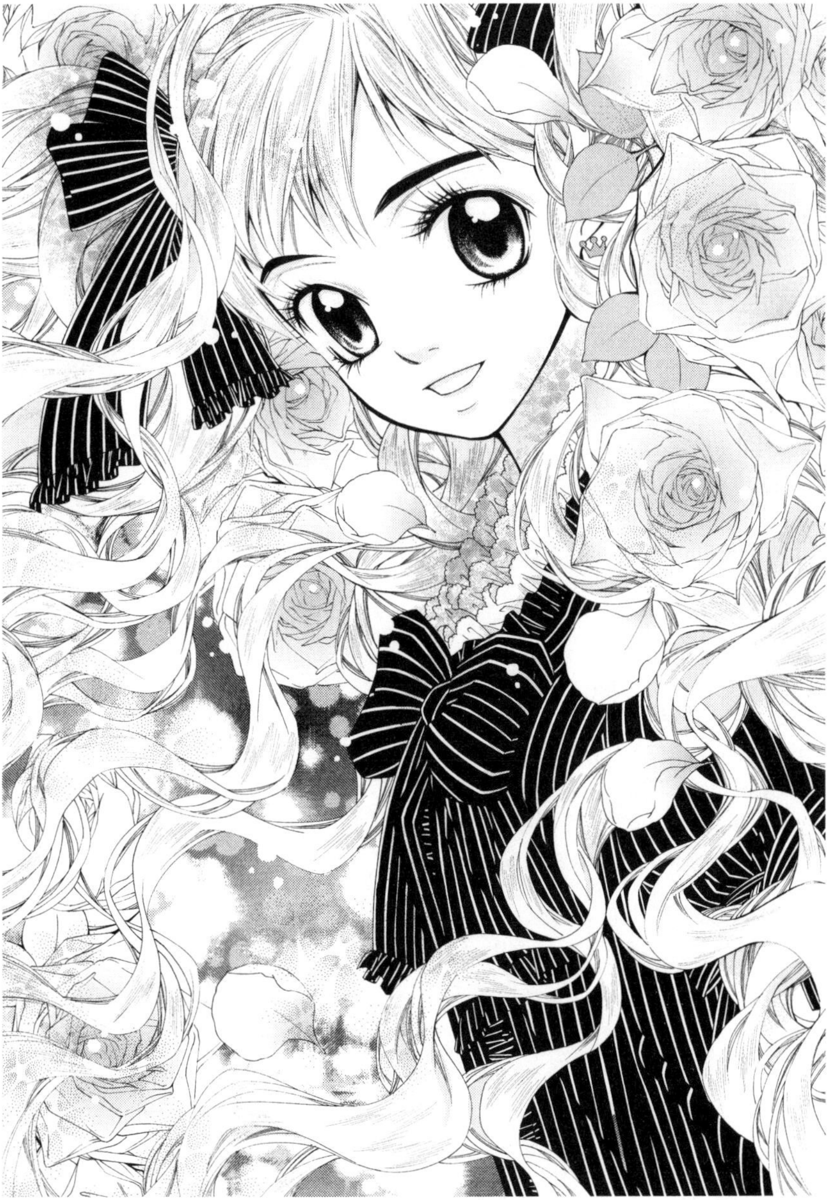

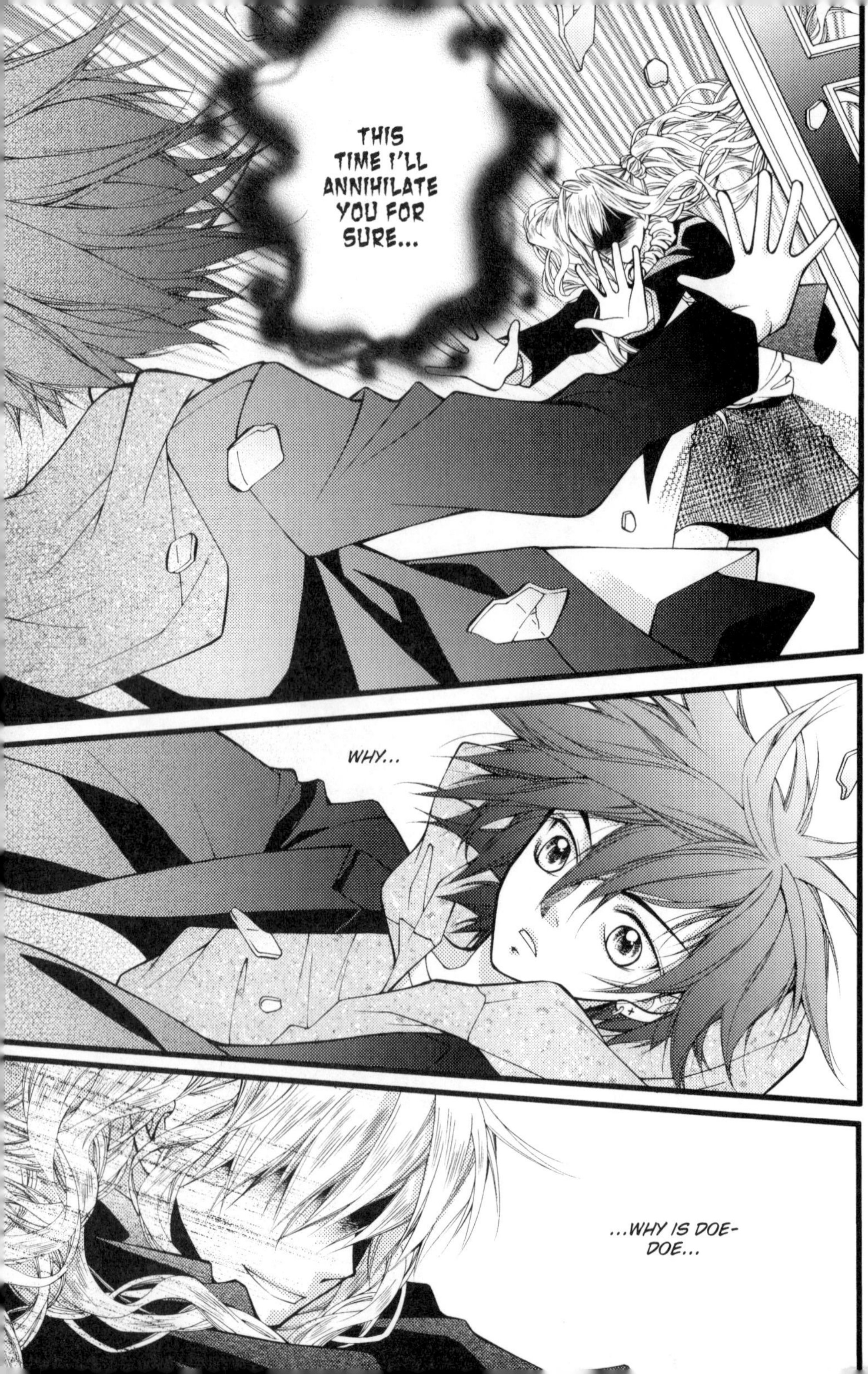
THIS TIME I'LL ANNIHILATE YOU FOR SURE...
WHY...
...WHY IS DOE-DOE...

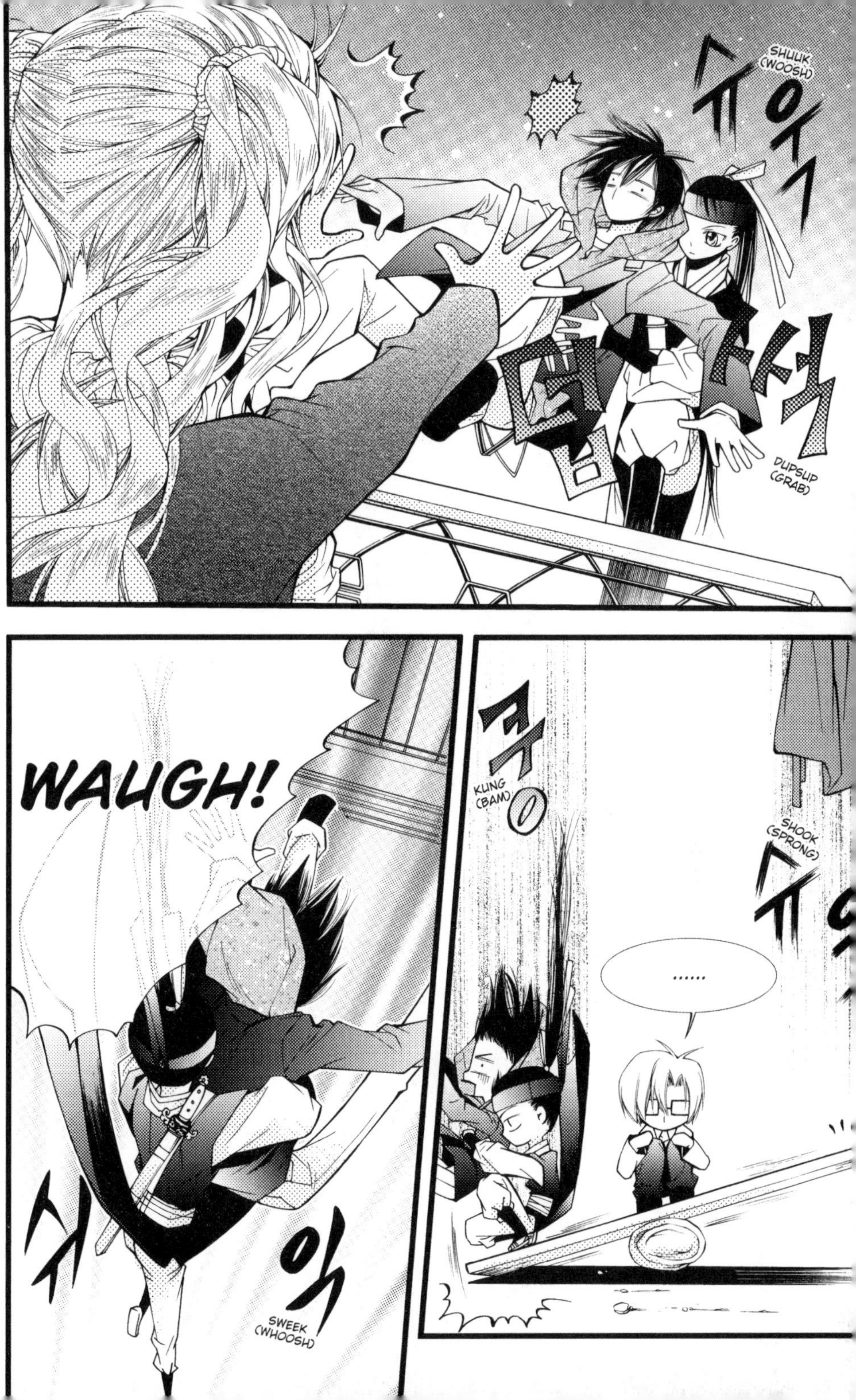
SHUUK (WOOSH)
DUPSUP (GRAB)
WAUGH!
SWEEK (WHOOSH)
KUNG (BAM)
SHOOK (SPRONG)
......

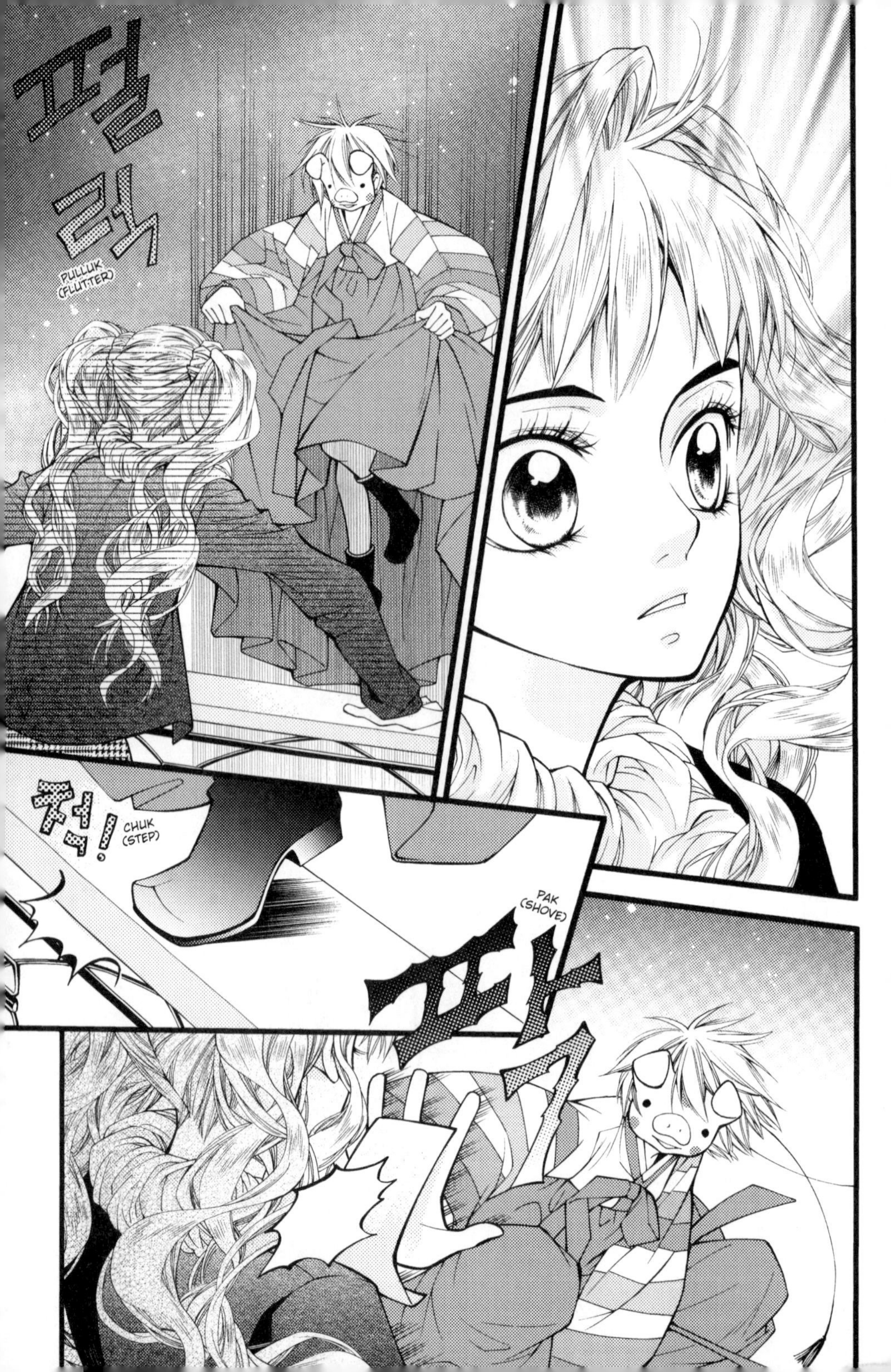
펄럭
PULLUK (FLUTTER)
척!
CHUK (STEP)
PAK (SHOVE)
팍

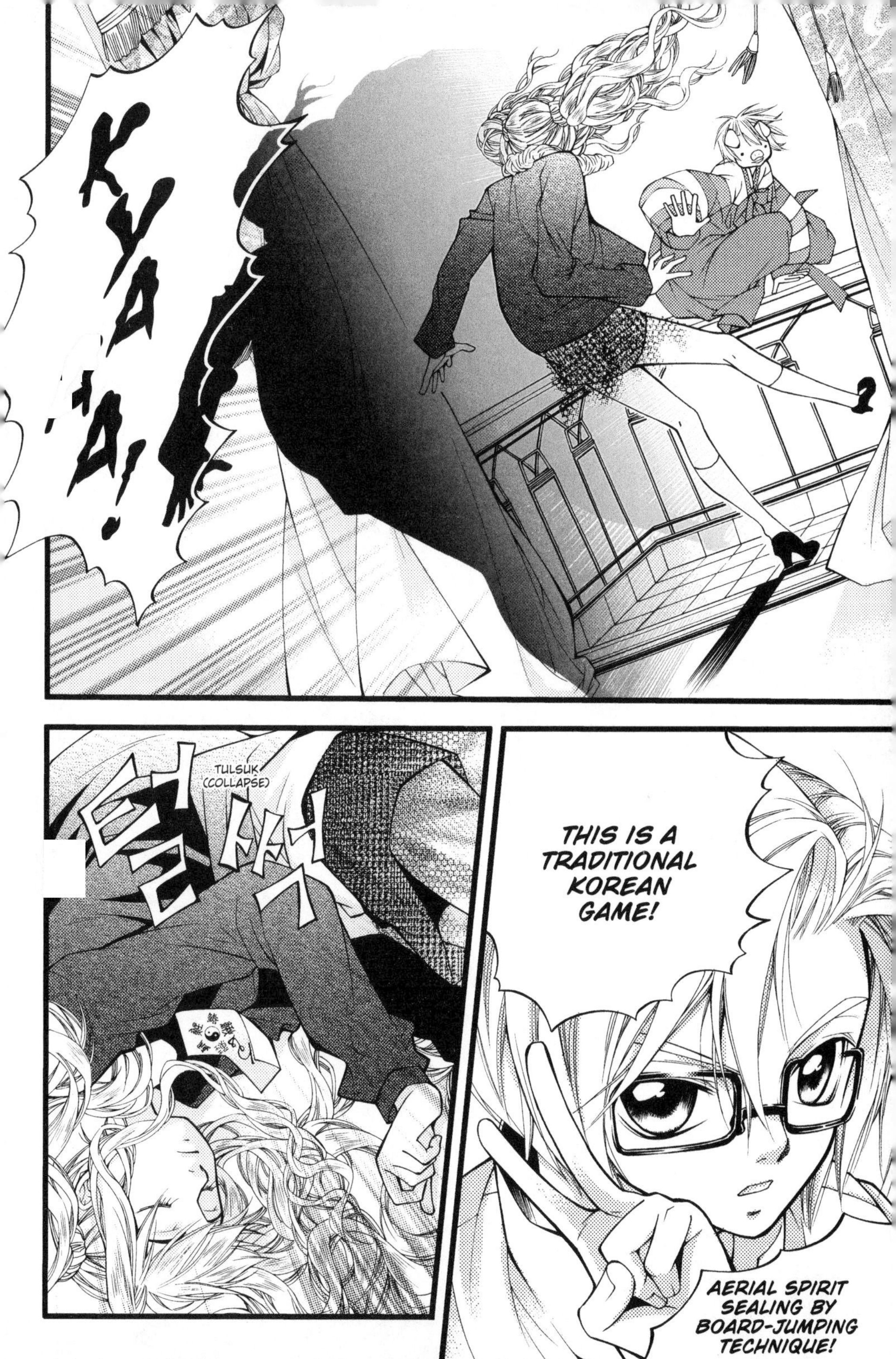
KYAAA!
털썩
TULSUK (COLLAPSE)
THIS IS A TRADITIONAL KOREAN GAME!
AERIAL SPIRIT SEALING BY BOARD-JUMPING TECHNIQUE!

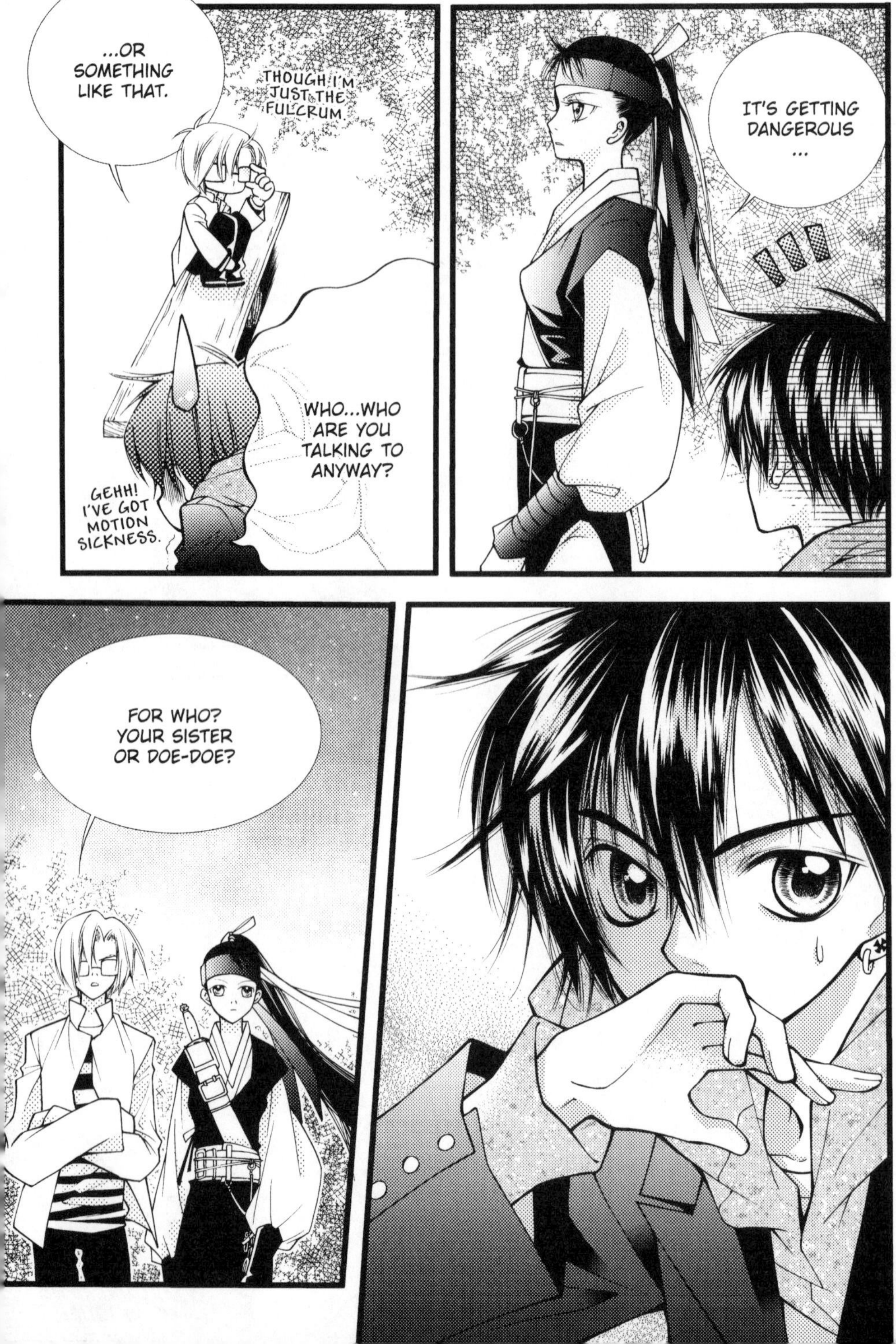
...OR SOMETHING LIKE THAT.
THOUGH I'M JUST THE FULCRUM.
WHO...WHO ARE YOU TALKING TO ANYWAY?
GEHH! I'VE GOT MOTION SICKNESS.
IT'S GETTING DANGEROUS ...
FOR WHO? YOUR SISTER OR DOE-DOE?

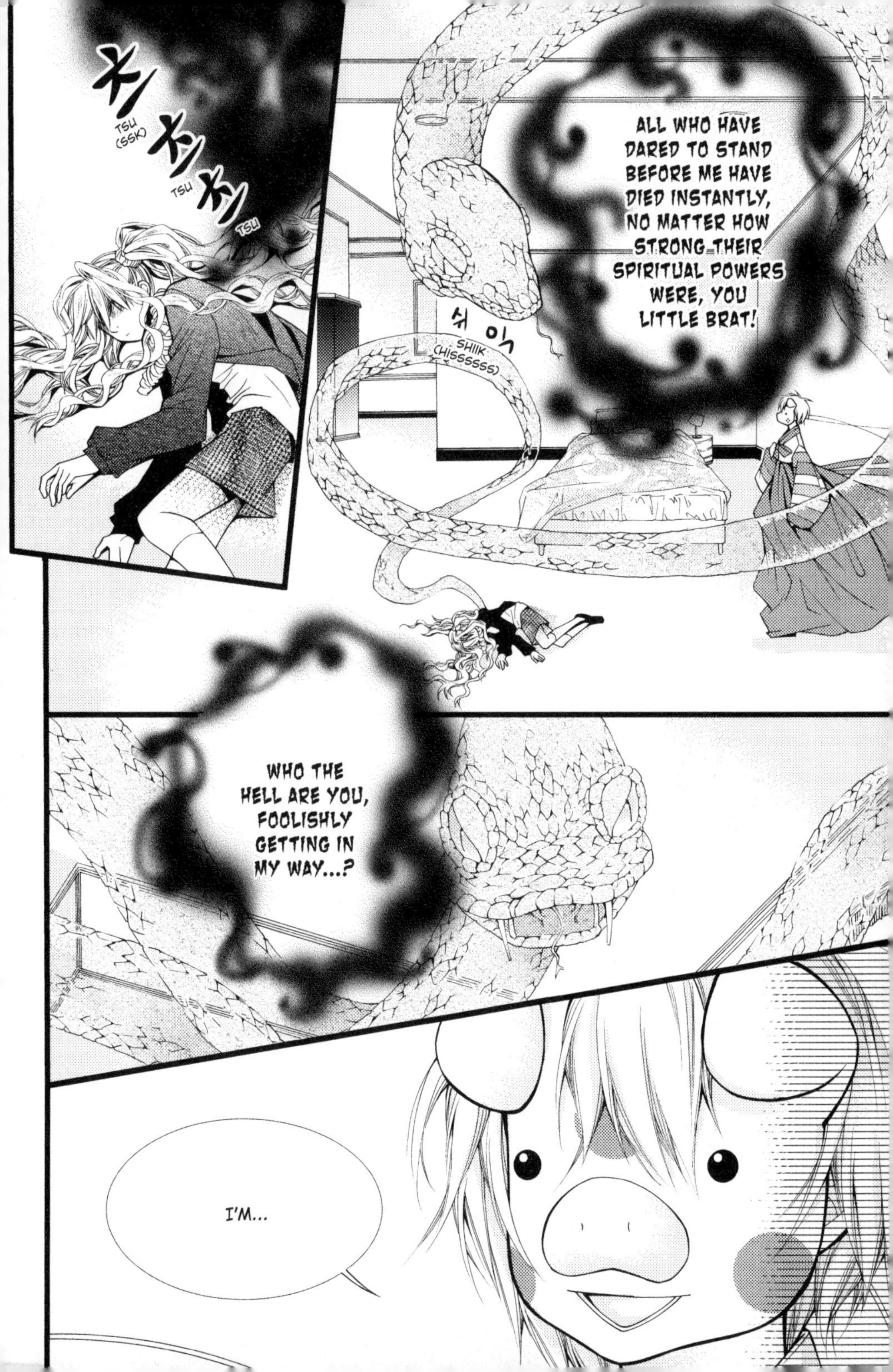

TSU (SSK)
TSU
TSU
쉬익
SHIIK (HISSSSSS)
ALL WHO HAVE DARED TO STAND BEFORE ME HAVE DIED INSTANTLY, NO MATTER HOW STRONG THEIR SPIRITUAL POWERS WERE, YOU LITTLE BRAT!
WHO THE HELL ARE YOU, FOOLISHLY GETTING IN MY WAY...?
I'M...

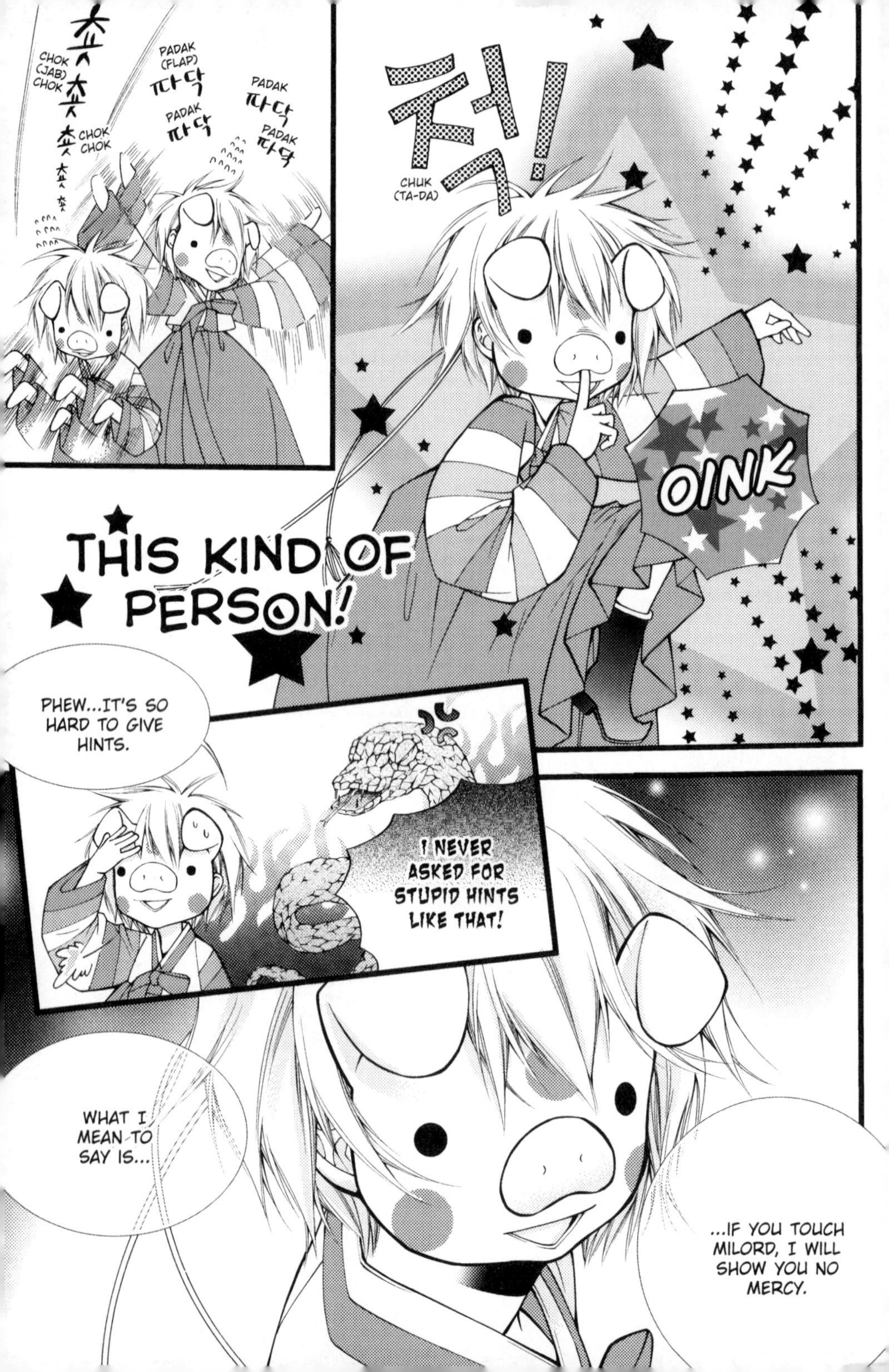

촉
CHOK (JAB) CHOK
촉
촉
CHOK CHOK
촉
촉
PADAK (FLAP)
파닥
PADAK
파닥
PADAK
파닥
PADAK
파닥
척!
CHUK (TA-DA)
THIS KIND OF PERSON!
OINK
PHEW...IT'S SO HARD TO GIVE HINTS.
I NEVER ASKED FOR STUPID HINTS LIKE THAT!
WHAT I MEAN TO SAY IS...
...IF YOU TOUCH MILORD, I WILL SHOW YOU NO MERCY.

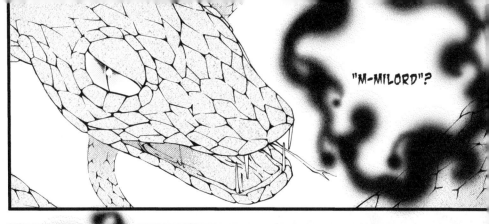

"M-MILORD"?

VERY FUNNY.
LAST TIME, I
MADE A MISTAKE,
BUT THIS TIME,
I'LL KILL YOU
WITH A SINGLE
BITE.

KIK
(SNICKER)

SHUUUK
(SWOOSH)

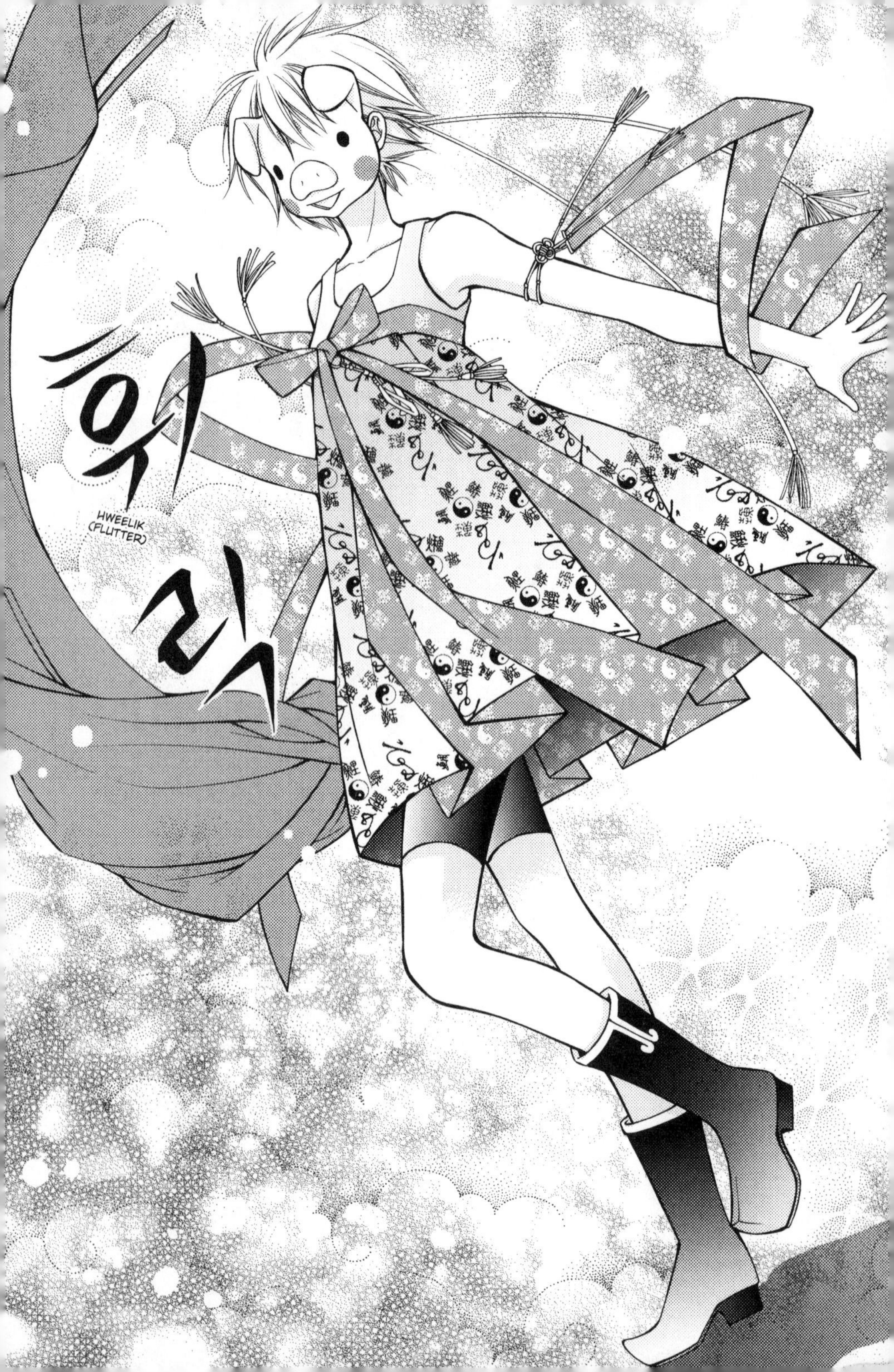
휘리릭
HWEELIK
(FLUTTER)

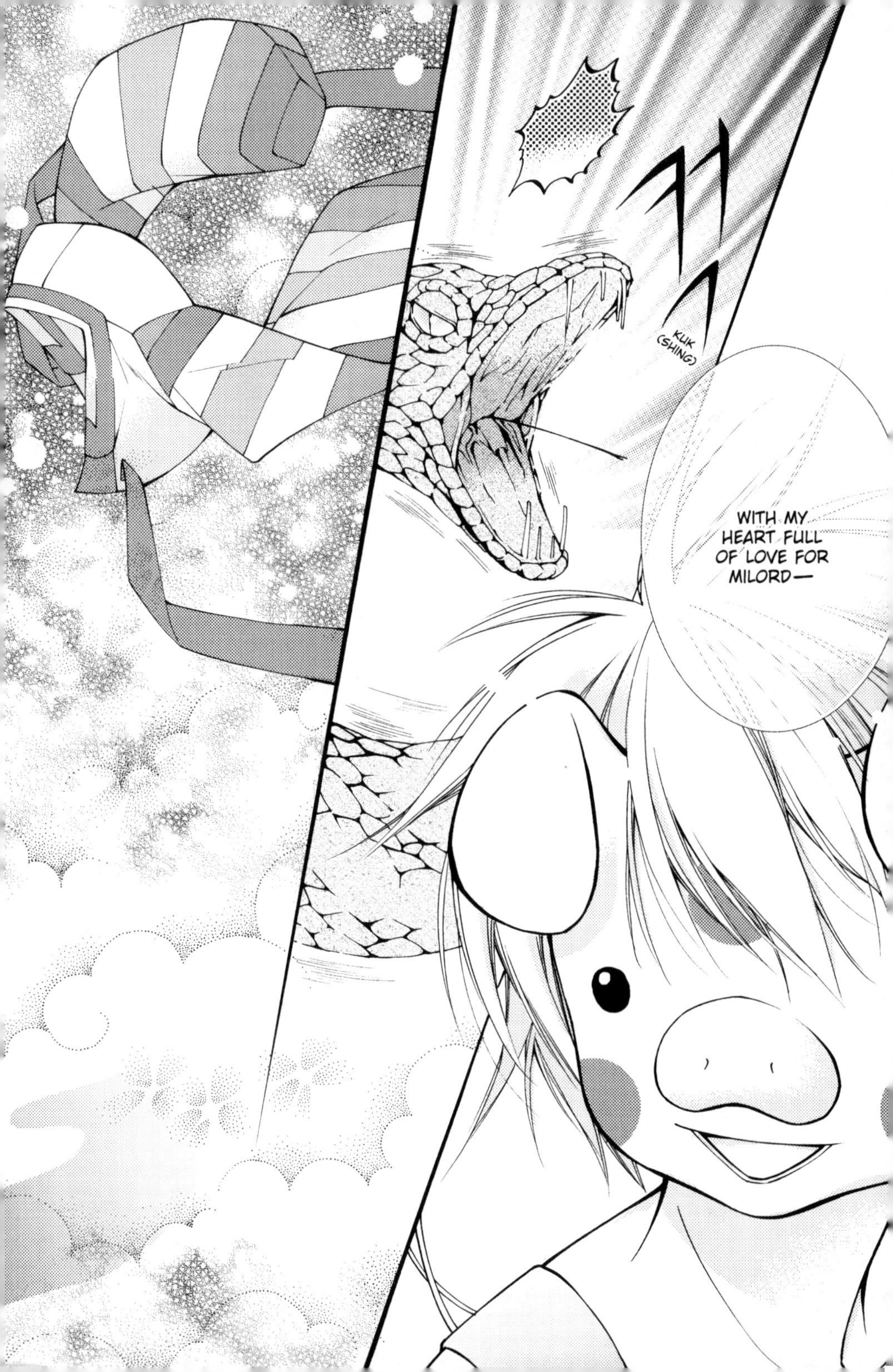
KUK
(SHING)
WITH MY HEART FULL OF LOVE FOR MILORD—

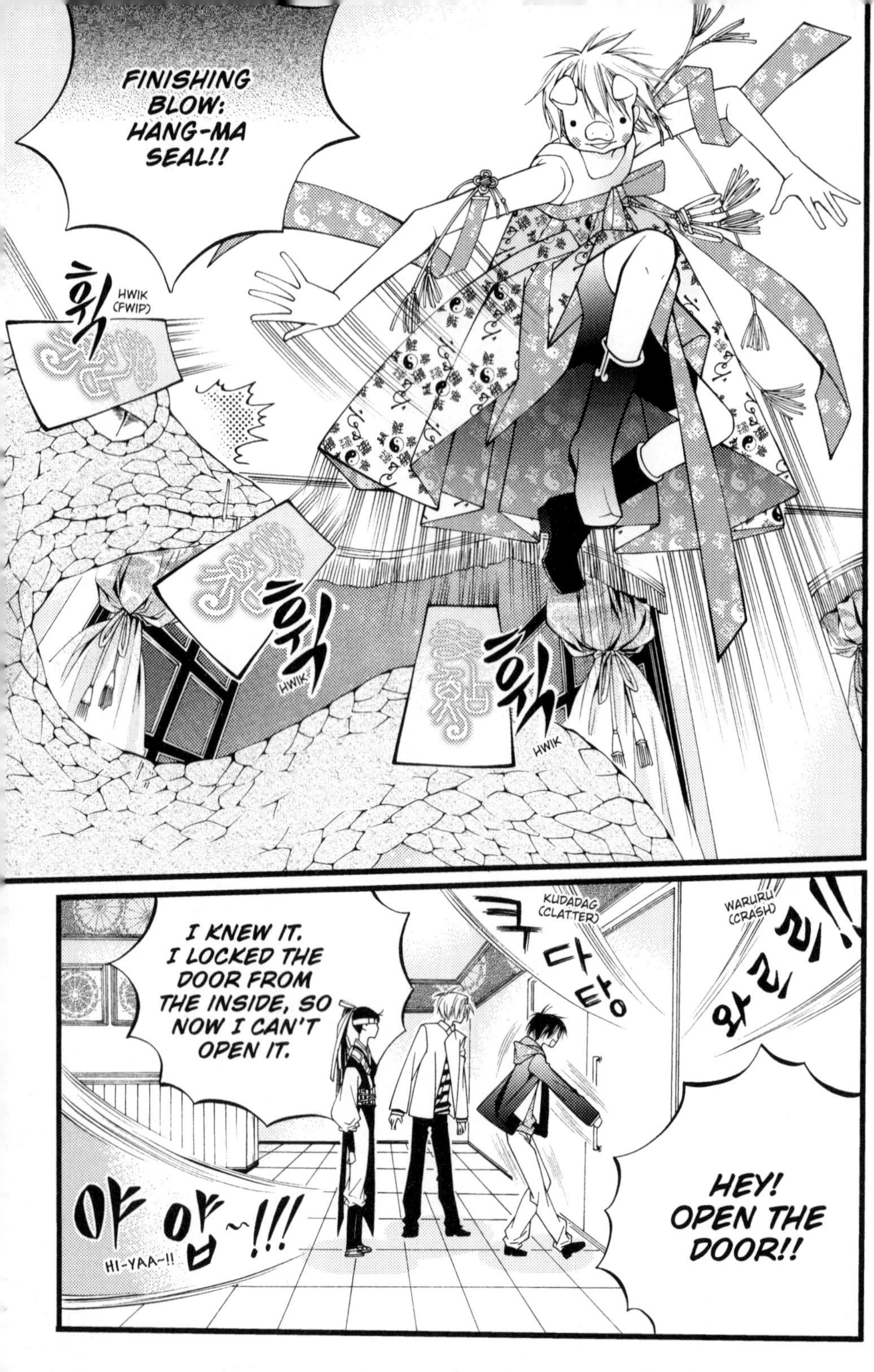
FINISHING BLOW: HANG-MA SEAL!!
휙
HWIK (FWIP)
휘익
HWIK
휘익
HWIK
I KNEW IT. I LOCKED THE DOOR FROM THE INSIDE, SO NOW I CAN'T OPEN IT.
쿠다당
KUDADAG (CLATTER)
와르르!!
WARURU (CRASH)
야압~!!!
HI-YAA~!!
HEY! OPEN THE DOOR!!

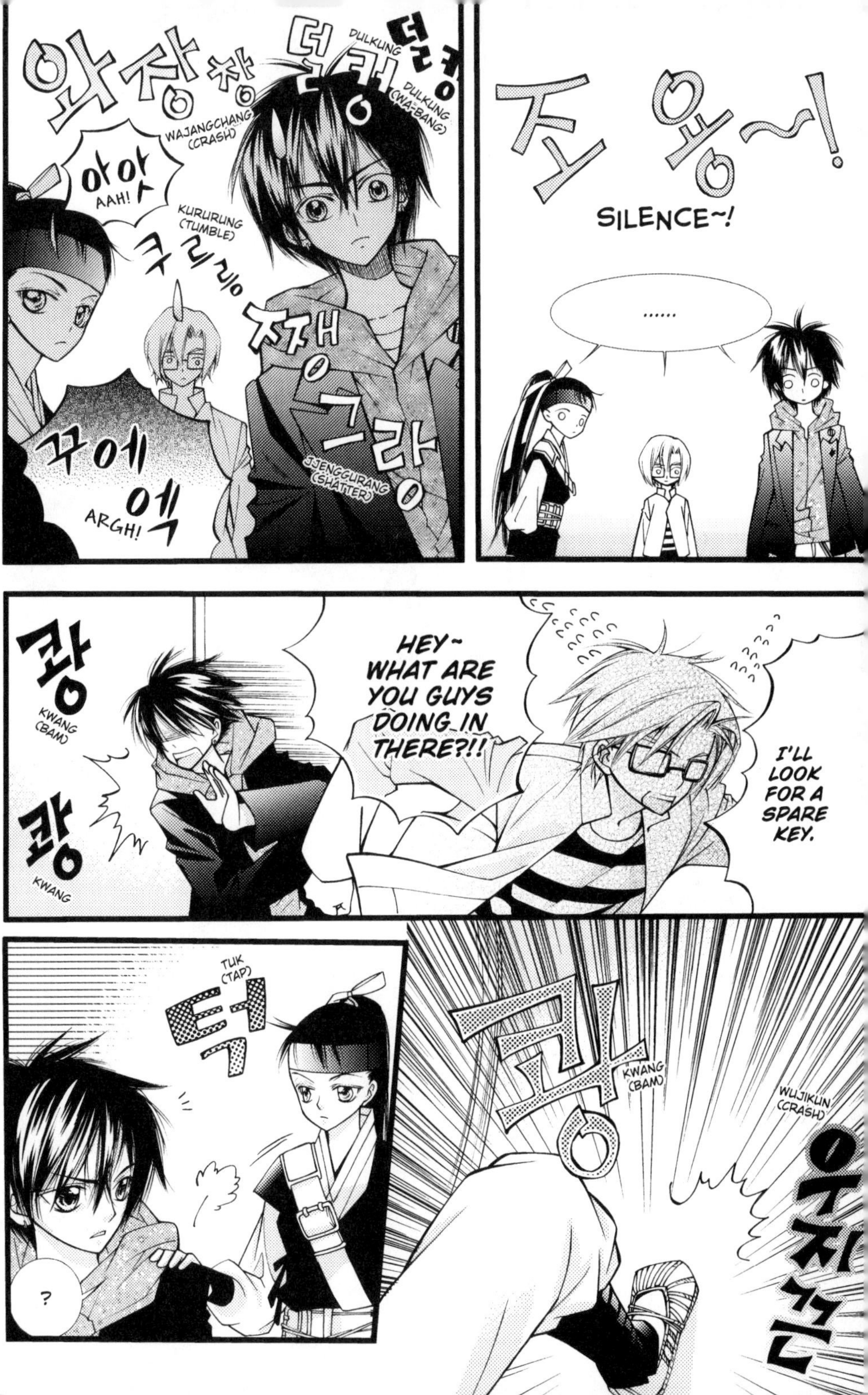

WAJANGCHANG (CRASH)
DULKUNG
DULKUNG (WA-BANG)
아악
AAH!
KURURUNG (TUMBLE)
JJENGGURANG (SHATTER)
ARGH!
SILENCE~!
......
쾅
KWANG (BAM)
쾅
KWANG
HEY~ WHAT ARE YOU GUYS DOING IN THERE?!!
I'LL LOOK FOR A SPARE KEY.
TUK (TAP)
?
KWANG (BAM)
WUJIKUN (CRASH)

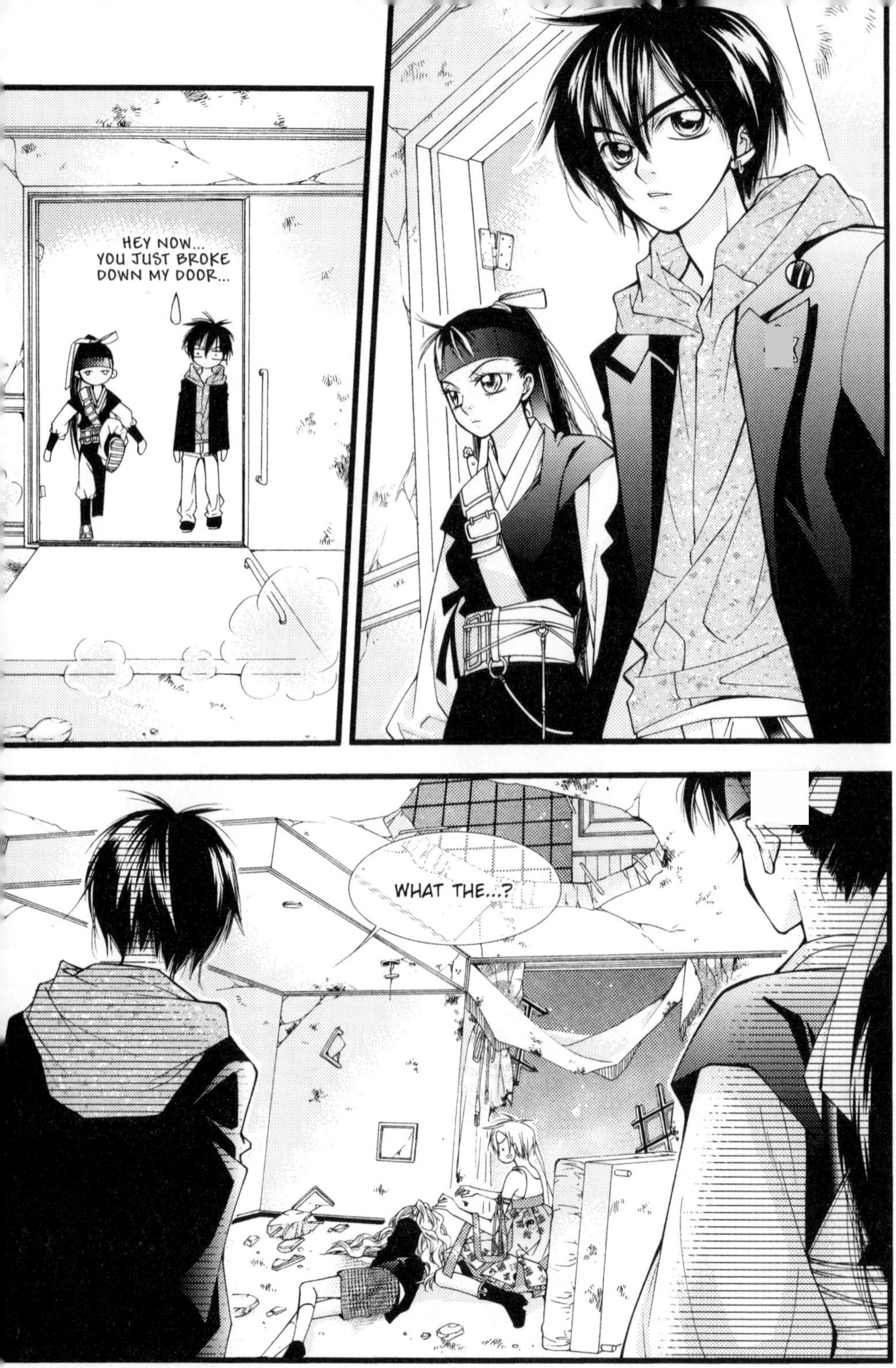
HEY NOW...
YOU JUST BROKE
DOWN MY DOOR...
WHAT THE...?

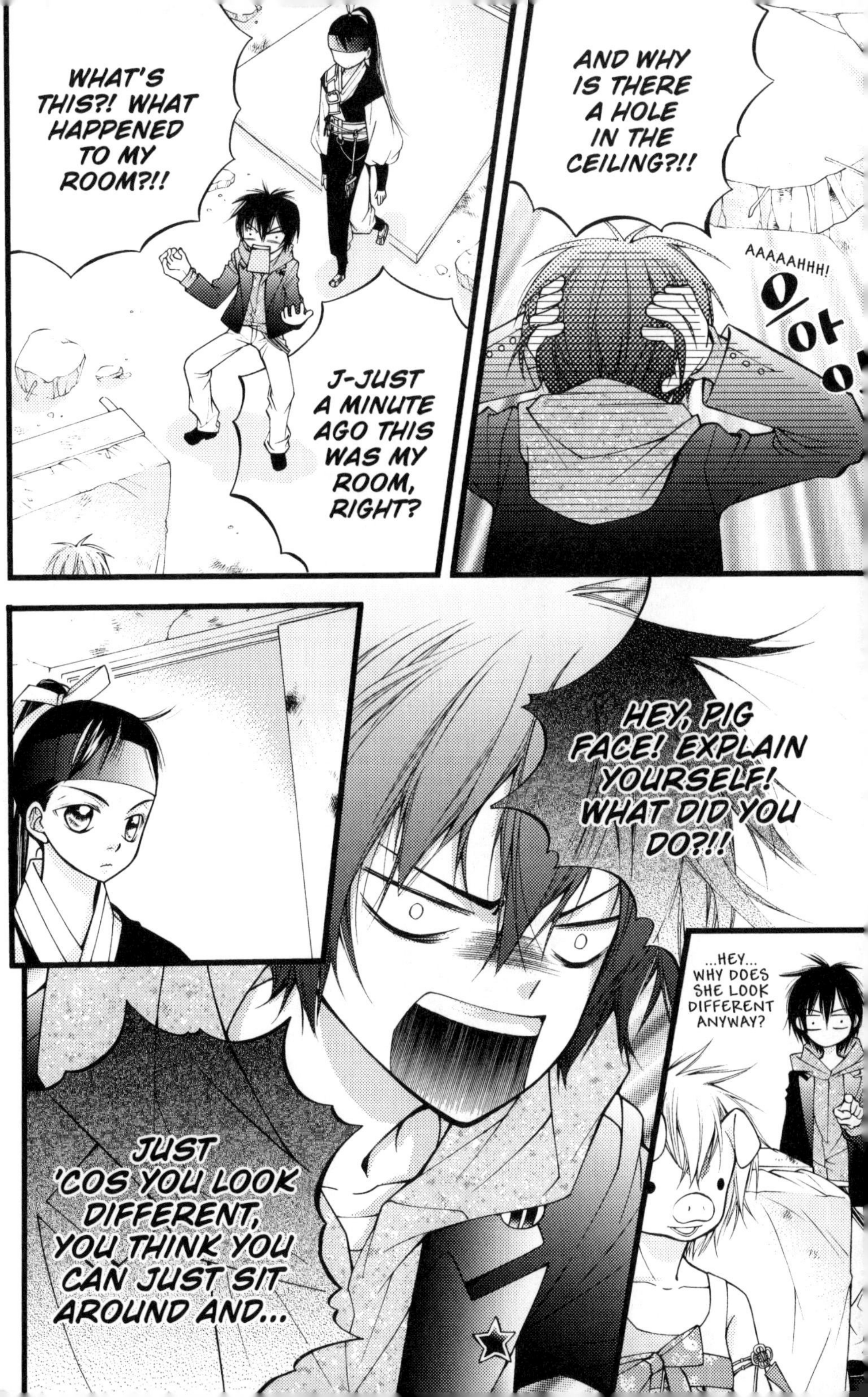
WHAT'S THIS?! WHAT HAPPENED TO MY ROOM?!!
J-JUST A MINUTE AGO THIS WAS MY ROOM, RIGHT?
AND WHY IS THERE A HOLE IN THE CEILING?!!
AAAAAHHH!
HEY, PIG FACE! EXPLAIN YOURSELF! WHAT DID YOU DO?!!
JUST 'COS YOU LOOK DIFFERENT, YOU THINK YOU CAN JUST SIT AROUND AND...
...HEY... WHY DOES SHE LOOK DIFFERENT ANYWAY?

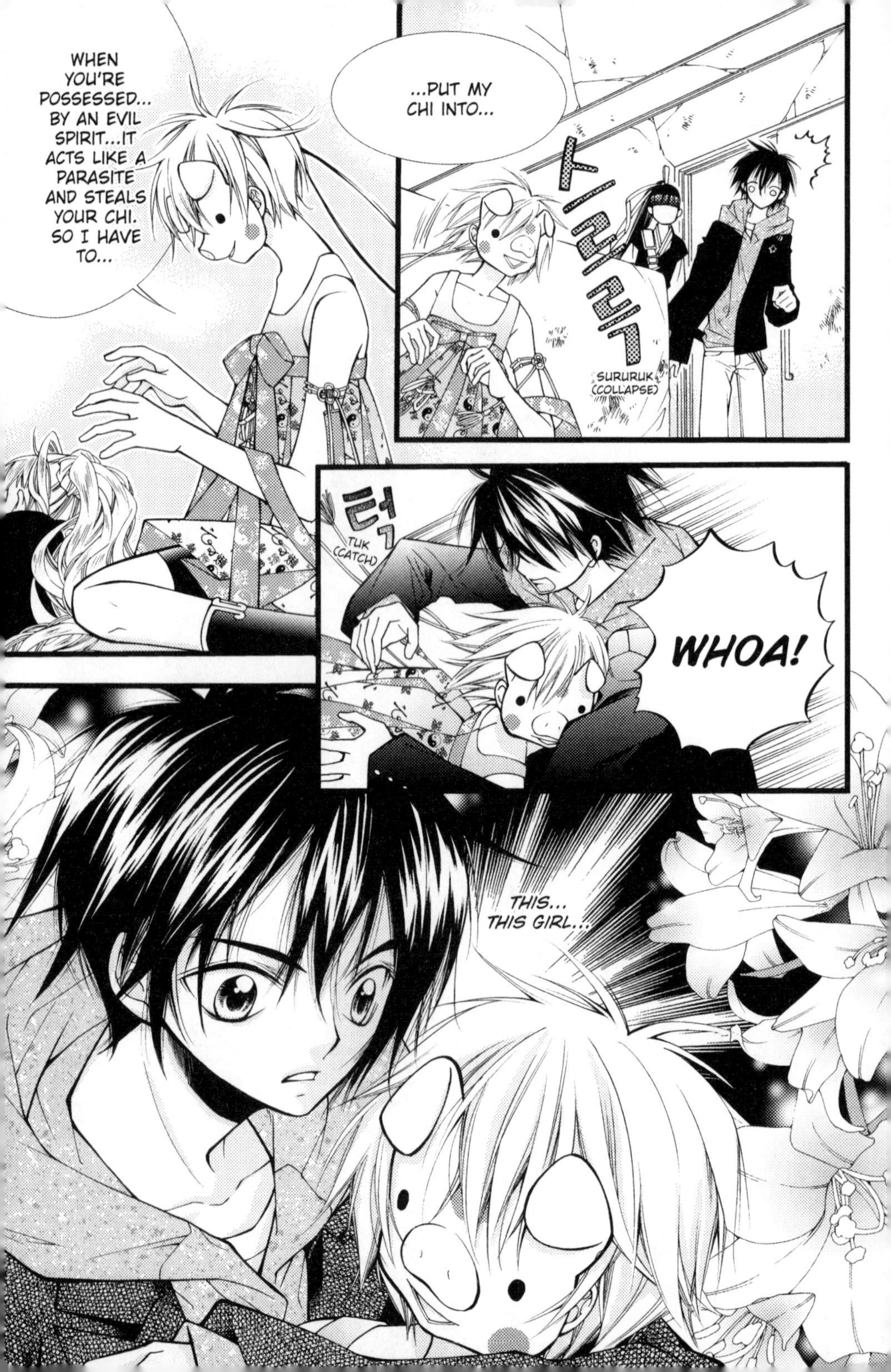
WHEN YOU'RE POSSESSED... BY AN EVIL SPIRIT...IT ACTS LIKE A PARASITE AND STEALS YOUR CHI. SO I HAVE TO...
...PUT MY CHI INTO...
스르륵
SURURUK (COLLAPSE)
턱
TUK (CATCH)
WHOA!
THIS... THIS GIRL...

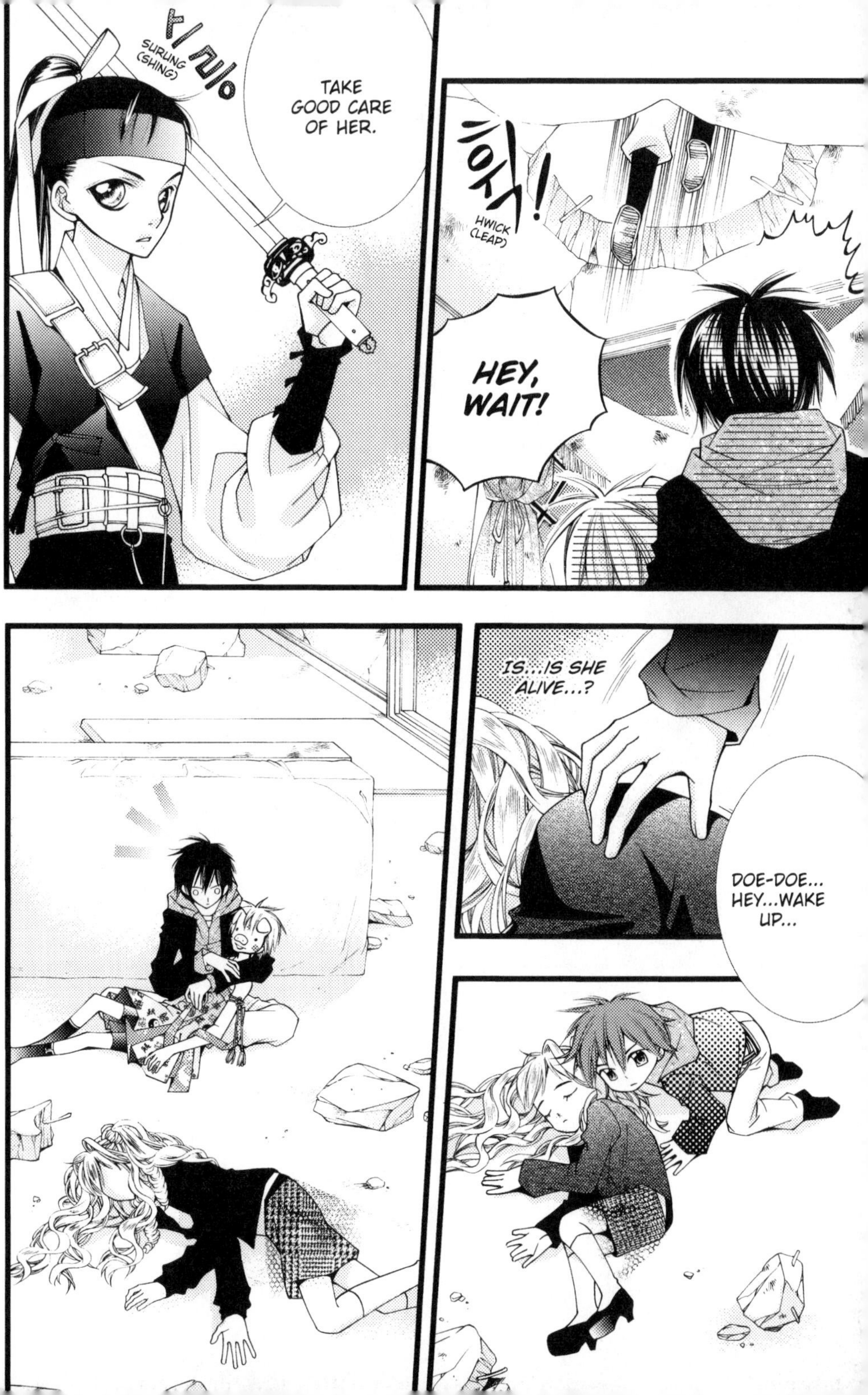
SURUNG (SHING)
TAKE GOOD CARE OF HER.
HWICK (LEAP)
HEY, WAIT!
IS...IS SHE ALIVE...?
DOE-DOE... HEY...WAKE UP...

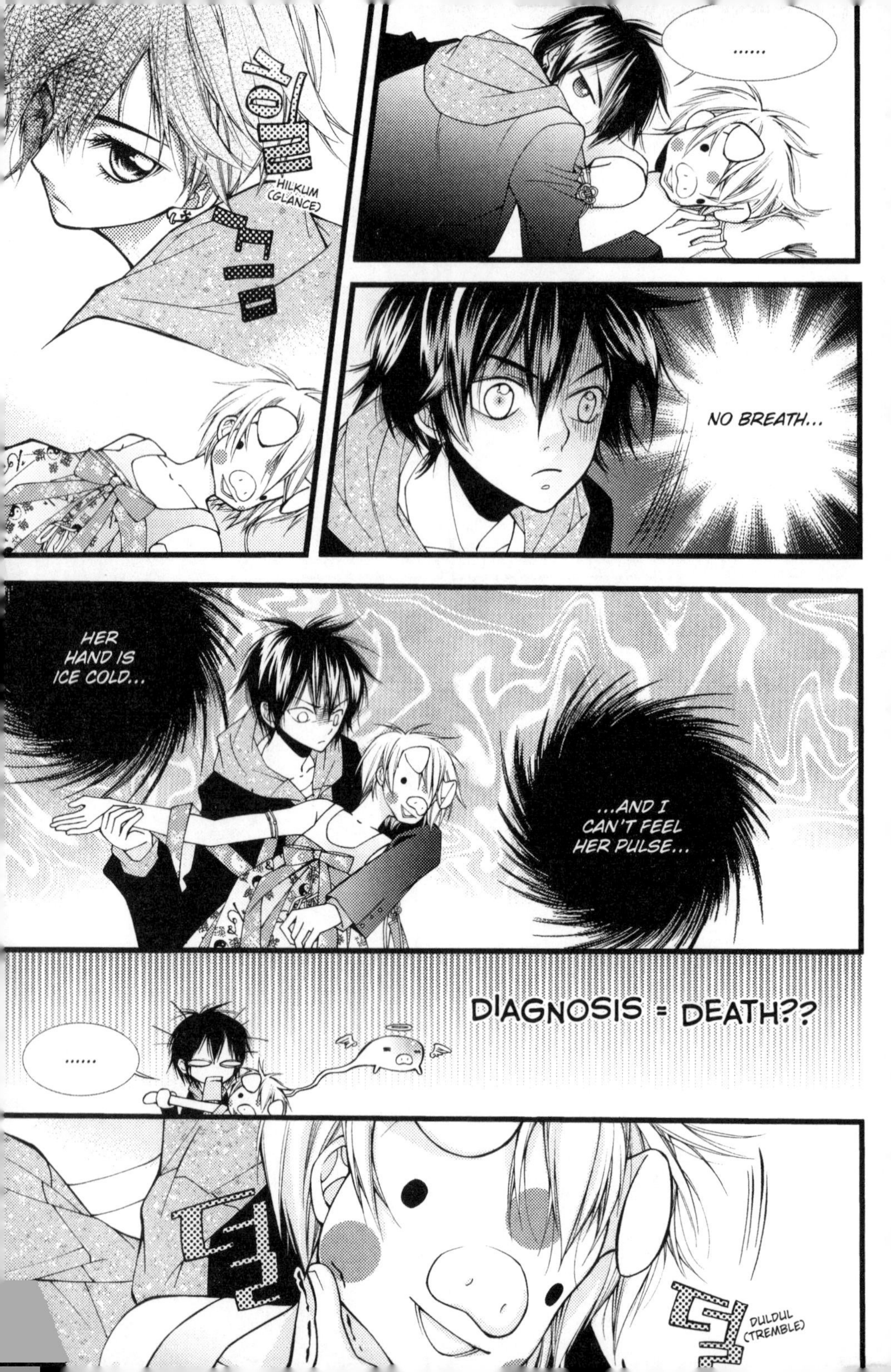
HILKUM (GLANCE)
......
NO BREATH...
HER HAND IS ICE COLD...
...AND I CAN'T FEEL HER PULSE...
DIAGNOSIS = DEATH??
......
DULDUL (TREMBLE)

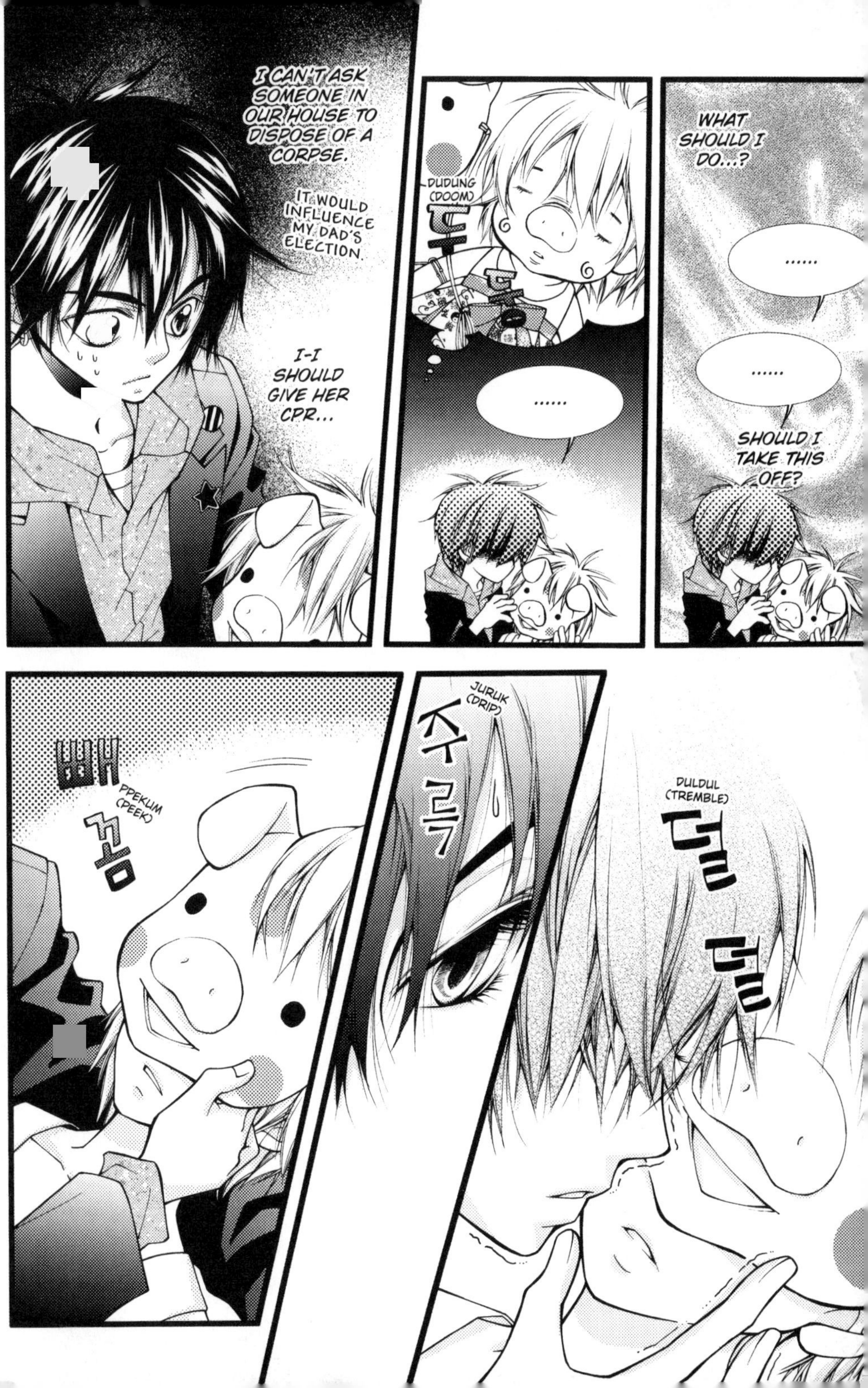
I CAN'T ASK SOMEONE IN OUR HOUSE TO DISPOSE OF A CORPSE.
IT WOULD INFLUENCE MY DAD'S ELECTION.
I-I SHOULD GIVE HER CPR...
DUDUNG (DOOM)
......
WHAT SHOULD I DO...?
......
......
SHOULD I TAKE THIS OFF?
PPEKUM (PEEK)
JURUK (DRIP)
DULDUL (TREMBLE)

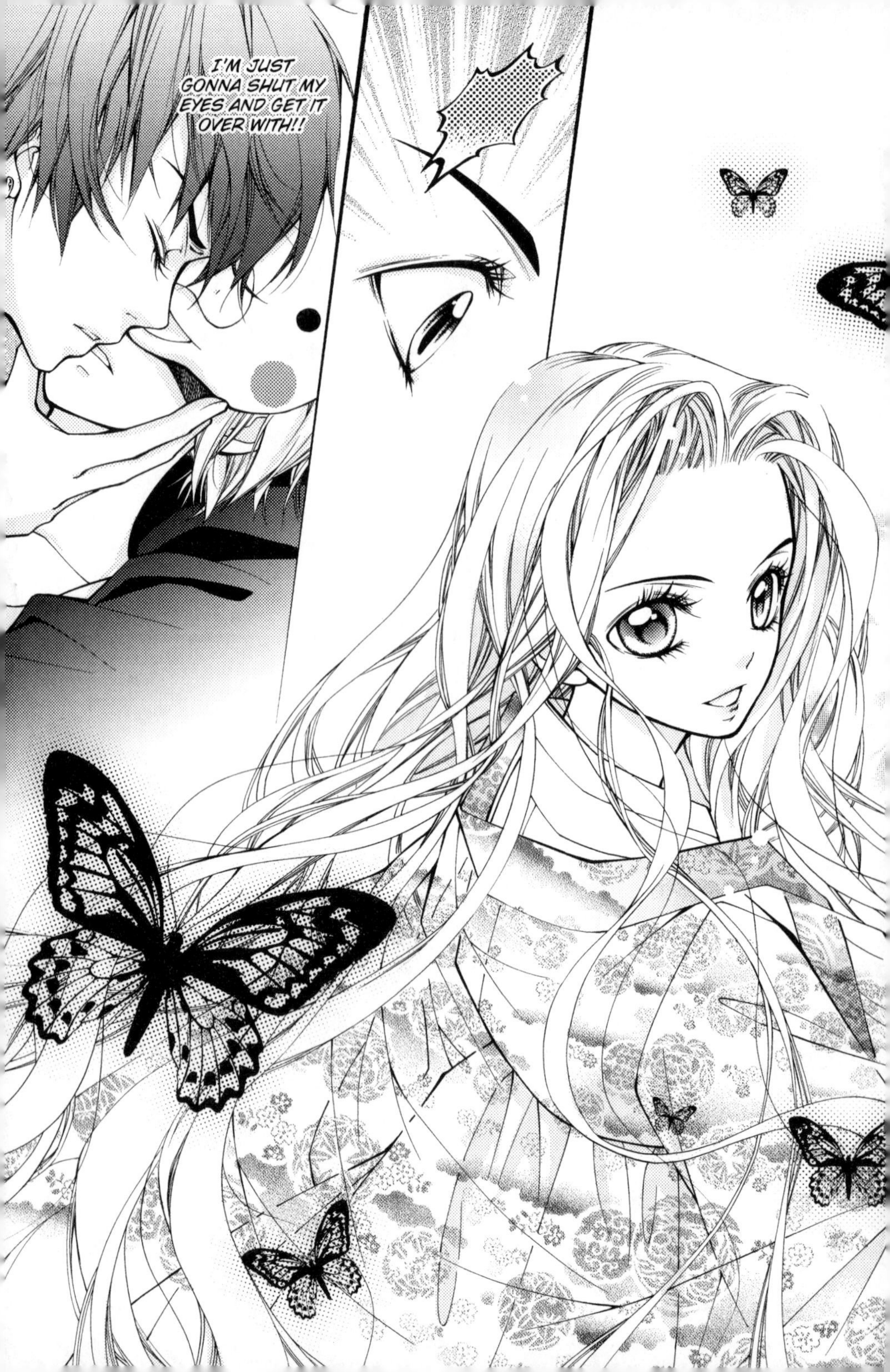
I'M JUST GONNA SHUT MY EYES AND GET IT OVER WITH!!

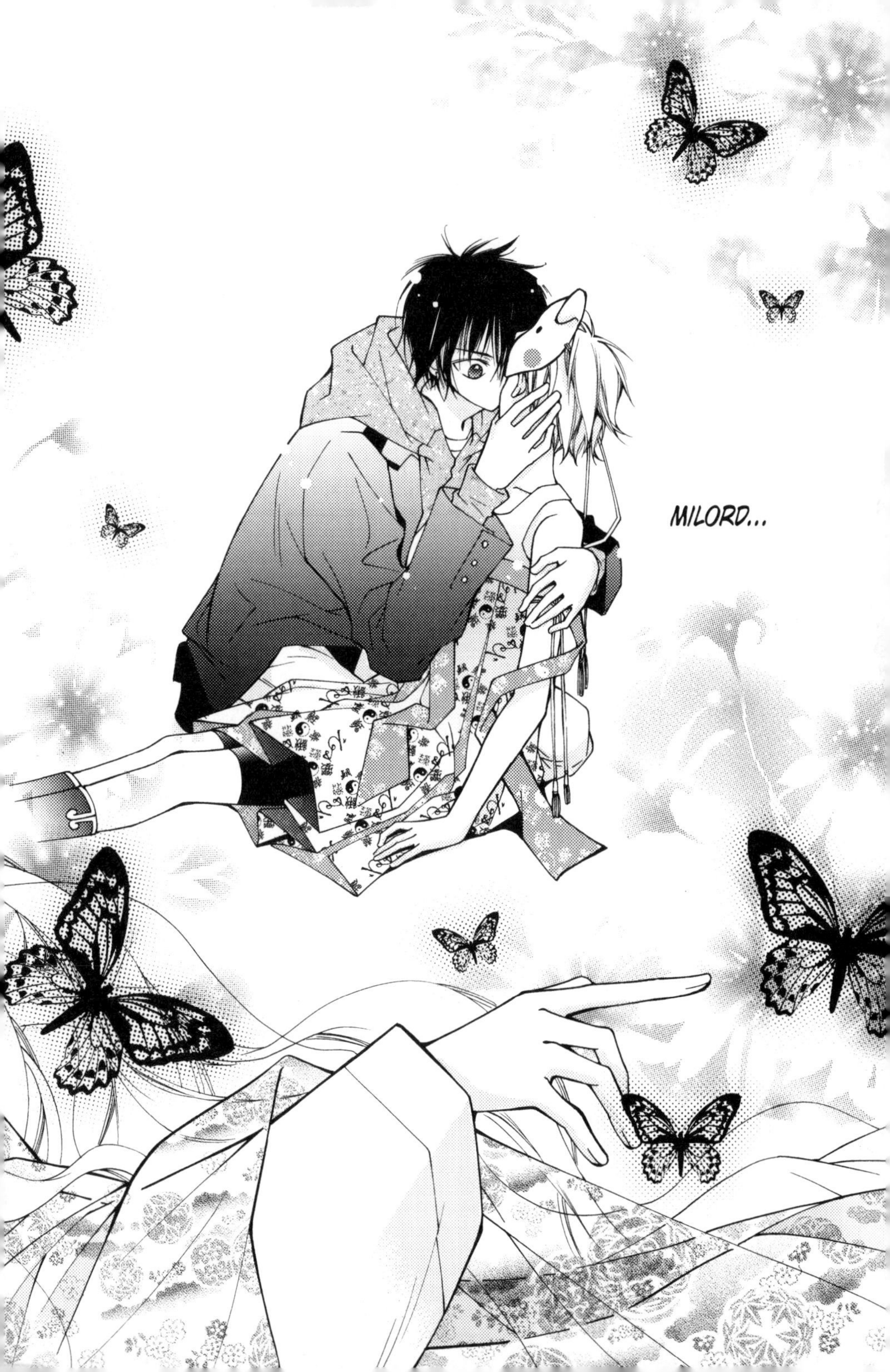
MILORD...

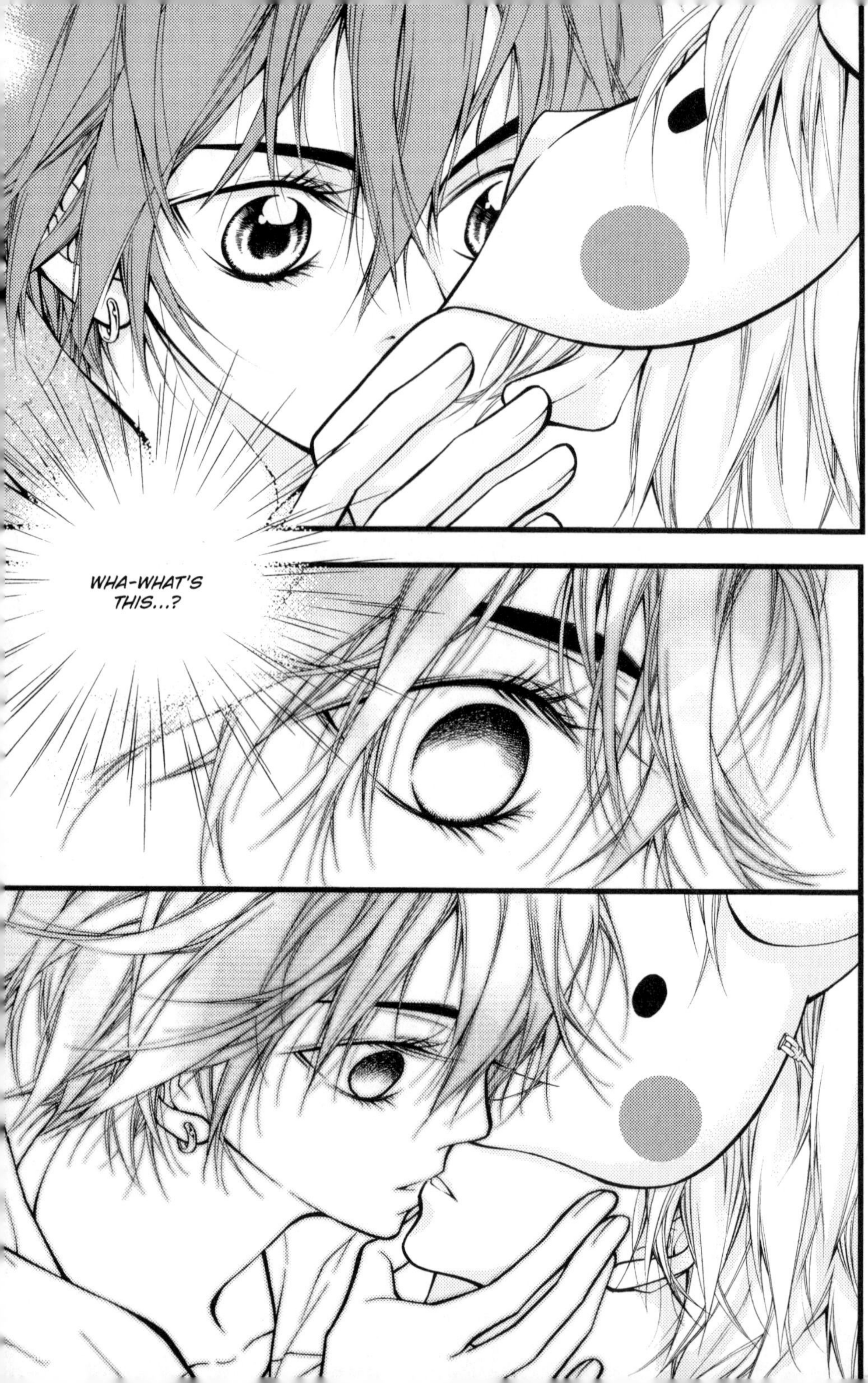
WHA-WHAT'S THIS...?

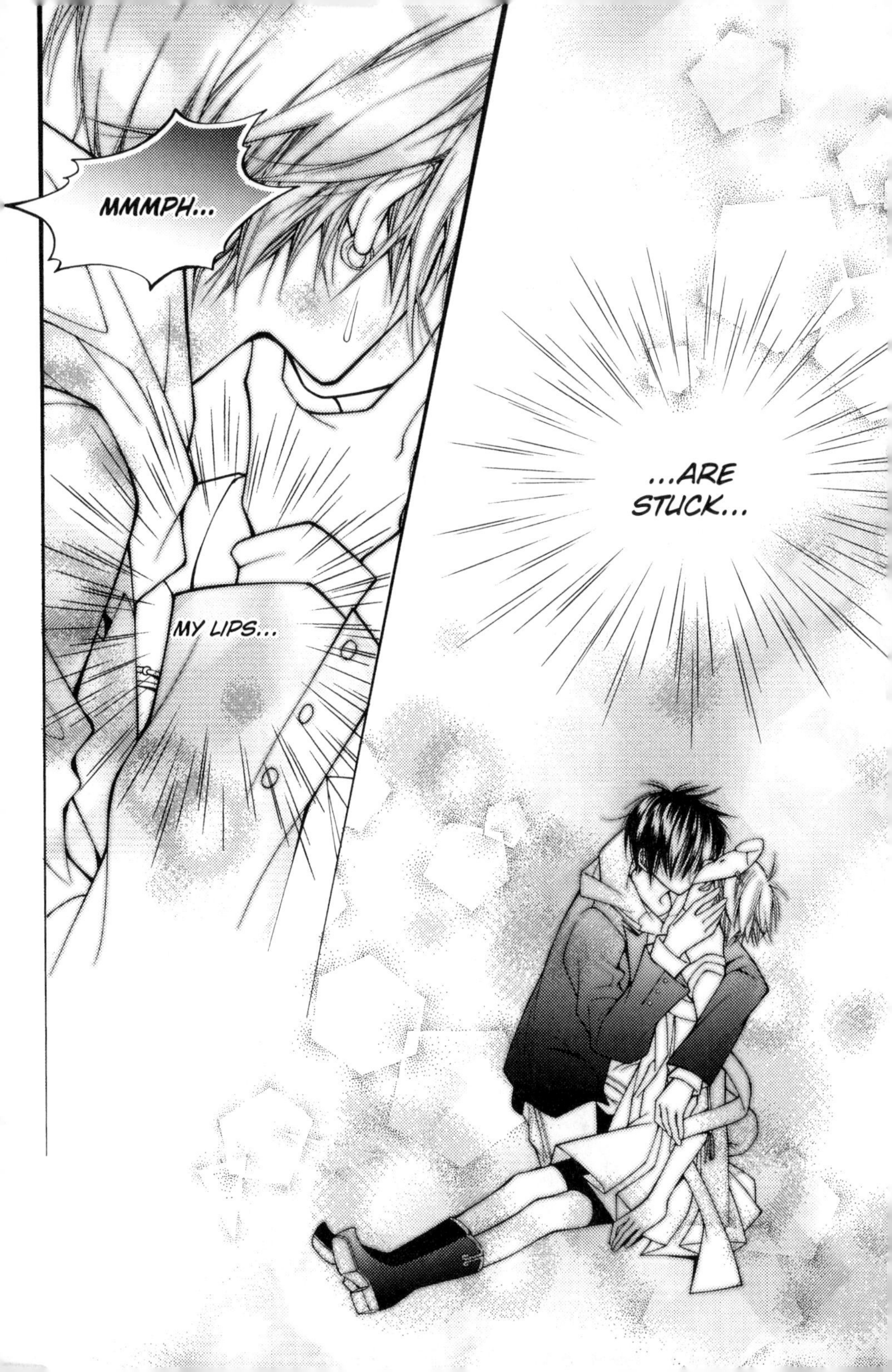
MMMPH...
MY LIPS...
...ARE STUCK...

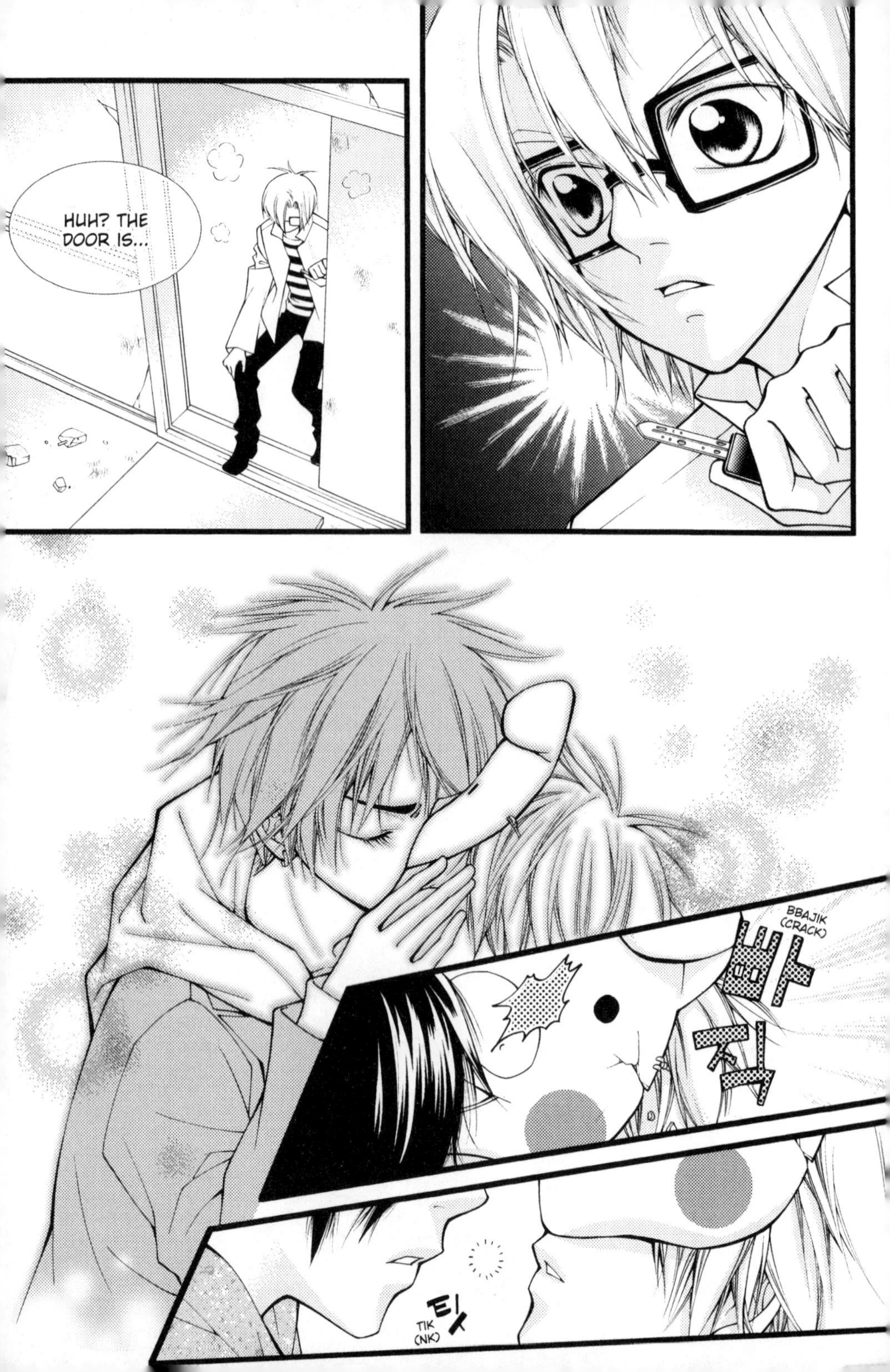
HUH? THE DOOR IS...
빠직
BBAJIK (CRACK)
티
TIK (NK)

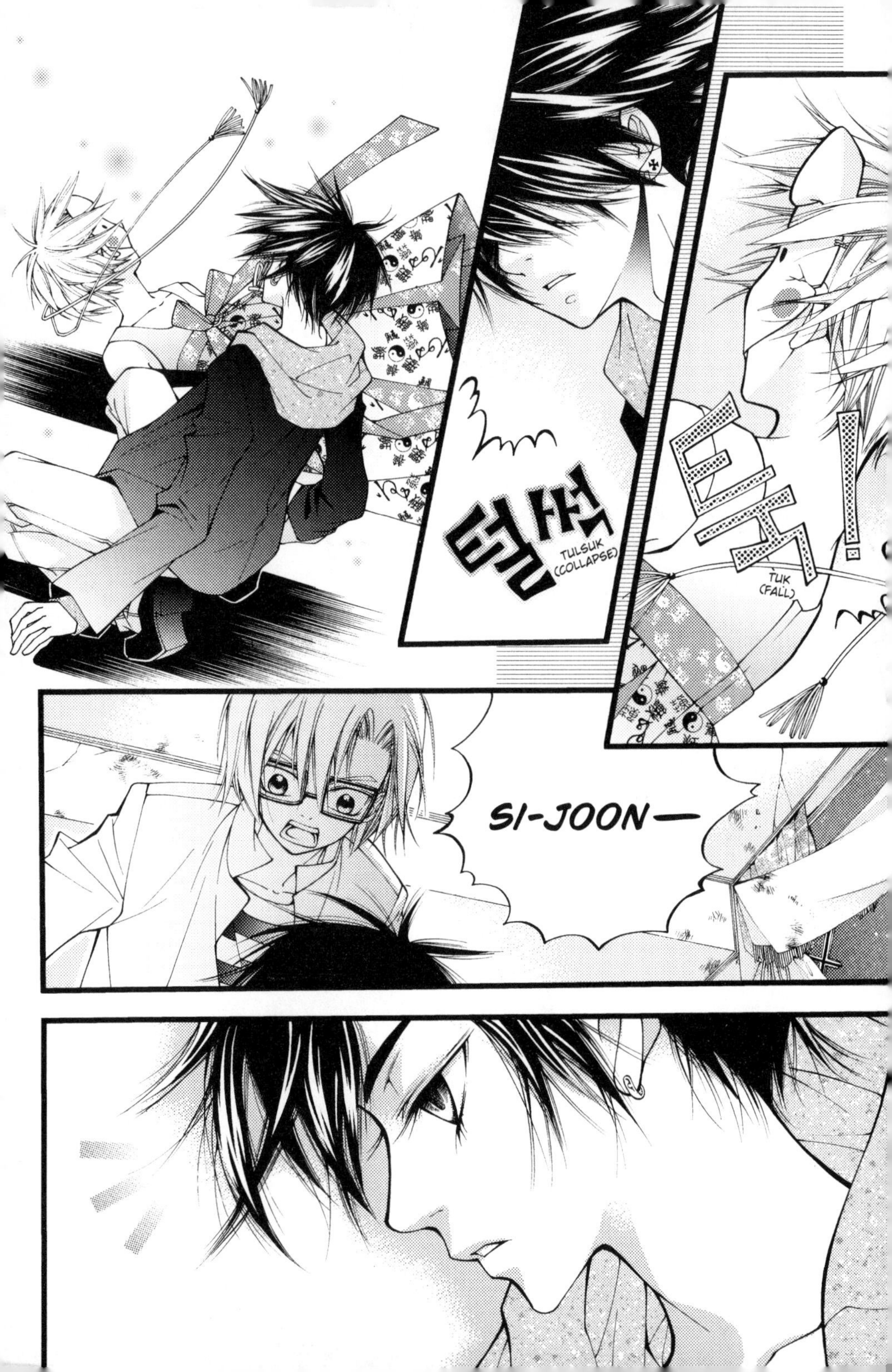
털썩
TULSUK (COLLAPSE)
탁!
TUK (FALL)
SI-JOON—

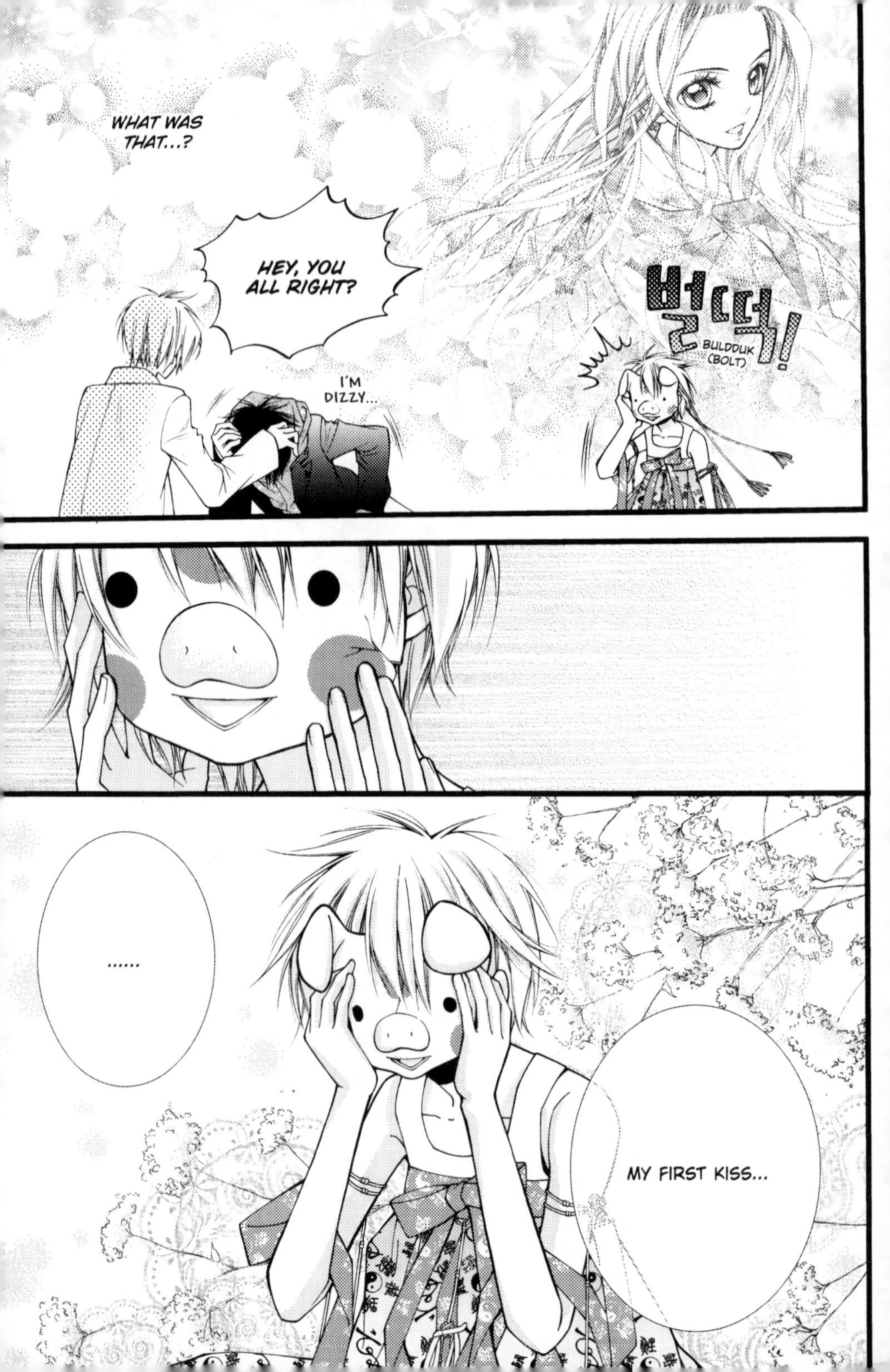
WHAT WAS THAT...?
HEY, YOU ALL RIGHT?
I'M DIZZY...
벌떡!
BULDDUK (BOLT)
......
MY FIRST KISS...

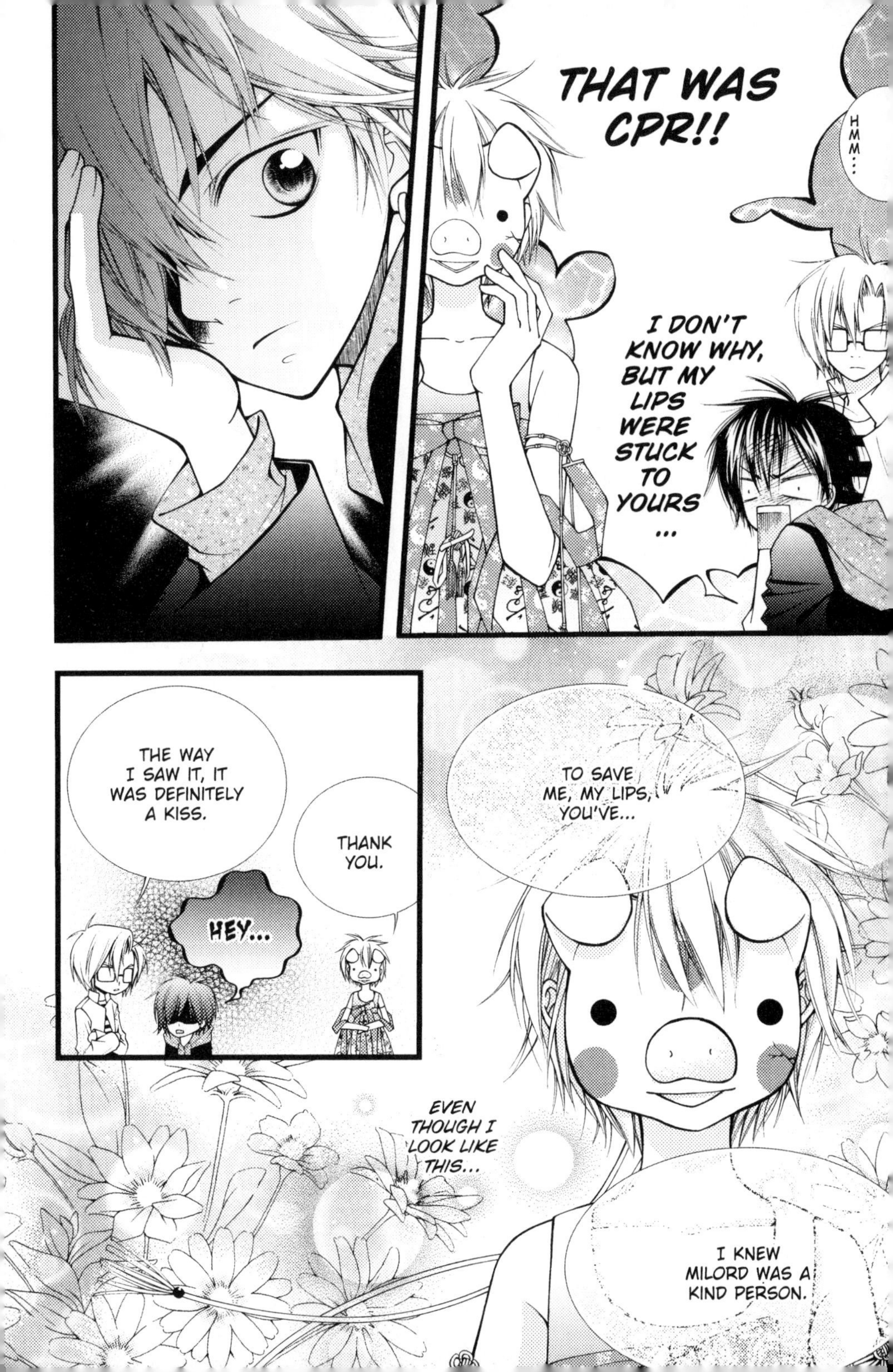
THAT WAS CPR!!
HMM...
I DON'T KNOW WHY, BUT MY LIPS WERE STUCK TO YOURS...
THE WAY I SAW IT, IT WAS DEFINITELY A KISS.
THANK YOU.
HEY...
TO SAVE ME, MY LIPS, YOU'VE...
EVEN THOUGH I LOOK LIKE THIS...
I KNEW MILORD WAS A KIND PERSON.

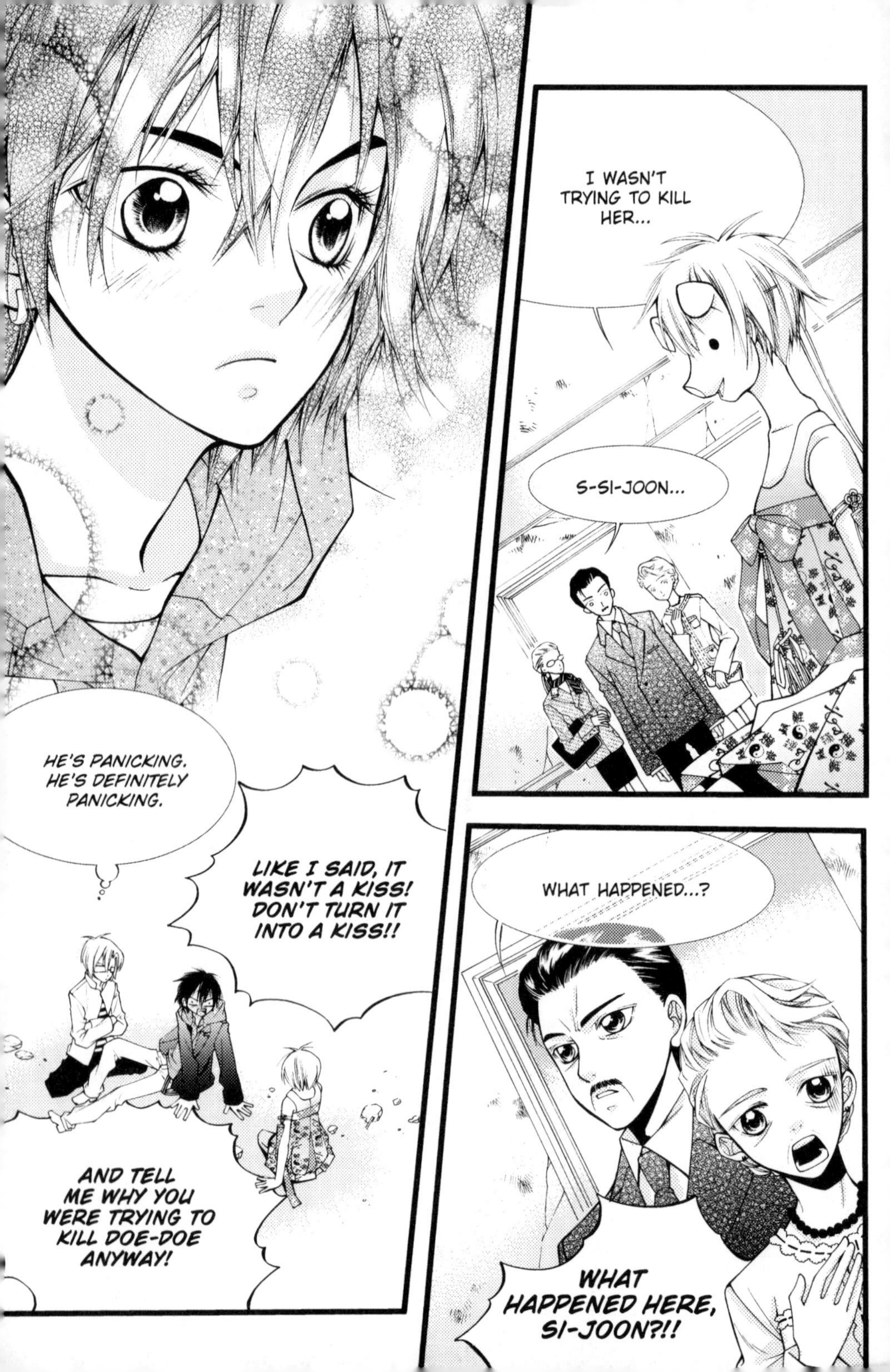
HE'S PANICKING. HE'S DEFINITELY PANICKING.
LIKE I SAID, IT WASN'T A KISS! DON'T TURN IT INTO A KISS!!
AND TELL ME WHY YOU WERE TRYING TO KILL DOE-DOE ANYWAY!
I WASN'T TRYING TO KILL HER...
S-SI-JOON...
WHAT HAPPENED...?
WHAT HAPPENED HERE, SI-JOON?!!

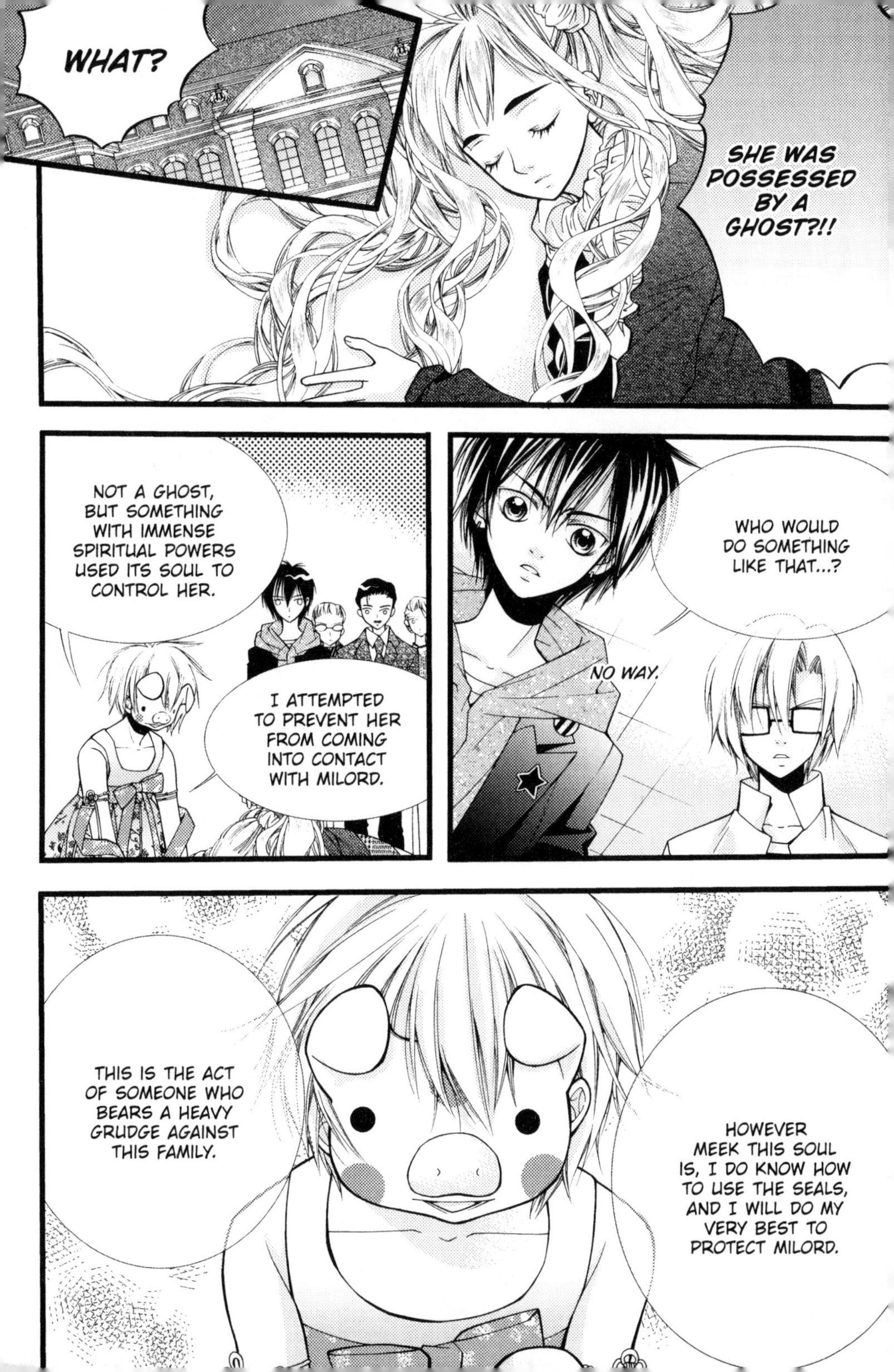
WHAT?
SHE WAS POSSESSED BY A GHOST?!!
NOT A GHOST, BUT SOMETHING WITH IMMENSE SPIRITUAL POWERS USED ITS SOUL TO CONTROL HER.
I ATTEMPTED TO PREVENT HER FROM COMING INTO CONTACT WITH MILORD.
WHO WOULD DO SOMETHING LIKE THAT...?
NO WAY.
THIS IS THE ACT OF SOMEONE WHO BEARS A HEAVY GRUDGE AGAINST THIS FAMILY.
HOWEVER MEEK THIS SOUL IS, I DO KNOW HOW TO USE THE SEALS, AND I WILL DO MY VERY BEST TO PROTECT MILORD.

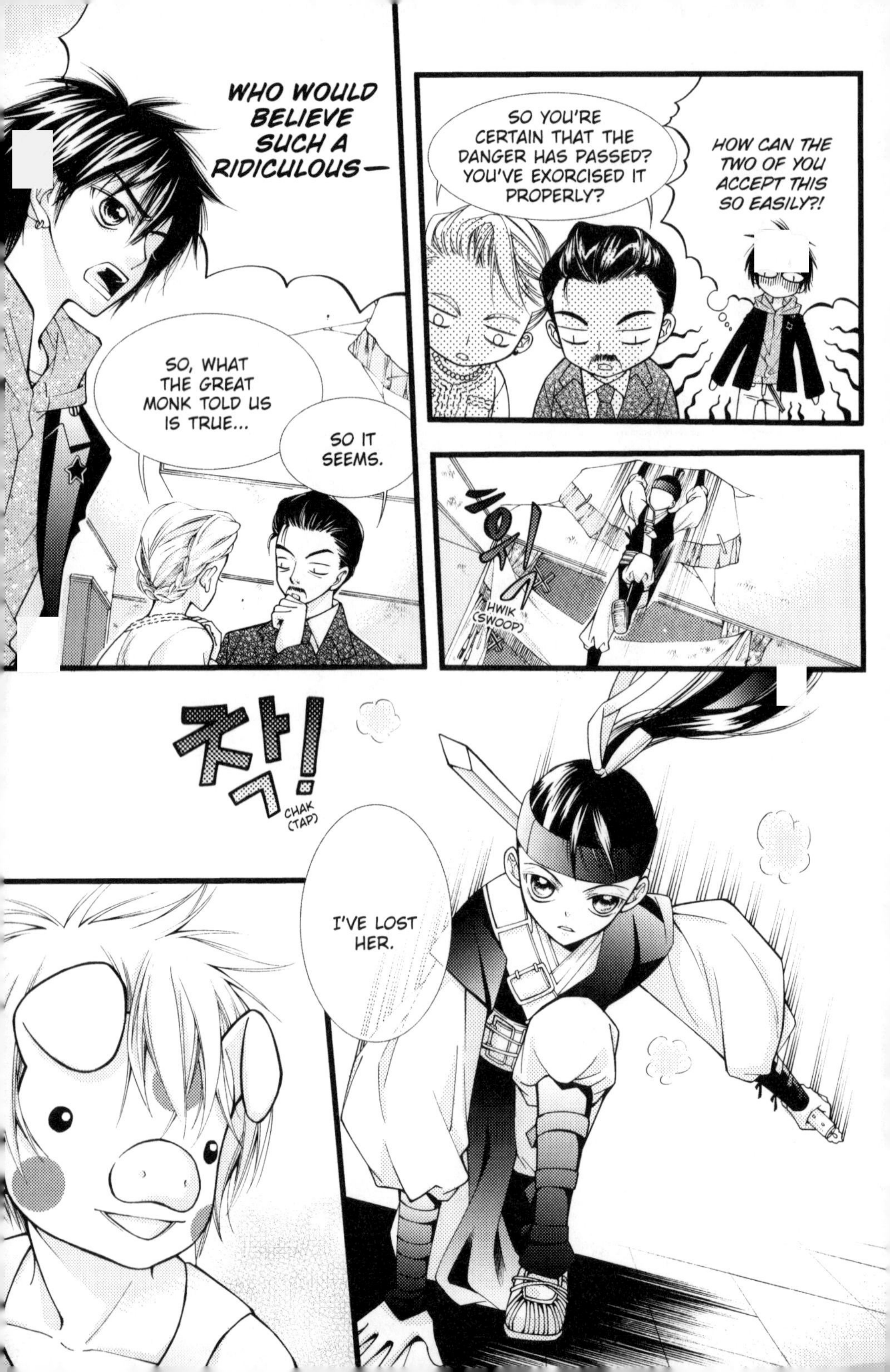
WHO WOULD BELIEVE SUCH A RIDICULOUS—
SO, WHAT THE GREAT MONK TOLD US IS TRUE...
SO IT SEEMS.
SO YOU'RE CERTAIN THAT THE DANGER HAS PASSED? YOU'VE EXORCISED IT PROPERLY?
HOW CAN THE TWO OF YOU ACCEPT THIS SO EASILY?!
HWIK (SWOOP)
착!
CHAK (TAP)
I'VE LOST HER.

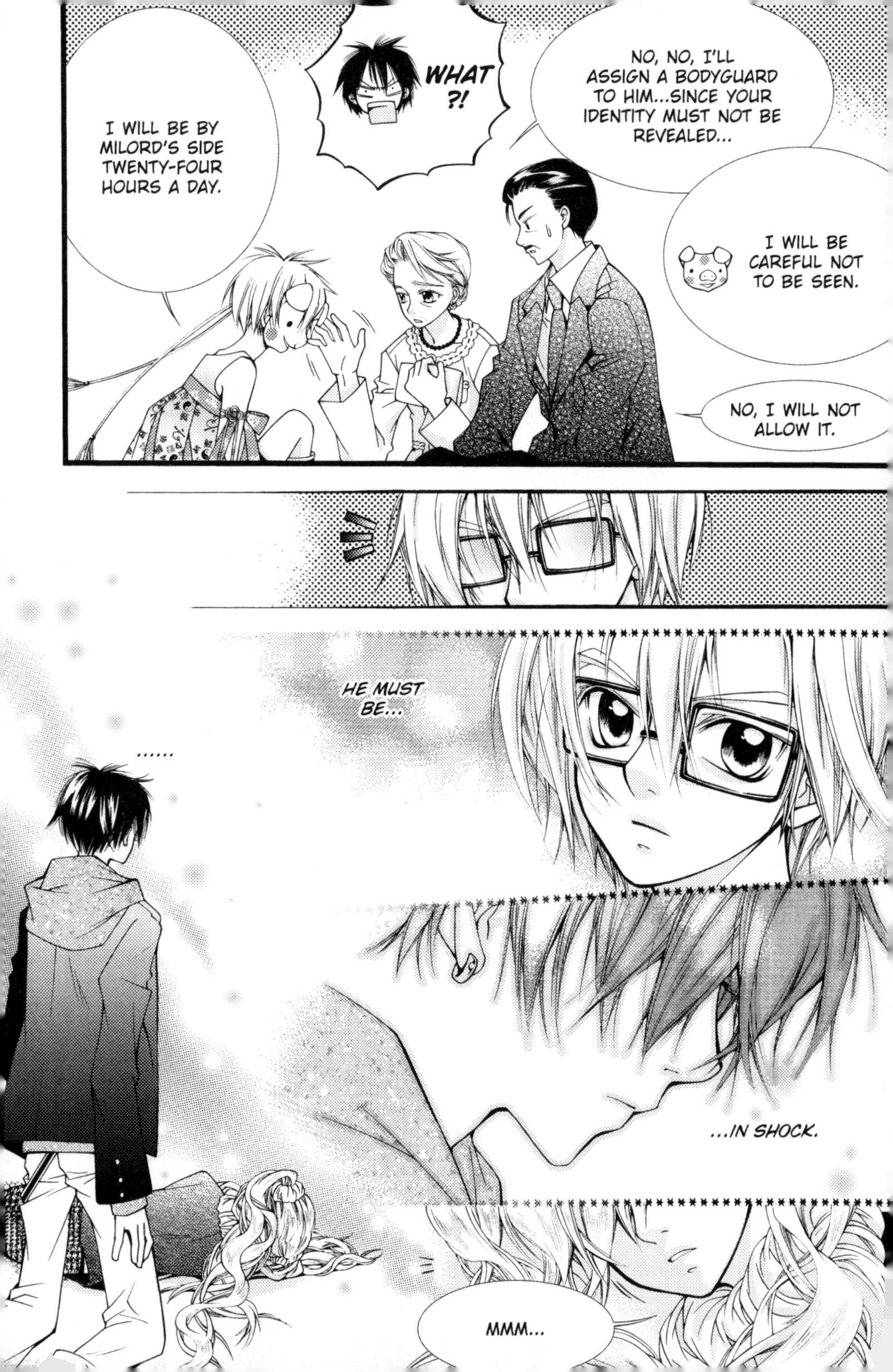
I WILL BE BY MILORD'S SIDE TWENTY-FOUR HOURS A DAY.
WHAT ?!
NO, NO, I'LL ASSIGN A BODYGUARD TO HIM...SINCE YOUR IDENTITY MUST NOT BE REVEALED...
I WILL BE CAREFUL NOT TO BE SEEN.
NO, I WILL NOT ALLOW IT.
......
HE MUST BE...
...IN SHOCK.
MMM...

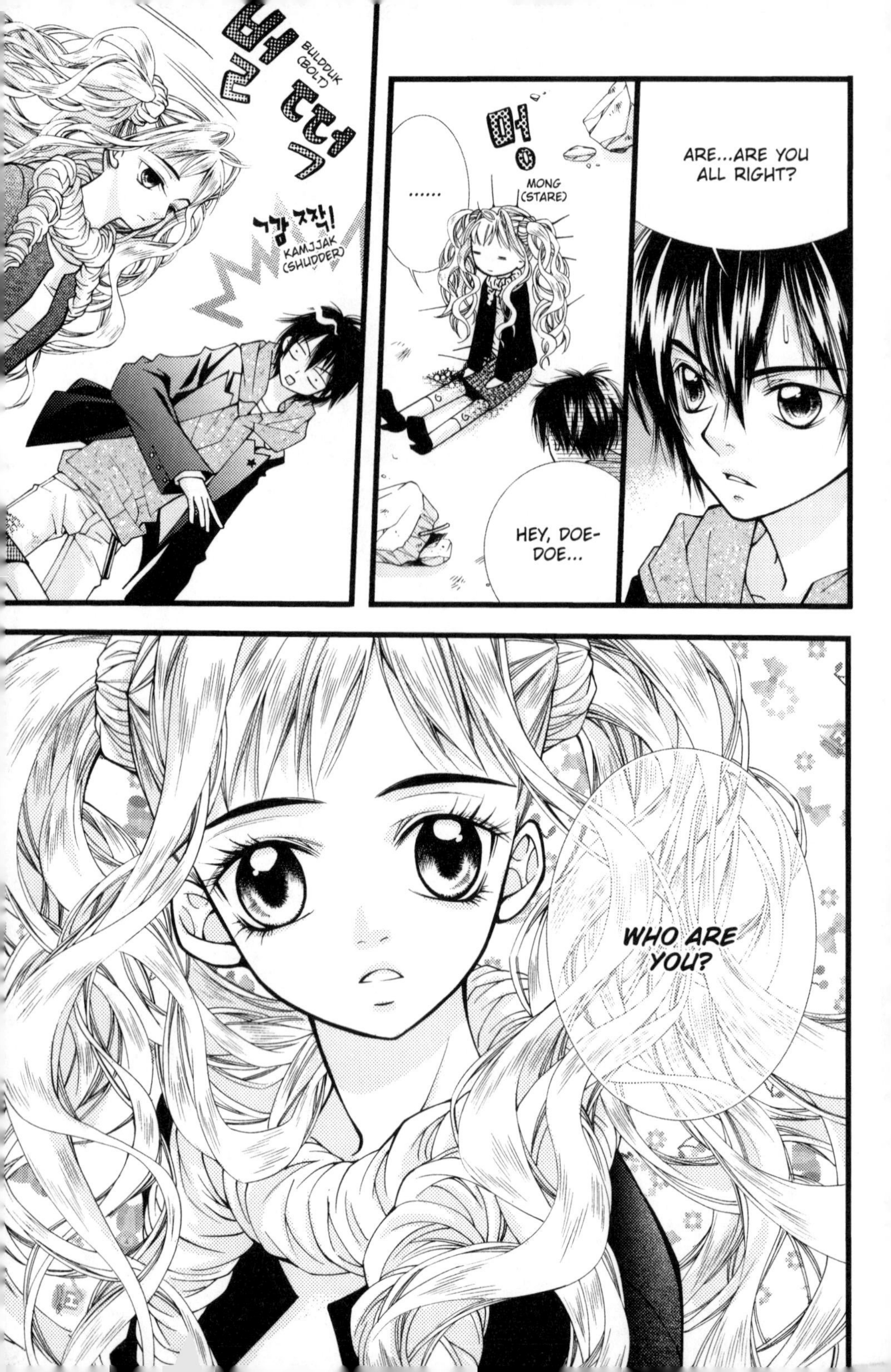
벌떡
BULDDUK (BOLT)
깜짝!
KAMJJAK (SHUDDER)
멍
MONG (STARE)
......
HEY, DOE-DOE...
ARE...ARE YOU ALL RIGHT?
WHO ARE YOU?

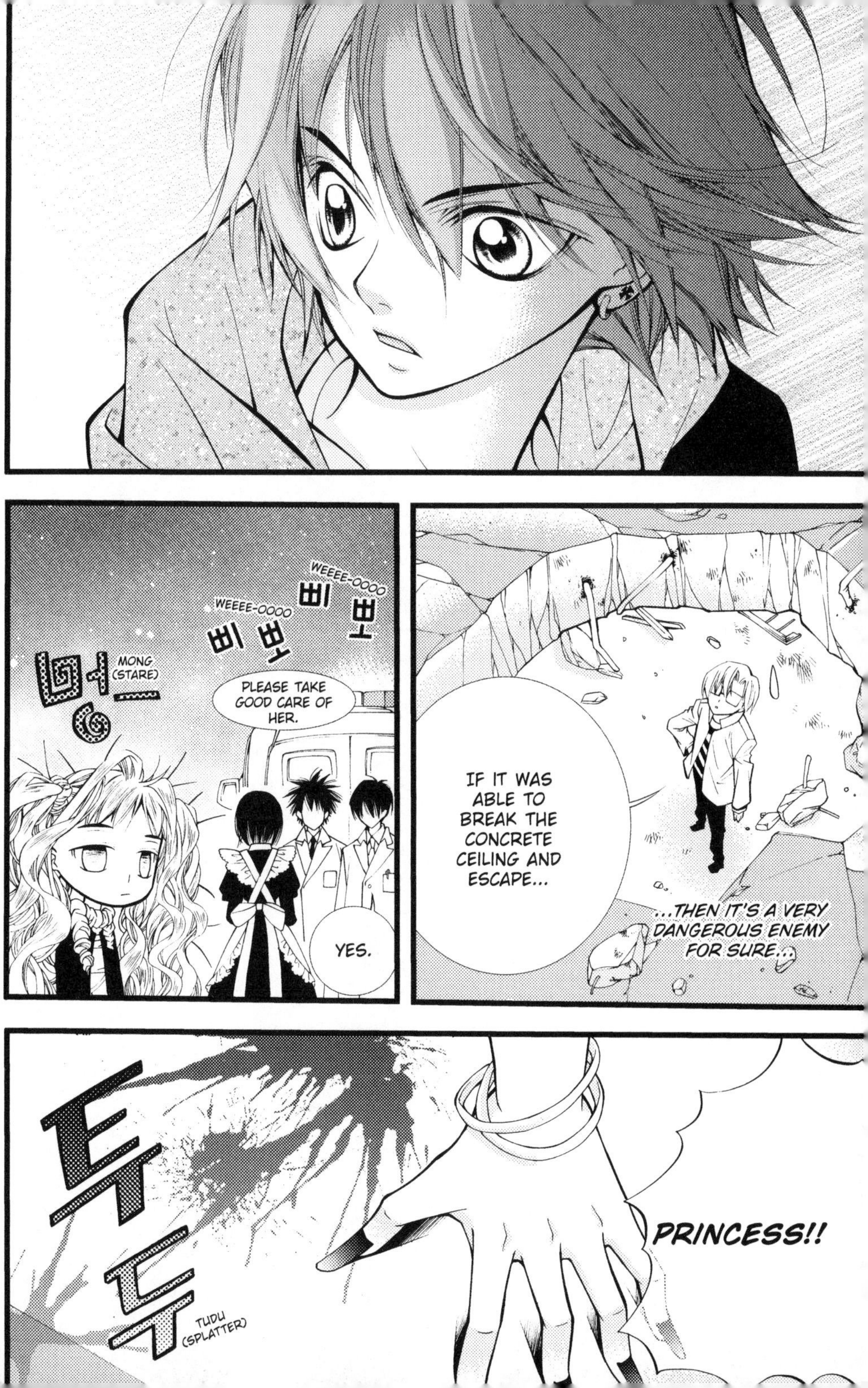
멍
MONG (STARE)
삐뽀
WEEEE-OOOO
삐뽀
WEEEE-OOOO
PLEASE TAKE GOOD CARE OF HER.
YES.
IF IT WAS ABLE TO BREAK THE CONCRETE CEILING AND ESCAPE...
...THEN IT'S A VERY DANGEROUS ENEMY FOR SURE...
투두
TUDU (SPLATTER)
PRINCESS!!

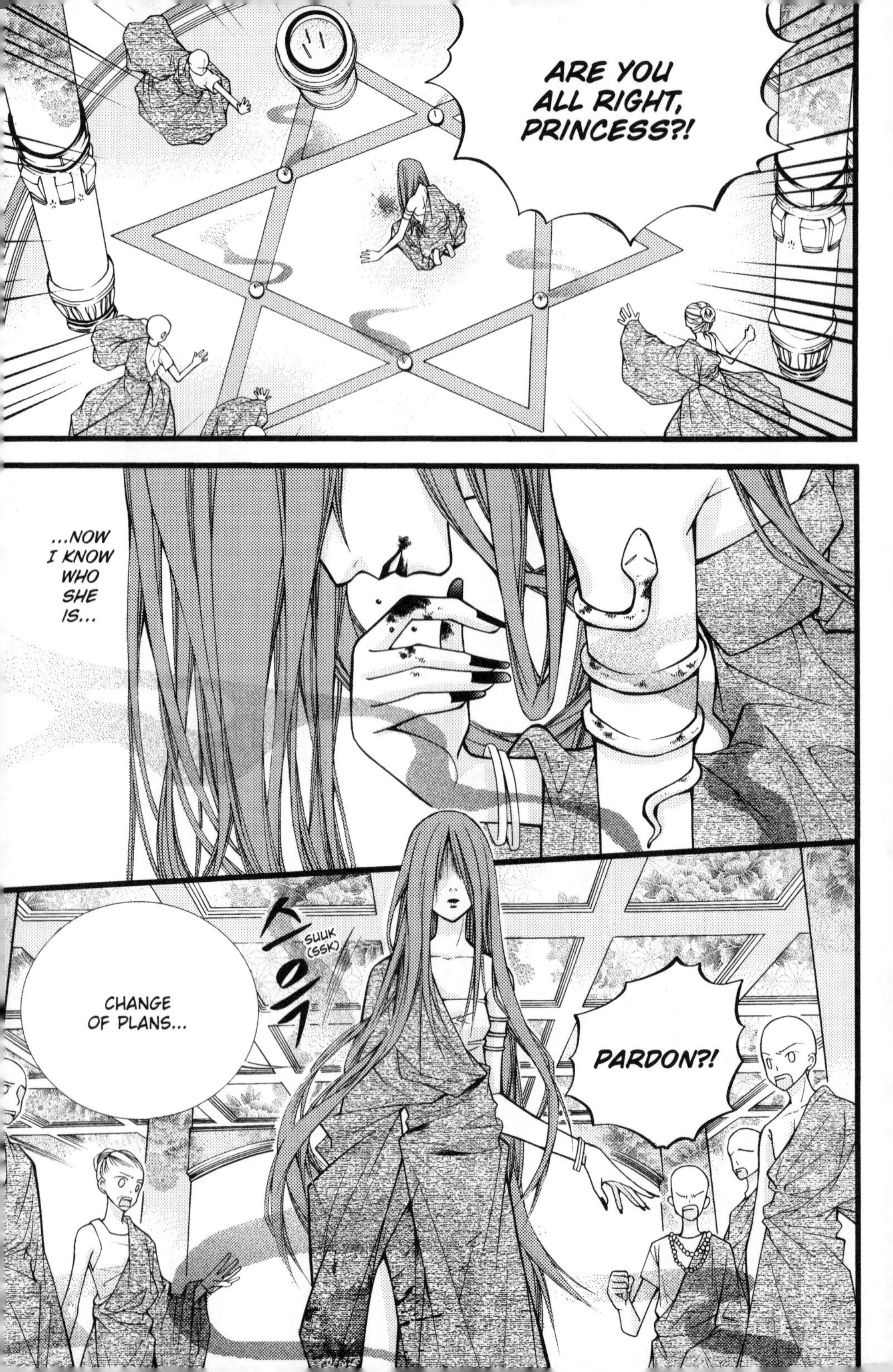
ARE YOU ALL RIGHT, PRINCESS?!
...NOW I KNOW WHO SHE IS...
CHANGE OF PLANS...
SUUK (SSK)
PARDON?!

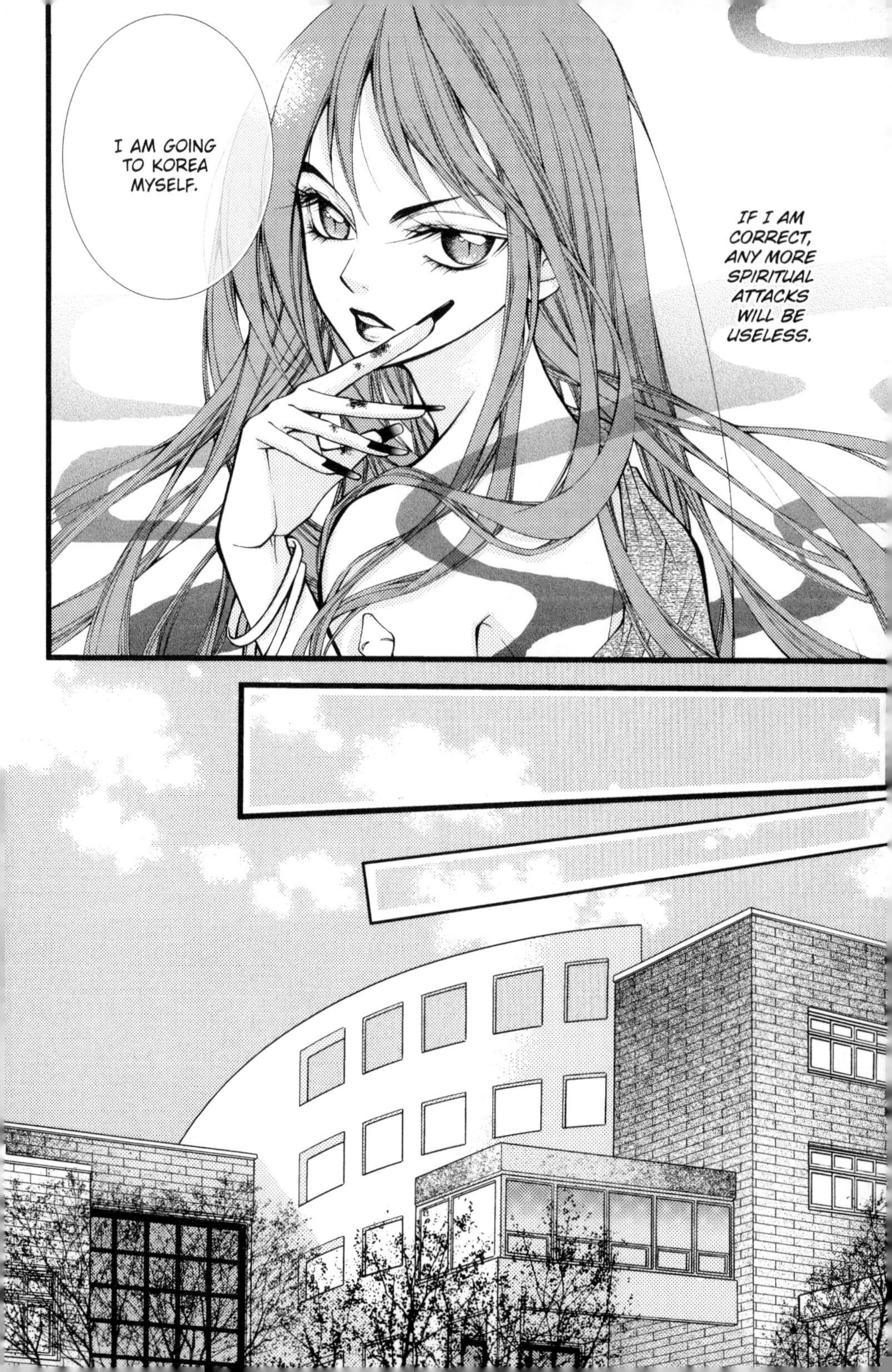
I AM GOING TO KOREA MYSELF.
IF I AM CORRECT, ANY MORE SPIRITUAL ATTACKS WILL BE USELESS.

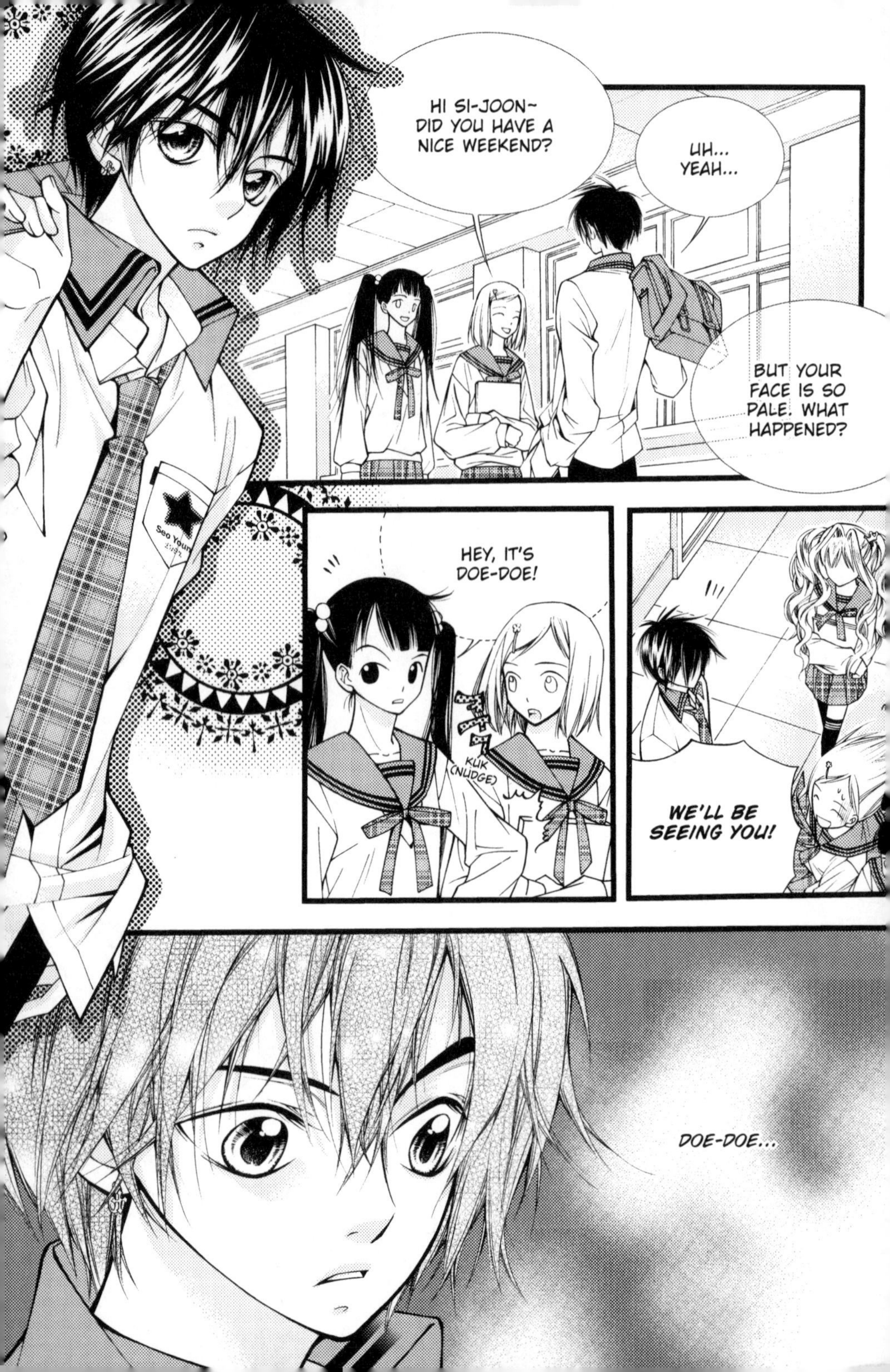
HI SI-JOON~ DID YOU HAVE A NICE WEEKEND?
UH... YEAH...
BUT YOUR FACE IS SO PALE. WHAT HAPPENED?
Seo Young
HEY, IT'S DOE-DOE!
KUK (NUDGE)
WE'LL BE SEEING YOU!
DOE-DOE...

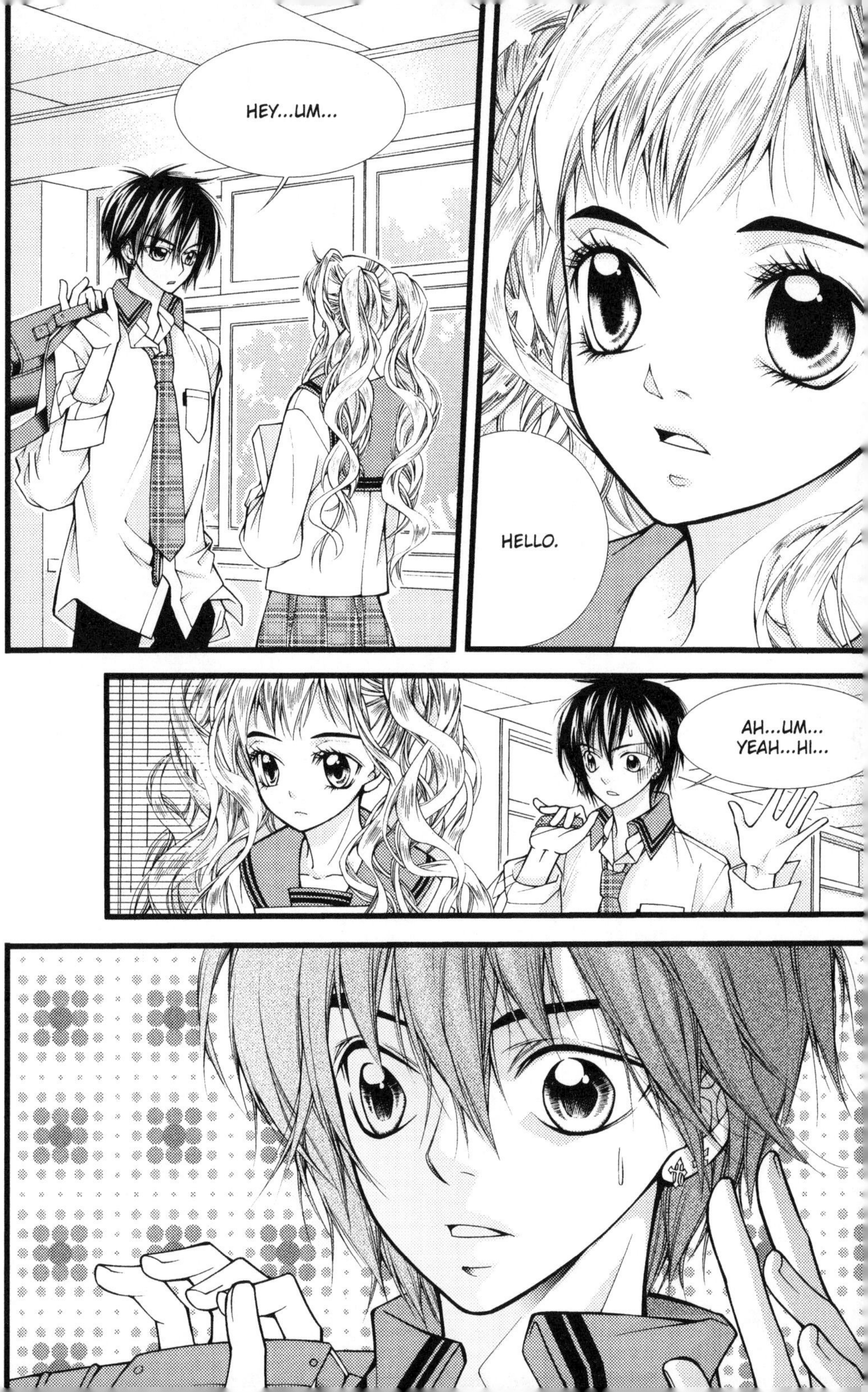
HEY...UM...
HELLO.
AH...UM... YEAH...HI...

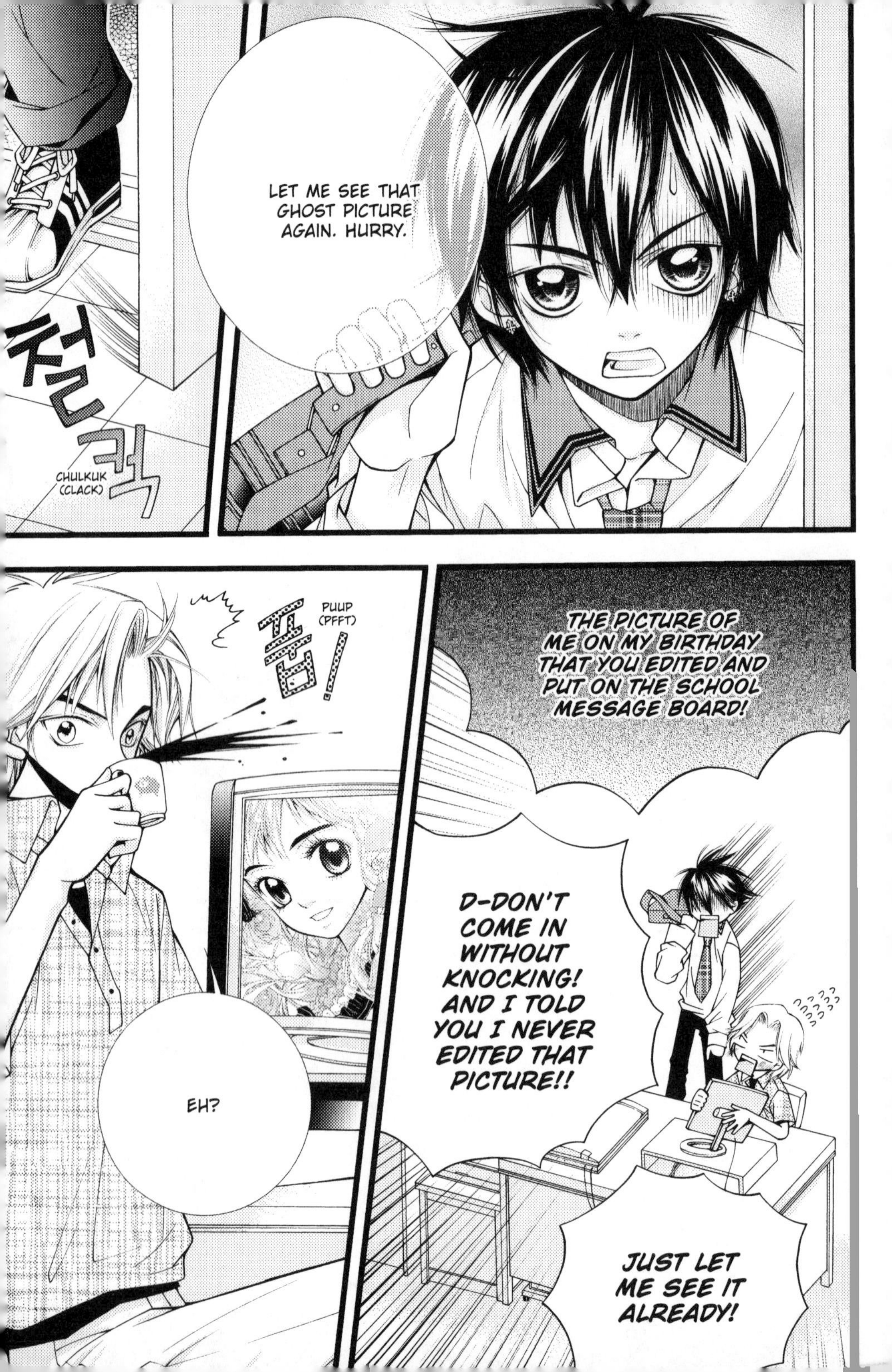
철컥
CHULKUK (CLACK)
LET ME SEE THAT GHOST PICTURE AGAIN. HURRY.
PUUP (PFFT)
EH?
THE PICTURE OF ME ON MY BIRTHDAY THAT YOU EDITED AND PUT ON THE SCHOOL MESSAGE BOARD!
D-DON'T COME IN WITHOUT KNOCKING! AND I TOLD YOU I NEVER EDITED THAT PICTURE!!
JUST LET ME SEE IT ALREADY!

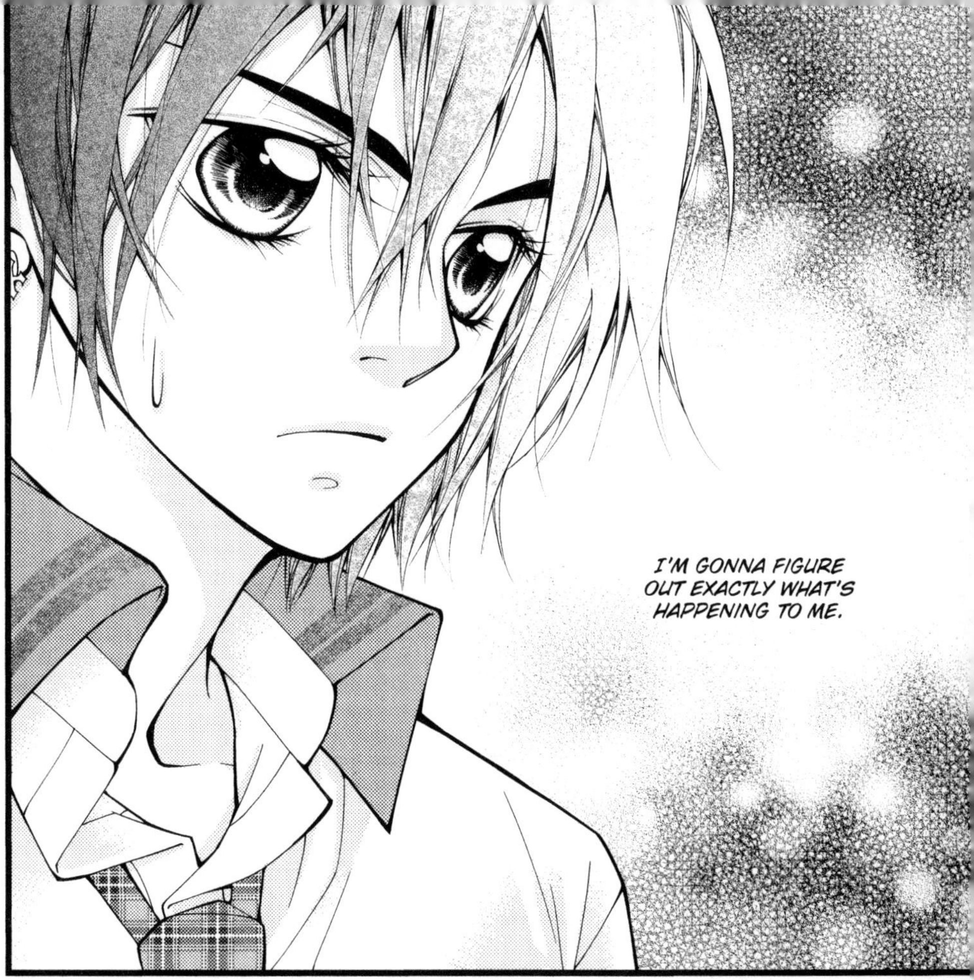
I'M GONNA FIGURE OUT EXACTLY WHAT'S HAPPENING TO ME.

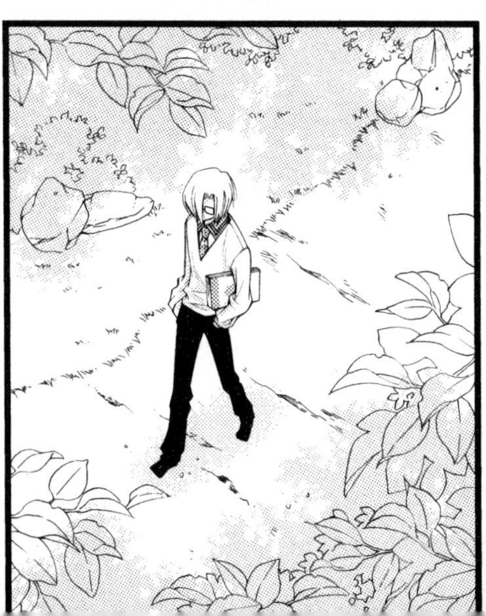

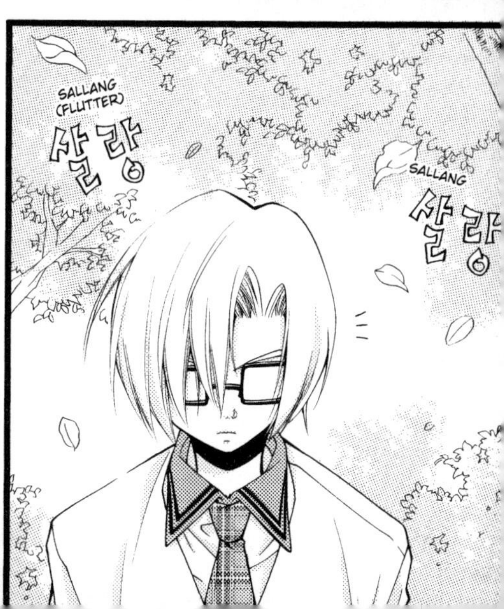
SALLANG (FLUTTER)
살랑
SALLANG
살랑

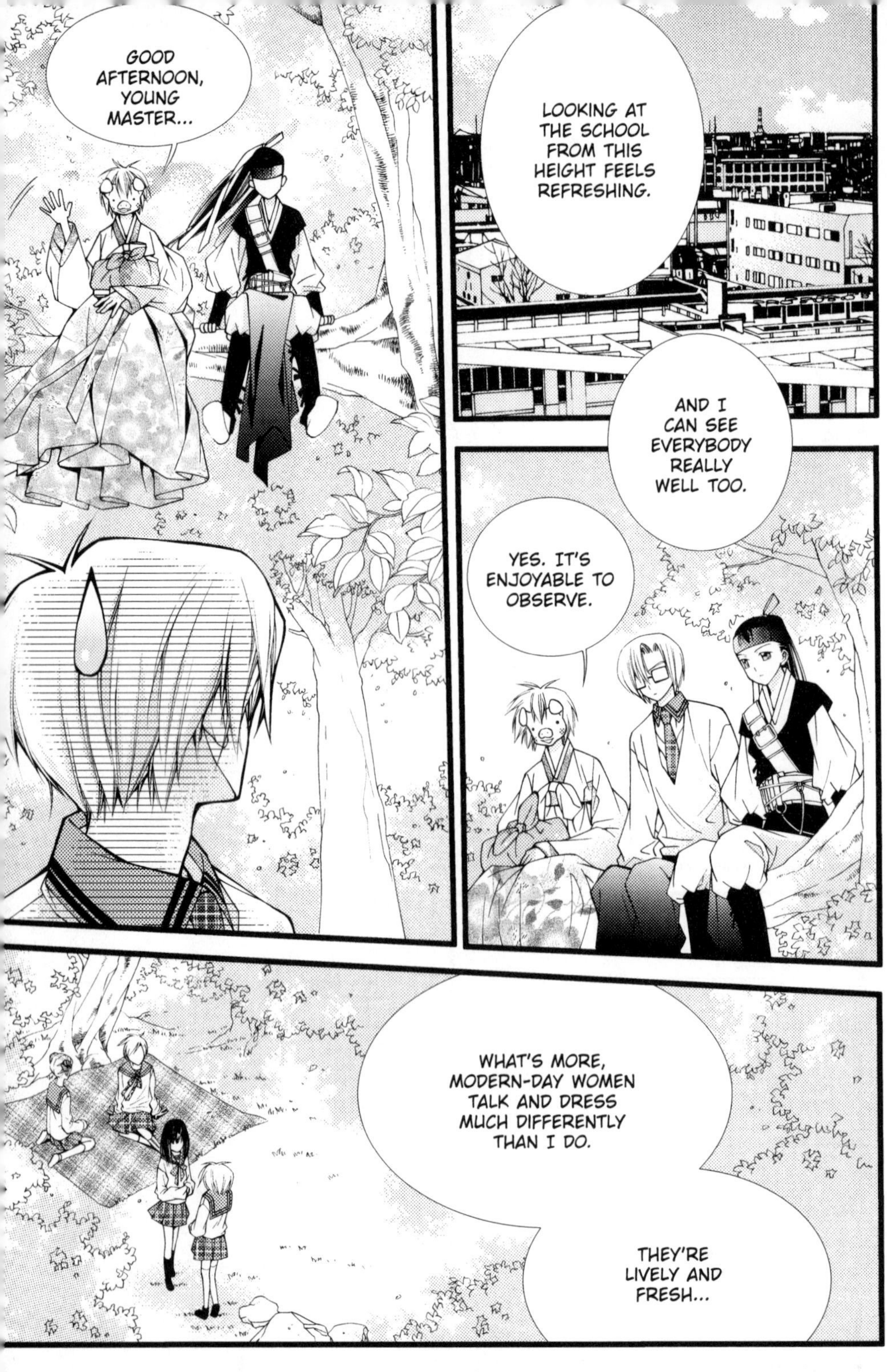
GOOD AFTERNOON, YOUNG MASTER...
LOOKING AT THE SCHOOL FROM THIS HEIGHT FEELS REFRESHING.
AND I CAN SEE EVERYBODY REALLY WELL TOO.
YES. IT'S ENJOYABLE TO OBSERVE.
WHAT'S MORE, MODERN-DAY WOMEN TALK AND DRESS MUCH DIFFERENTLY THAN I DO.
THEY'RE LIVELY AND FRESH...

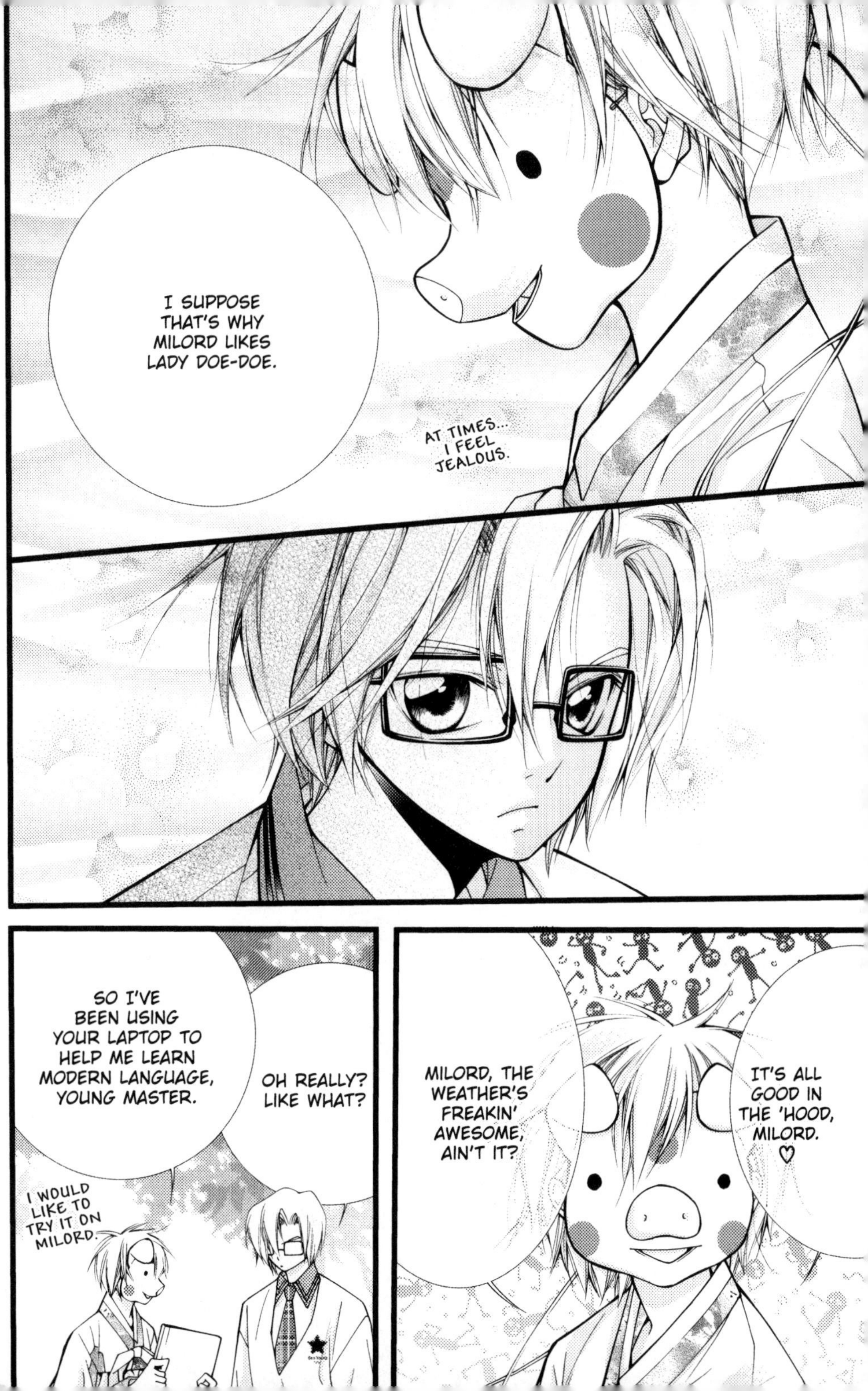
I SUPPOSE THAT'S WHY MILORD LIKES LADY DOE-DOE.
AT TIMES... I FEEL JEALOUS.
SO I'VE BEEN USING YOUR LAPTOP TO HELP ME LEARN MODERN LANGUAGE, YOUNG MASTER.
OH REALLY? LIKE WHAT?
I WOULD LIKE TO TRY IT ON MILORD.
MILORD, THE WEATHER'S FREAKIN' AWESOME, AIN'T IT?
IT'S ALL GOOD IN THE 'HOOD, MILORD. ♡

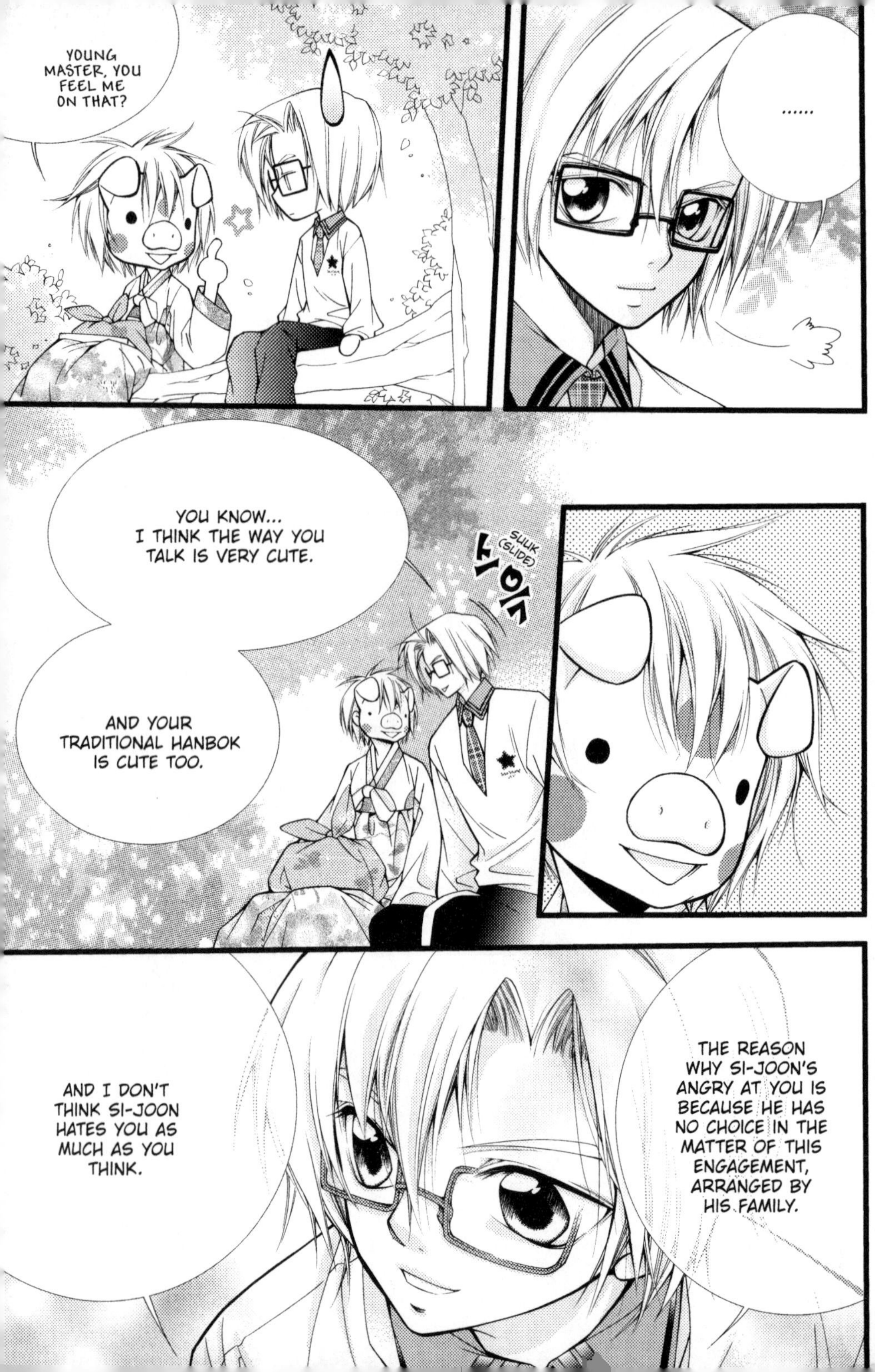
YOUNG MASTER, YOU FEEL ME ON THAT?
......
YOU KNOW... I THINK THE WAY YOU TALK IS VERY CUTE.
AND YOUR TRADITIONAL HANBOK IS CUTE TOO.
SUUK (SLIDE)
AND I DON'T THINK SI-JOON HATES YOU AS MUCH AS YOU THINK.
THE REASON WHY SI-JOON'S ANGRY AT YOU IS BECAUSE HE HAS NO CHOICE IN THE MATTER OF THIS ENGAGEMENT, ARRANGED BY HIS FAMILY.

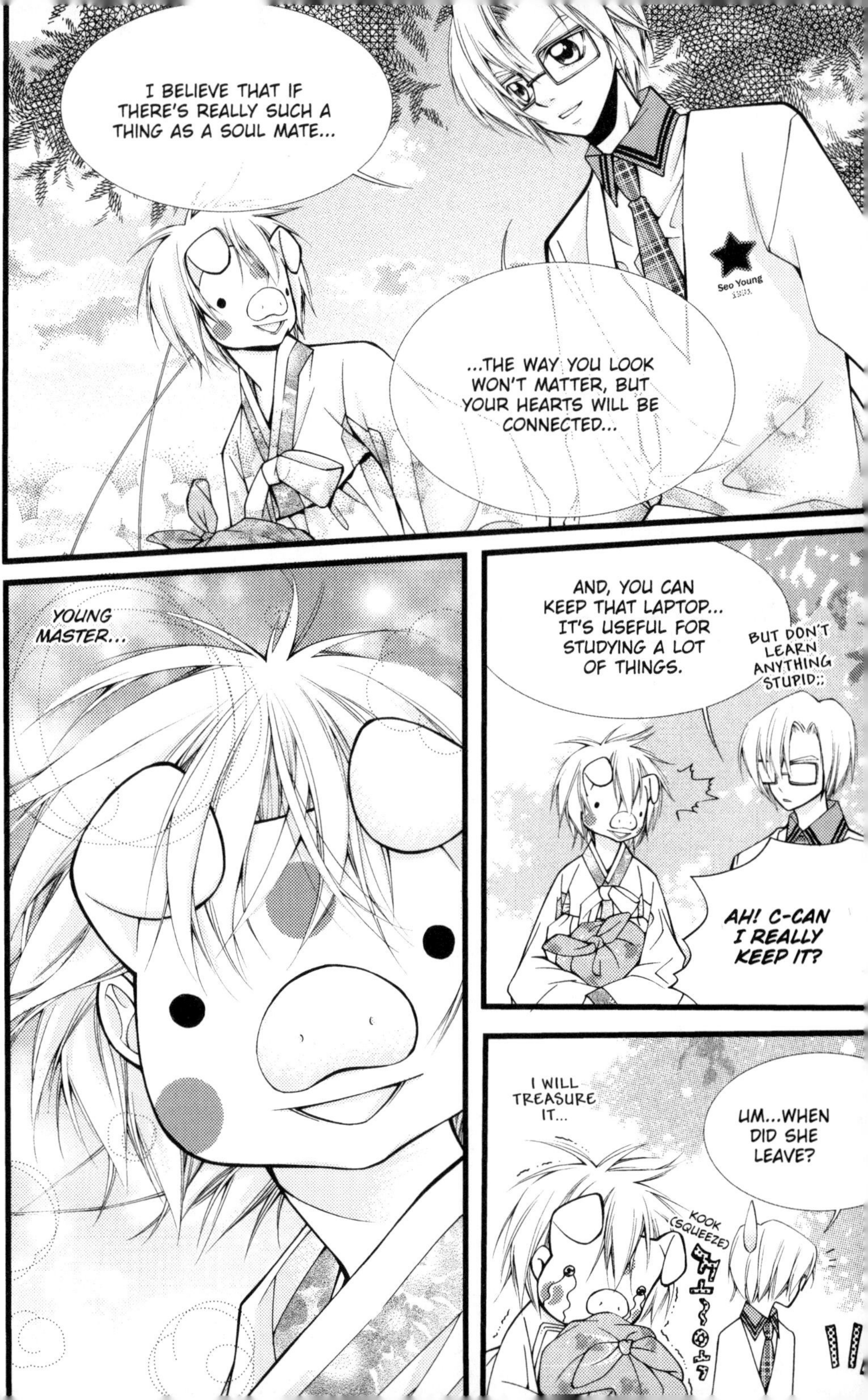

I BELIEVE THAT IF THERE'S REALLY SUCH A THING AS A SOUL MATE...
Seo Young
...THE WAY YOU LOOK WON'T MATTER, BUT YOUR HEARTS WILL BE CONNECTED...
YOUNG MASTER...
AND, YOU CAN KEEP THAT LAPTOP... IT'S USEFUL FOR STUDYING A LOT OF THINGS.
BUT DON'T LEARN ANYTHING STUPID;;
AH! C-CAN I REALLY KEEP IT?
I WILL TREASURE IT...
UM...WHEN DID SHE LEAVE?
KOOK (SQUEEZE)

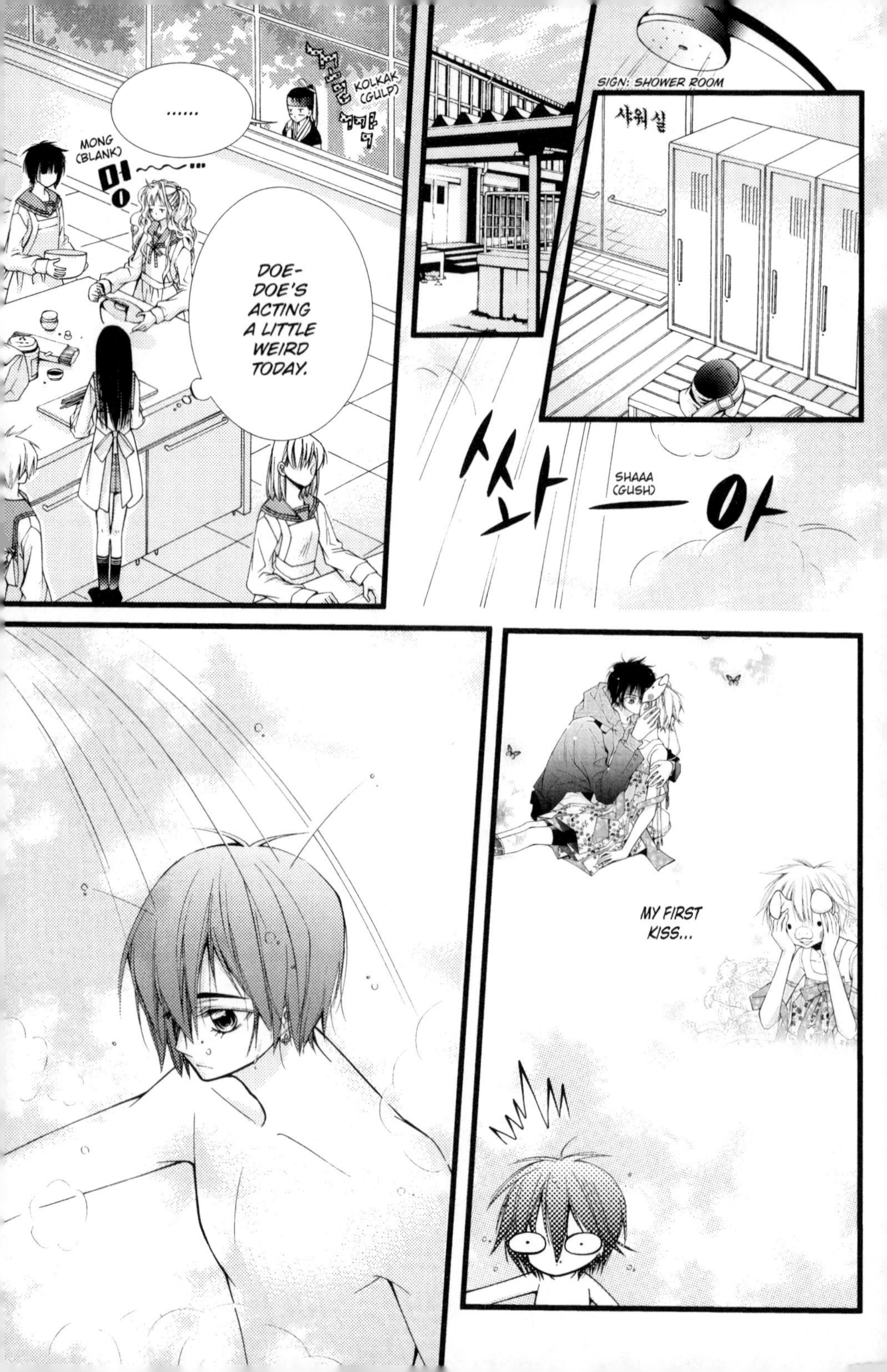

......
KOLKAK (GULP)
MONG (BLANK)
DOE-DOE'S ACTING A LITTLE WEIRD TODAY.
SIGN: SHOWER ROOM
샤워실
쏴 아
SHAAA (GUSH)
MY FIRST KISS...

PADAK (SHAKE) 파닥 PADAK 파닥 파닥 PADAK

PADAK 파닥

파닥 PADAK

THAT WAS JUST CPR.

IF THAT WAS A KISS, THAT WAS... MY...FIRST... FIRST...

WHY DO I KEEP RE-MEMBERING IT?!!

달 칵 DALKAK (CLICK)

IS THAT YOU, JI-OH? CAN YOU HAND ME A TOWEL?

THANKS.

IT IS NOT A PROBLEM...

싸 SHHAK (SHUDDER)

아

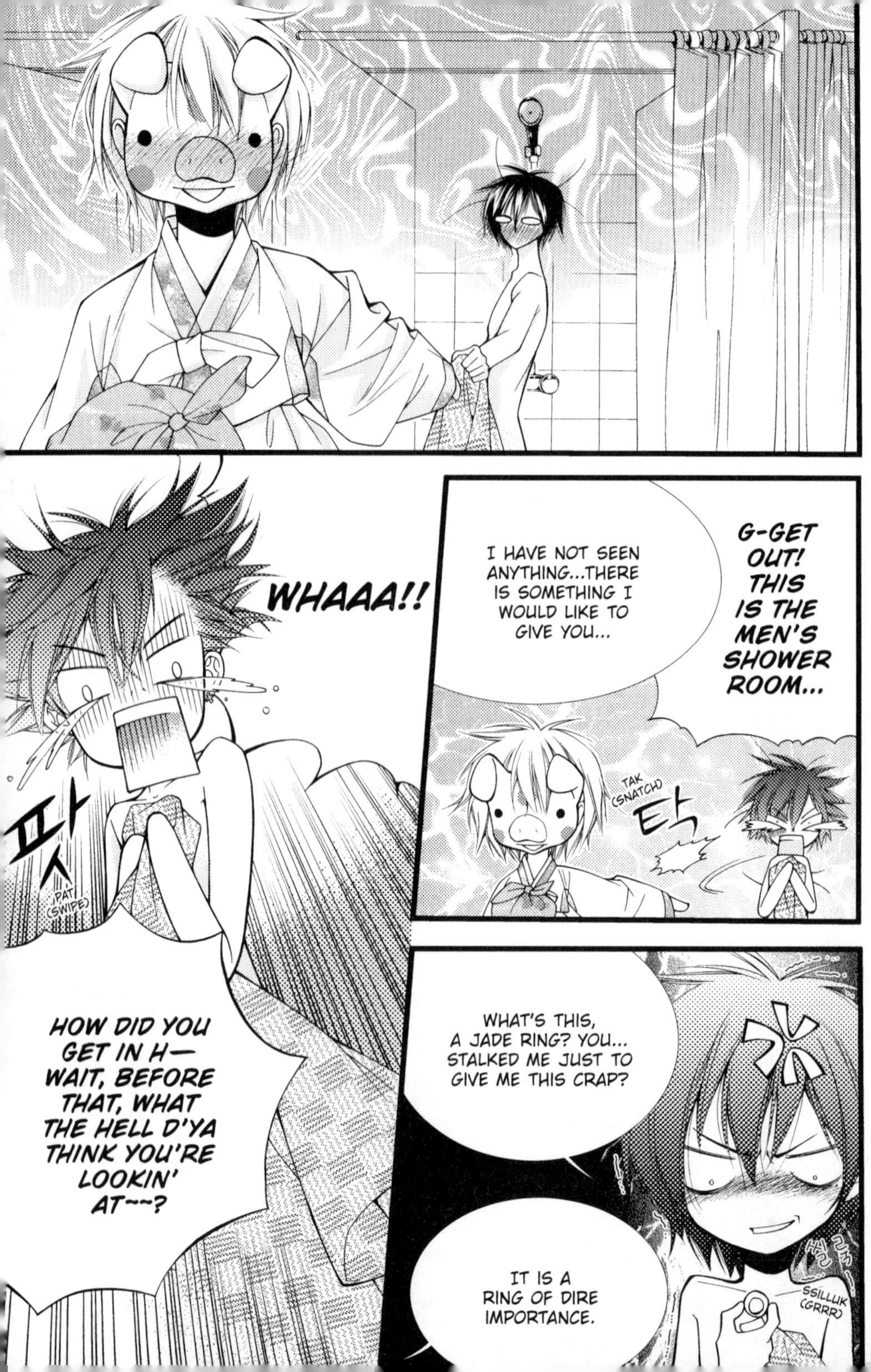
WHAAA!!
파
스
PAT
(SWIPE)
HOW DID YOU GET IN H— WAIT, BEFORE THAT, WHAT THE HELL D'YA THINK YOU'RE LOOKIN' AT~~?
I HAVE NOT SEEN ANYTHING...THERE IS SOMETHING I WOULD LIKE TO GIVE YOU...
G-GET OUT! THIS IS THE MEN'S SHOWER ROOM...
TAK
(SNATCH)
탁
WHAT'S THIS, A JADE RING? YOU... STALKED ME JUST TO GIVE ME THIS CRAP?
IT IS A RING OF DIRE IMPORTANCE.
SSILLUK
(GRRR)

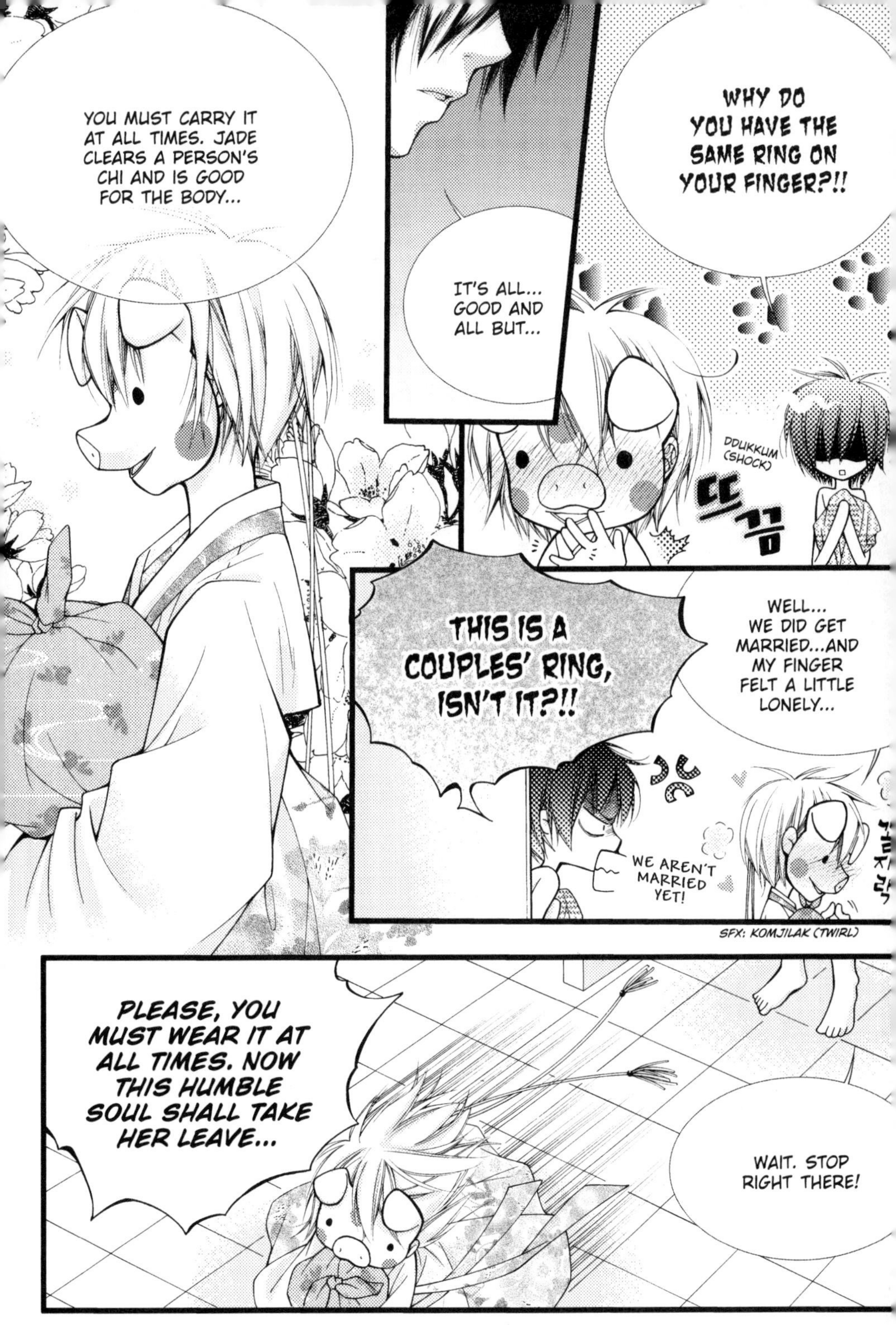
YOU MUST CARRY IT AT ALL TIMES. JADE CLEARS A PERSON'S CHI AND IS GOOD FOR THE BODY...
IT'S ALL... GOOD AND ALL BUT...
WHY DO YOU HAVE THE SAME RING ON YOUR FINGER?!!
DDUKKUM (SHOCK)
THIS IS A COUPLES' RING, ISN'T IT?!!
WELL... WE DID GET MARRIED...AND MY FINGER FELT A LITTLE LONELY...
WE AREN'T MARRIED YET!
SFX: KOMJILAK (TWIRL)
PLEASE, YOU MUST WEAR IT AT ALL TIMES. NOW THIS HUMBLE SOUL SHALL TAKE HER LEAVE...
WAIT. STOP RIGHT THERE!

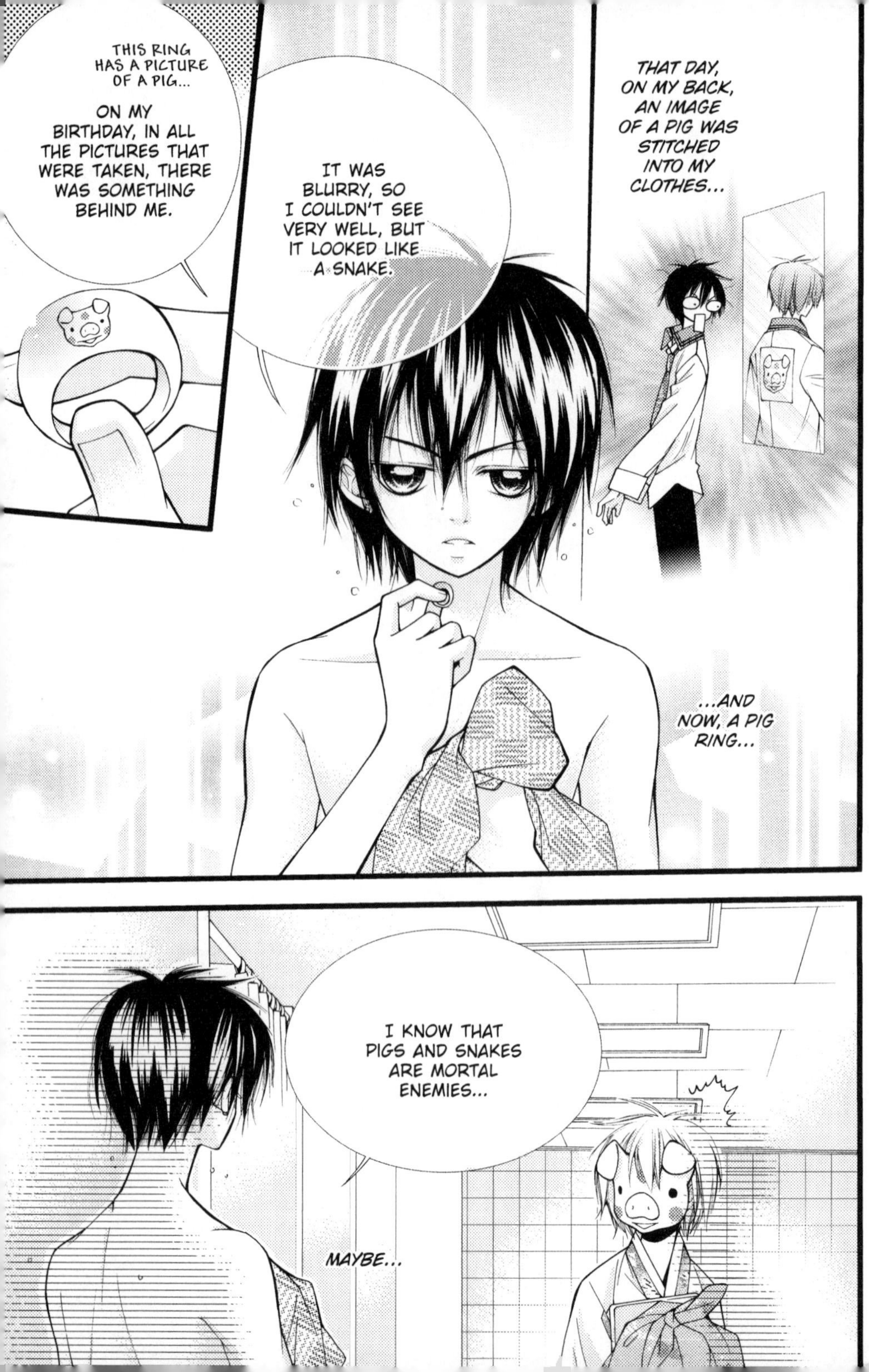
THIS RING HAS A PICTURE OF A PIG...
ON MY BIRTHDAY, IN ALL THE PICTURES THAT WERE TAKEN, THERE WAS SOMETHING BEHIND ME.
IT WAS BLURRY, SO I COULDN'T SEE VERY WELL, BUT IT LOOKED LIKE A SNAKE.
THAT DAY, ON MY BACK, AN IMAGE OF A PIG WAS STITCHED INTO MY CLOTHES...
...AND NOW, A PIG RING...
I KNOW THAT PIGS AND SNAKES ARE MORTAL ENEMIES...
MAYBE...

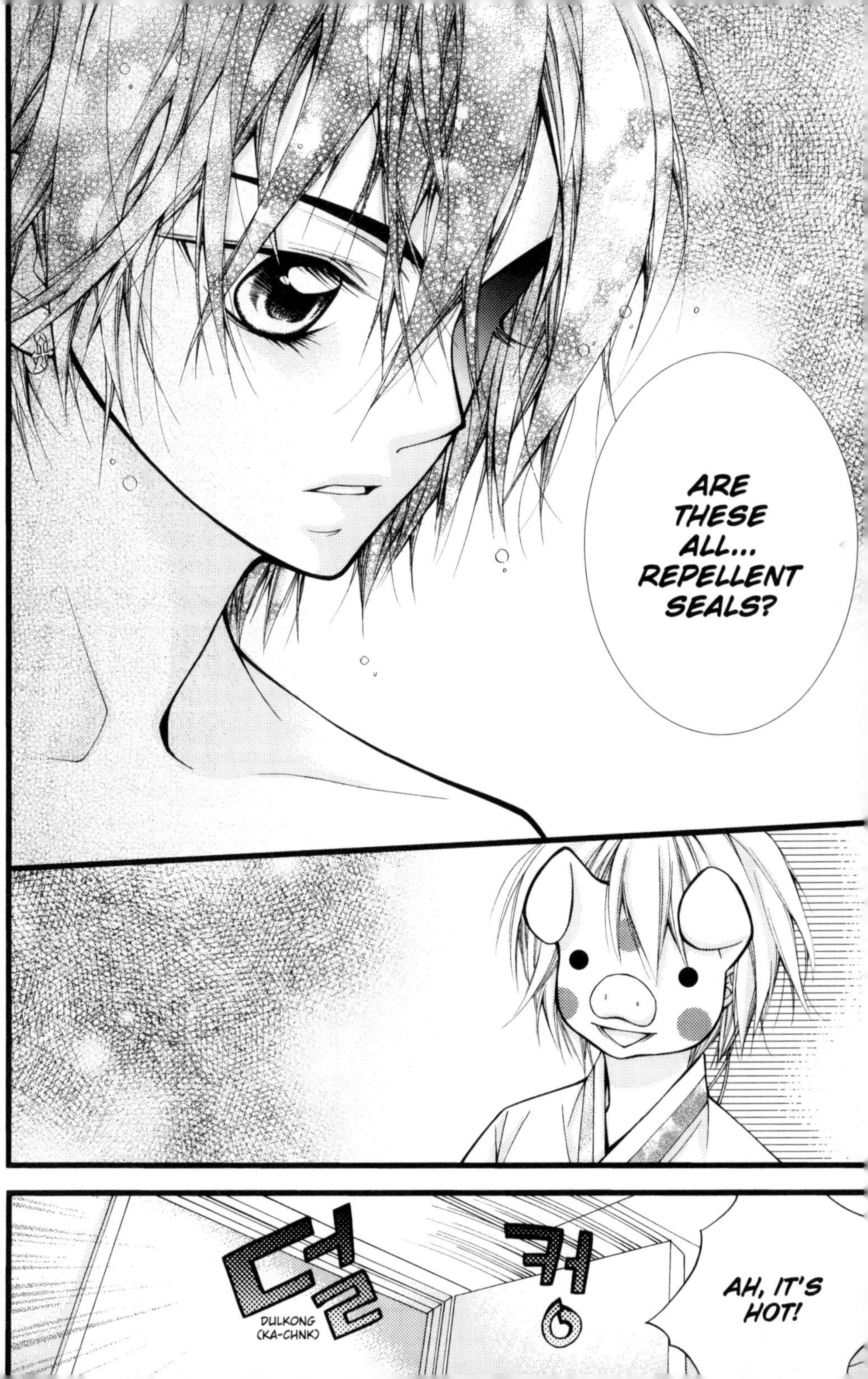
ARE THESE ALL... REPELLENT SEALS?
DULKONG (KA-CHNK)
AH, IT'S HOT!

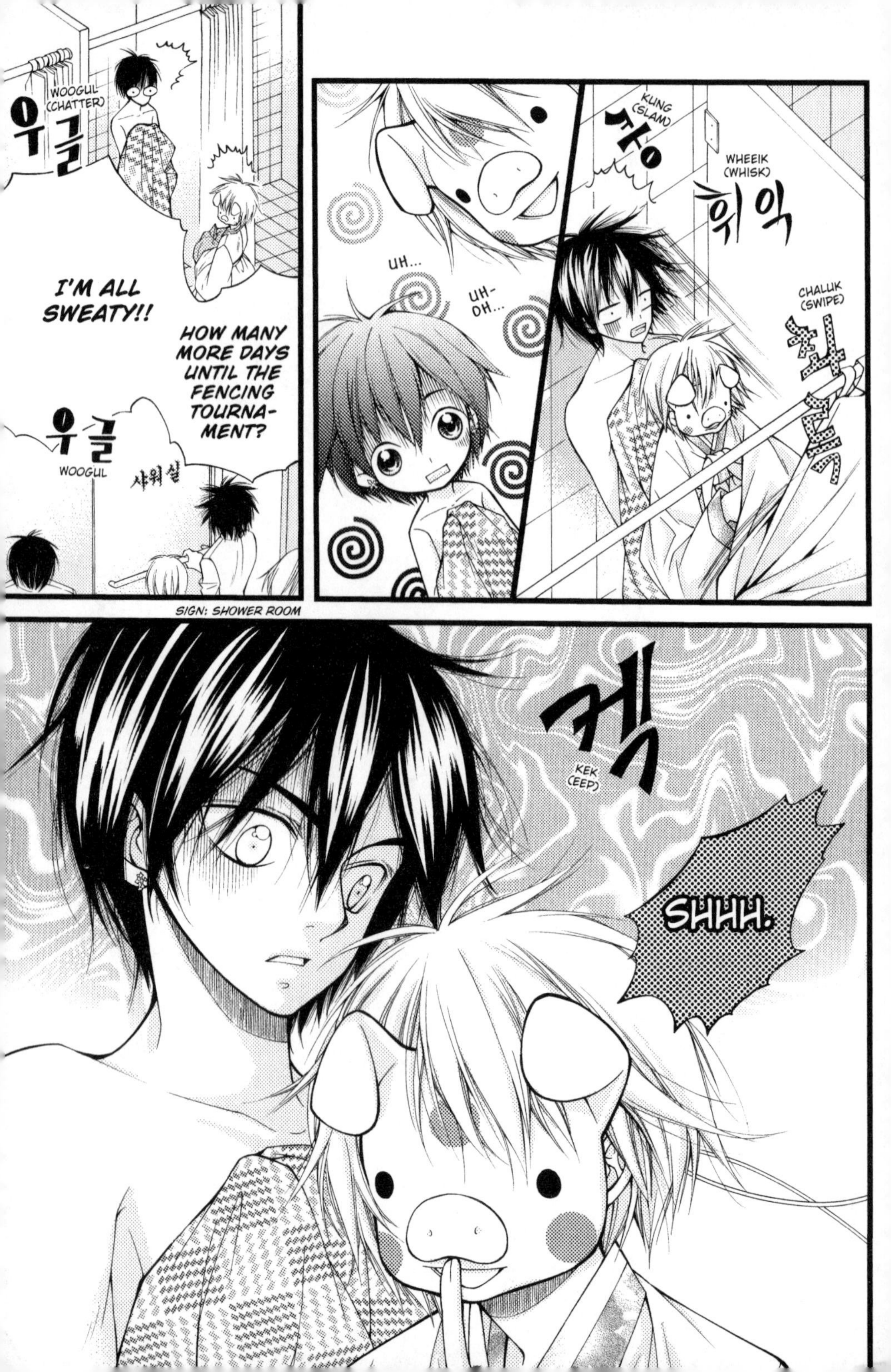
우글
WOOGUL (CHATTER)
I'M ALL SWEATY!!
HOW MANY MORE DAYS UNTIL THE FENCING TOURNA-MENT?
우글
WOOGUL
샤워실
SIGN: SHOWER ROOM
UH...
UH-OH...
쾅
KUNG (SLAM)
휘익
WHEEIK (WHISK)
CHALUK (SWIPE)
켁
KEK (EEP)
SHHH.

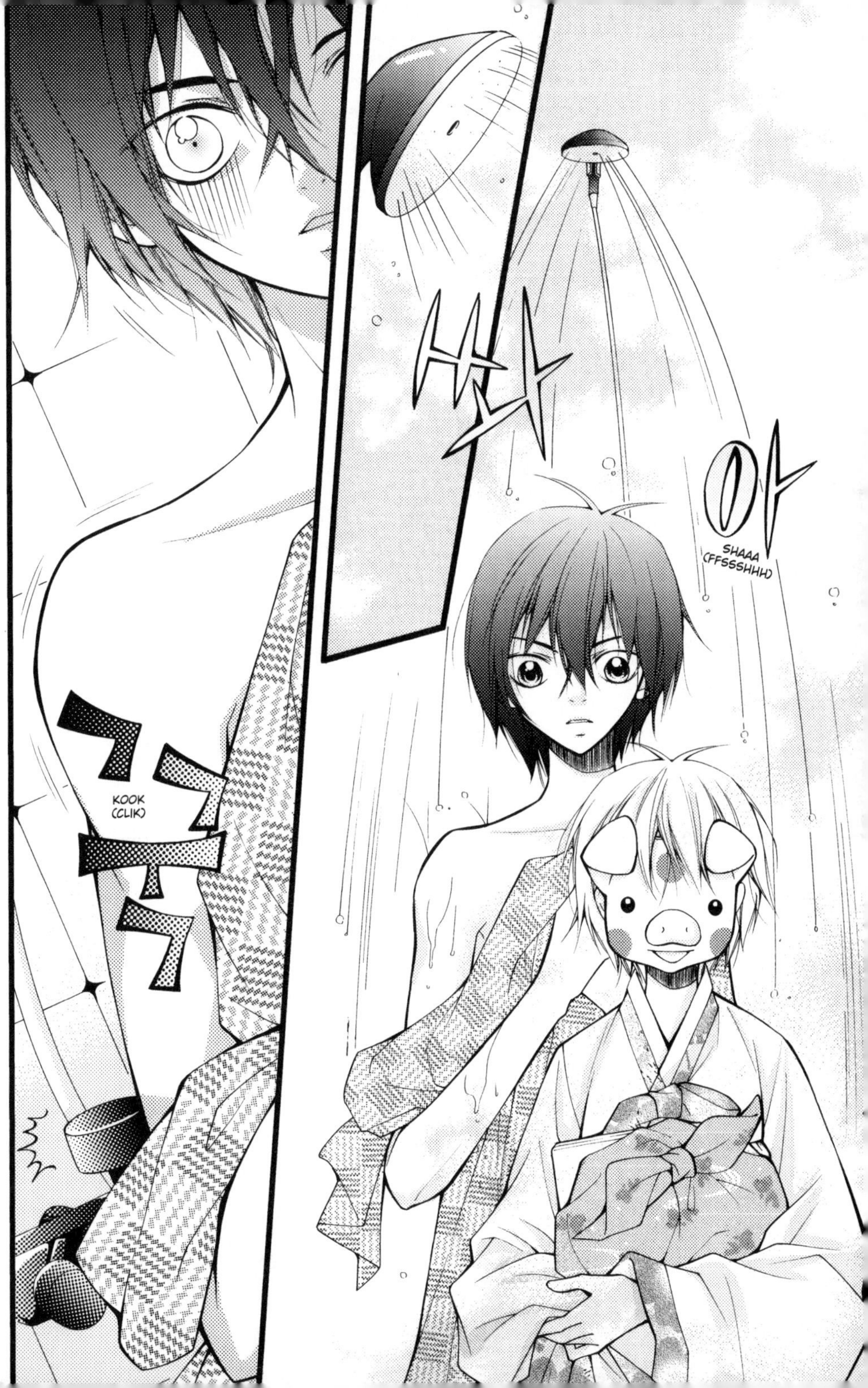
KOOK
(CLIK)
SHAAA
(FFSSSHHH)

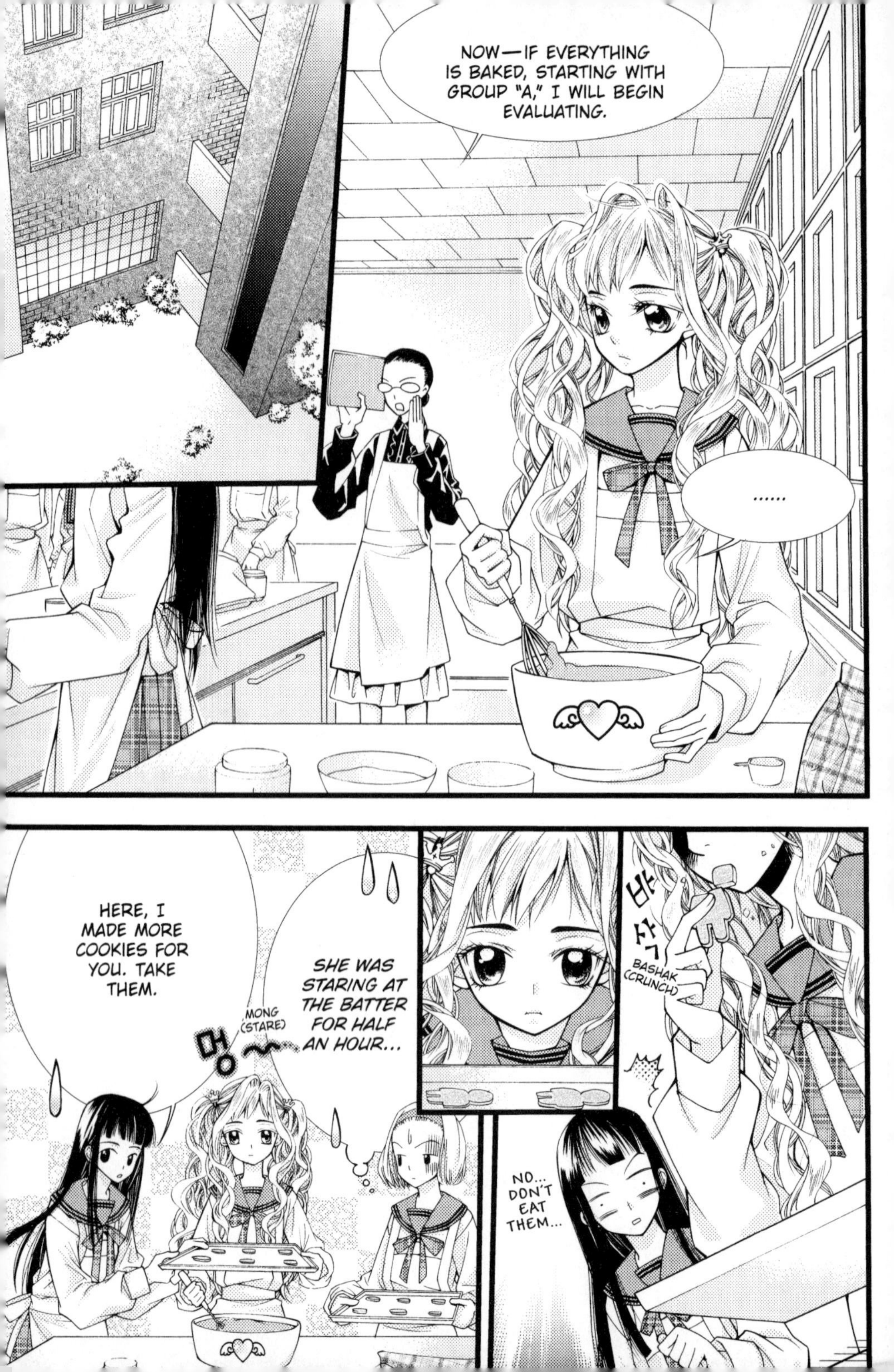
NOW—IF EVERYTHING IS BAKED, STARTING WITH GROUP "A," I WILL BEGIN EVALUATING.
......
HERE, I MADE MORE COOKIES FOR YOU. TAKE THEM.
SHE WAS STARING AT THE BATTER FOR HALF AN HOUR...
멍
MONG (STARE)
바삭
BASHAK (CRUNCH)
NO... DON'T EAT THEM...

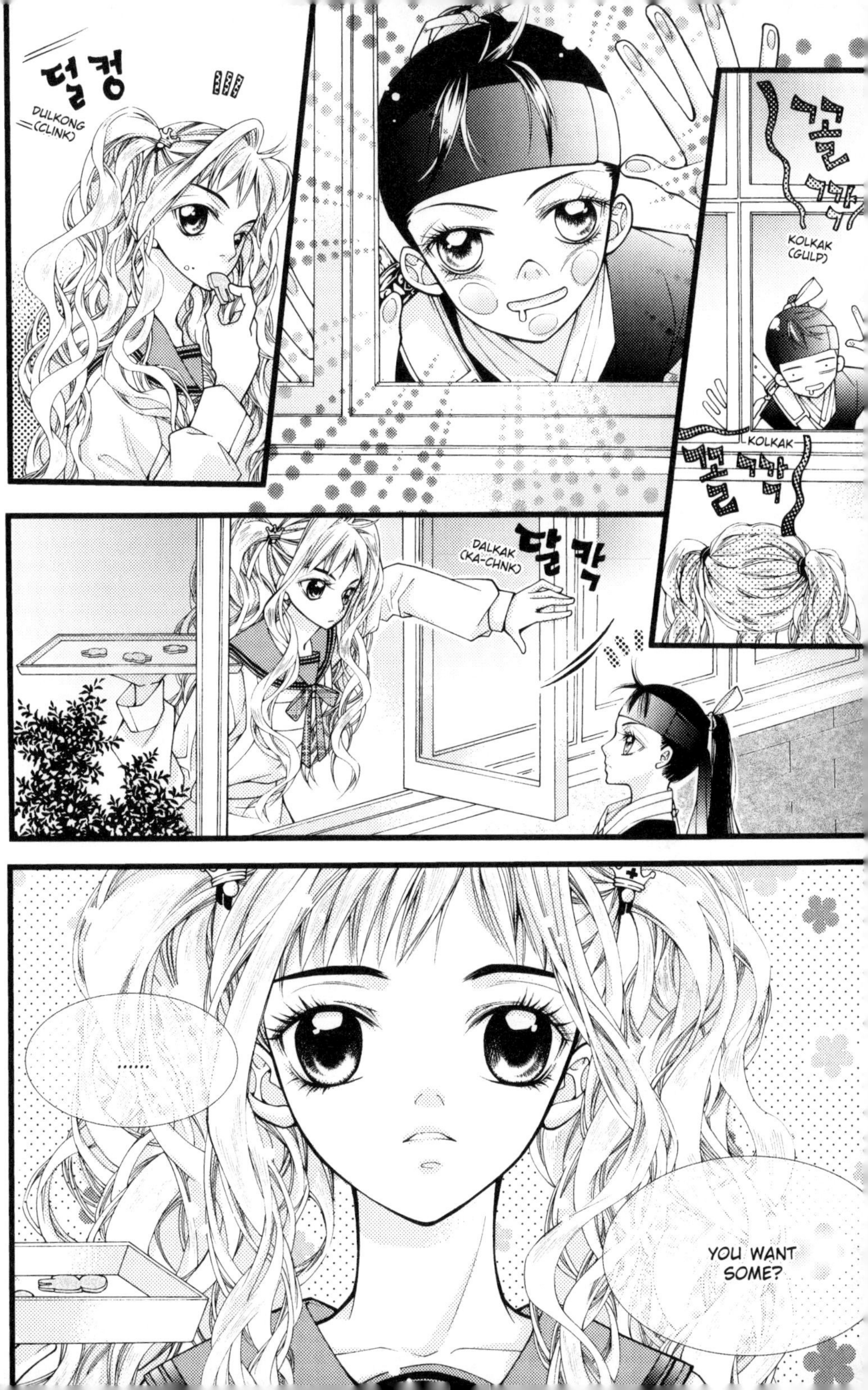
덜컹
DULKONG (CLINK)
!!!
꼴깍
KOLKAK (GULP)
KOLKAK
꼴깍
달칵
DALKAK (KA-CHNK)
!!
......
YOU WANT SOME?

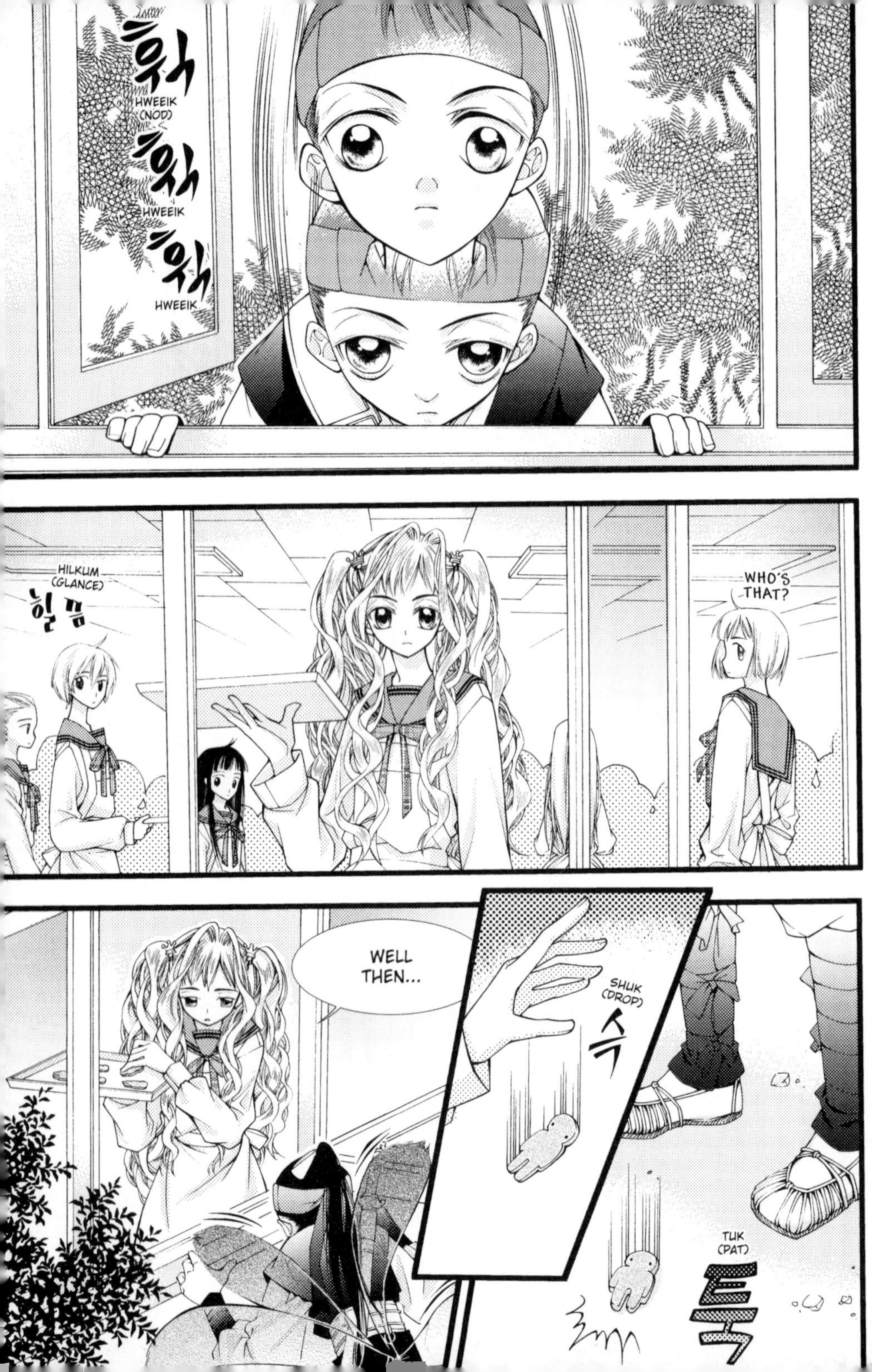
휘익
HWEEIK (NOD)
휘익
HWEEIK
휘익
HWEEIK
HILKUM (GLANCE)
힐끔
WHO'S THAT?
WELL THEN...
SHUK (DROP)
슥
TUK (PAT)
톡

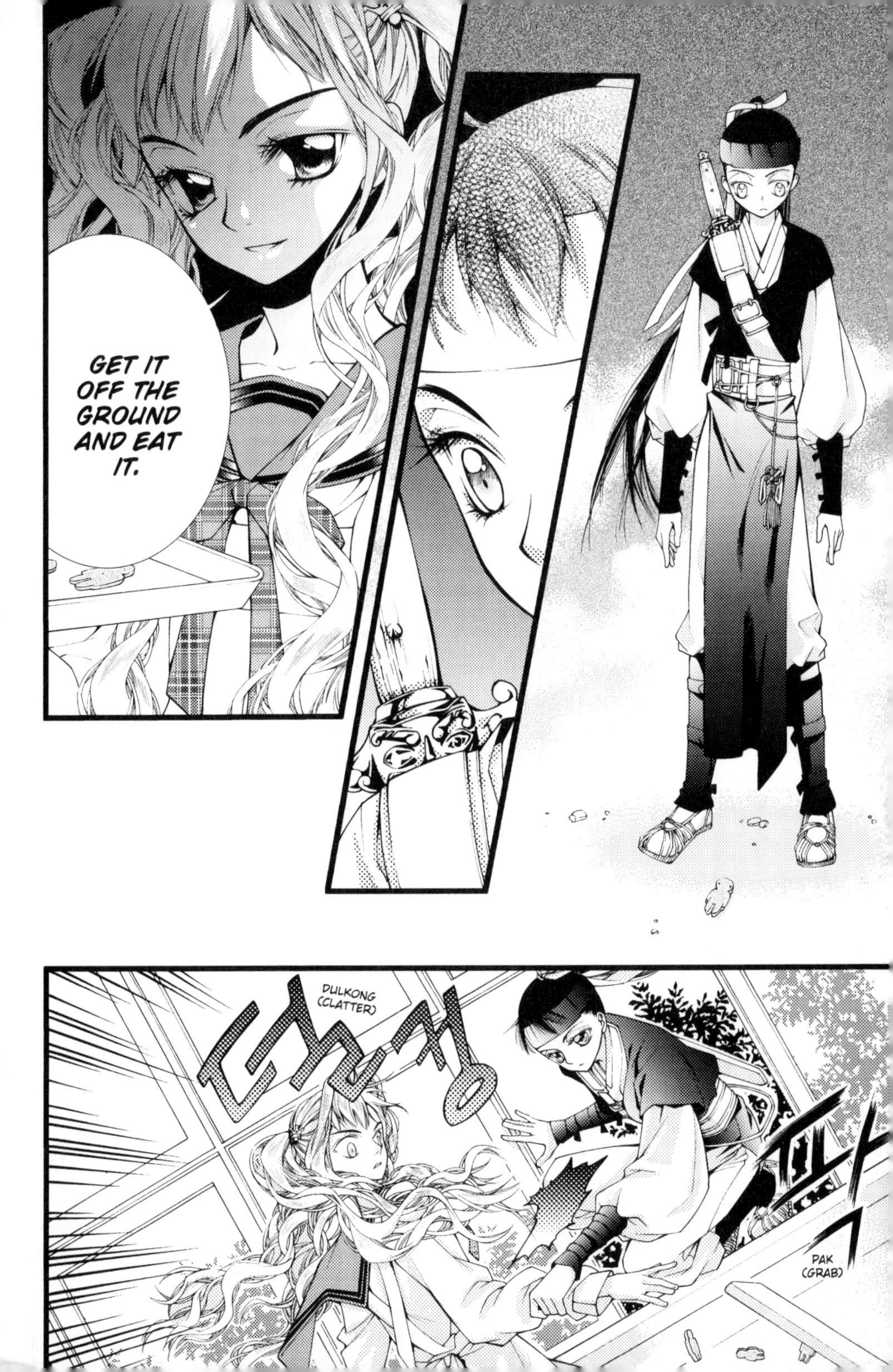
GET IT OFF THE GROUND AND EAT IT.
DULKONG (CLATTER)
PAK (GRAB)

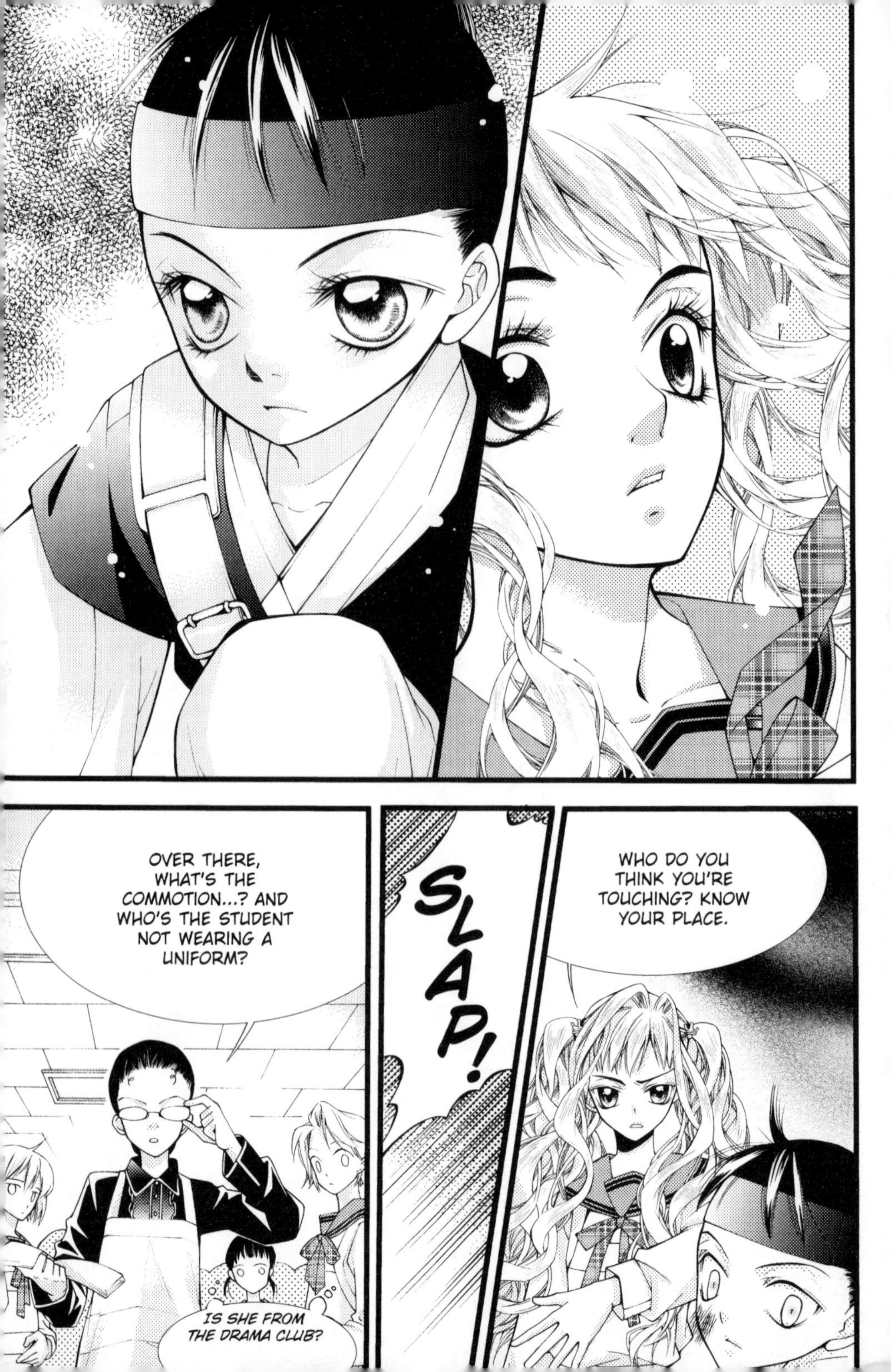

OVER THERE, WHAT'S THE COMMOTION...? AND WHO'S THE STUDENT NOT WEARING A UNIFORM?
IS SHE FROM THE DRAMA CLUB?
SLAP!
WHO DO YOU THINK YOU'RE TOUCHING? KNOW YOUR PLACE.

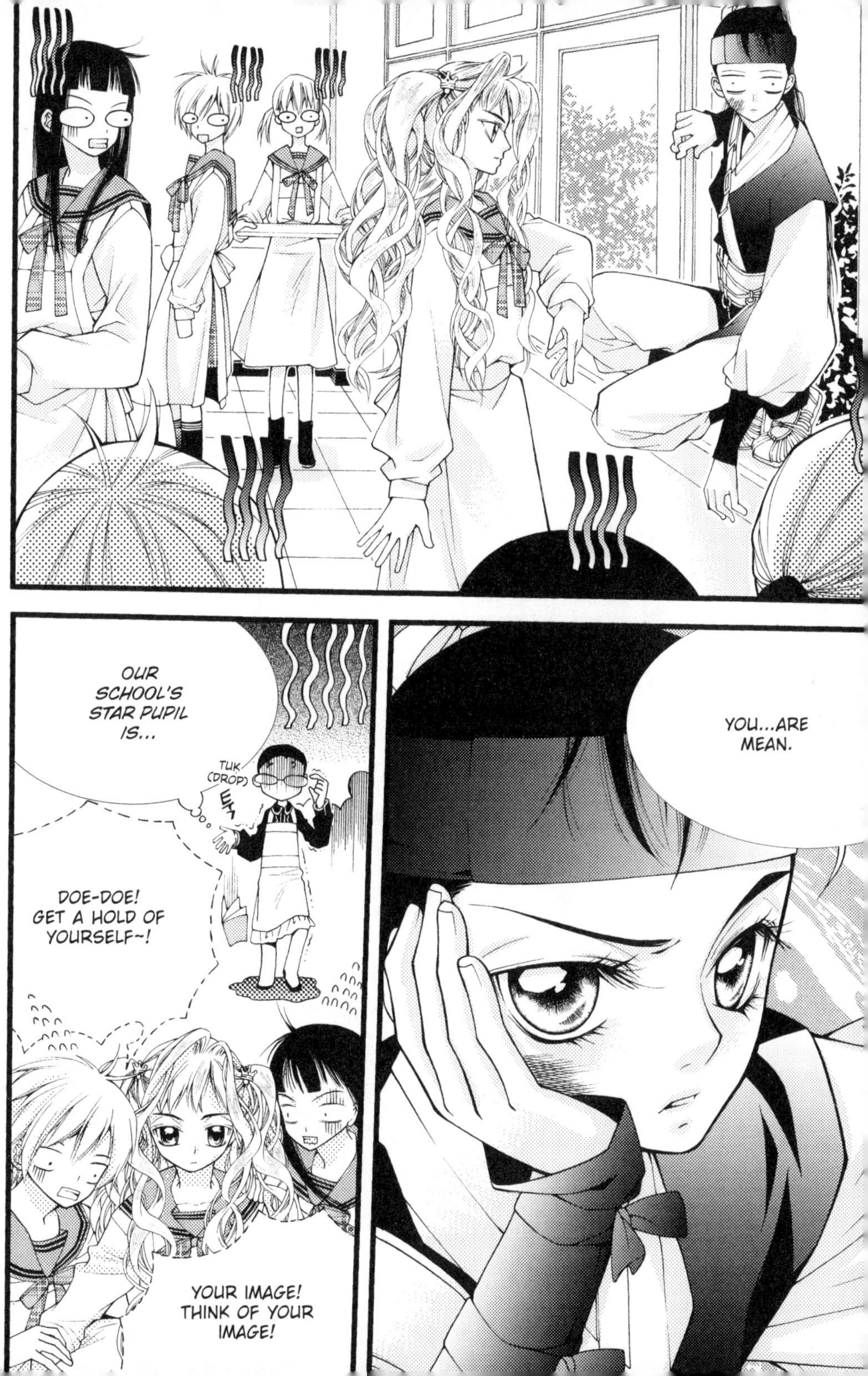
OUR SCHOOL'S STAR PUPIL IS...
TUK (DROP)
DOE-DOE! GET A HOLD OF YOURSELF~!
YOUR IMAGE! THINK OF YOUR IMAGE!
YOU...ARE MEAN.

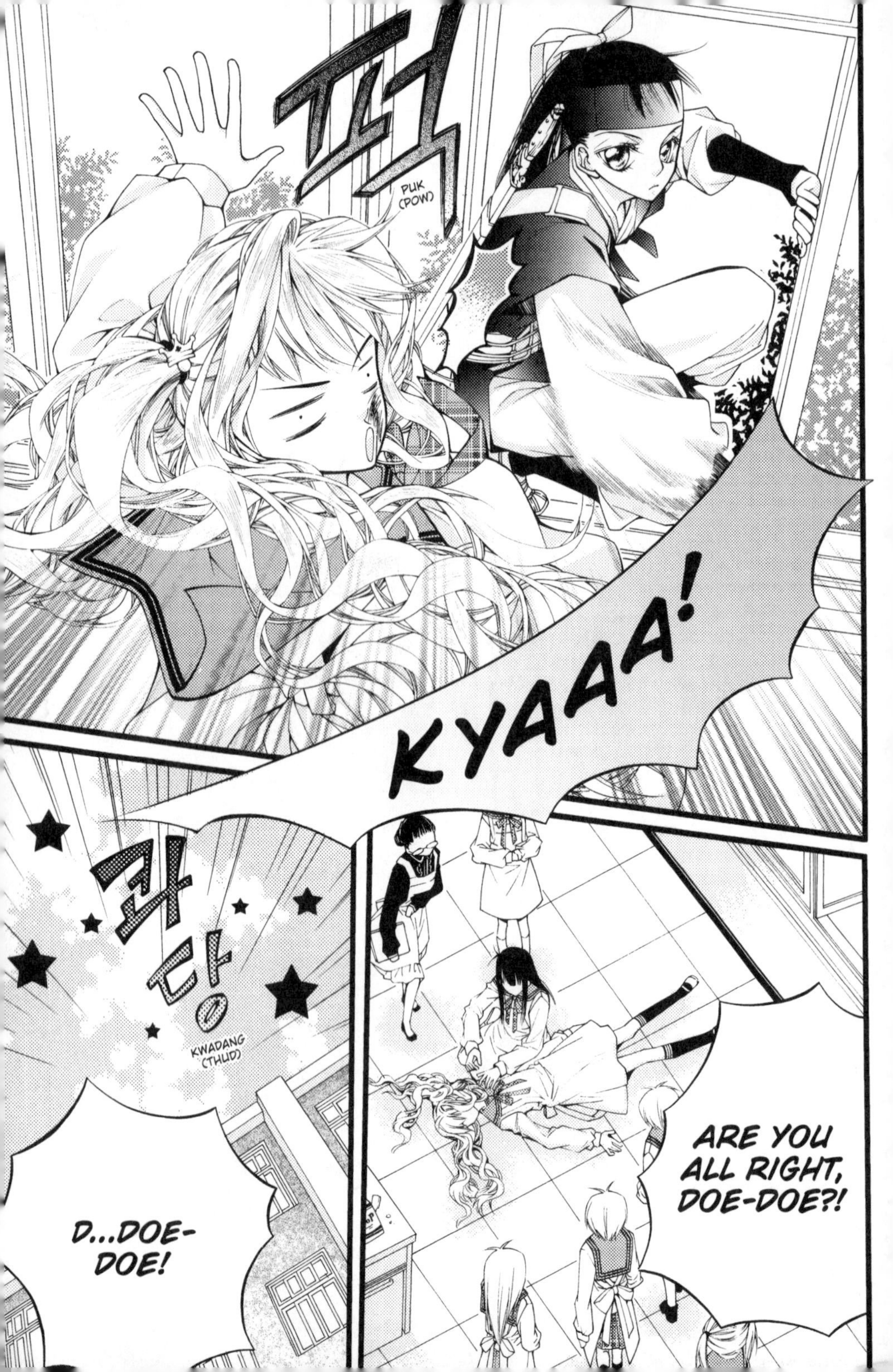
퍽
PUK (POW)
KYAAA!
콰당
KWADANG (THUD)
D...DOE-DOE!
ARE YOU ALL RIGHT, DOE-DOE?!

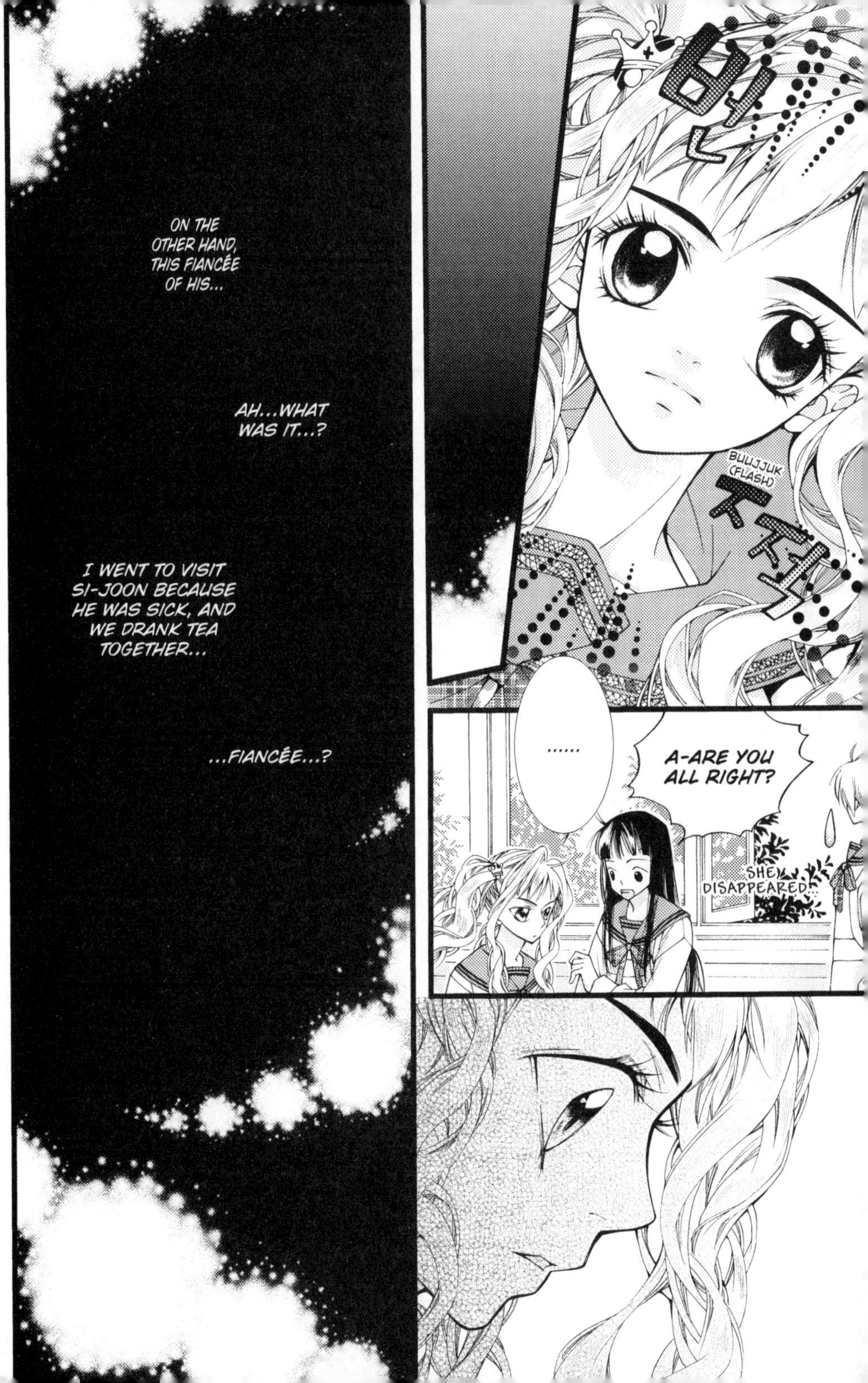

ON THE OTHER HAND, THIS FIANCÉE OF HIS...
AH...WHAT WAS IT...?
I WENT TO VISIT SI-JOON BECAUSE HE WAS SICK, AND WE DRANK TEA TOGETHER...
...FIANCÉE...?
BUUJJUK (FLASH)
......
A-ARE YOU ALL RIGHT?
SHE DISAPPEARED...

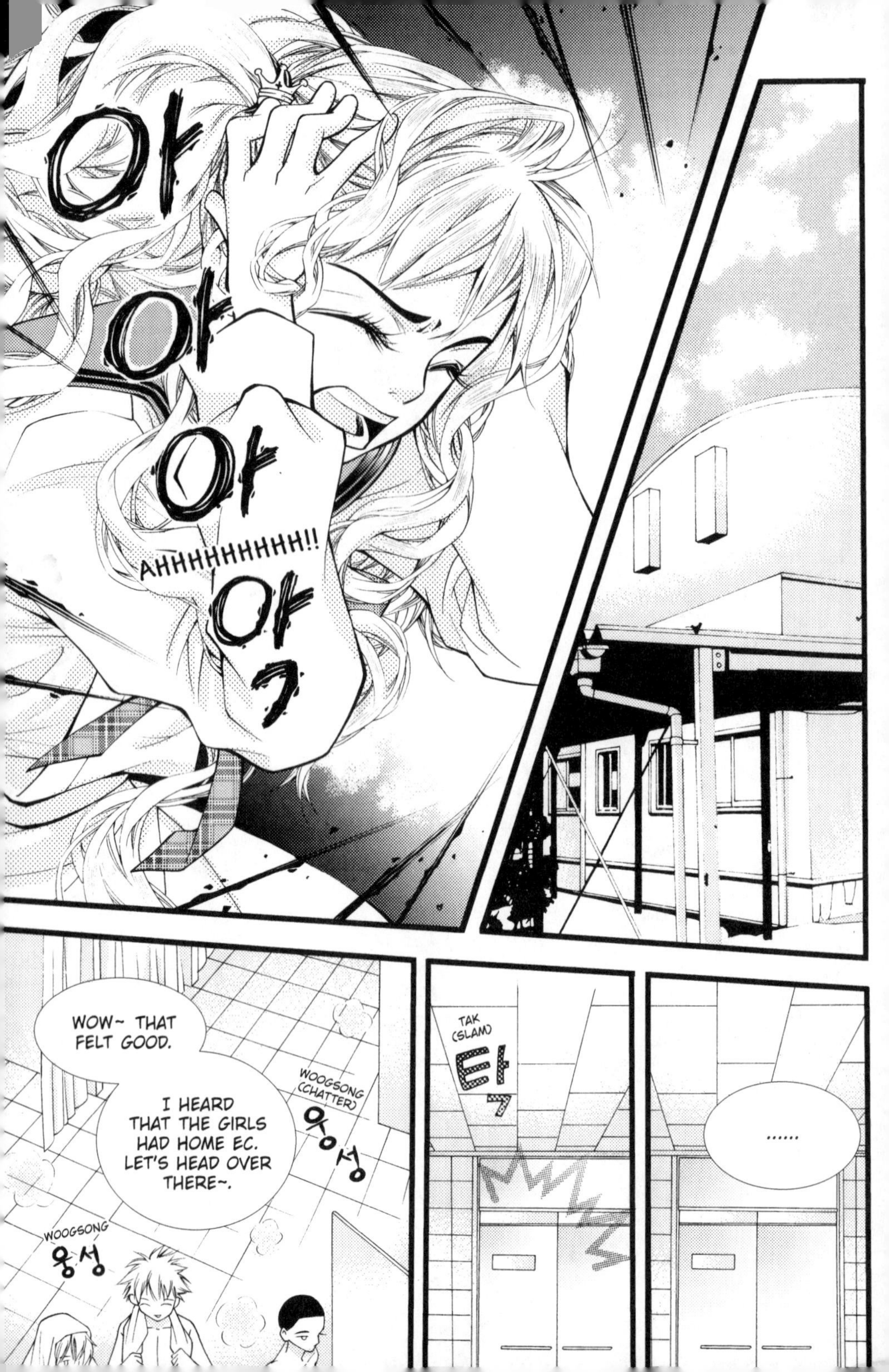

아아아아악
AHHHHHHHHH!!
WOW~ THAT FELT GOOD.
I HEARD THAT THE GIRLS HAD HOME EC. LET'S HEAD OVER THERE~.
WOOGSONG (CHATTER)
웅성
WOOGSONG
웅성
TAK (SLAM)
탁
......

PAT (WHOOSH)
I-I'M SO SORRY...I-I DIDN'T EXPECT PEOPLE TO COME IN AT THAT MOMENT...
DDUK (DRIP)
뚝
DDUK
뚝
UM...ARE YOU ALL RIGHT...? YOUR FACE IS...
BITEUL (TWITCH)
비틀
......
......

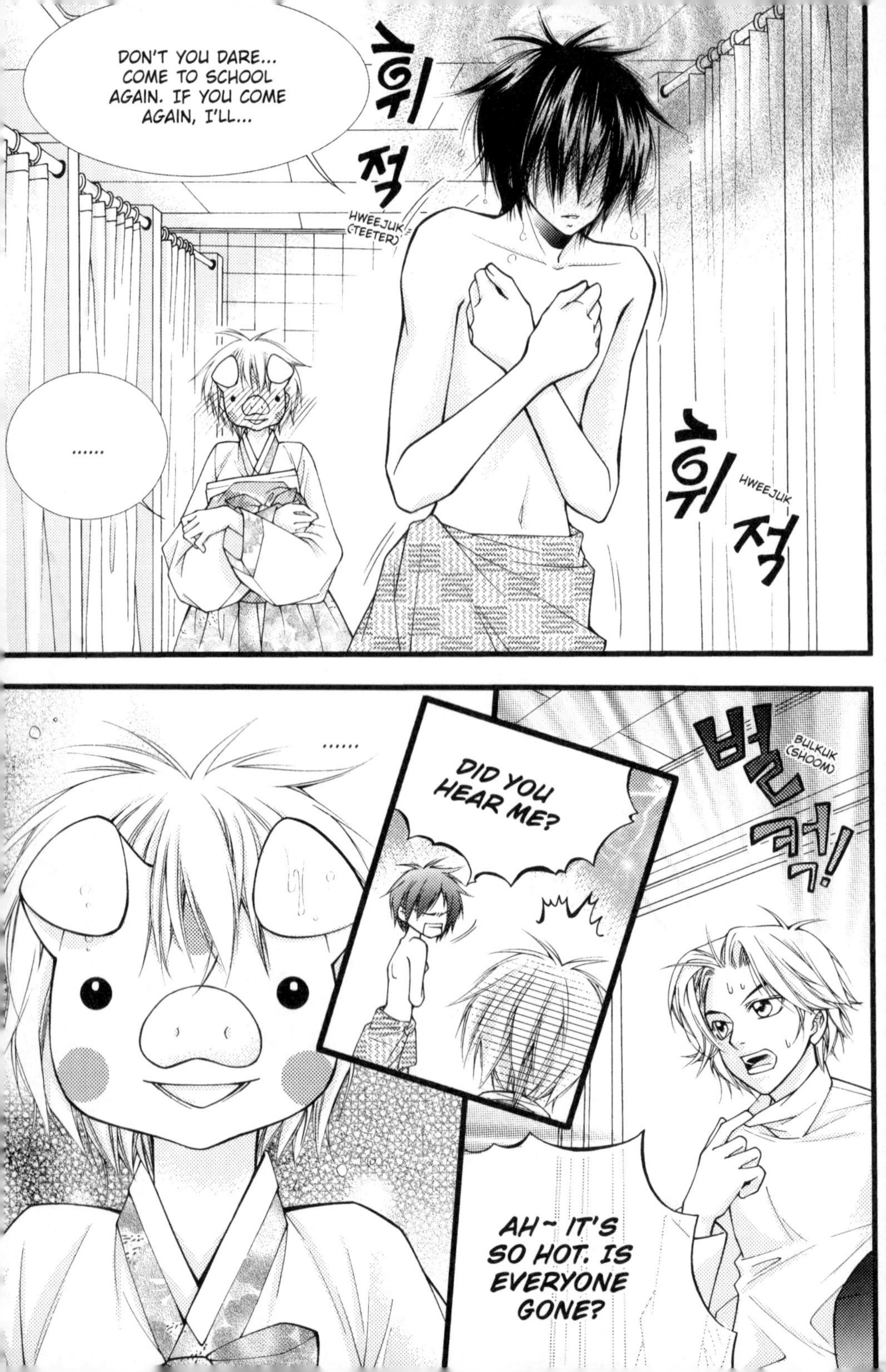
DON'T YOU DARE... COME TO SCHOOL AGAIN. IF YOU COME AGAIN, I'LL...
휘적
HWEEJUK (TEETER)
......
휘적
HWEEJUK
......
DID YOU HEAR ME?
벌컥!
BULKUK (SHOOM)
AH~ IT'S SO HOT. IS EVERYONE GONE?

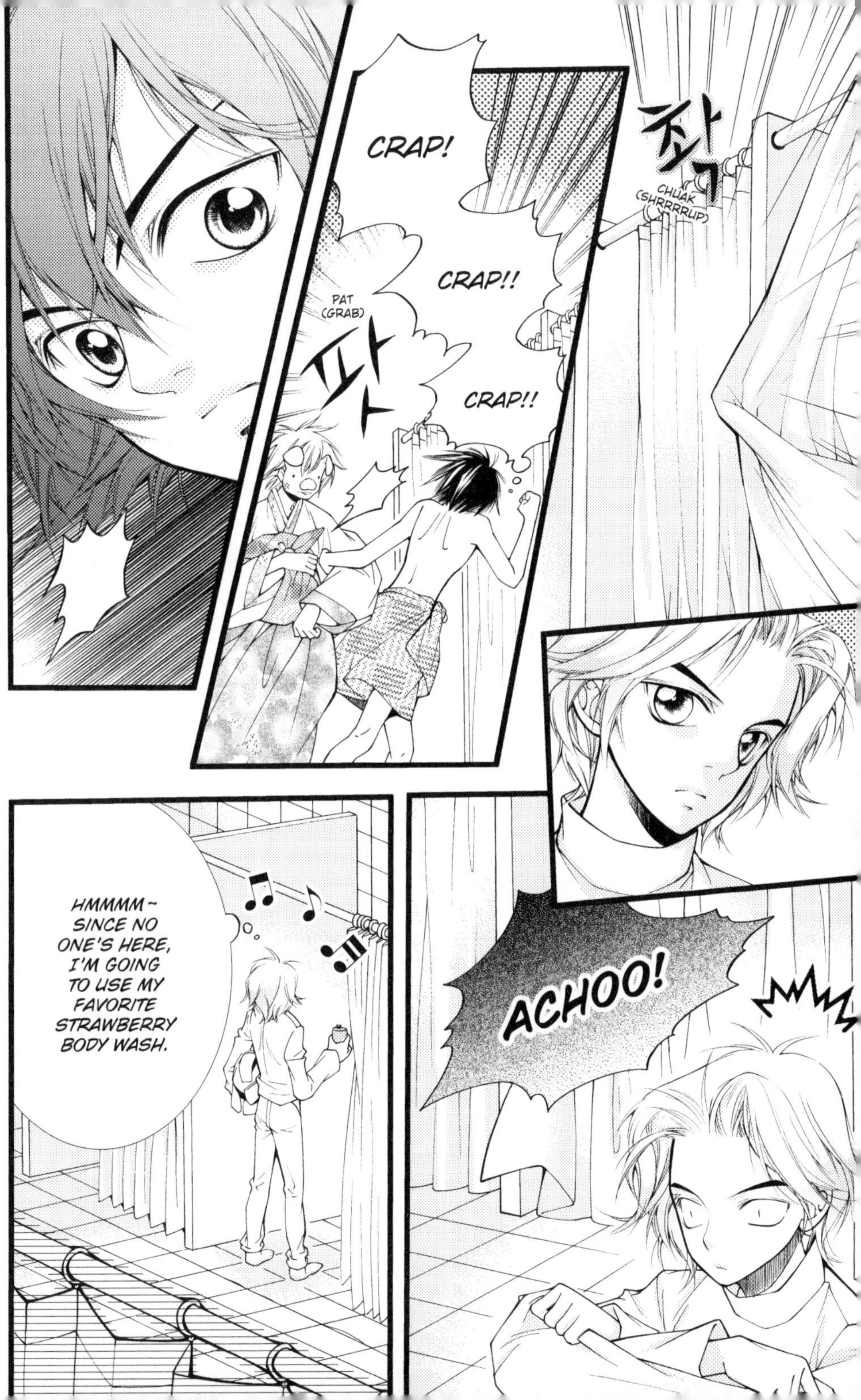
CRAP!
CRAP!!
PAT (GRAB)
CRAP!!
좍
CHUAK (SHRRRRUP)
HMMMM~ SINCE NO ONE'S HERE, I'M GOING TO USE MY FAVORITE STRAWBERRY BODY WASH.
ACHOO!

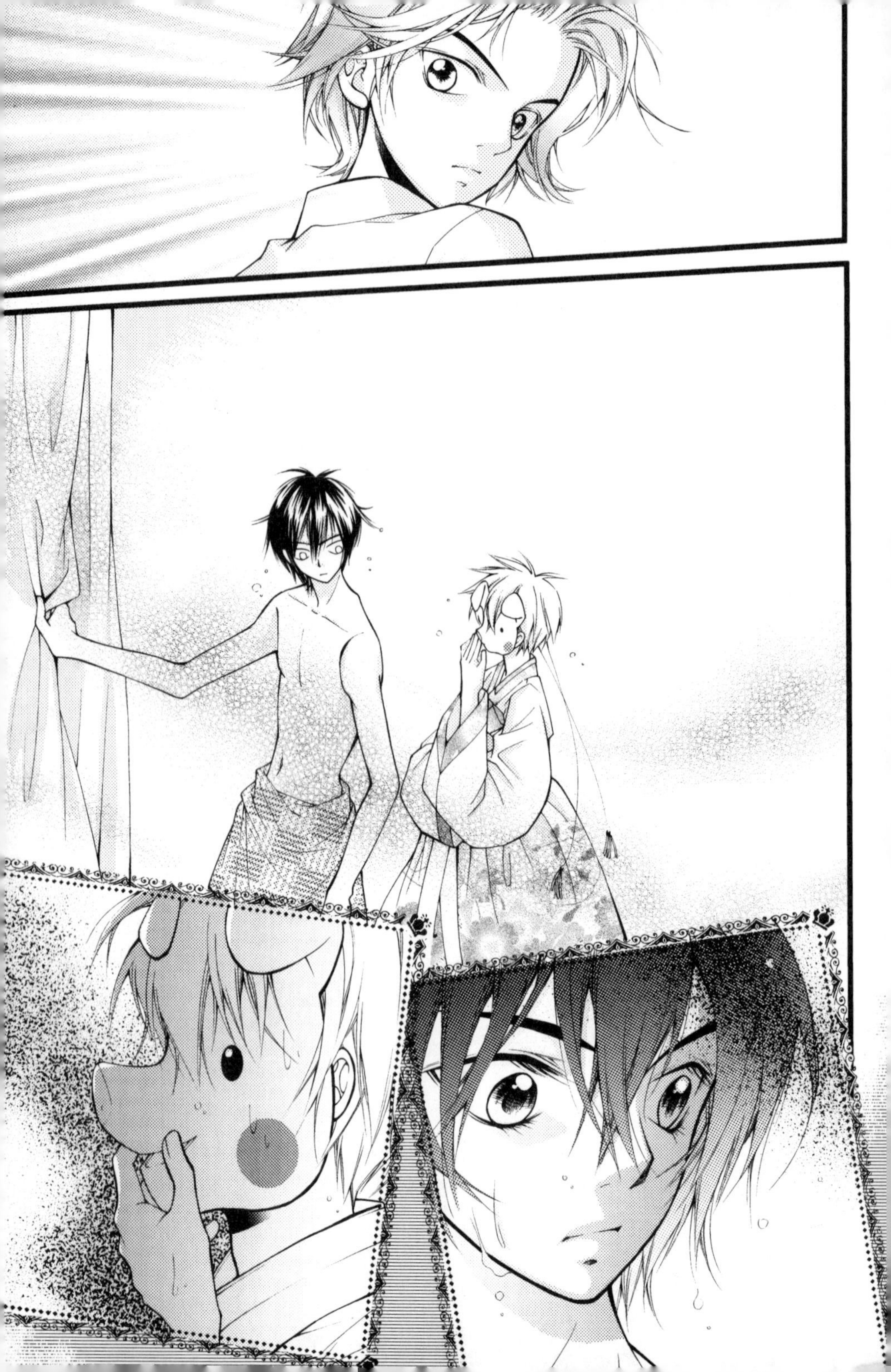

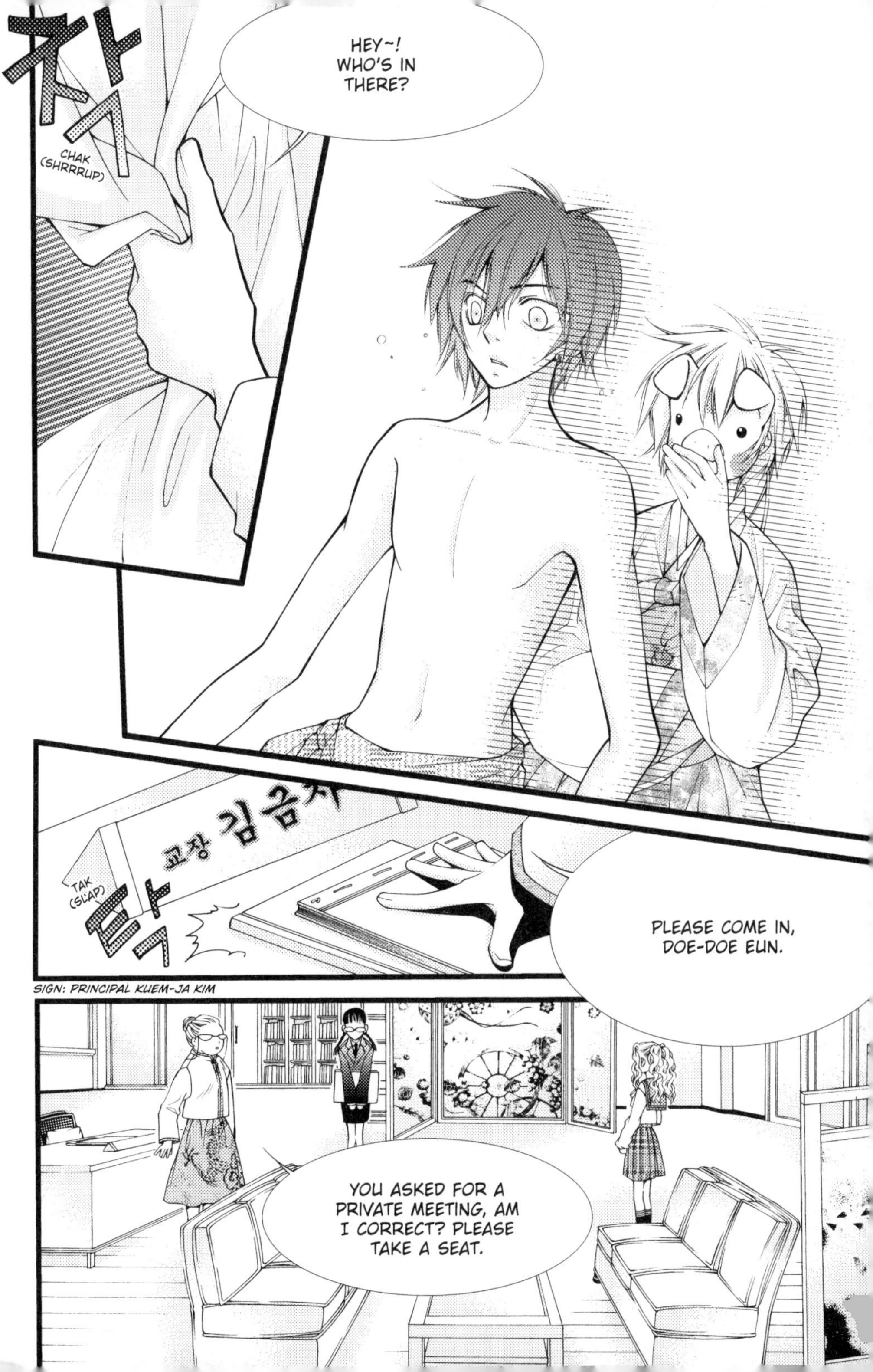

착
CHAK (SHRRRUP)
HEY~! WHO'S IN THERE?
교장 김금자
탁
TAK (SLAP)
PLEASE COME IN, DOE-DOE EUN.
SIGN: PRINCIPAL KUEM-JA KIM
YOU ASKED FOR A PRIVATE MEETING, AM I CORRECT? PLEASE TAKE A SEAT.

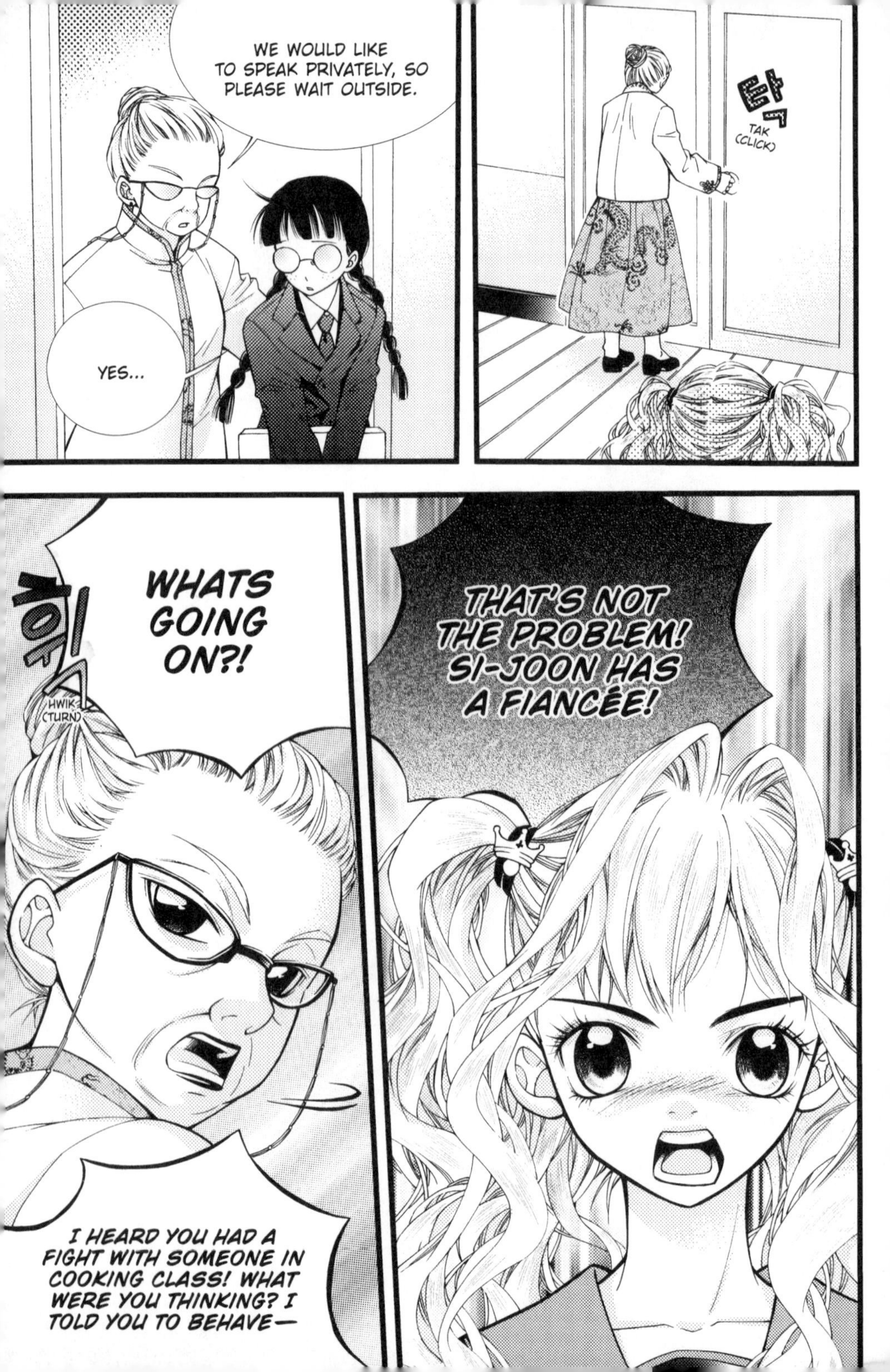
WE WOULD LIKE TO SPEAK PRIVATELY, SO PLEASE WAIT OUTSIDE.
YES...
탁
TAK (CLICK)
WHATS GOING ON?!
HWIK (TURN)
I HEARD YOU HAD A FIGHT WITH SOMEONE IN COOKING CLASS! WHAT WERE YOU THINKING? I TOLD YOU TO BEHAVE—
THAT'S NOT THE PROBLEM! SI-JOON HAS A FIANCÉE!

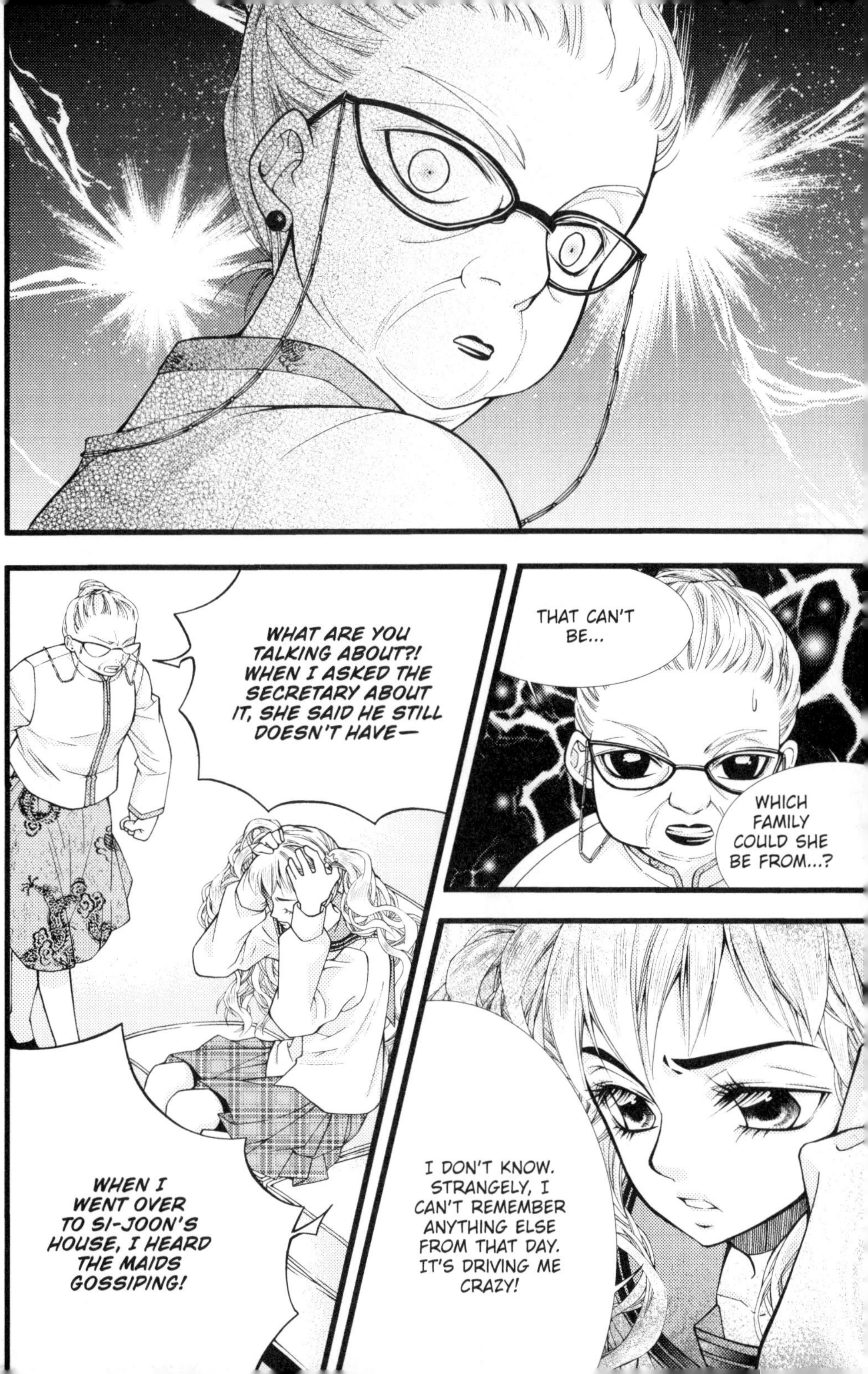
WHAT ARE YOU TALKING ABOUT?! WHEN I ASKED THE SECRETARY ABOUT IT, SHE SAID HE STILL DOESN'T HAVE—
WHEN I WENT OVER TO SI-JOON'S HOUSE, I HEARD THE MAIDS GOSSIPING!
THAT CAN'T BE...
WHICH FAMILY COULD SHE BE FROM...?
I DON'T KNOW. STRANGELY, I CAN'T REMEMBER ANYTHING ELSE FROM THAT DAY. IT'S DRIVING ME CRAZY!

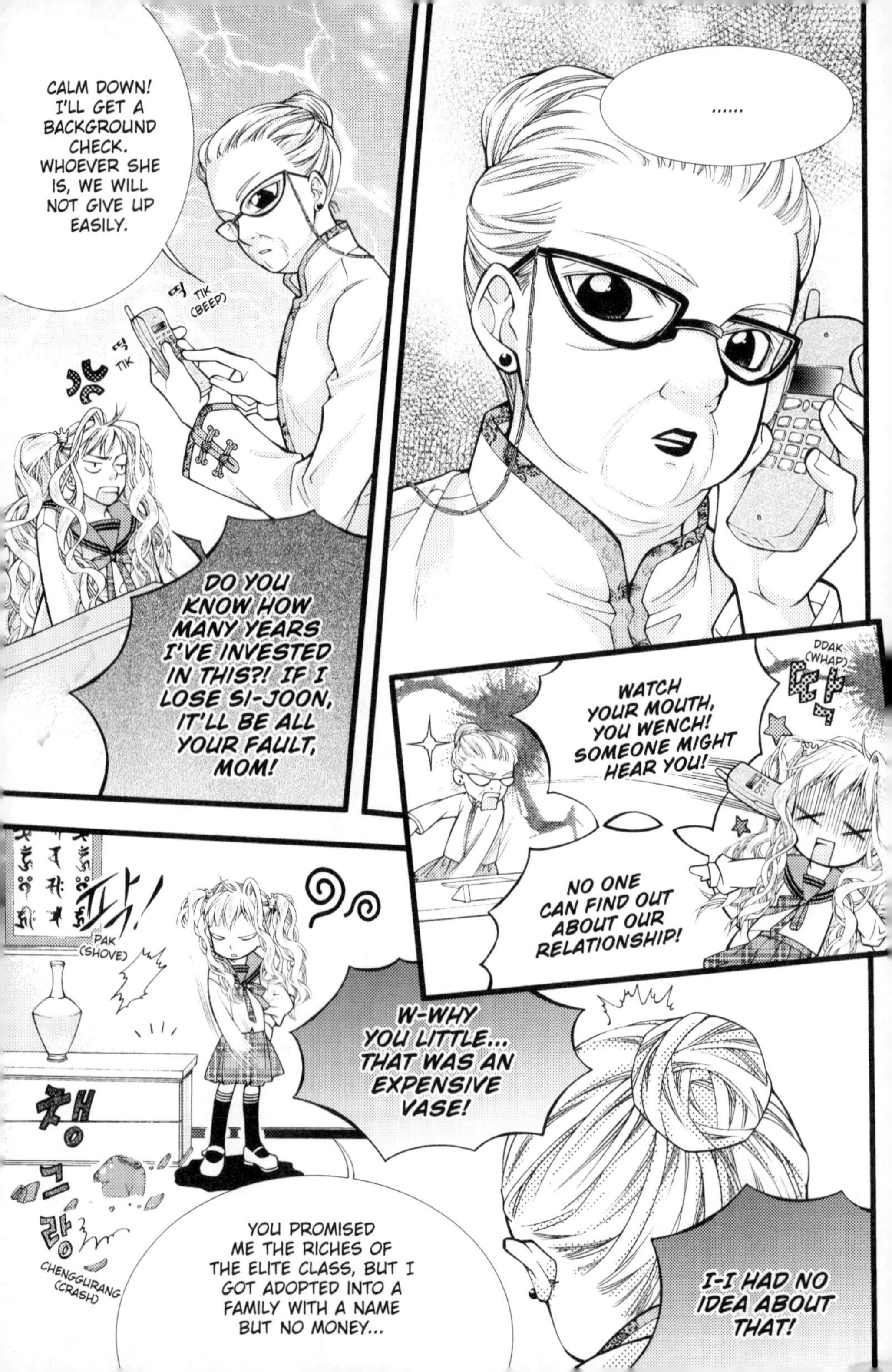
CALM DOWN! I'LL GET A BACKGROUND CHECK. WHOEVER SHE IS, WE WILL NOT GIVE UP EASILY.
TIK (BEEP)
TIK
DO YOU KNOW HOW MANY YEARS I'VE INVESTED IN THIS?! IF I LOSE SI-JOON, IT'LL BE ALL YOUR FAULT, MOM!
......
DDAK (WHAP)
WATCH YOUR MOUTH, YOU WENCH! SOMEONE MIGHT HEAR YOU!
NO ONE CAN FIND OUT ABOUT OUR RELATIONSHIP!
PAK (SHOVE)
CHENGGURANG (CRASH)
W-WHY YOU LITTLE... THAT WAS AN EXPENSIVE VASE!
YOU PROMISED ME THE RICHES OF THE ELITE CLASS, BUT I GOT ADOPTED INTO A FAMILY WITH A NAME BUT NO MONEY...
I-I HAD NO IDEA ABOUT THAT!

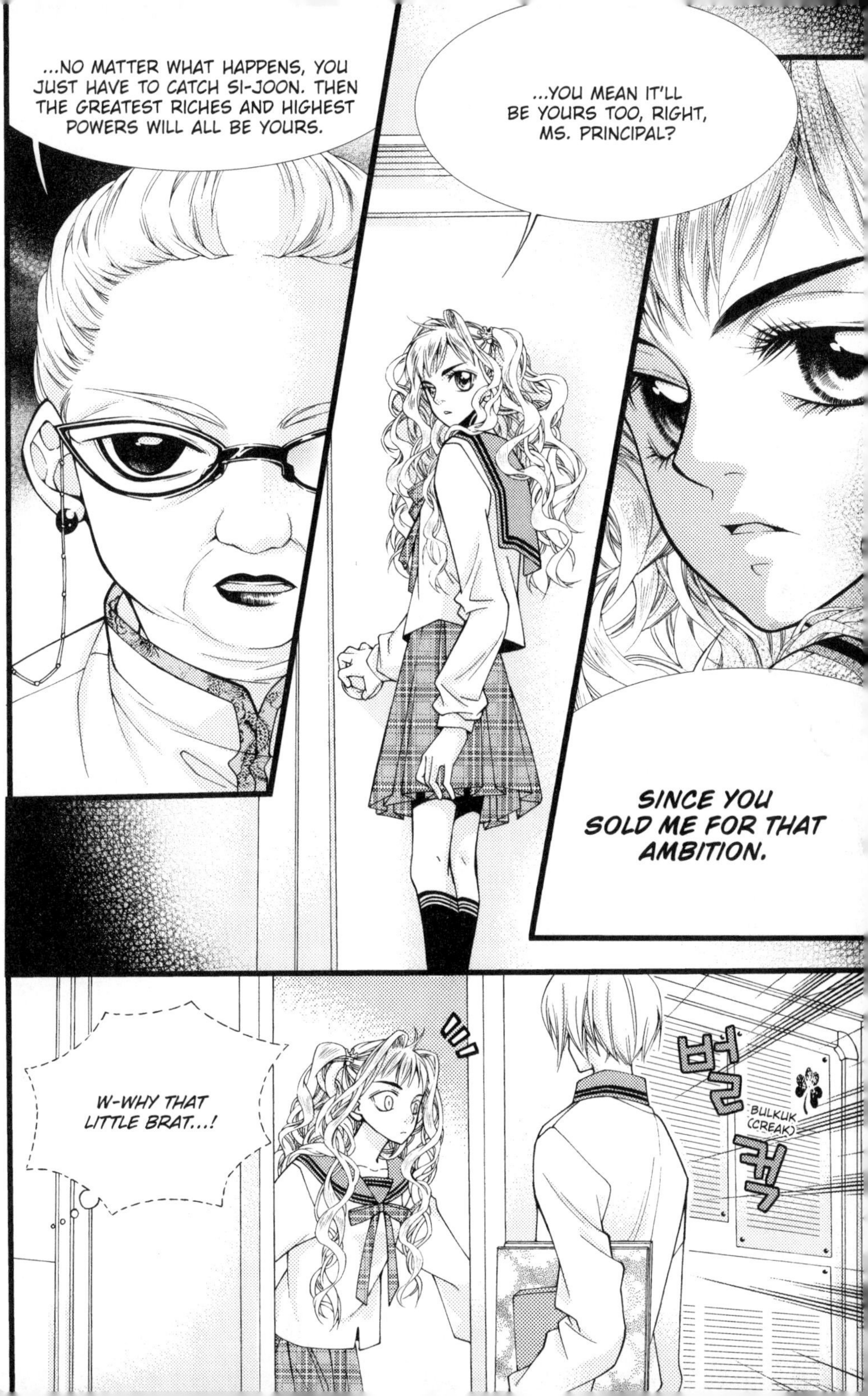
...NO MATTER WHAT HAPPENS, YOU JUST HAVE TO CATCH SI-JOON. THEN THE GREATEST RICHES AND HIGHEST POWERS WILL ALL BE YOURS.
...YOU MEAN IT'LL BE YOURS TOO, RIGHT, MS. PRINCIPAL?
SINCE YOU SOLD ME FOR THAT AMBITION.
W-WHY THAT LITTLE BRAT...!
벌컥
BULKUK (CREAK)

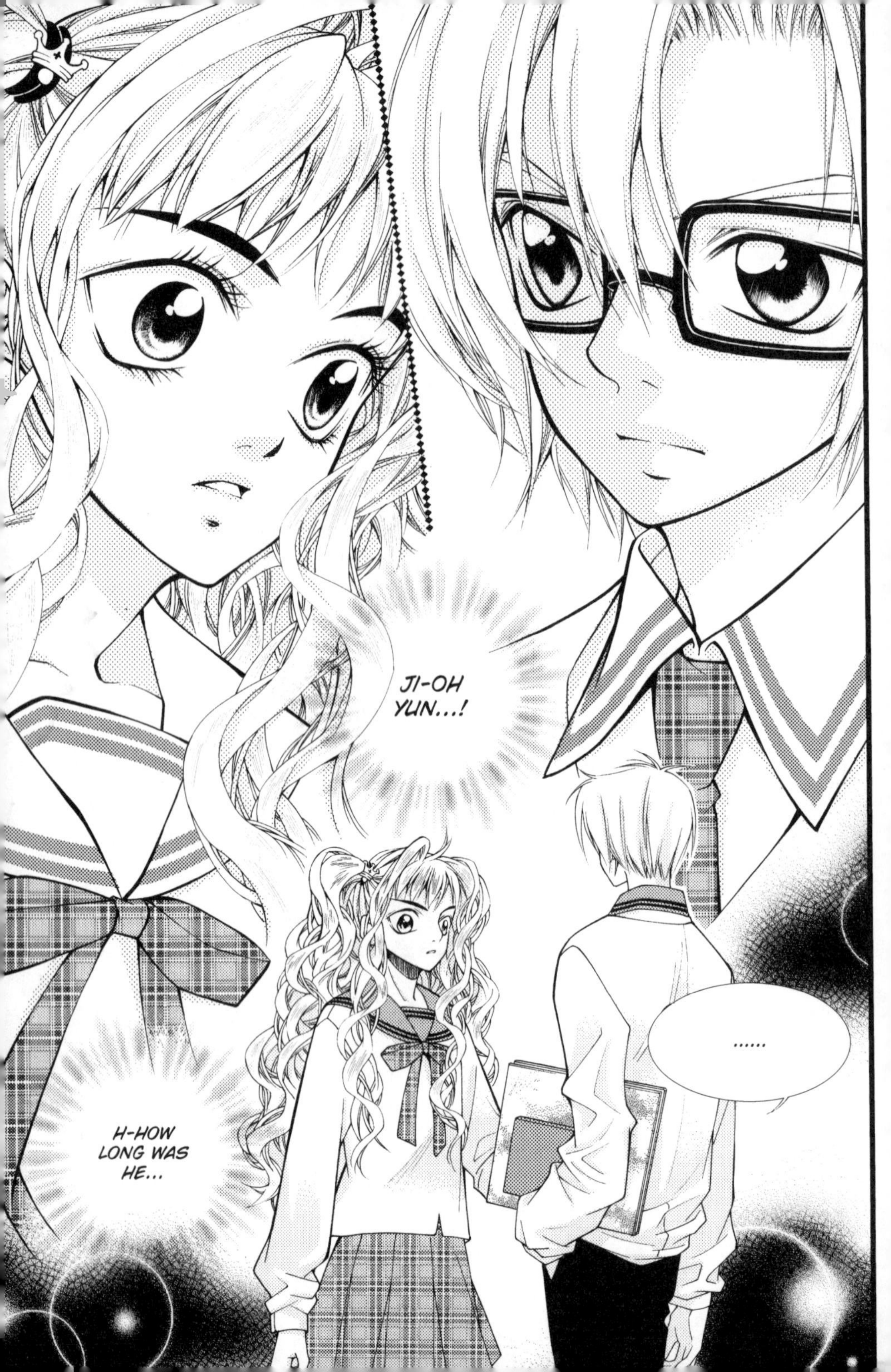
JI-OH YUN...!
H-HOW LONG WAS HE...
......

I BROUGHT THE REPORTS FROM THE CLASS REPRESENTATIVE MEETING.

KNOCK

KNOCK

...DID HE HEAR EVERYTHING?

VICE PRESIDENT JI-OH, PLEASE COME IN.

HOW IS YOUR MOTHER? DID SHE GIVE YOU ANYTHING TO SEND TO ME? HO-HO~.

ELEGANT~ 고상~

......

AH, NO, THERE WASN'T ANYTHING...

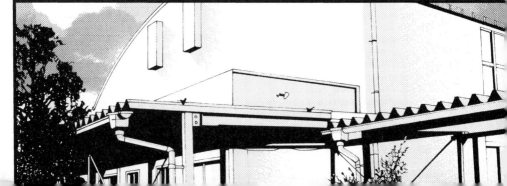

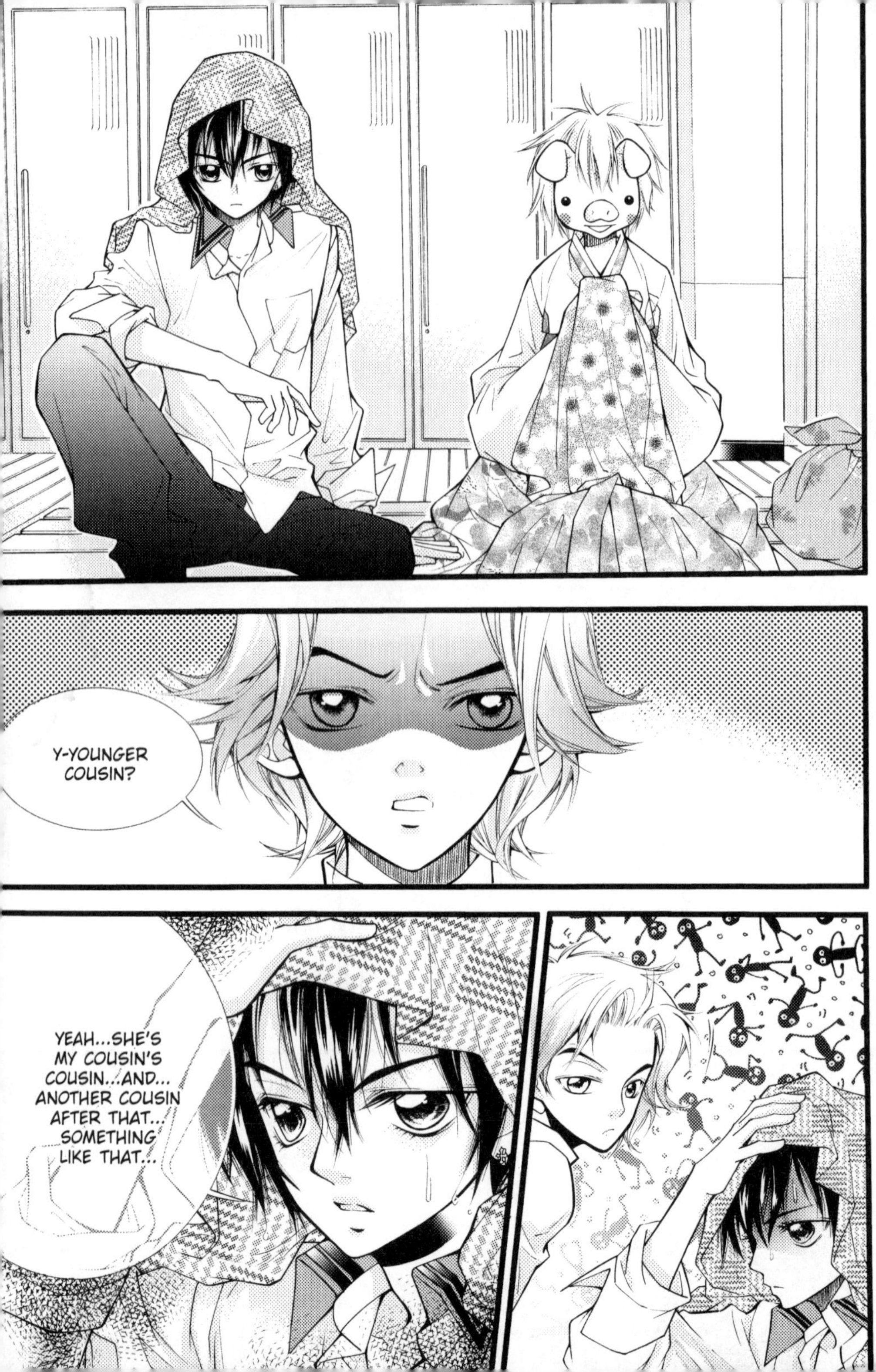
Y-YOUNGER COUSIN?
YEAH...SHE'S MY COUSIN'S COUSIN...AND... ANOTHER COUSIN AFTER THAT... SOMETHING LIKE THAT...

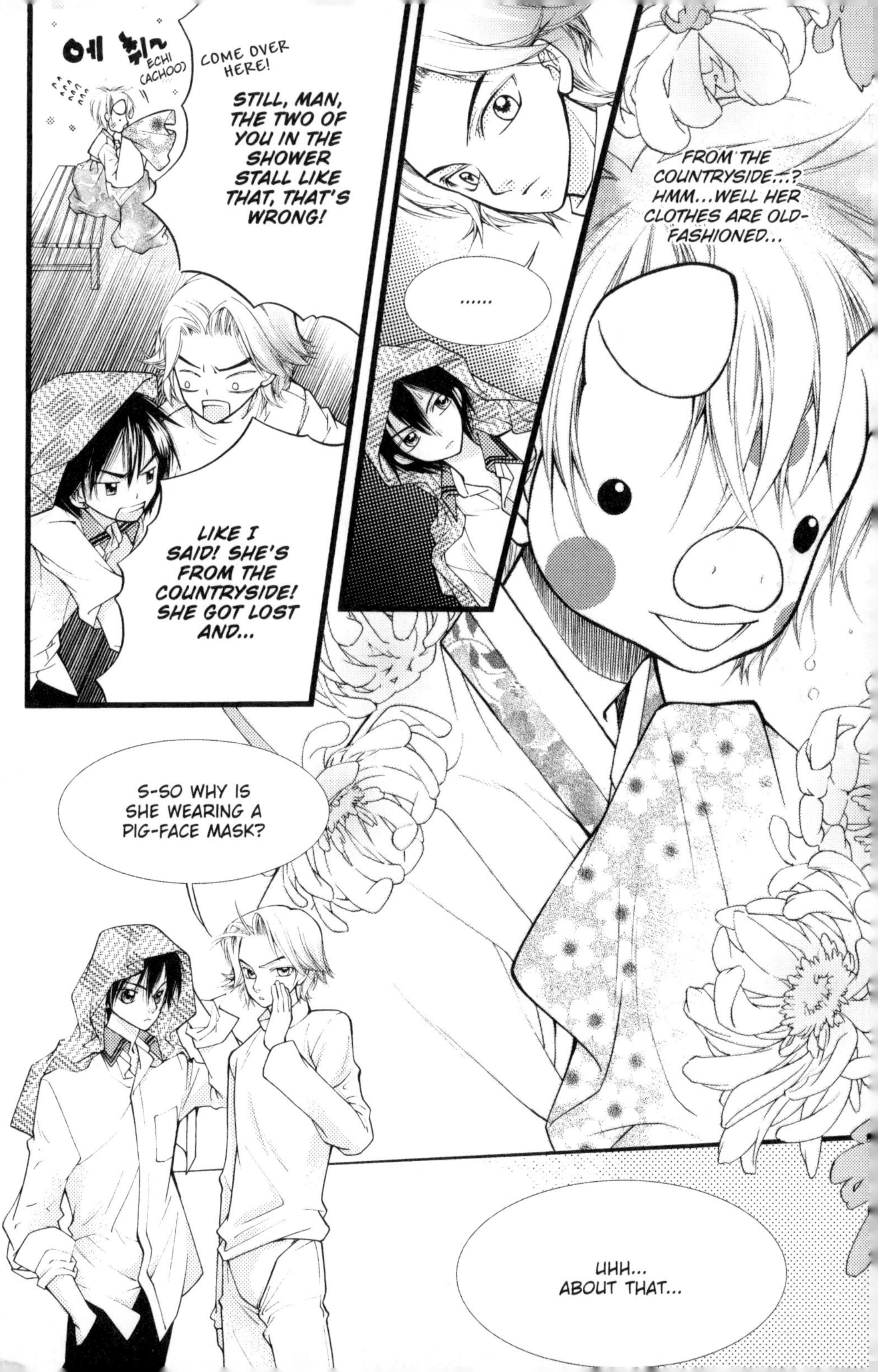

에취~
ECHI (ACHOO)
COME OVER HERE!
STILL, MAN, THE TWO OF YOU IN THE SHOWER STALL LIKE THAT, THAT'S WRONG!
LIKE I SAID! SHE'S FROM THE COUNTRYSIDE! SHE GOT LOST AND...
......
FROM THE COUNTRYSIDE...? HMM...WELL HER CLOTHES ARE OLD-FASHIONED...
S-SO WHY IS SHE WEARING A PIG-FACE MASK?
UHH... ABOUT THAT...

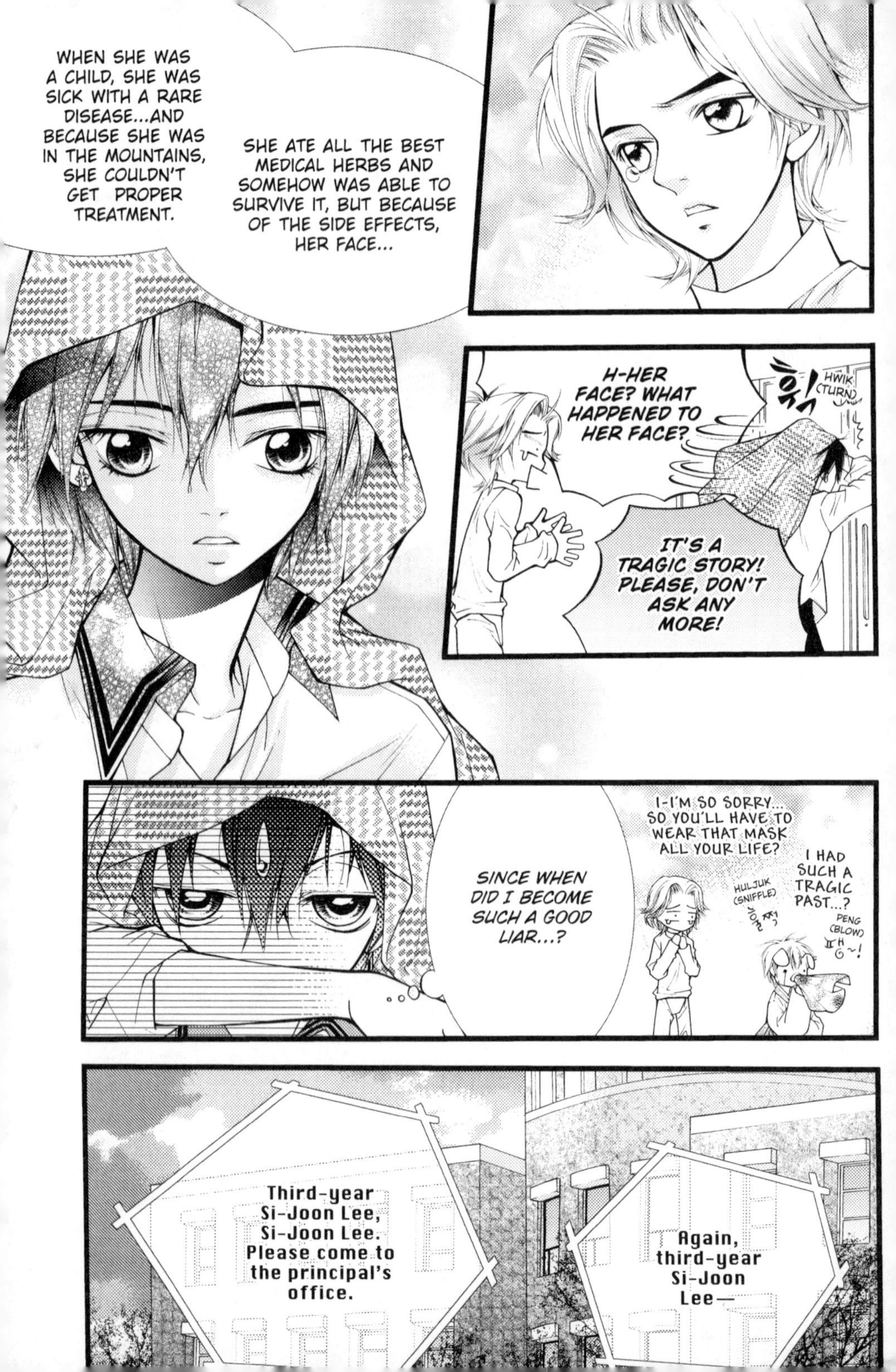

WHEN SHE WAS A CHILD, SHE WAS SICK WITH A RARE DISEASE...AND BECAUSE SHE WAS IN THE MOUNTAINS, SHE COULDN'T GET PROPER TREATMENT.
SHE ATE ALL THE BEST MEDICAL HERBS AND SOMEHOW WAS ABLE TO SURVIVE IT, BUT BECAUSE OF THE SIDE EFFECTS, HER FACE...
H-HER FACE? WHAT HAPPENED TO HER FACE?
HWIK (TURN)
IT'S A TRAGIC STORY! PLEASE, DON'T ASK ANY MORE!
SINCE WHEN DID I BECOME SUCH A GOOD LIAR...?
I-I'M SO SORRY... SO YOU'LL HAVE TO WEAR THAT MASK ALL YOUR LIFE?
HULJUK (SNIFFLE)
I HAD SUCH A TRAGIC PAST...?
PENG (BLOW)
Third-year Si-Joon Lee, Si-Joon Lee. Please come to the principal's office.
Again, third-year Si-Joon Lee—

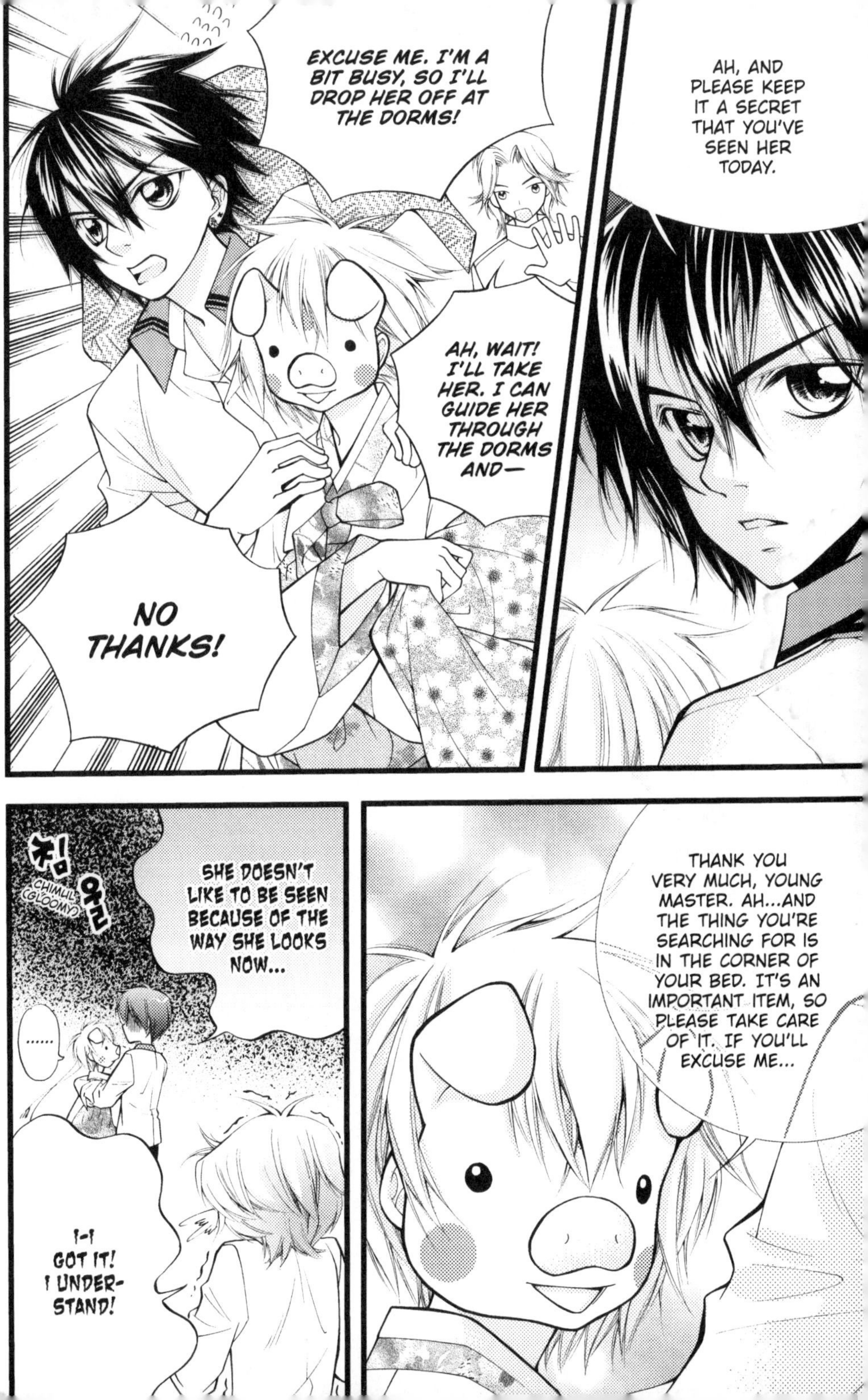
EXCUSE ME. I'M A BIT BUSY, SO I'LL DROP HER OFF AT THE DORMS!
AH, WAIT! I'LL TAKE HER. I CAN GUIDE HER THROUGH THE DORMS AND—
NO THANKS!
AH, AND PLEASE KEEP IT A SECRET THAT YOU'VE SEEN HER TODAY.
침울
CHIMUL (GLOOMY)
SHE DOESN'T LIKE TO BE SEEN BECAUSE OF THE WAY SHE LOOKS NOW...
......
I-I GOT IT! I UNDER-STAND!
THANK YOU VERY MUCH, YOUNG MASTER. AH...AND THE THING YOU'RE SEARCHING FOR IS IN THE CORNER OF YOUR BED. IT'S AN IMPORTANT ITEM, SO PLEASE TAKE CARE OF IT. IF YOU'LL EXCUSE ME...

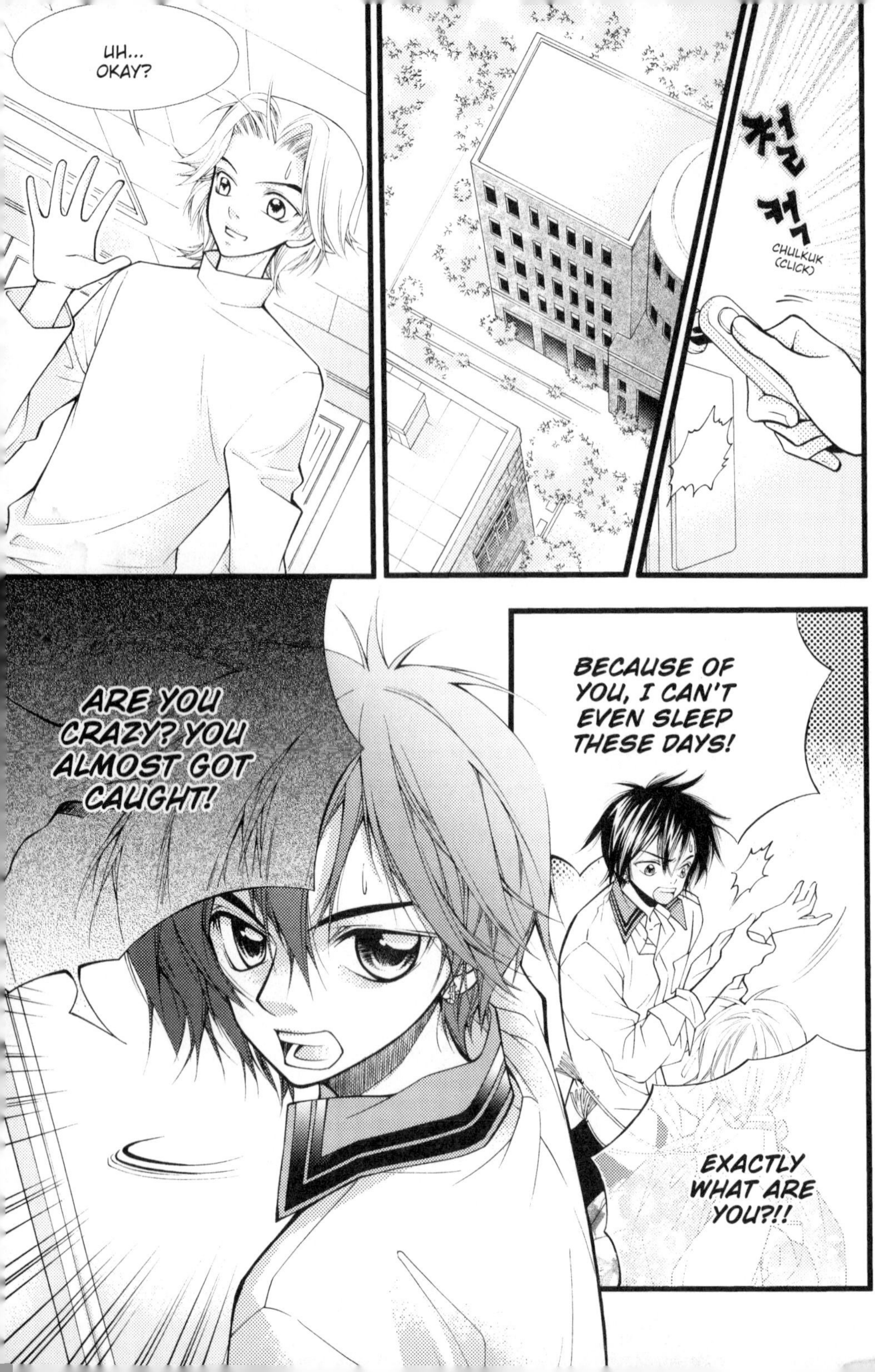
UH... OKAY?
철컥
CHULKUK (CLICK)
ARE YOU CRAZY? YOU ALMOST GOT CAUGHT!
BECAUSE OF YOU, I CAN'T EVEN SLEEP THESE DAYS!
EXACTLY WHAT ARE YOU?!!

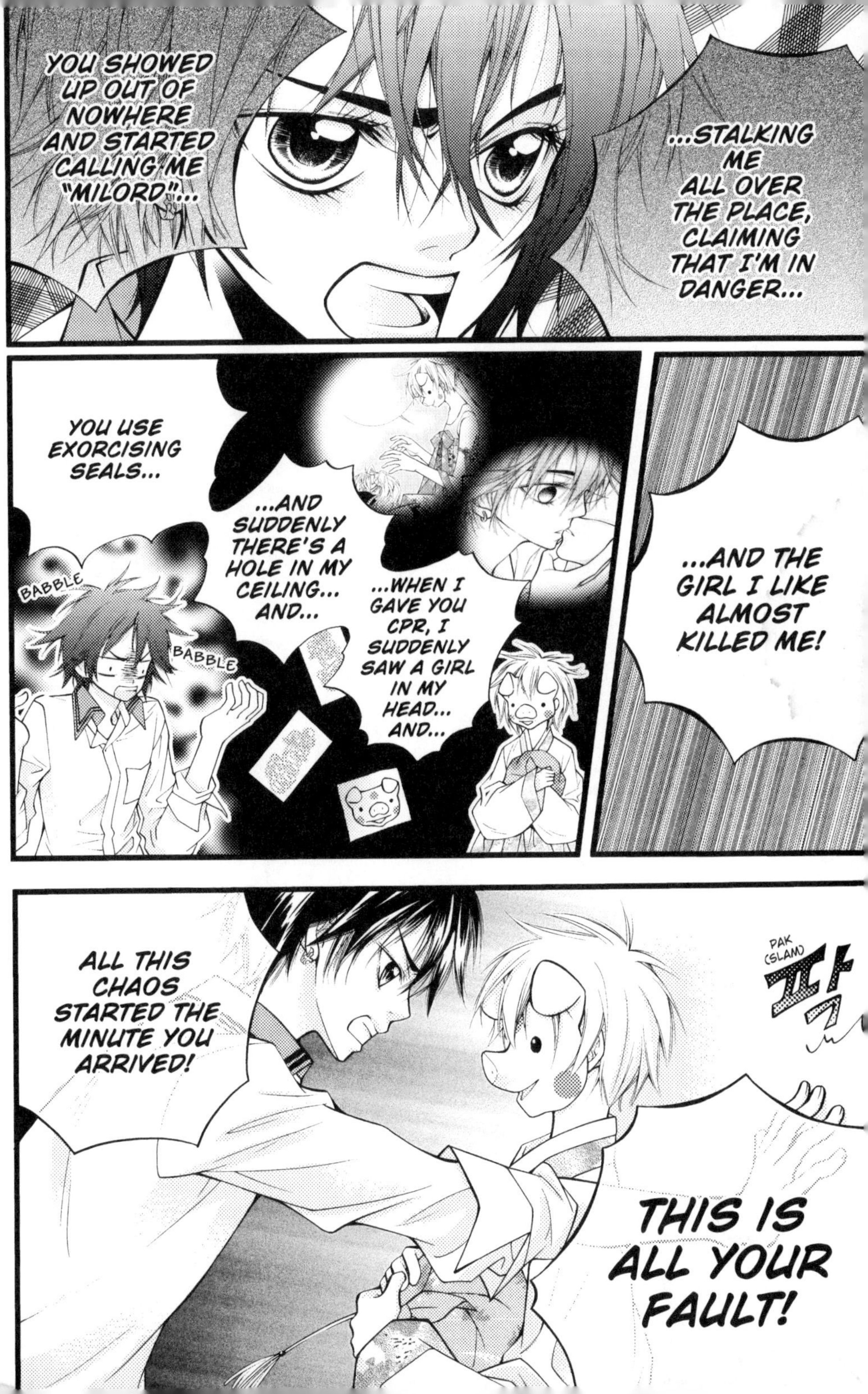
YOU SHOWED UP OUT OF NOWHERE AND STARTED CALLING ME "MILORD"...
...STALKING ME ALL OVER THE PLACE, CLAIMING THAT I'M IN DANGER...
YOU USE EXORCISING SEALS...
BABBLE
BABBLE
...AND SUDDENLY THERE'S A HOLE IN MY CEILING... AND...
...WHEN I GAVE YOU CPR, I SUDDENLY SAW A GIRL IN MY HEAD... AND...
...AND THE GIRL I LIKE ALMOST KILLED ME!
ALL THIS CHAOS STARTED THE MINUTE YOU ARRIVED!
PAK (SLAM)
팍
THIS IS ALL YOUR FAULT!

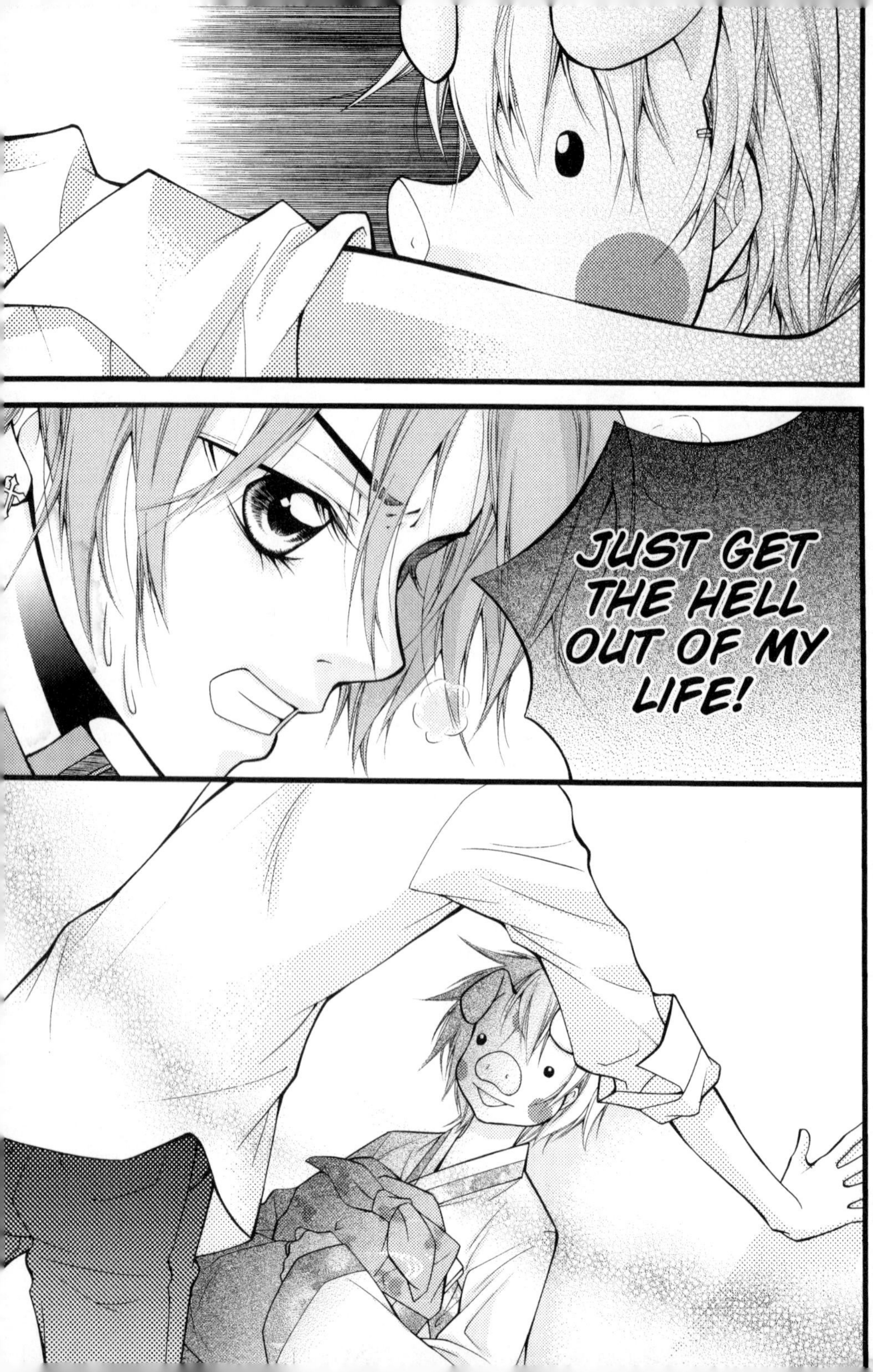
JUST GET THE HELL OUT OF MY LIFE!

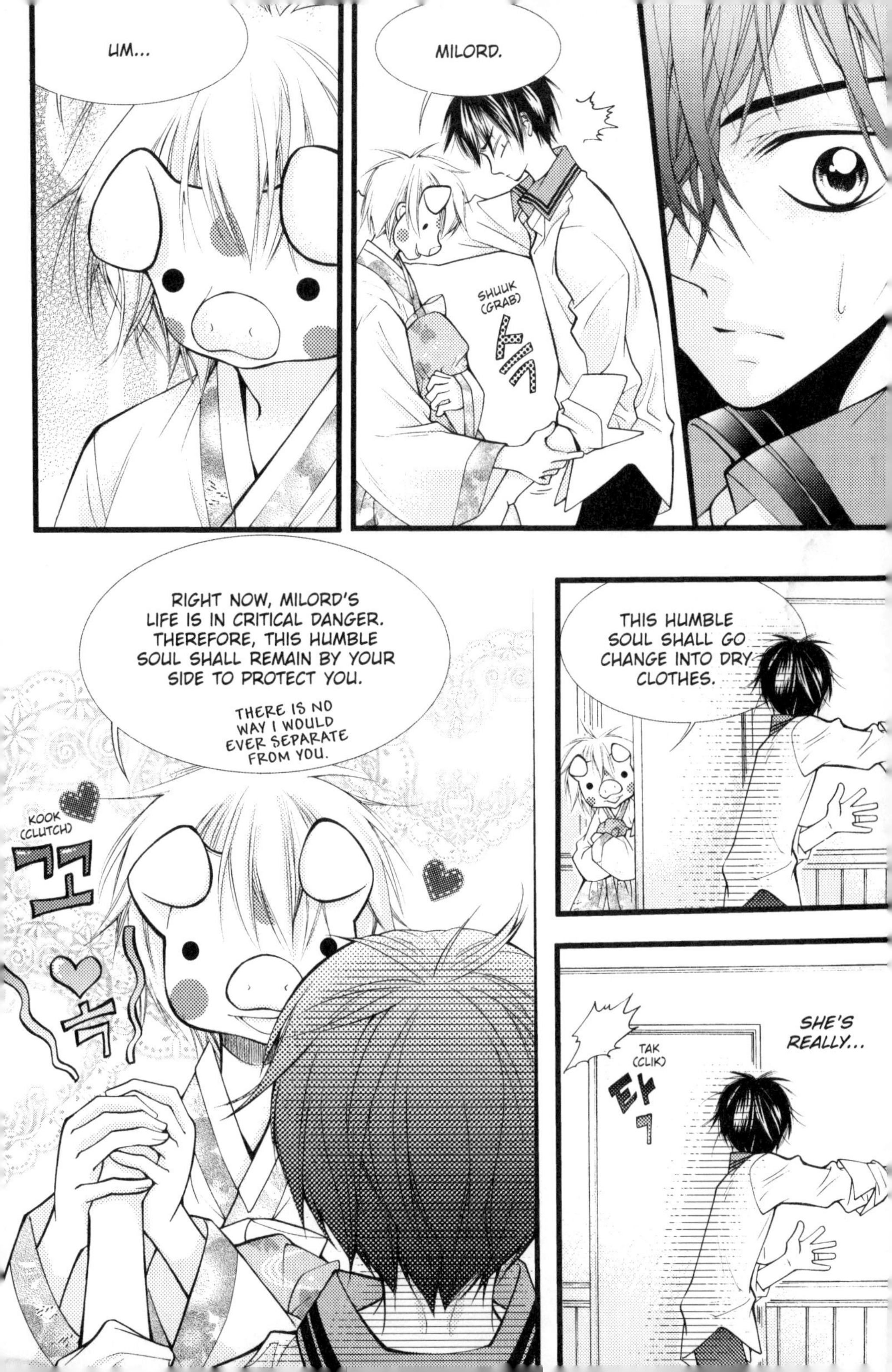
UM...
MILORD.
SHUUK (GRAB)
RIGHT NOW, MILORD'S LIFE IS IN CRITICAL DANGER. THEREFORE, THIS HUMBLE SOUL SHALL REMAIN BY YOUR SIDE TO PROTECT YOU.
THERE IS NO WAY I WOULD EVER SEPARATE FROM YOU.
KOOK (CLUTCH)
THIS HUMBLE SOUL SHALL GO CHANGE INTO DRY CLOTHES.
TAK (CLIK)
SHE'S REALLY...

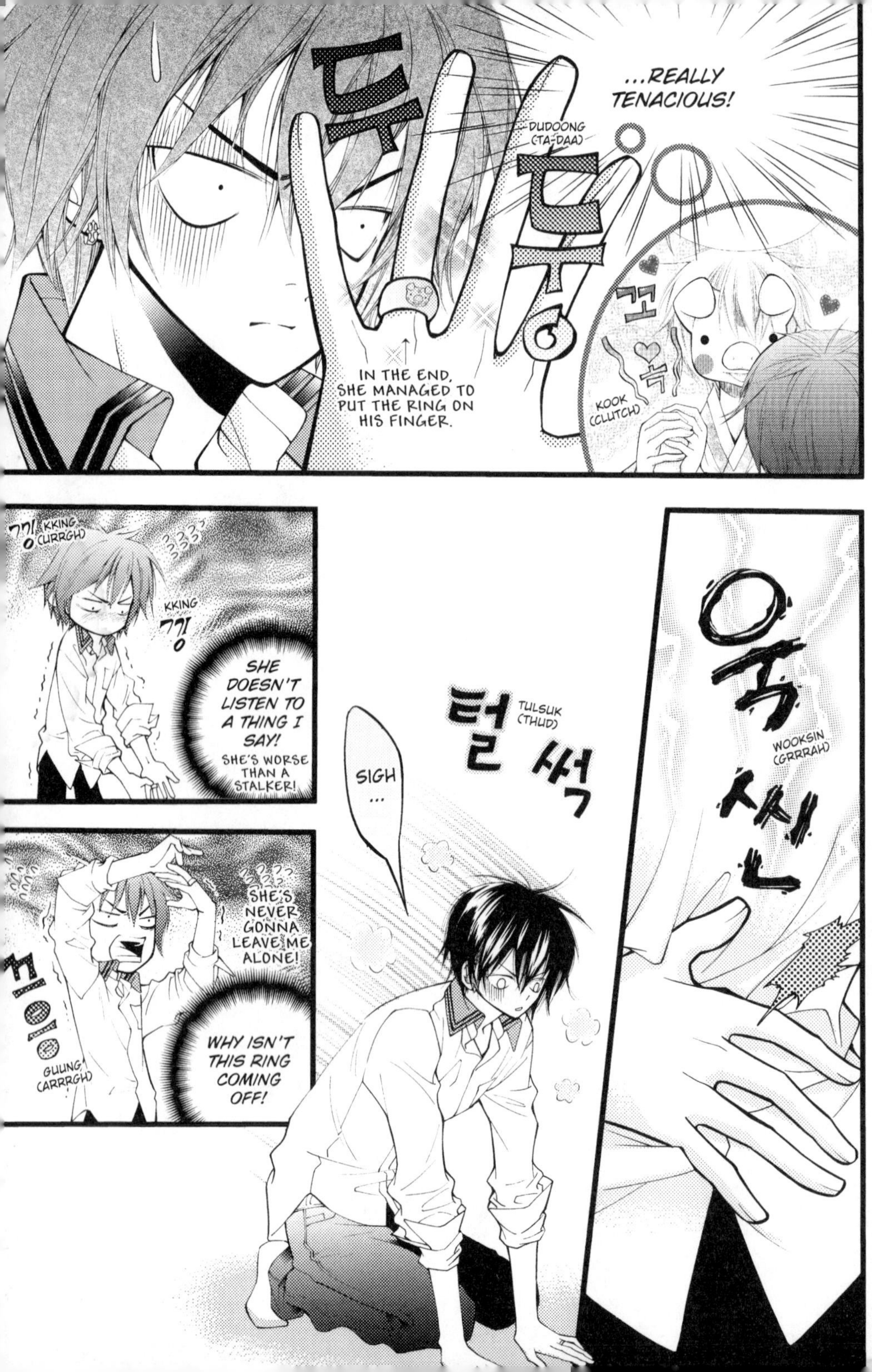

두둥
...REALLY TENACIOUS!
DUDOONG (TA-DAA)
IN THE END, SHE MANAGED TO PUT THE RING ON HIS FINGER.
KOOK (CLUTCH)
KKING (CURRGH)
KKING
SHE DOESN'T LISTEN TO A THING I SAY!
SHE'S WORSE THAN A STALKER!
SHE'S NEVER GONNA LEAVE ME ALONE!
WHY ISN'T THIS RING COMING OFF!
GUUNG (ARRRGH)
SIGH...
털썩
TULSUK (THUD)
WOOKSIN (GRRRAH)

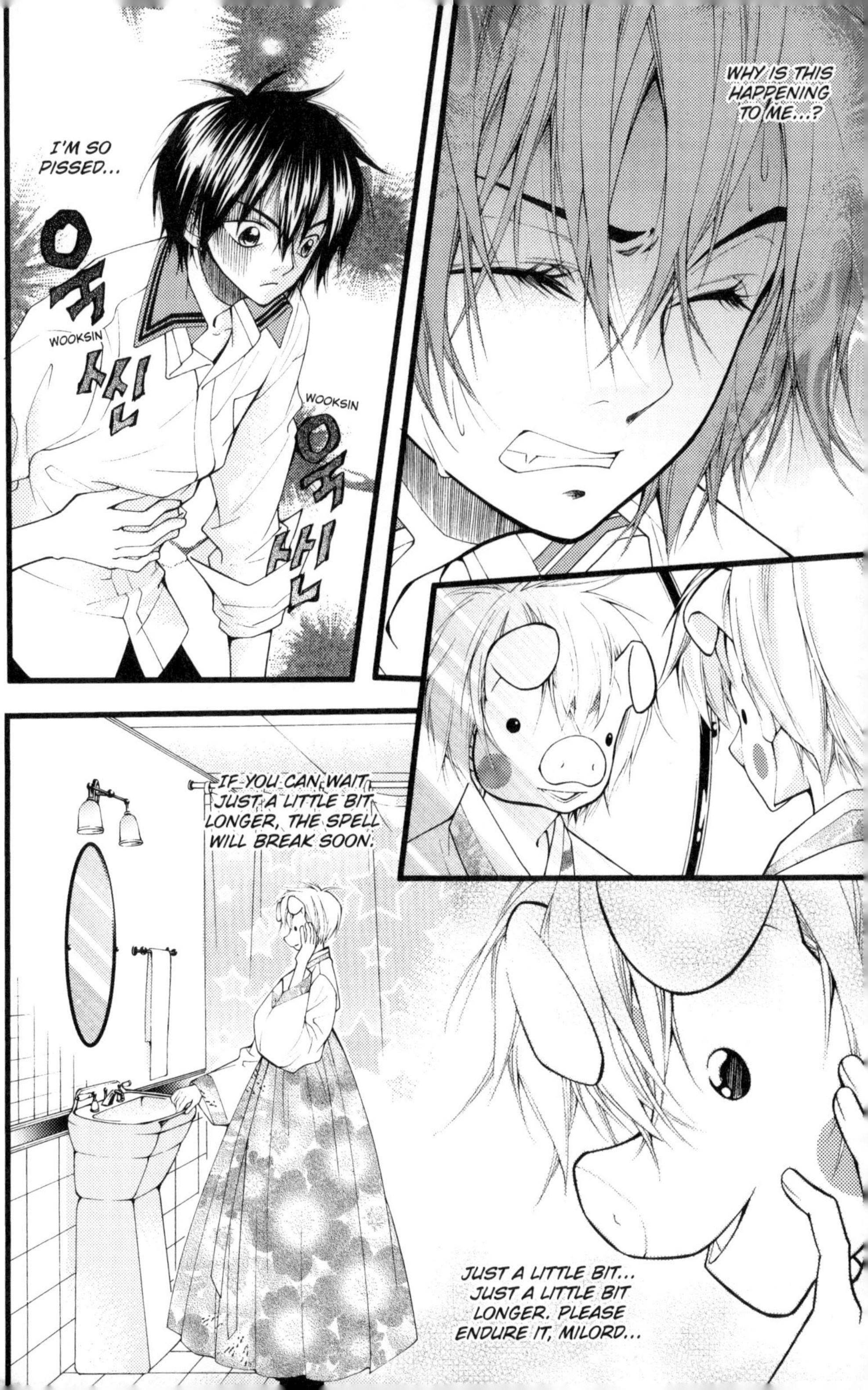
I'M SO PISSED...
WOOKSIN
WOOKSIN
WHY IS THIS HAPPENING TO ME...?
IF YOU CAN WAIT JUST A LITTLE BIT LONGER, THE SPELL WILL BREAK SOON.
JUST A LITTLE BIT... JUST A LITTLE BIT LONGER. PLEASE ENDURE IT, MILORD...

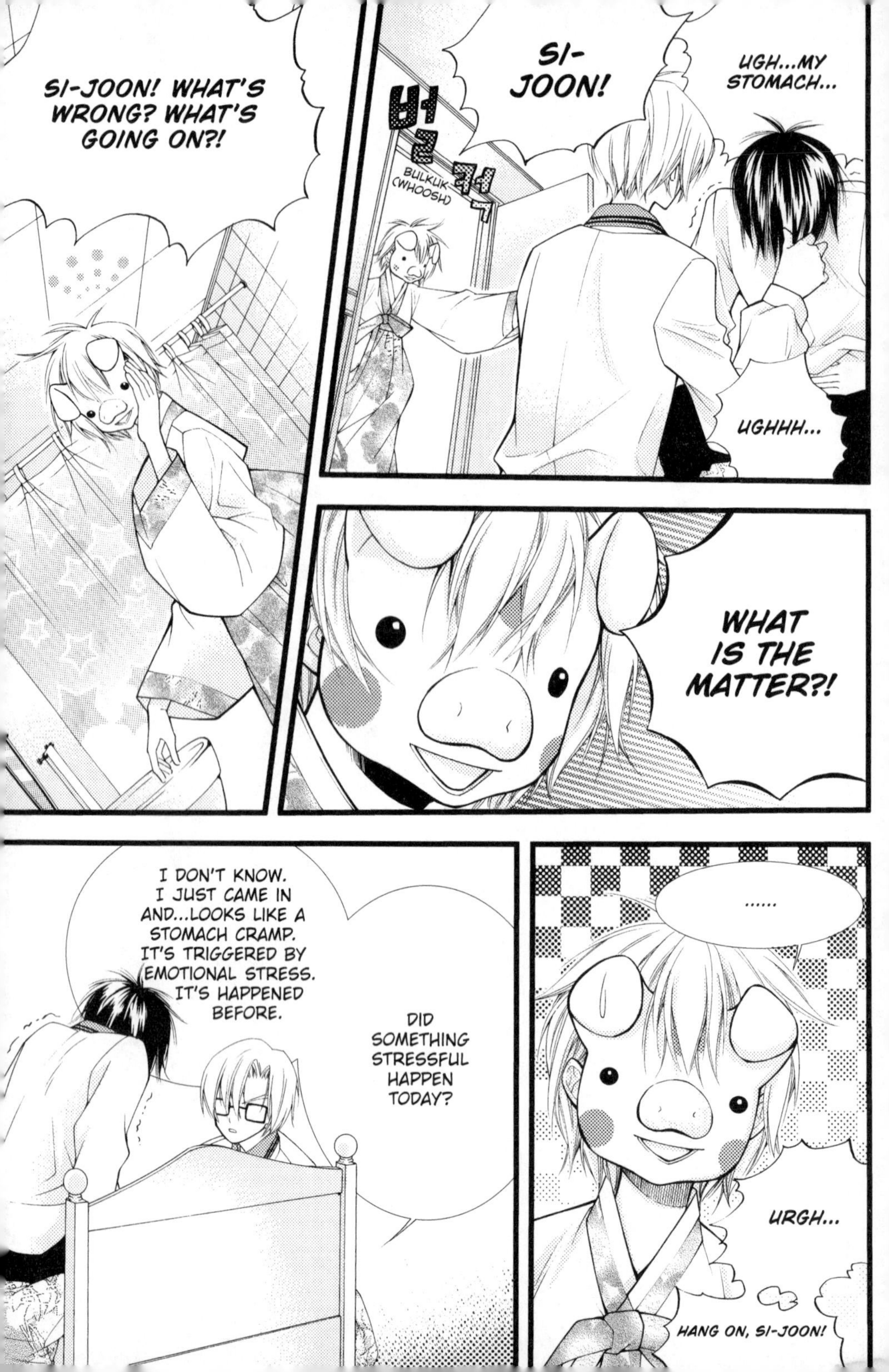
SI-JOON! WHAT'S WRONG? WHAT'S GOING ON?!
SI-JOON!
BULKUK (WHOOSH)
UGH...MY STOMACH...
UGHHH...
WHAT IS THE MATTER?!
I DON'T KNOW. I JUST CAME IN AND...LOOKS LIKE A STOMACH CRAMP. IT'S TRIGGERED BY EMOTIONAL STRESS. IT'S HAPPENED BEFORE.
DID SOMETHING STRESSFUL HAPPEN TODAY?
......
URGH...
HANG ON, SI-JOON!

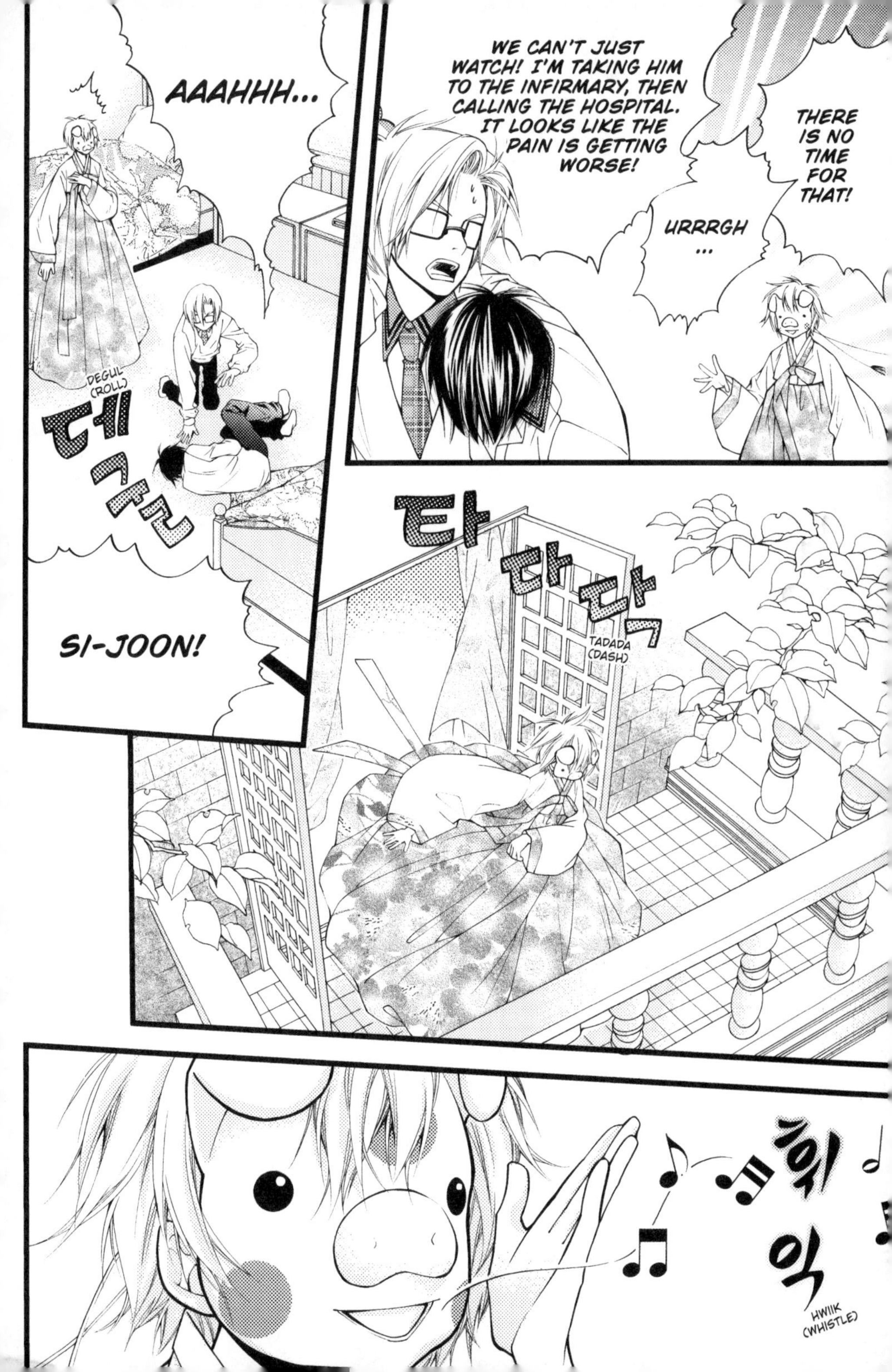
AAAHHH...
DEGUL (ROLL)
데굴
SI-JOON!
WE CAN'T JUST WATCH! I'M TAKING HIM TO THE INFIRMARY, THEN CALLING THE HOSPITAL. IT LOOKS LIKE THE PAIN IS GETTING WORSE!
URRRGH ...
THERE IS NO TIME FOR THAT!
타다닥
TADADA (DASH)
휘익
HWIIK (WHISTLE)

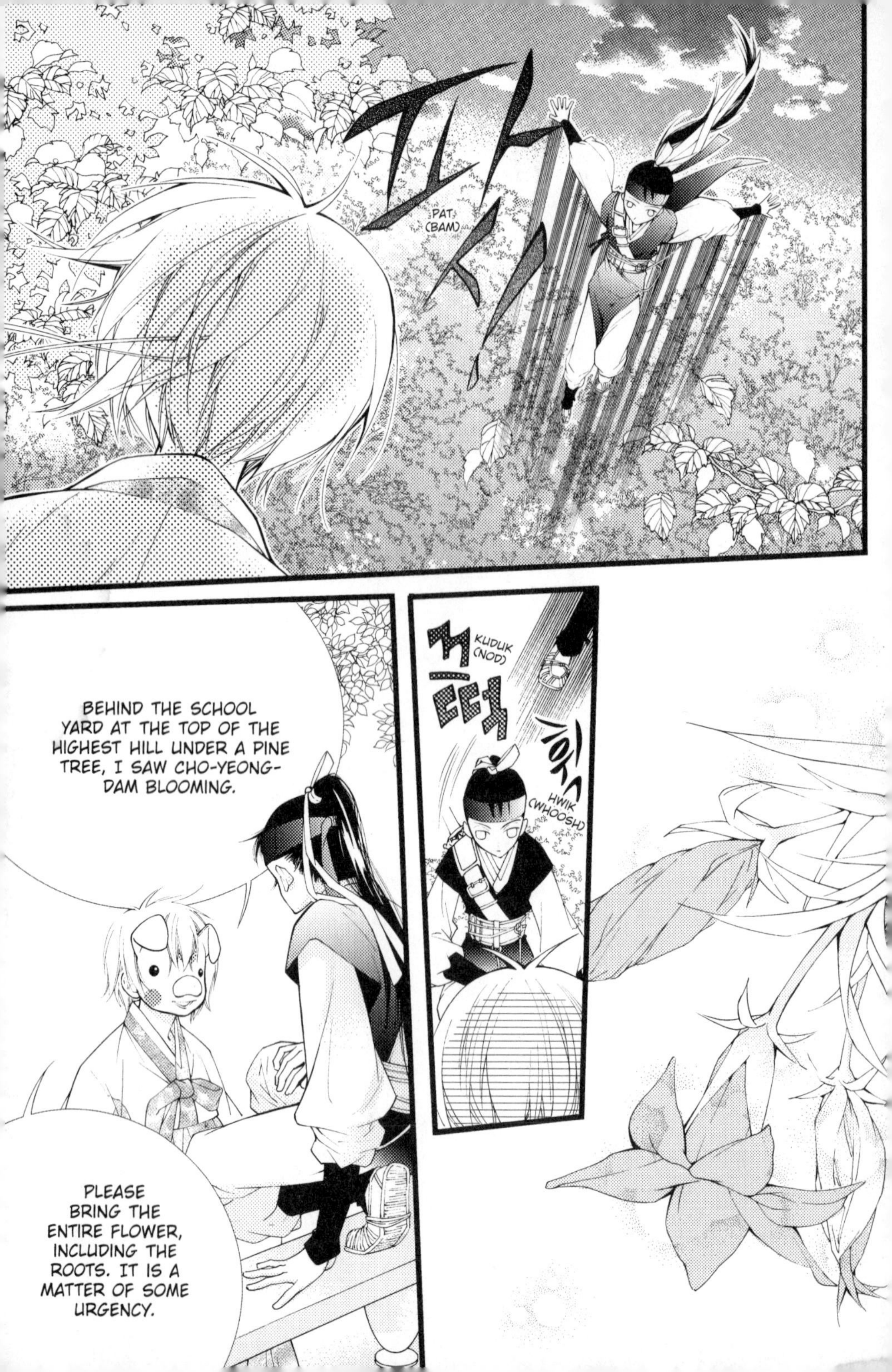
PAT (BAM)
BEHIND THE SCHOOL YARD AT THE TOP OF THE HIGHEST HILL UNDER A PINE TREE, I SAW CHO-YEONG-DAM BLOOMING.
PLEASE BRING THE ENTIRE FLOWER, INCLUDING THE ROOTS. IT IS A MATTER OF SOME URGENCY.
KUDUK (NOD)
HWIK (WHOOSH)

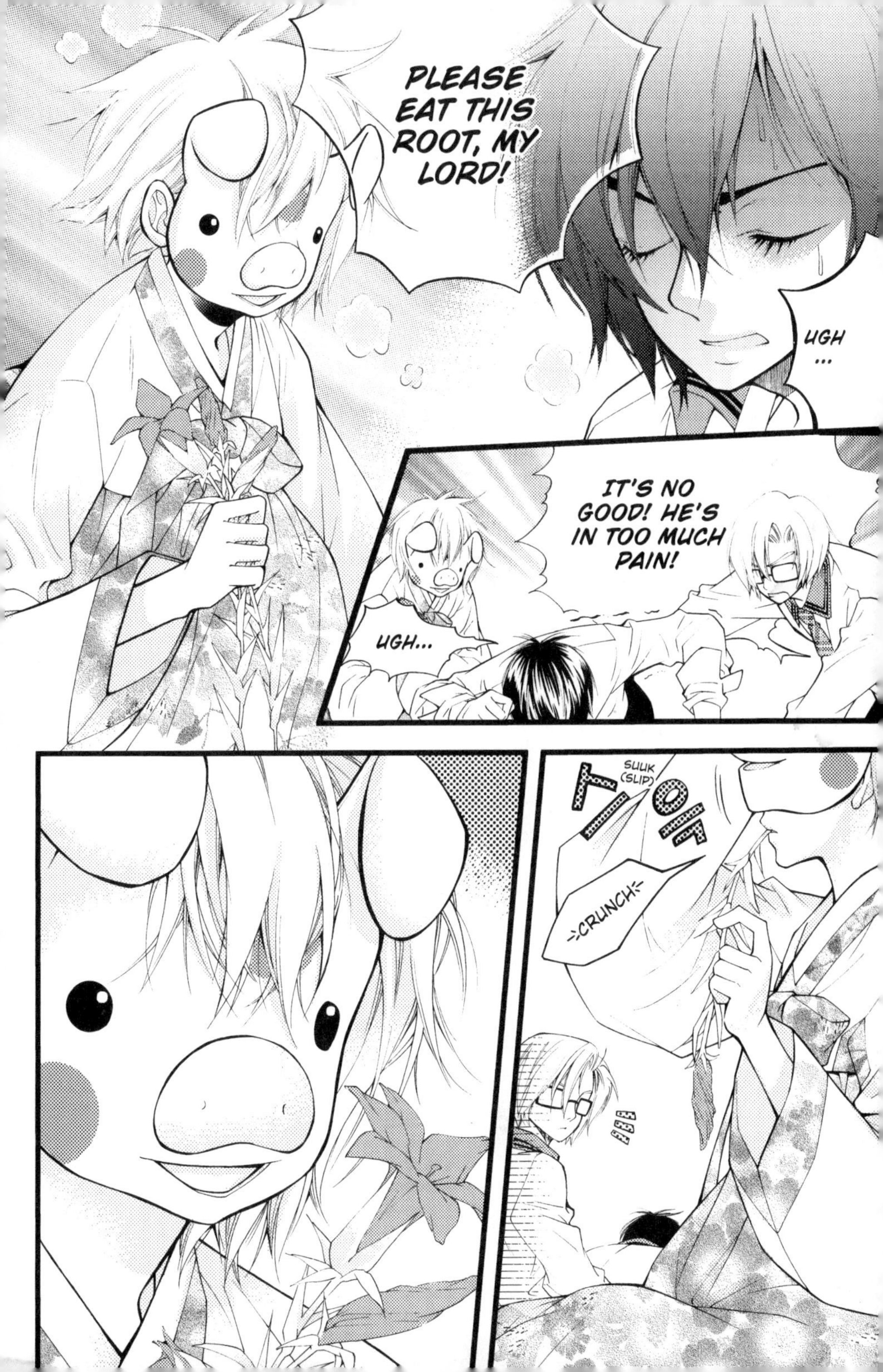
PLEASE EAT THIS ROOT, MY LORD!
UGH ...
IT'S NO GOOD! HE'S IN TOO MUCH PAIN!
UGH...
SUUK (SLIP)
CRUNCH

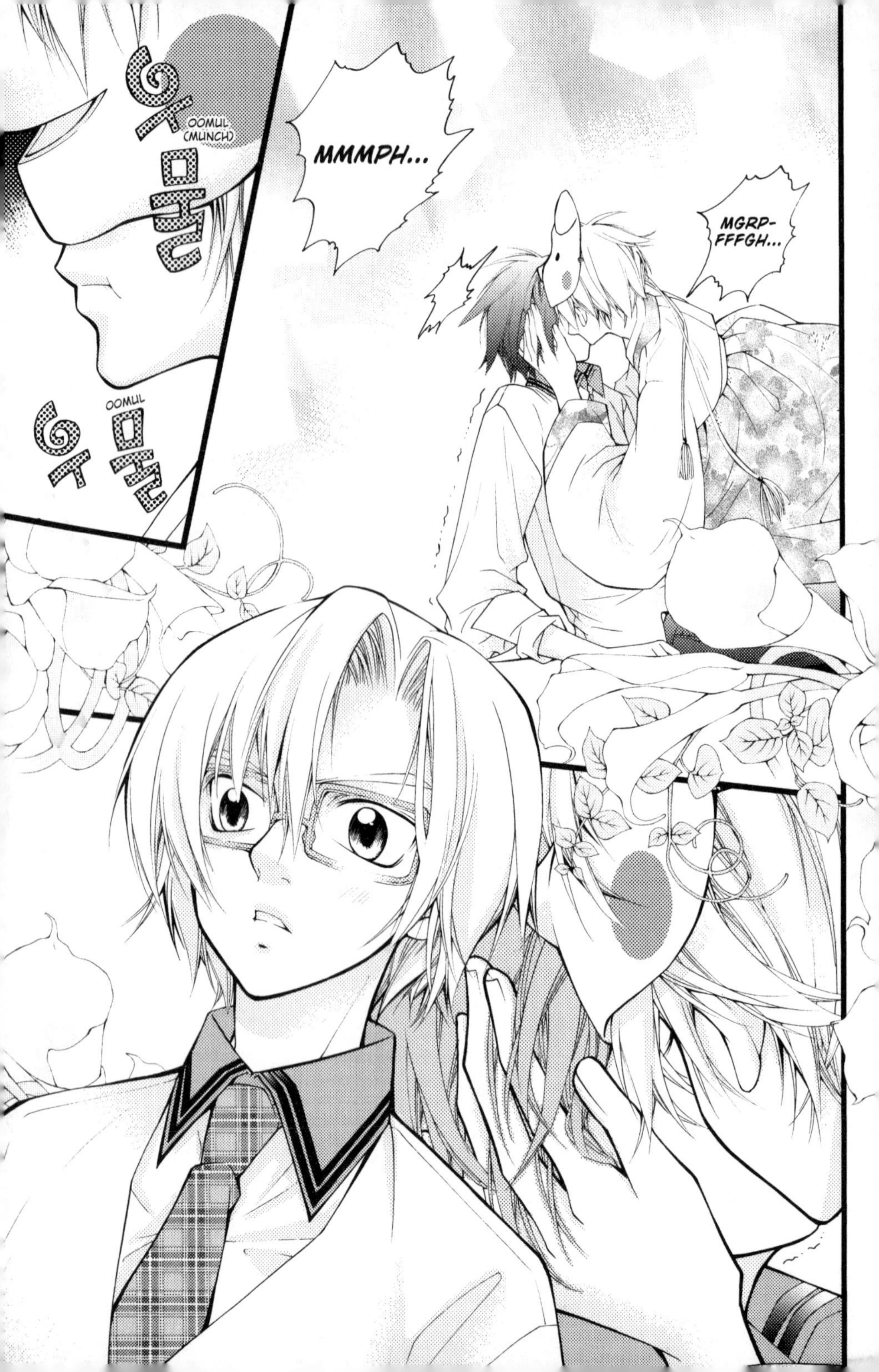
OOMUL (MUNCH)
OOMUL
MMMPH...
MGRP-FFFGH...

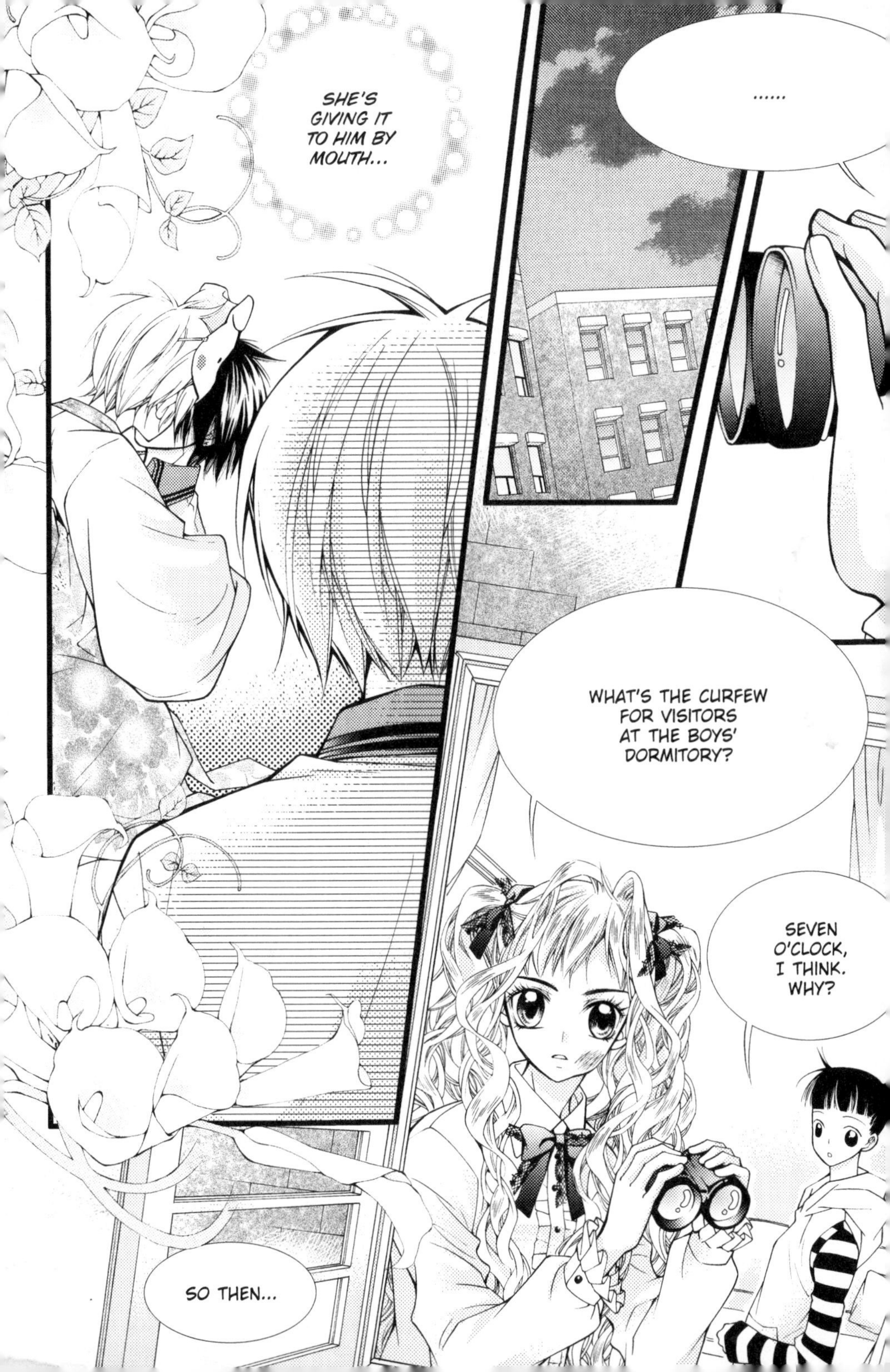
SHE'S GIVING IT TO HIM BY MOUTH...
......
WHAT'S THE CURFEW FOR VISITORS AT THE BOYS' DORMITORY?
SEVEN O'CLOCK, I THINK. WHY?
SO THEN...

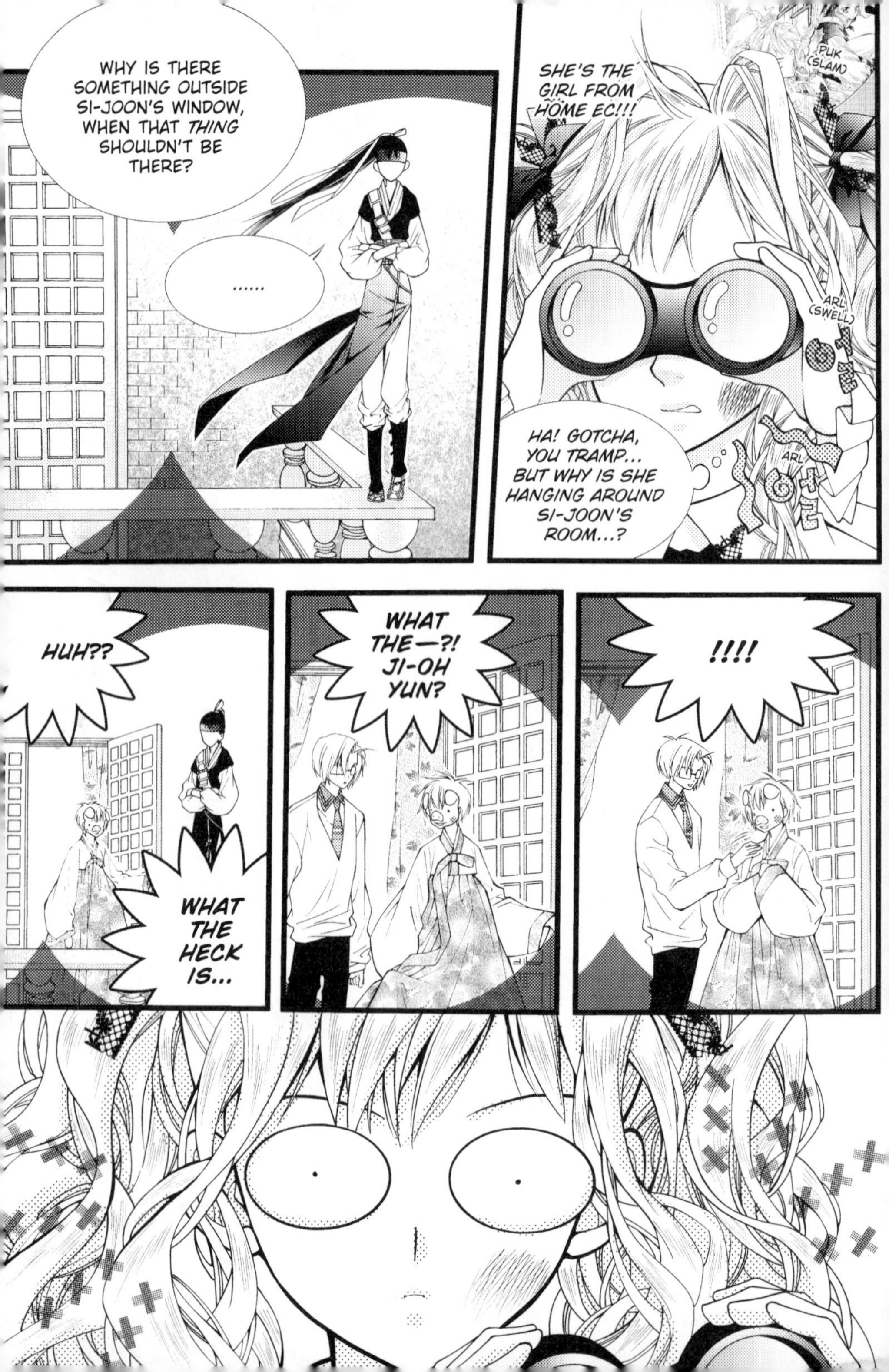
WHY IS THERE SOMETHING OUTSIDE SI-JOON'S WINDOW, WHEN THAT *THING* SHOULDN'T BE THERE?
......
SHE'S THE GIRL FROM HOME EC!!!
PUK (SLAM)
ARL (SWELL)
ARL
HA! GOTCHA, YOU TRAMP... BUT WHY IS SHE HANGING AROUND SI-JOON'S ROOM...?
HUH??
WHAT THE HECK IS...
WHAT THE—?! JI-OH YUN?
!!!!

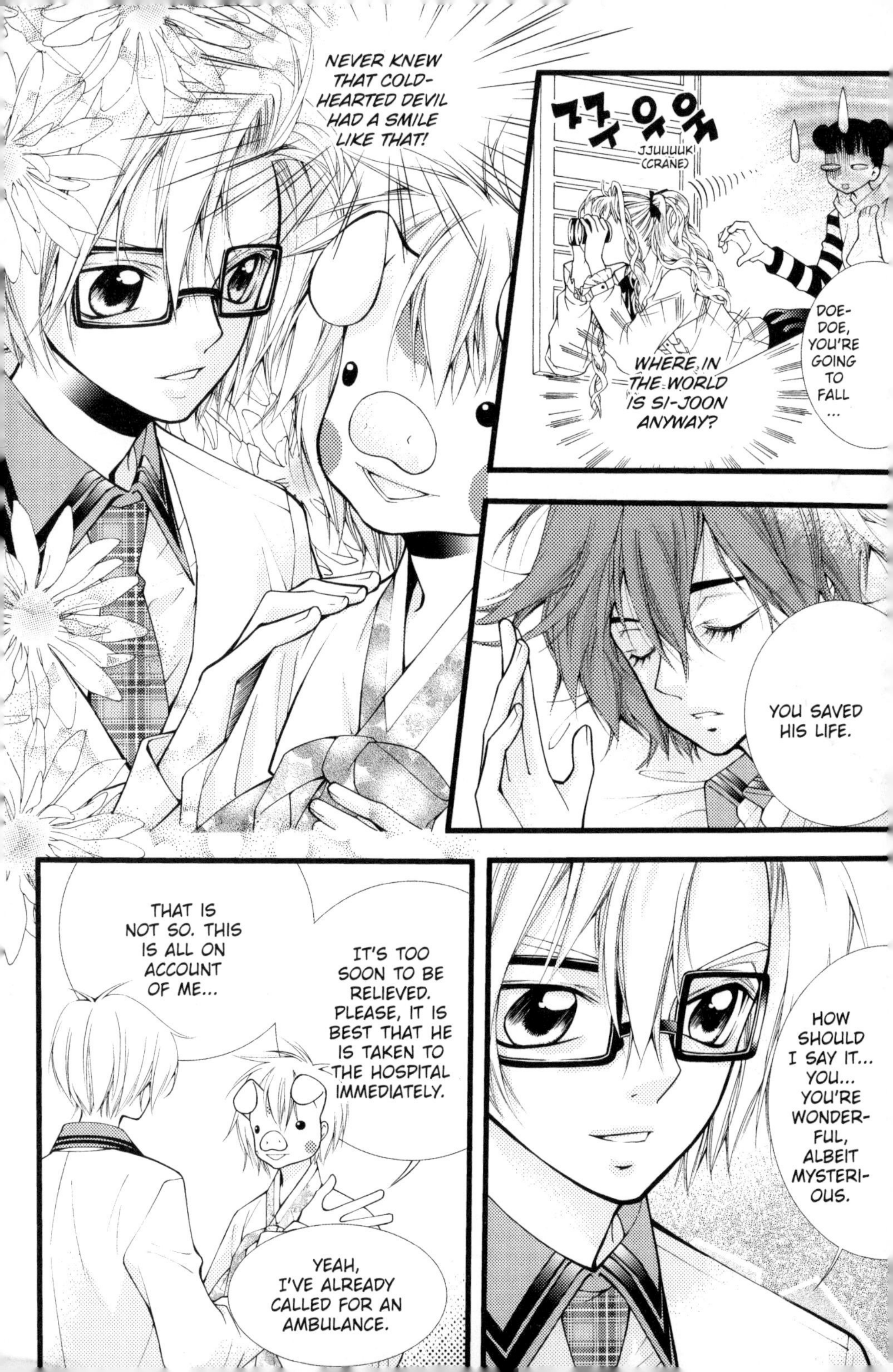
NEVER KNEW THAT COLD-HEARTED DEVIL HAD A SMILE LIKE THAT!
JJUUUUK (CRANE)
WHERE IN THE WORLD IS SI-JOON ANYWAY?
DOE-DOE, YOU'RE GOING TO FALL ...
YOU SAVED HIS LIFE.
THAT IS NOT SO. THIS IS ALL ON ACCOUNT OF ME...
IT'S TOO SOON TO BE RELIEVED. PLEASE, IT IS BEST THAT HE IS TAKEN TO THE HOSPITAL IMMEDIATELY.
YEAH, I'VE ALREADY CALLED FOR AN AMBULANCE.
HOW SHOULD I SAY IT... YOU... YOU'RE WONDER-FUL, ALBEIT MYSTERI-OUS.

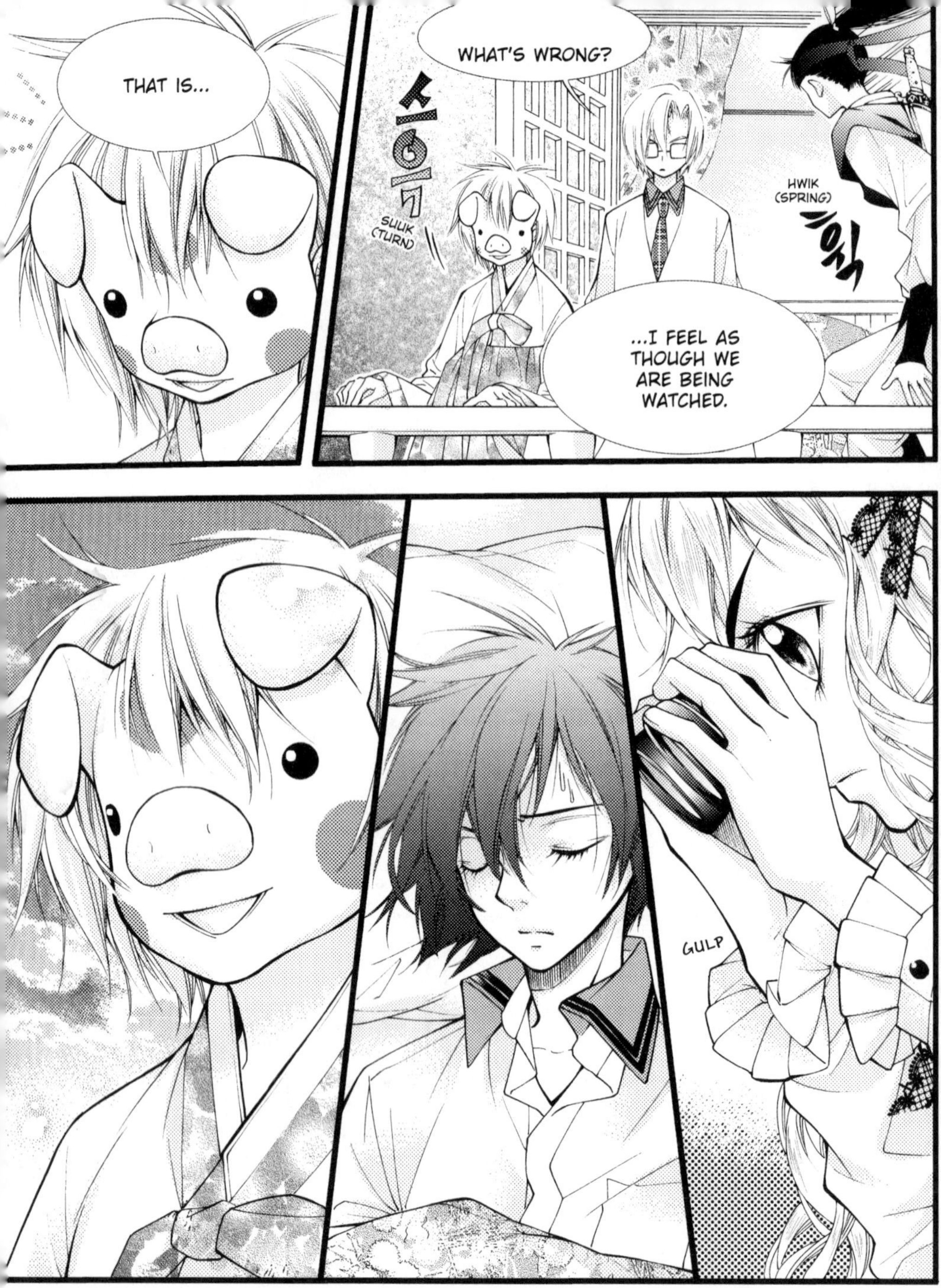
THAT IS...
WHAT'S WRONG?
스윽
SUUK (TURN)
HWIK (SPRING)
...I FEEL AS THOUGH WE ARE BEING WATCHED.
GULP

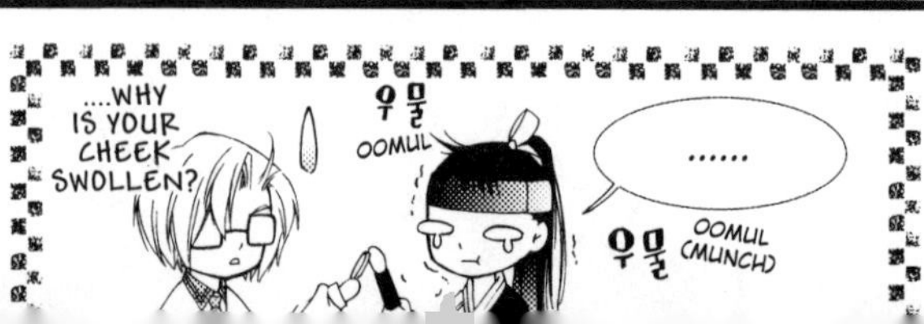
....WHY IS YOUR CHEEK SWOLLEN?
우물
OOMUL
......
우물
OOMUL (MUNCH)

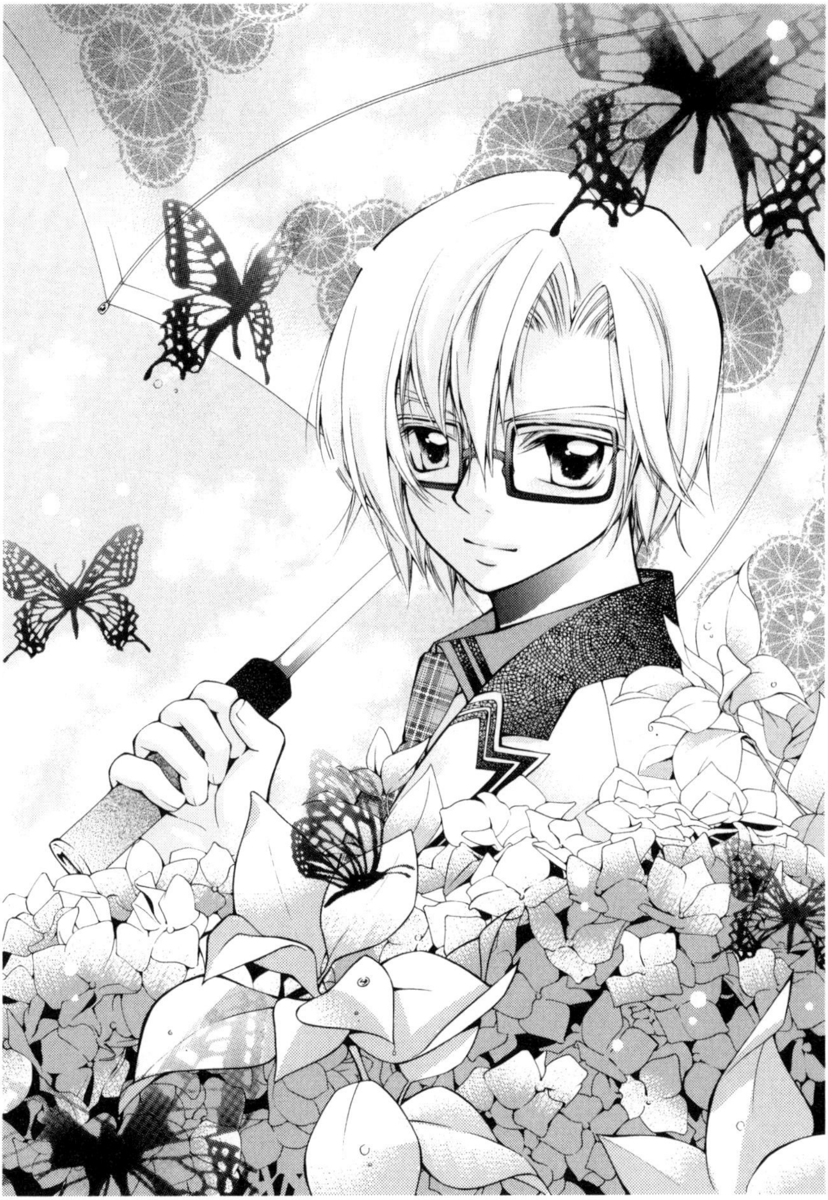

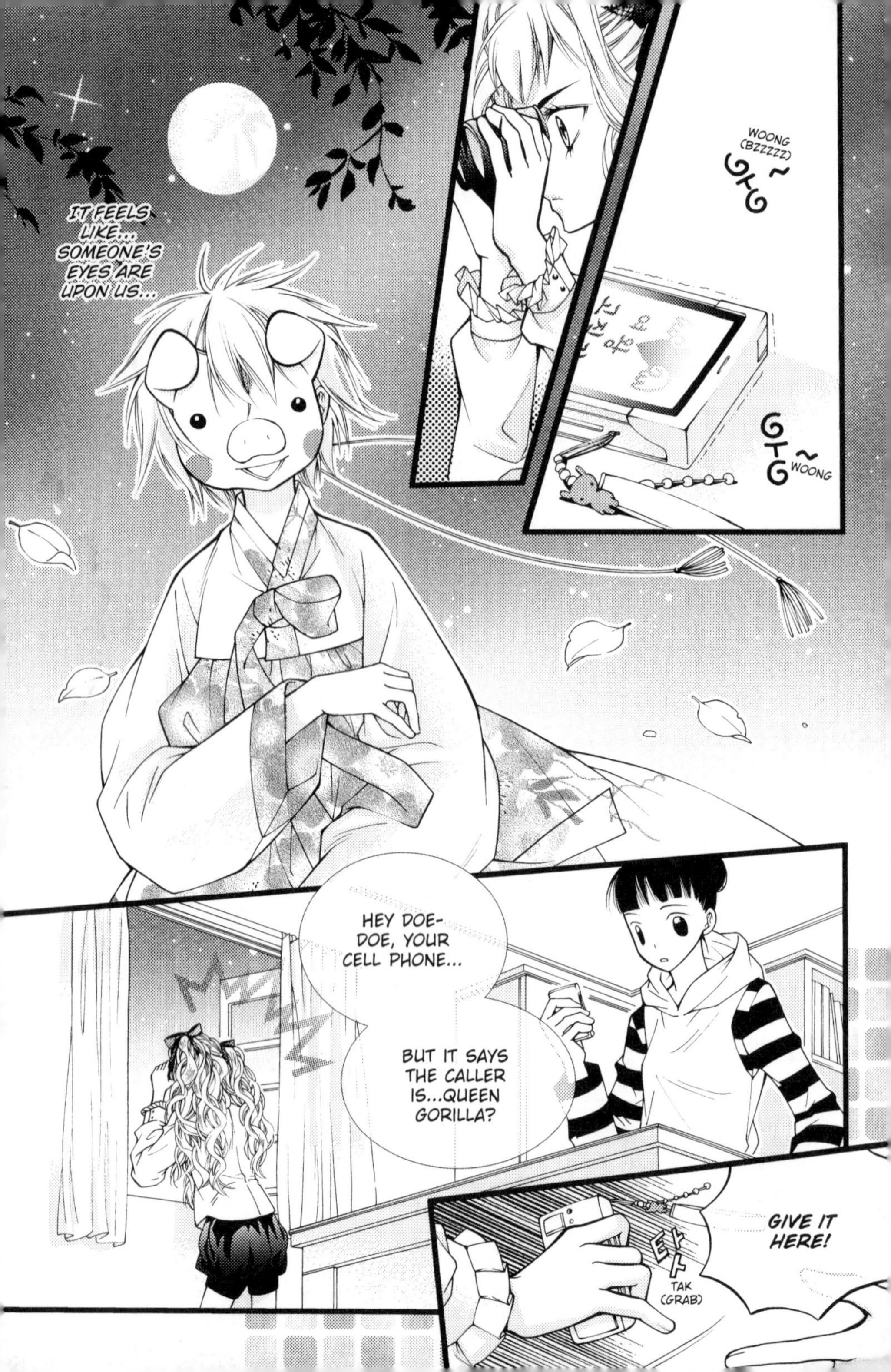

IT FEELS LIKE... SOMEONE'S EYES ARE UPON US...
WOONG (BZZZZZ)
WOONG
HEY DOE-DOE, YOUR CELL PHONE...
BUT IT SAYS THE CALLER IS...QUEEN GORILLA?
TAK (GRAB)
GIVE IT HERE!

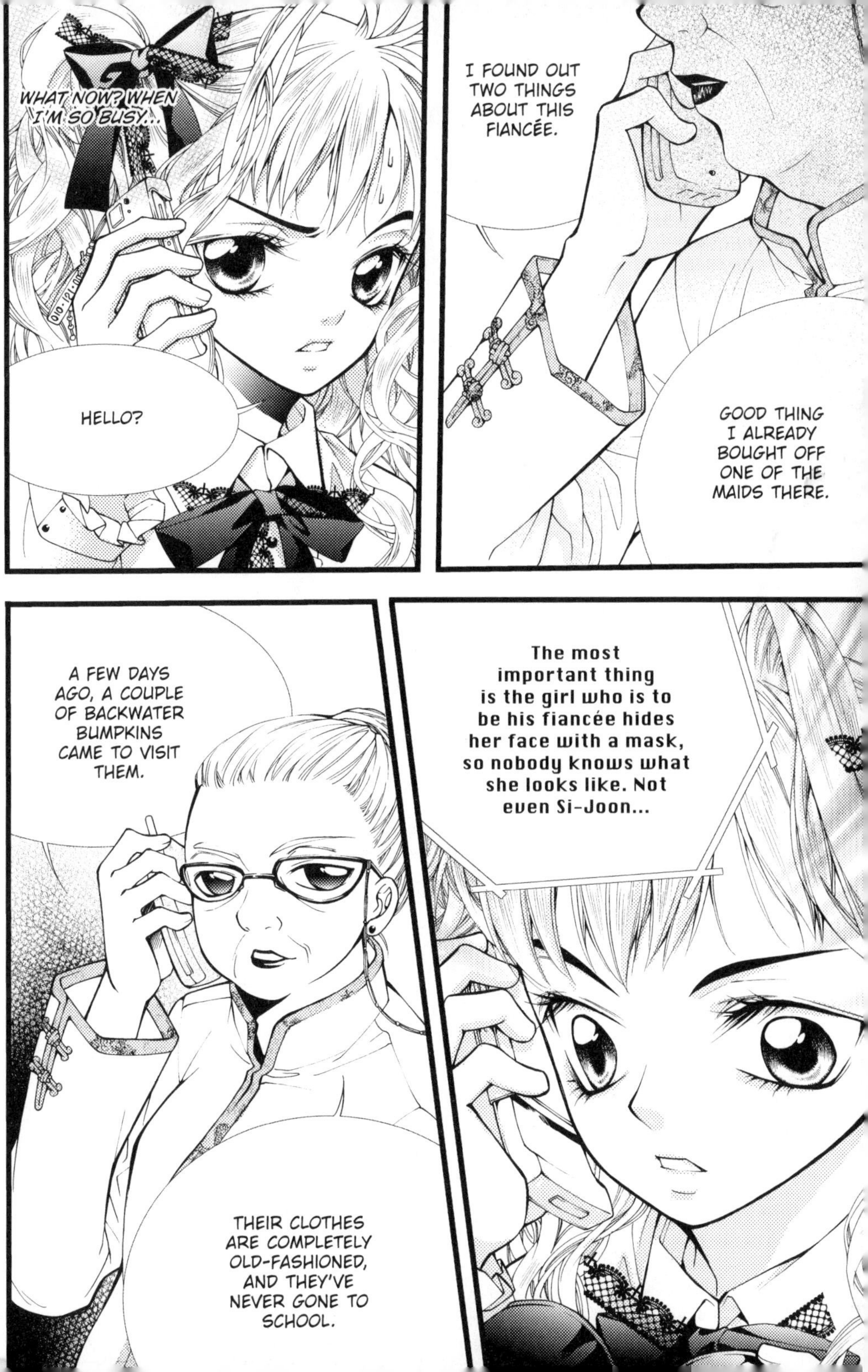
WHAT NOW? WHEN I'M SO BUSY...
HELLO?
I FOUND OUT TWO THINGS ABOUT THIS FIANCÉE.
GOOD THING I ALREADY BOUGHT OFF ONE OF THE MAIDS THERE.
A FEW DAYS AGO, A COUPLE OF BACKWATER BUMPKINS CAME TO VISIT THEM.
THEIR CLOTHES ARE COMPLETELY OLD-FASHIONED, AND THEY'VE NEVER GONE TO SCHOOL.
The most important thing is the girl who is to be his fiancée hides her face with a mask, so nobody knows what she looks like. Not even Si-Joon...

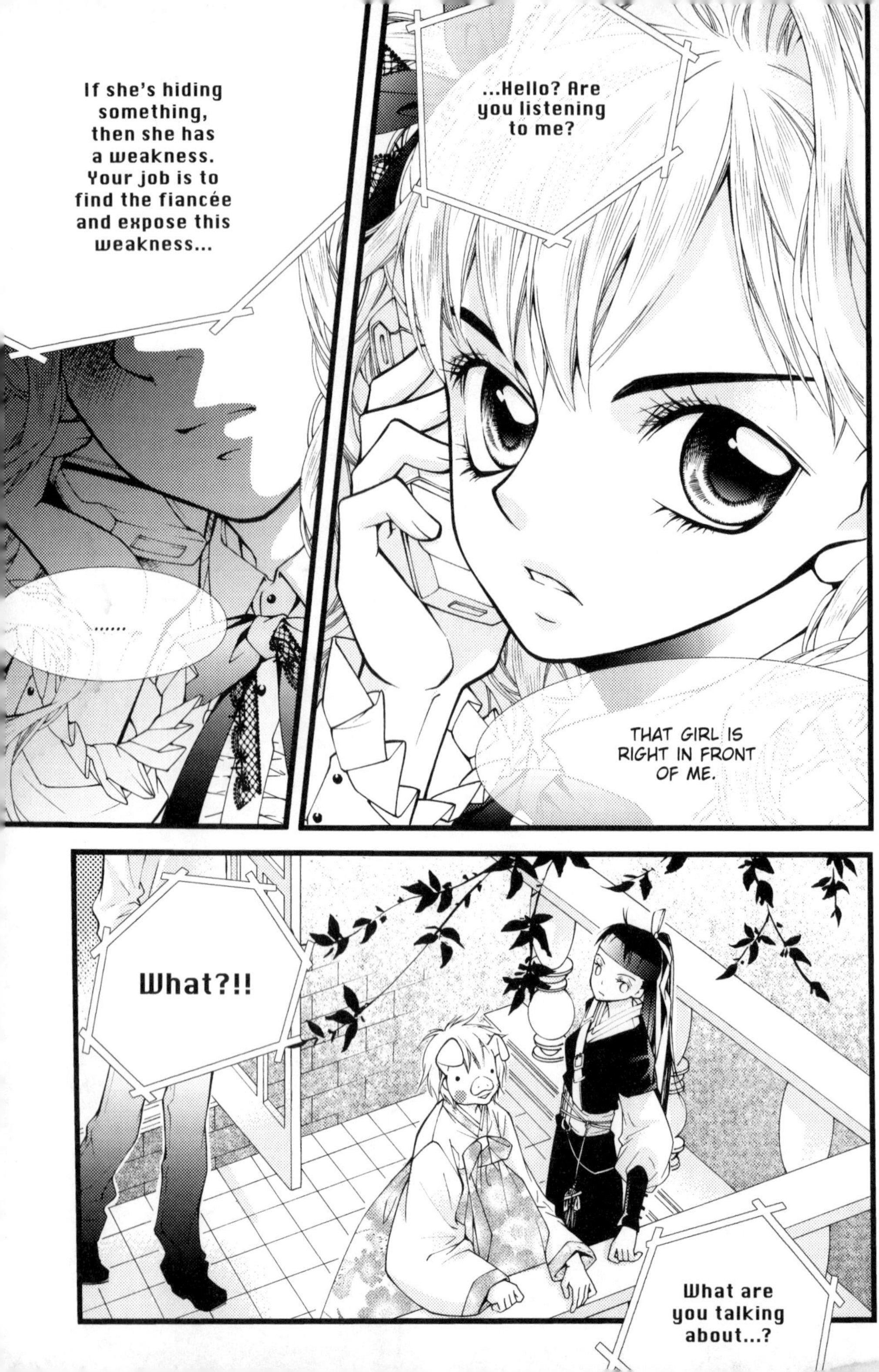
If she's hiding something, then she has a weakness. Your job is to find the fiancée and expose this weakness...
......
...Hello? Are you listening to me?
THAT GIRL IS RIGHT IN FRONT OF ME.
What?!!
What are you talking about...?

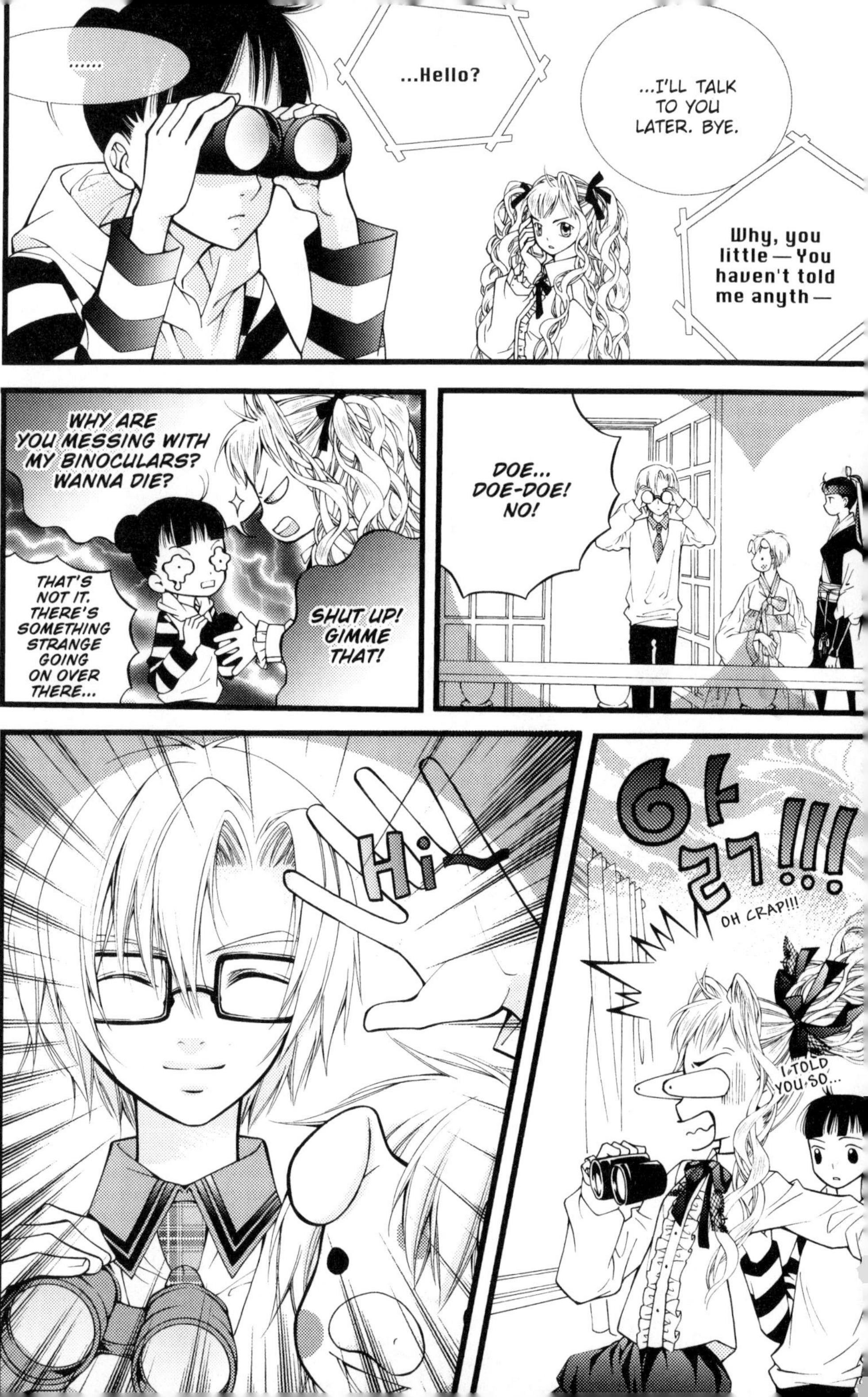
......
...Hello?
...I'LL TALK TO YOU LATER. BYE.
Why, you little — You haven't told me anyth —
WHY ARE YOU MESSING WITH MY BINOCULARS? WANNA DIE?
THAT'S NOT IT. THERE'S SOMETHING STRANGE GOING ON OVER THERE...
SHUT UP! GIMME THAT!
DOE... DOE-DOE! NO!
Hi~
아카!!!
OH CRAP!!!
I TOLD YOU SO...

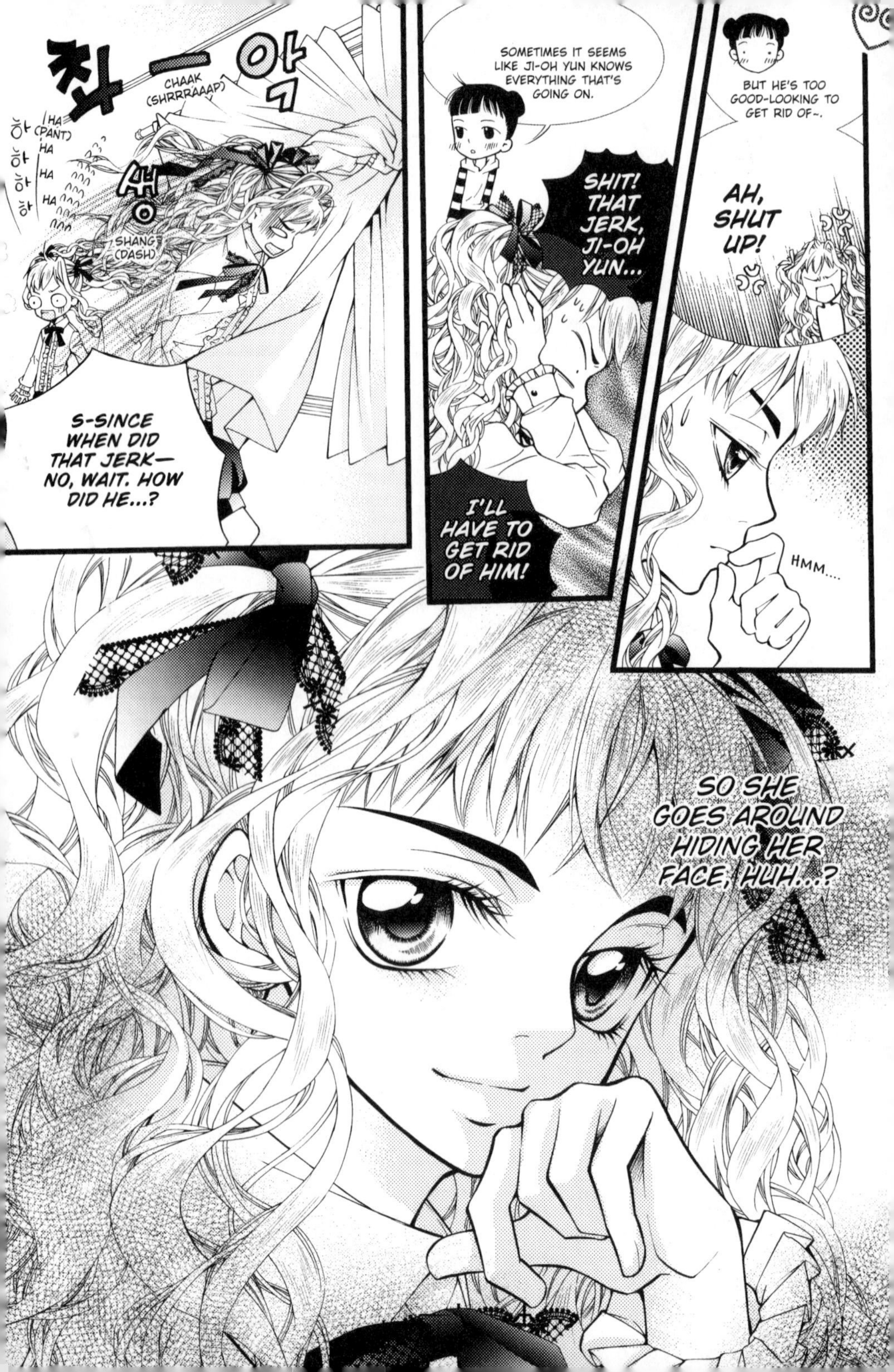
CHAAK (SHRRRAAAP)
HA (PANT) HA HA HA
SHANG (DASH)
S-SINCE WHEN DID THAT JERK— NO, WAIT. HOW DID HE...?
SOMETIMES IT SEEMS LIKE JI-OH YUN KNOWS EVERYTHING THAT'S GOING ON.
SHIT! THAT JERK, JI-OH YUN...
I'LL HAVE TO GET RID OF HIM!
BUT HE'S TOO GOOD-LOOKING TO GET RID OF~.
AH, SHUT UP!
HMM...
SO SHE GOES AROUND HIDING HER FACE, HUH...?

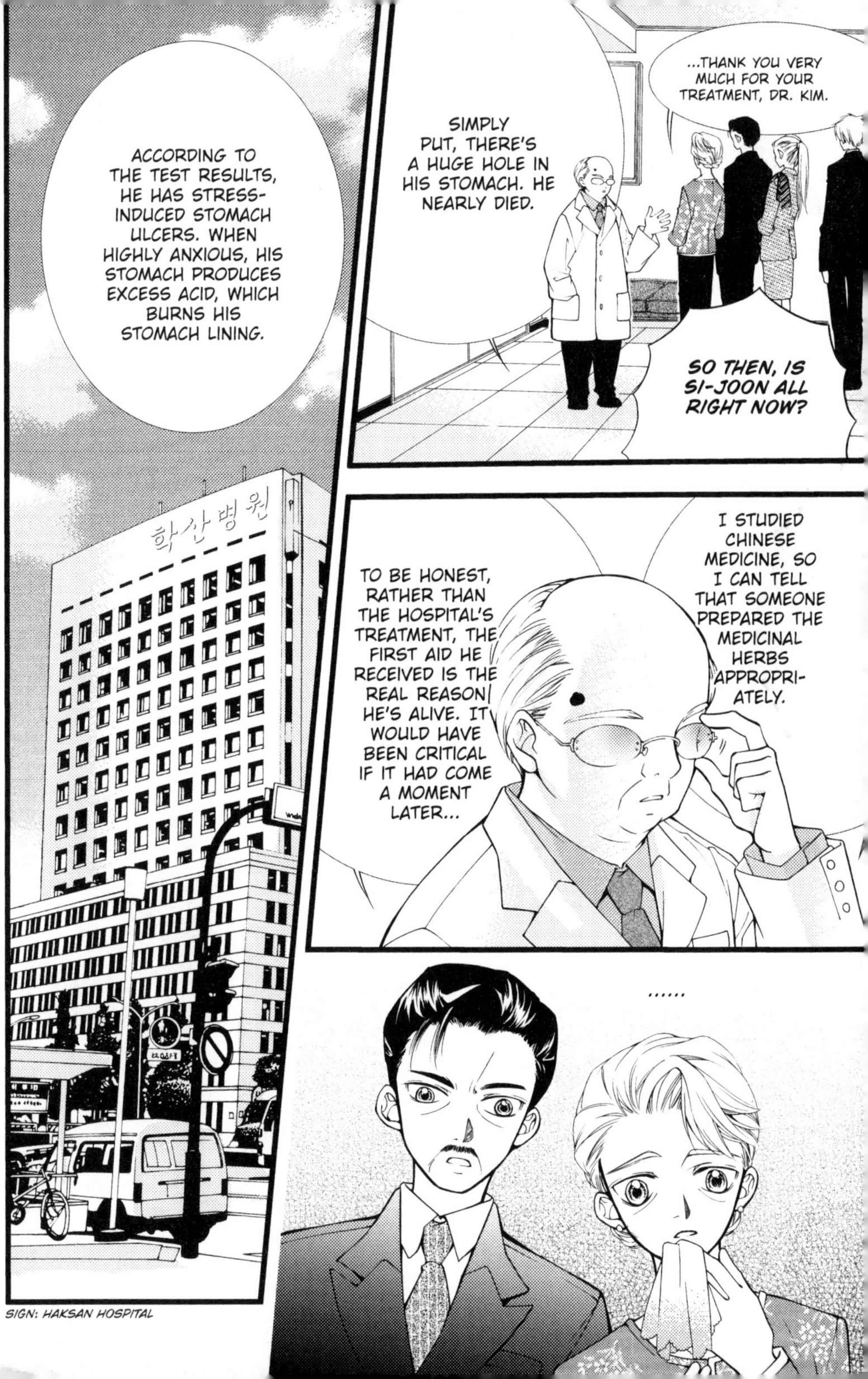
ACCORDING TO THE TEST RESULTS, HE HAS STRESS-INDUCED STOMACH ULCERS. WHEN HIGHLY ANXIOUS, HIS STOMACH PRODUCES EXCESS ACID, WHICH BURNS HIS STOMACH LINING.
학산병원
SIMPLY PUT, THERE'S A HUGE HOLE IN HIS STOMACH. HE NEARLY DIED.
...THANK YOU VERY MUCH FOR YOUR TREATMENT, DR. KIM.
SO THEN, IS SI-JOON ALL RIGHT NOW?
TO BE HONEST, RATHER THAN THE HOSPITAL'S TREATMENT, THE FIRST AID HE RECEIVED IS THE REAL REASON HE'S ALIVE. IT WOULD HAVE BEEN CRITICAL IF IT HAD COME A MOMENT LATER...
I STUDIED CHINESE MEDICINE, SO I CAN TELL THAT SOMEONE PREPARED THE MEDICINAL HERBS APPROPRI-ATELY.
......
SIGN: HAKSAN HOSPITAL

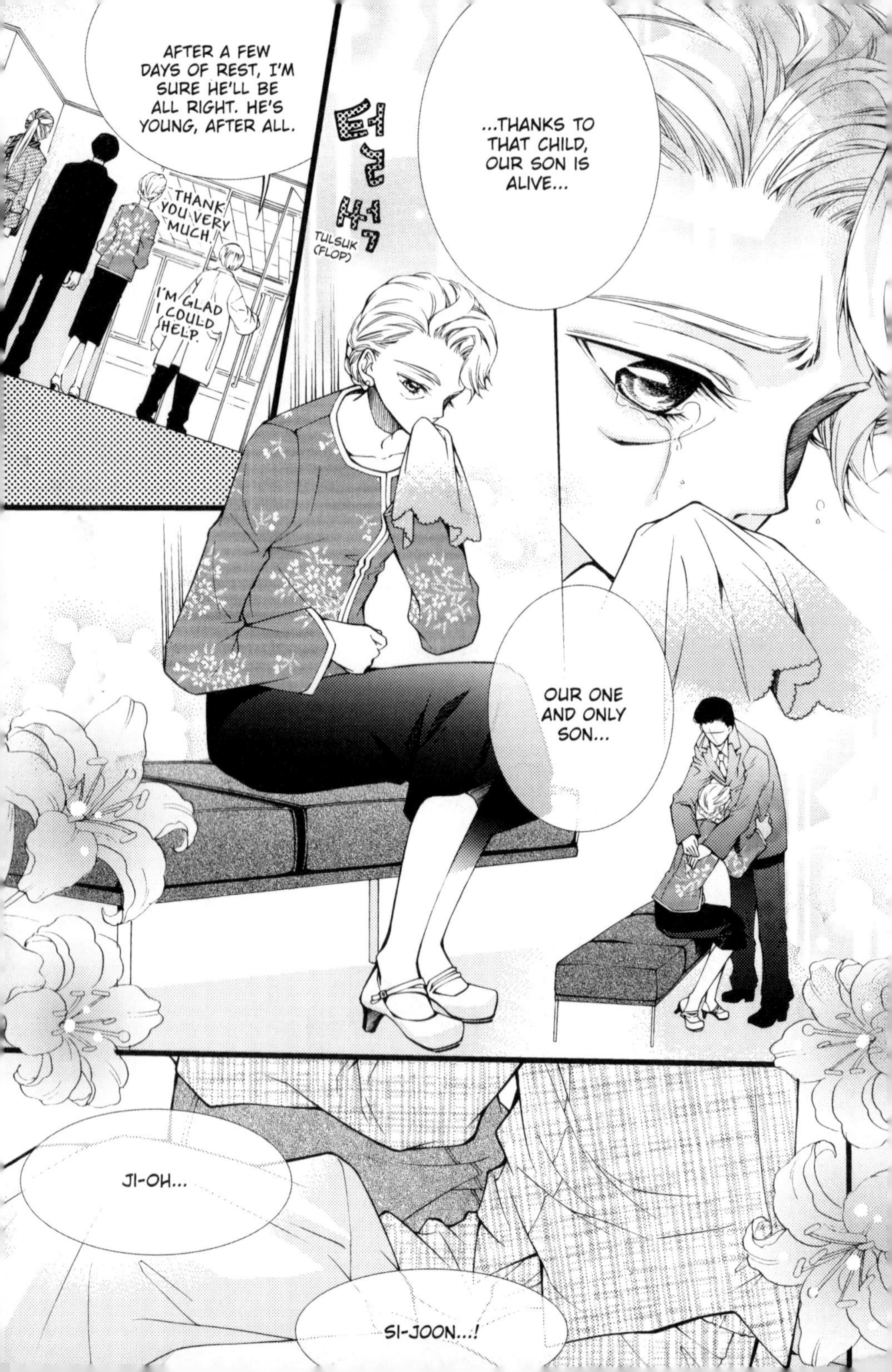
AFTER A FEW DAYS OF REST, I'M SURE HE'LL BE ALL RIGHT. HE'S YOUNG, AFTER ALL.
THANK YOU VERY MUCH.
I'M GLAD I COULD HELP.
털썩
TULSUK (FLOP)
...THANKS TO THAT CHILD, OUR SON IS ALIVE...
OUR ONE AND ONLY SON...
JI-OH...
SI-JOON...!

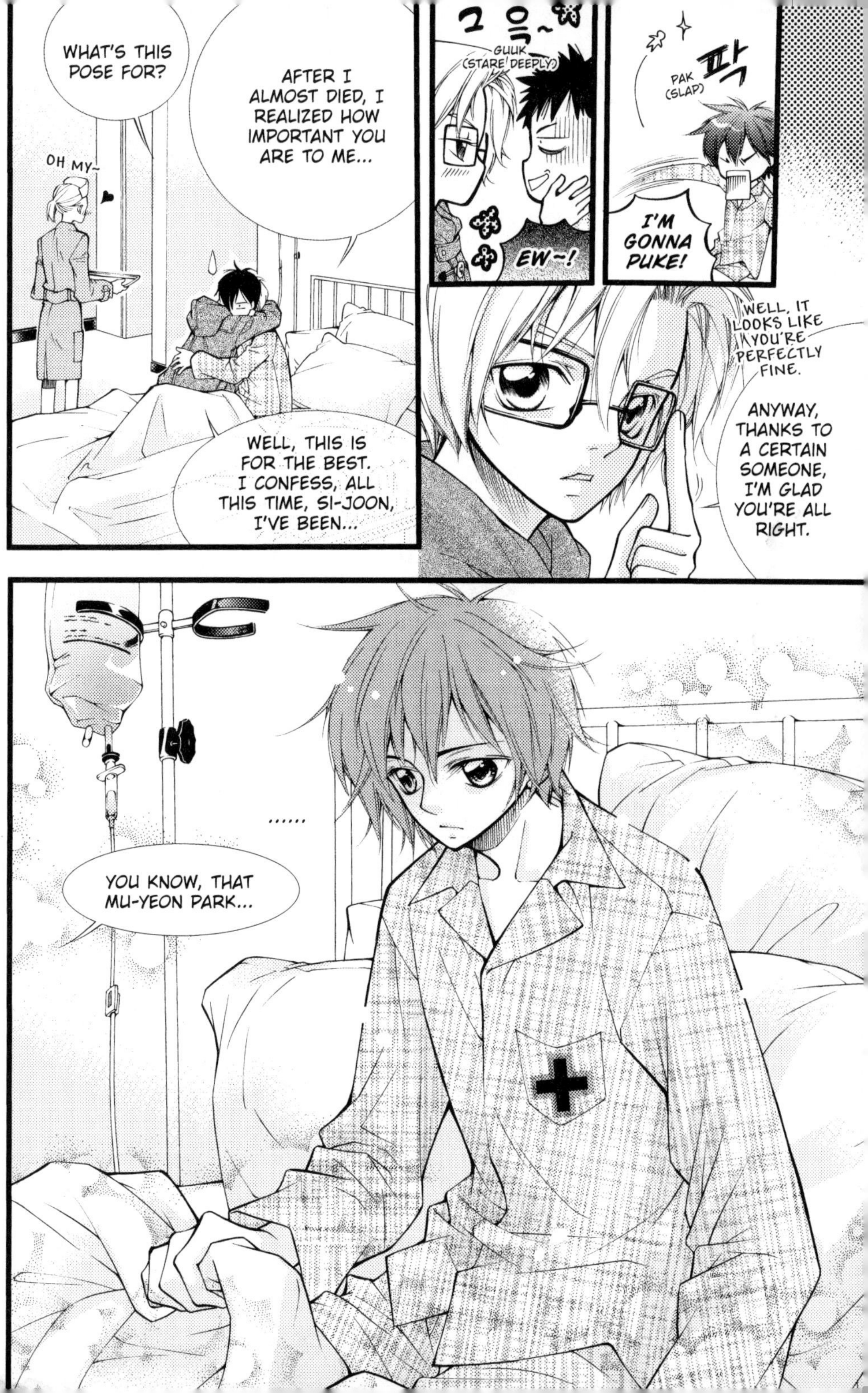
WHAT'S THIS POSE FOR?
AFTER I ALMOST DIED, I REALIZED HOW IMPORTANT YOU ARE TO ME...
OH MY~
WELL, THIS IS FOR THE BEST. I CONFESS, ALL THIS TIME, SI-JOON, I'VE BEEN...
그윽~
GUUK (STARE DEEPLY)
EW~!
팍
PAK (SLAP)
I'M GONNA PUKE!
WELL, IT LOOKS LIKE YOU'RE PERFECTLY FINE.
ANYWAY, THANKS TO A CERTAIN SOMEONE, I'M GLAD YOU'RE ALL RIGHT.
......
YOU KNOW, THAT MU-YEON PARK...

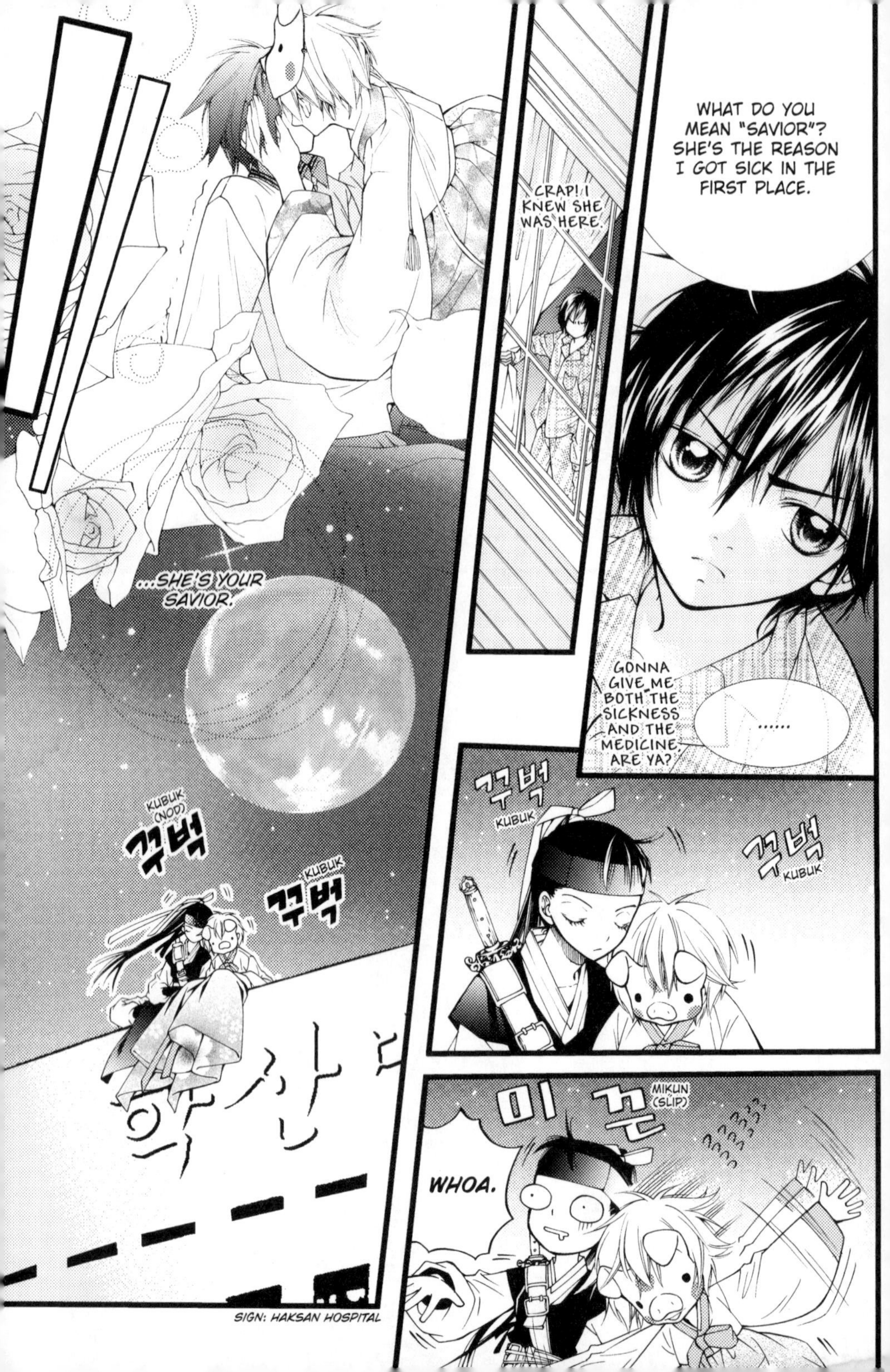

...SHE'S YOUR SAVIOR.
KUBUK (NOD)
꾸벅
KUBUK
꾸벅
SIGN: HAKSAN HOSPITAL
CRAP! I KNEW SHE WAS HERE.
WHAT DO YOU MEAN "SAVIOR"? SHE'S THE REASON I GOT SICK IN THE FIRST PLACE.
GONNA GIVE ME BOTH THE SICKNESS AND THE MEDICINE, ARE YA?
......
꾸벅
KUBUK
꾸벅
KUBUK
미끈
MIKUN (SLIP)
WHOA.

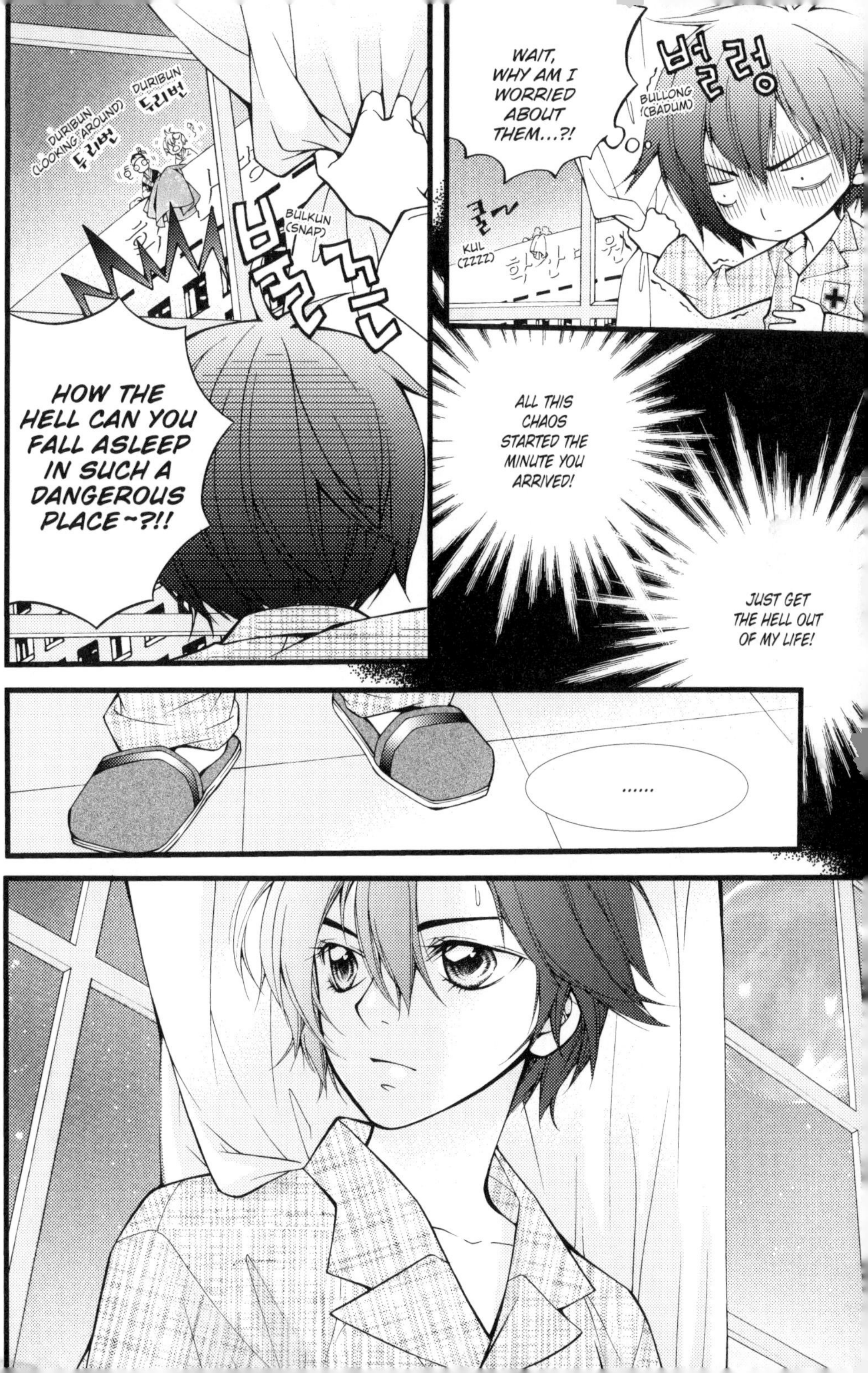
DURIBUN (LOOKING AROUND)
두리번
DURIBUN
두리번
BULKUN (SNAP)
HOW THE HELL CAN YOU FALL ASLEEP IN SUCH A DANGEROUS PLACE~?!!
WAIT, WHY AM I WORRIED ABOUT THEM...?!
벌렁
BULLONG (BADUM)
KUL (ZZZZ)
ALL THIS CHAOS STARTED THE MINUTE YOU ARRIVED!
JUST GET THE HELL OUT OF MY LIFE!
......

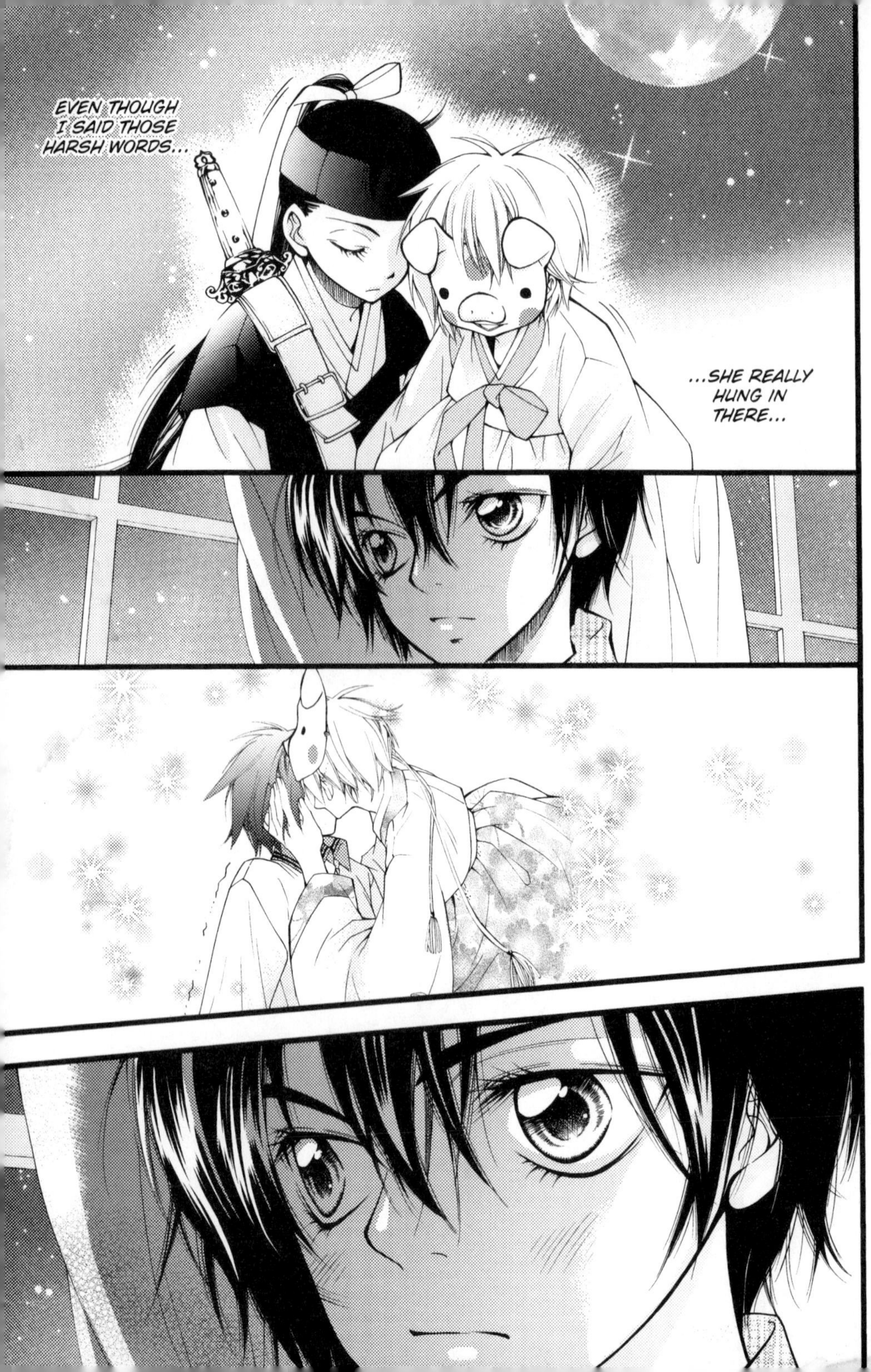
EVEN THOUGH I SAID THOSE HARSH WORDS...
...SHE REALLY HUNG IN THERE...

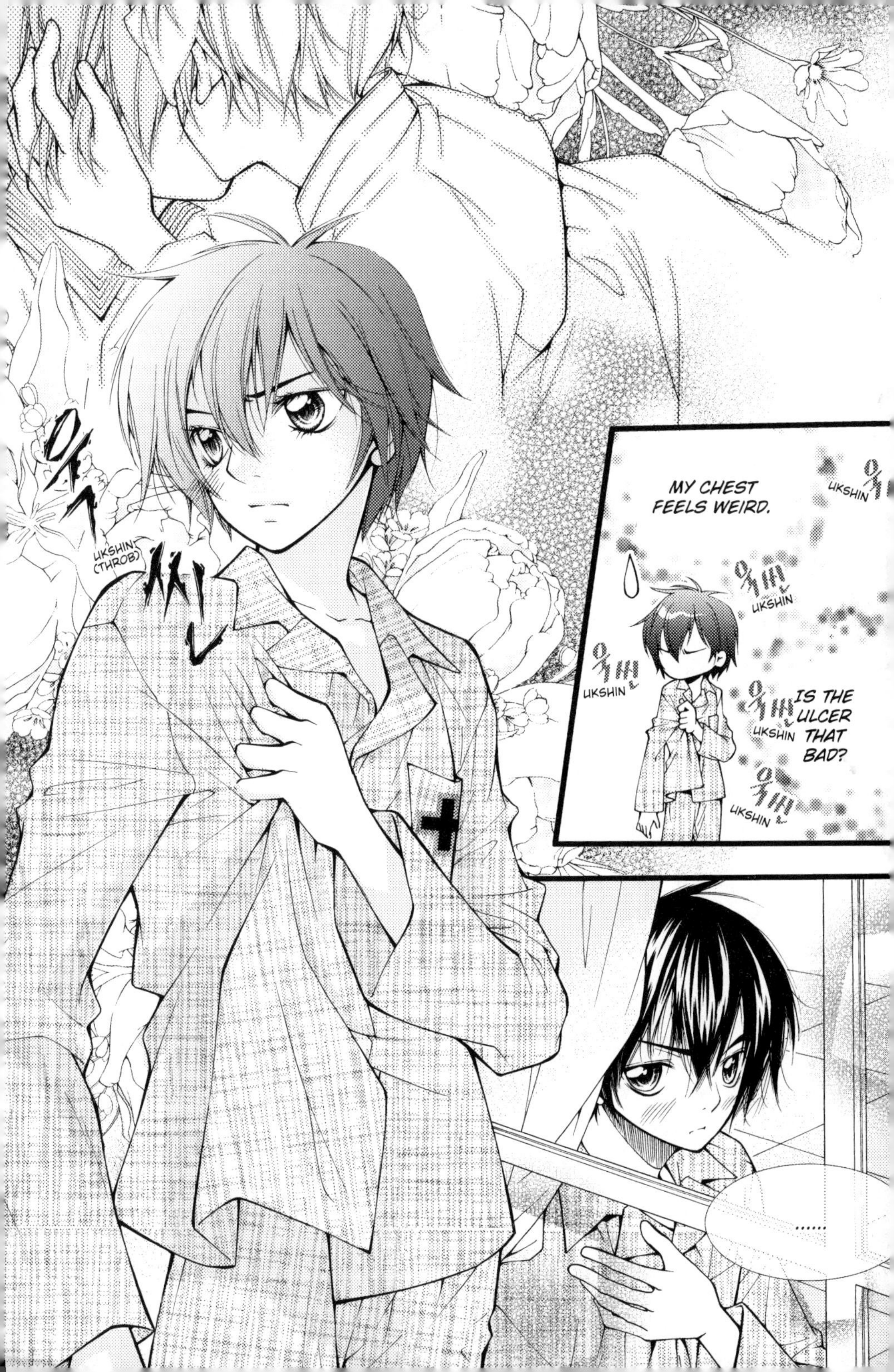

UKSHIN (THROB)
MY CHEST FEELS WEIRD.
UKSHIN
UKSHIN
UKSHIN
UKSHIN
IS THE ULCER THAT BAD?
UKSHIN
......

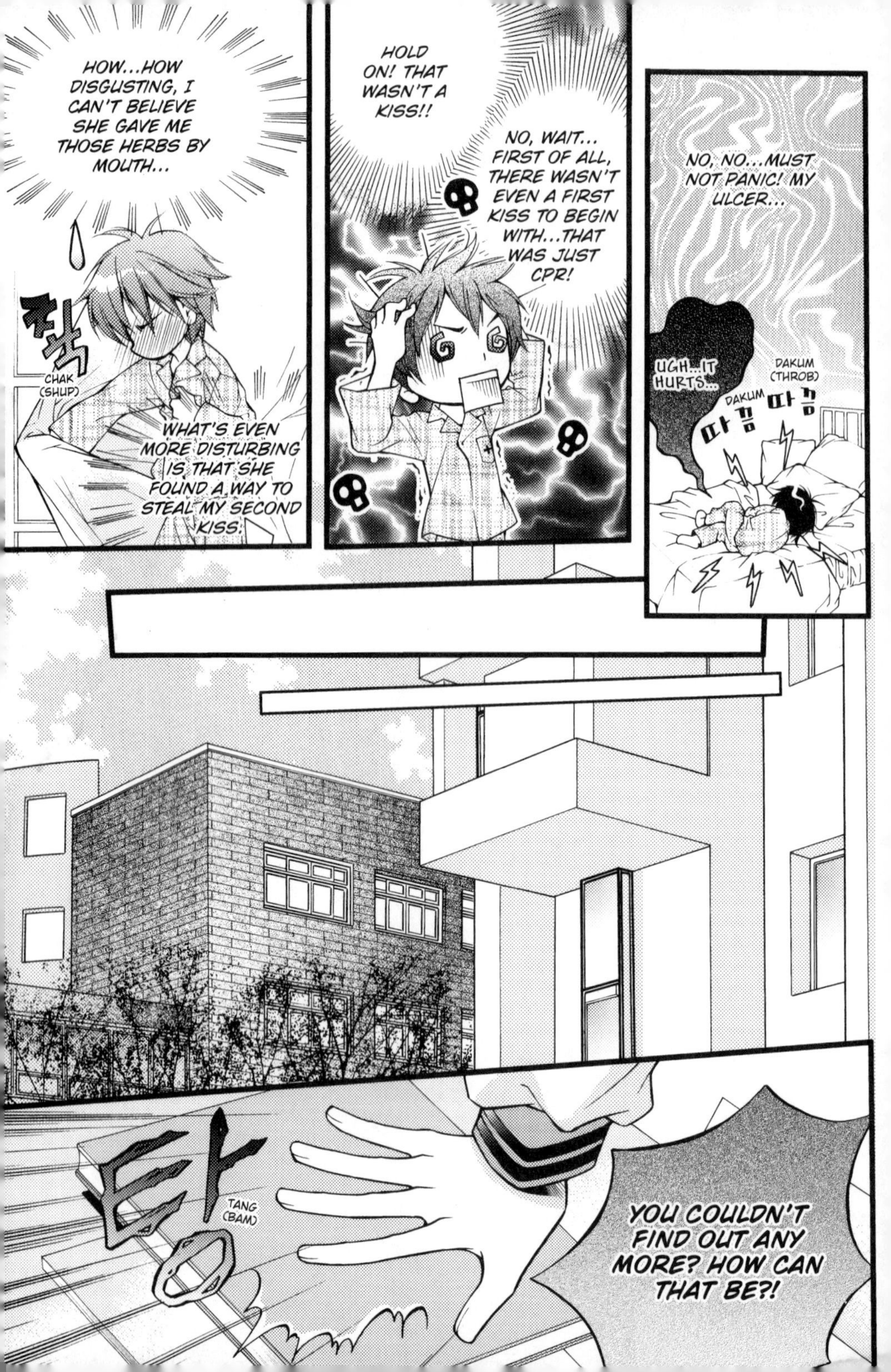
HOW...HOW DISGUSTING, I CAN'T BELIEVE SHE GAVE ME THOSE HERBS BY MOUTH...
CHAK (SHUP)
WHAT'S EVEN MORE DISTURBING IS THAT SHE FOUND A WAY TO STEAL MY SECOND KISS.
HOLD ON! THAT WASN'T A KISS!!
NO, WAIT... FIRST OF ALL, THERE WASN'T EVEN A FIRST KISS TO BEGIN WITH...THAT WAS JUST CPR!
NO, NO...MUST NOT PANIC! MY ULCER...
UGH...IT HURTS...
DAKUM (THROB)
DAKUM
따끔 따끔
TANG (BAM)
YOU COULDN'T FIND OUT ANY MORE? HOW CAN THAT BE?!

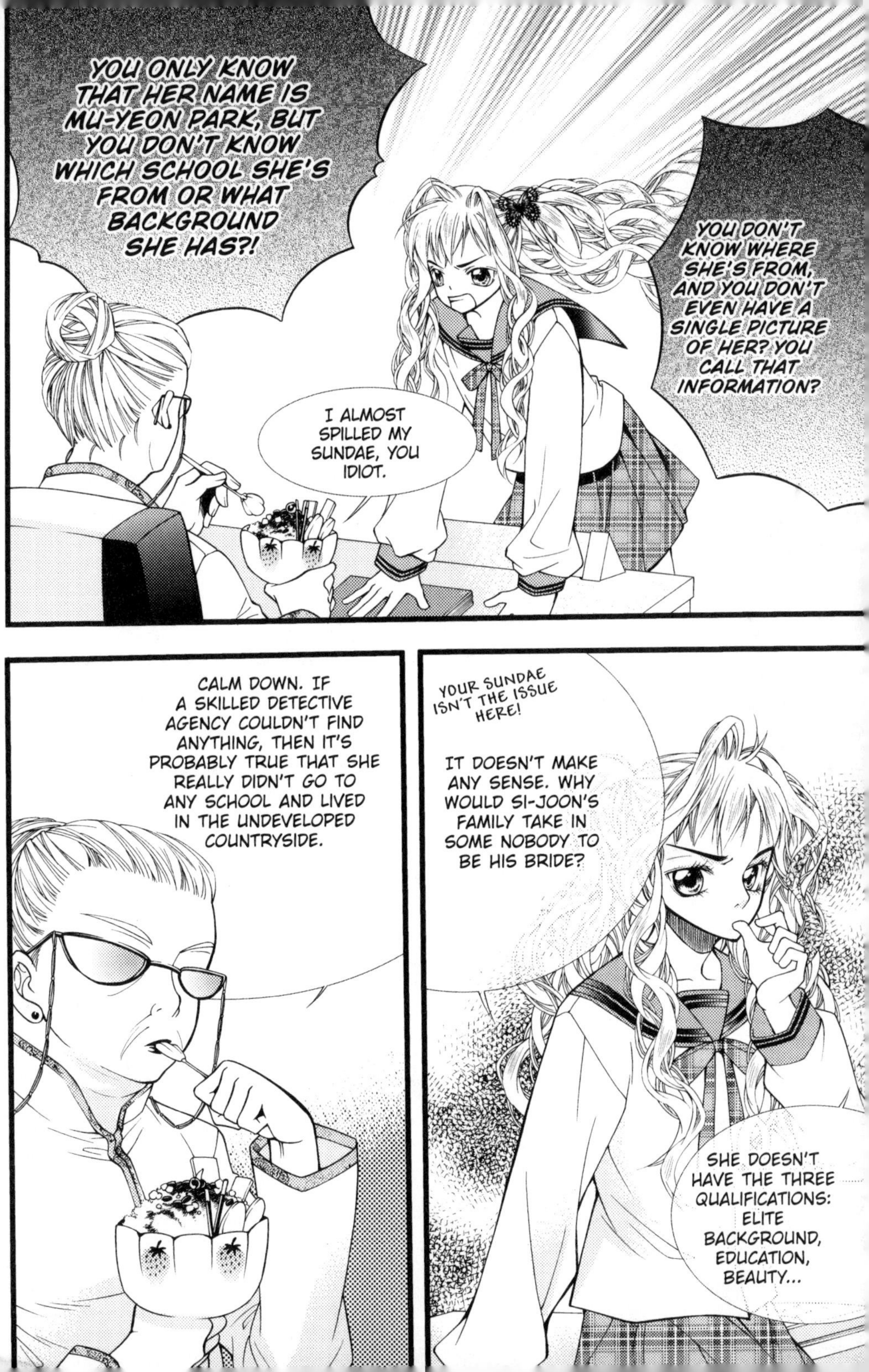
YOU ONLY KNOW THAT HER NAME IS MU-YEON PARK, BUT YOU DON'T KNOW WHICH SCHOOL SHE'S FROM OR WHAT BACKGROUND SHE HAS?!
YOU DON'T KNOW WHERE SHE'S FROM, AND YOU DON'T EVEN HAVE A SINGLE PICTURE OF HER? YOU CALL THAT INFORMATION?
I ALMOST SPILLED MY SUNDAE, YOU IDIOT.
CALM DOWN. IF A SKILLED DETECTIVE AGENCY COULDN'T FIND ANYTHING, THEN IT'S PROBABLY TRUE THAT SHE REALLY DIDN'T GO TO ANY SCHOOL AND LIVED IN THE UNDEVELOPED COUNTRYSIDE.
YOUR SUNDAE ISN'T THE ISSUE HERE!
IT DOESN'T MAKE ANY SENSE. WHY WOULD SI-JOON'S FAMILY TAKE IN SOME NOBODY TO BE HIS BRIDE?
SHE DOESN'T HAVE THE THREE QUALIFICATIONS: ELITE BACKGROUND, EDUCATION, BEAUTY...

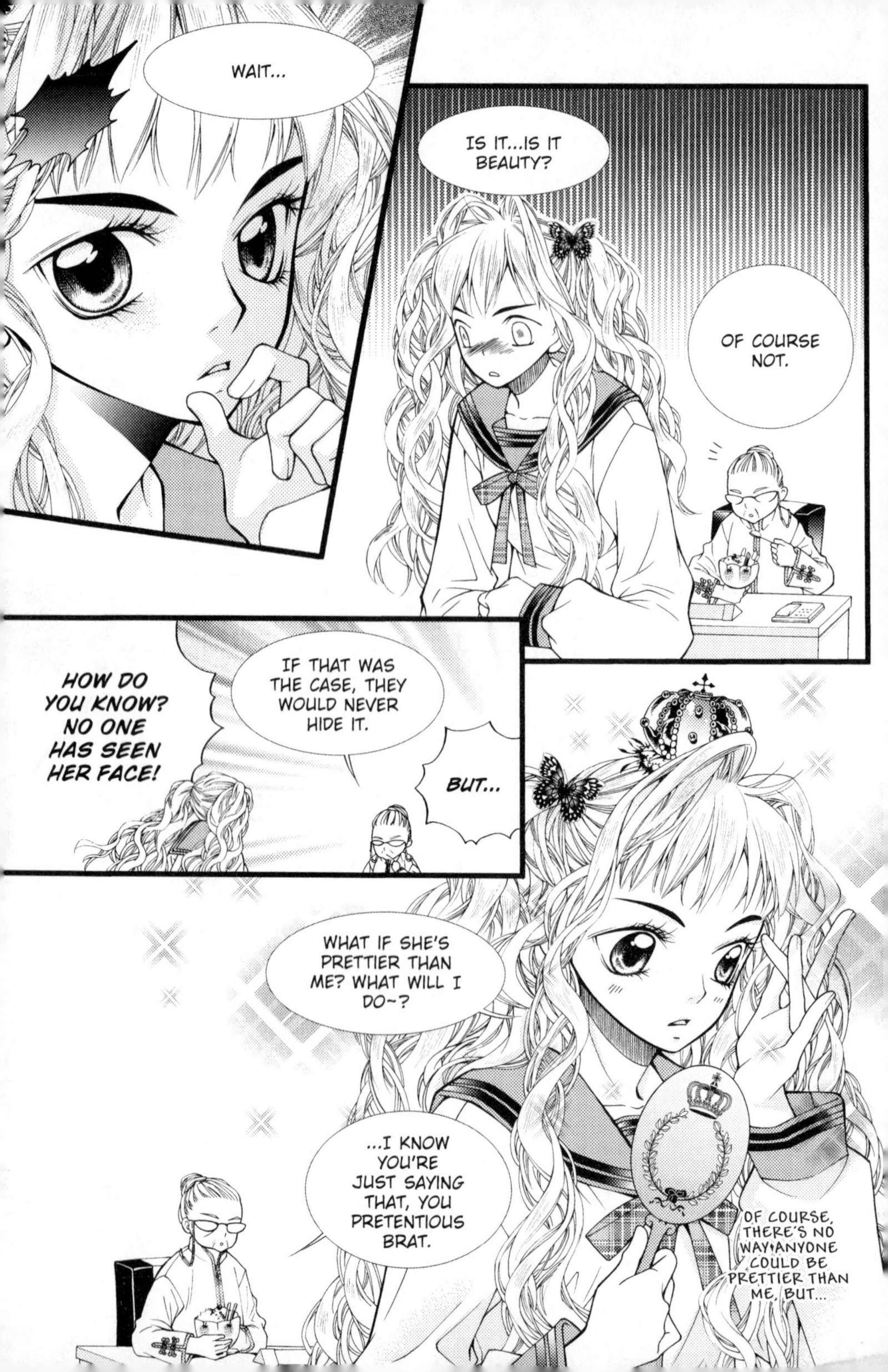
WAIT...
IS IT...IS IT BEAUTY?
OF COURSE NOT.
IF THAT WAS THE CASE, THEY WOULD NEVER HIDE IT.
BUT...
HOW DO YOU KNOW? NO ONE HAS SEEN HER FACE!
WHAT IF SHE'S PRETTIER THAN ME? WHAT WILL I DO~?
...I KNOW YOU'RE JUST SAYING THAT, YOU PRETENTIOUS BRAT.
OF COURSE, THERE'S NO WAY ANYONE COULD BE PRETTIER THAN ME, BUT...

THERE'S SOMETHING I WANT YOU TO SEE.

IS THE RESIDENT ADVISOR HERE YET?

TAK (CLINK)

Ah yes, just arrived.

TIK (CLICK)

HOO... IT'S HOT...

DID YOU SEND FOR ME?

THE STORY YOU TOLD ME BEFORE, COULD YOU REPEAT IT NOW?

WOTOOK (STRAIGHTEN)

GASP! D-DOE-DOE...

ABOUT SI-JOON LEE'S COUSIN.

AH— YOU MEAN THE TIME WHEN SI-JOON'S COUSIN CAME TO SCHOOL?

BBUT (STIFFEN)

BBUT

KULSONG (SNIFFLE)

THAT IS, SHE HAS SUCH A SAD, TRAGIC PAST. WHEN SHE WAS A CHILD, SHE CAME DOWN WITH A HORRIBLE SICKNESS, AND HER FACE BECAME SO DISTORTED THAT SHE HAD TO HIDE IT WITH A MASK.

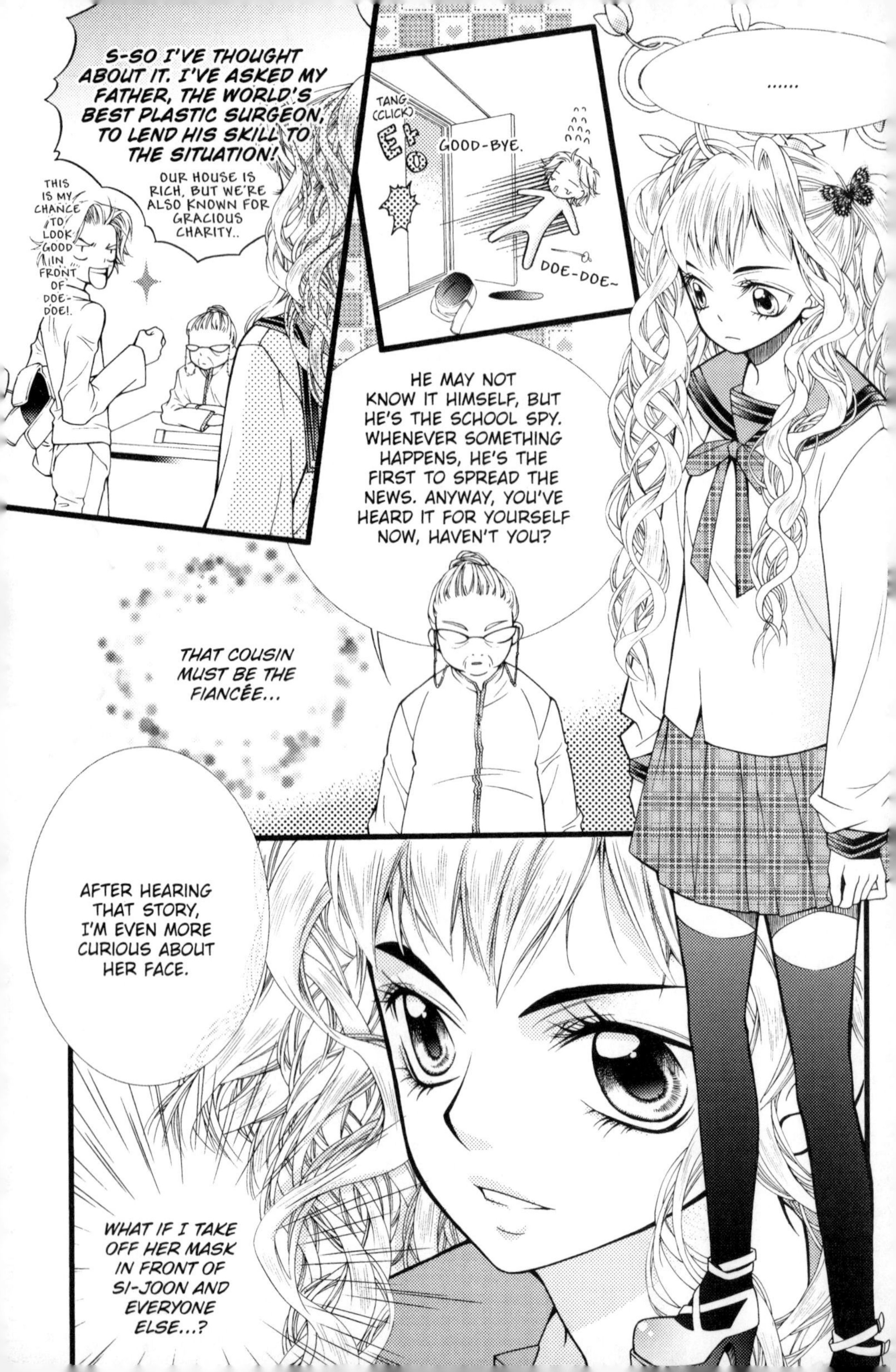
S-SO I'VE THOUGHT ABOUT IT. I'VE ASKED MY FATHER, THE WORLD'S BEST PLASTIC SURGEON, TO LEND HIS SKILL TO THE SITUATION!
THIS IS MY CHANCE TO LOOK GOOD IN FRONT OF DOE-DOE!.
OUR HOUSE IS RICH, BUT WE'RE ALSO KNOWN FOR GRACIOUS CHARITY..
TANG (CLICK)
GOOD-BYE.
DOE-DOE~
......
HE MAY NOT KNOW IT HIMSELF, BUT HE'S THE SCHOOL SPY. WHENEVER SOMETHING HAPPENS, HE'S THE FIRST TO SPREAD THE NEWS. ANYWAY, YOU'VE HEARD IT FOR YOURSELF NOW, HAVEN'T YOU?
THAT COUSIN MUST BE THE FIANCÉE...
AFTER HEARING THAT STORY, I'M EVEN MORE CURIOUS ABOUT HER FACE.
WHAT IF I TAKE OFF HER MASK IN FRONT OF SI-JOON AND EVERYONE ELSE...?

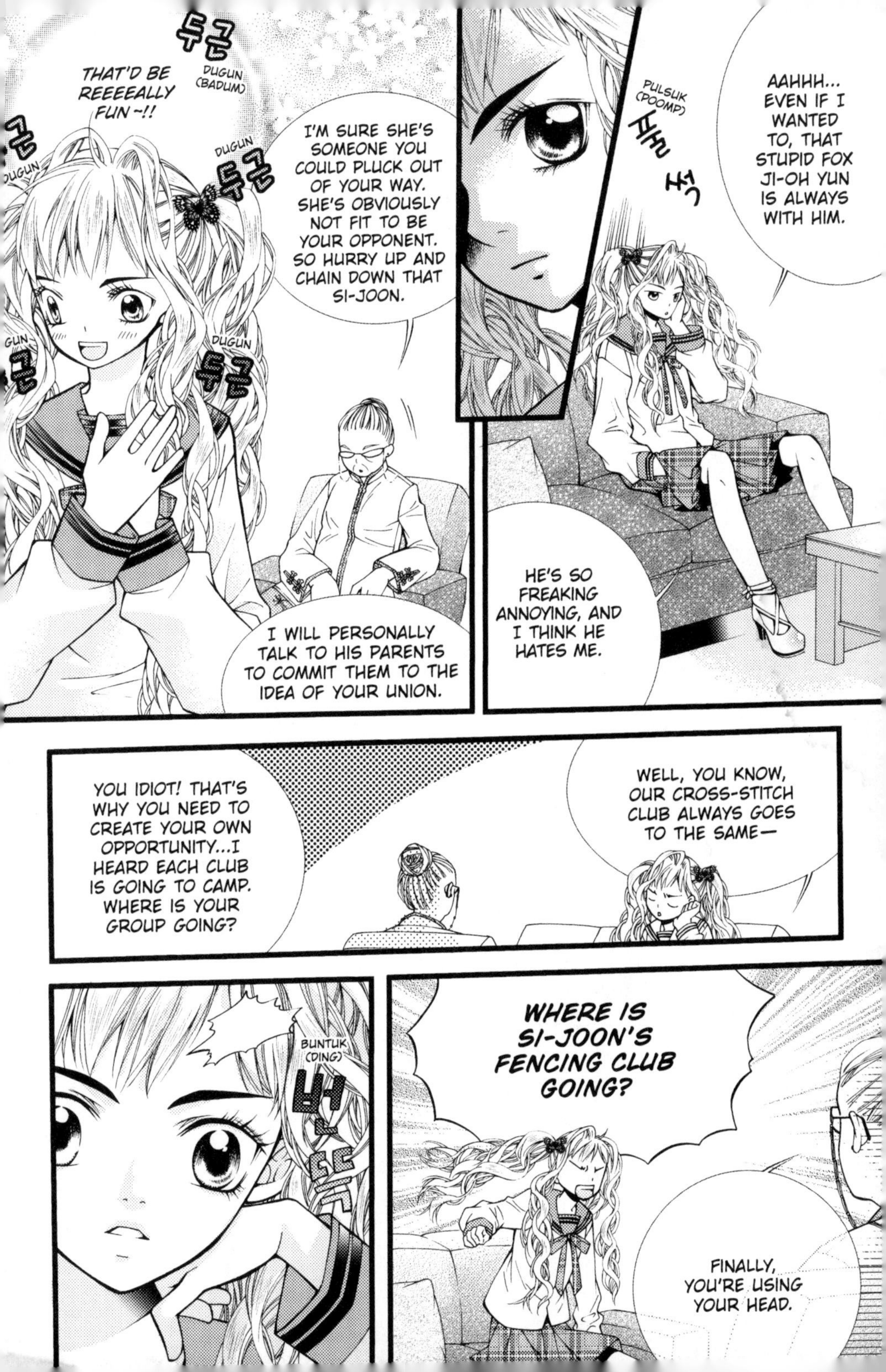
THAT'D BE REEEEALLY FUN~!!
두근
DUGUN (BADUM)
두근
DUGUN
두근
DUGUN
I'M SURE SHE'S SOMEONE YOU COULD PLUCK OUT OF YOUR WAY. SHE'S OBVIOUSLY NOT FIT TO BE YOUR OPPONENT. SO HURRY UP AND CHAIN DOWN THAT SI-JOON.
I WILL PERSONALLY TALK TO HIS PARENTS TO COMMIT THEM TO THE IDEA OF YOUR UNION.
PULSUK (POOMP)
AAHHH... EVEN IF I WANTED TO, THAT STUPID FOX JI-OH YUN IS ALWAYS WITH HIM.
HE'S SO FREAKING ANNOYING, AND I THINK HE HATES ME.
YOU IDIOT! THAT'S WHY YOU NEED TO CREATE YOUR OWN OPPORTUNITY...I HEARD EACH CLUB IS GOING TO CAMP. WHERE IS YOUR GROUP GOING?
WELL, YOU KNOW, OUR CROSS-STITCH CLUB ALWAYS GOES TO THE SAME—
BUNTUK (DING)
WHERE IS SI-JOON'S FENCING CLUB GOING?
FINALLY, YOU'RE USING YOUR HEAD.

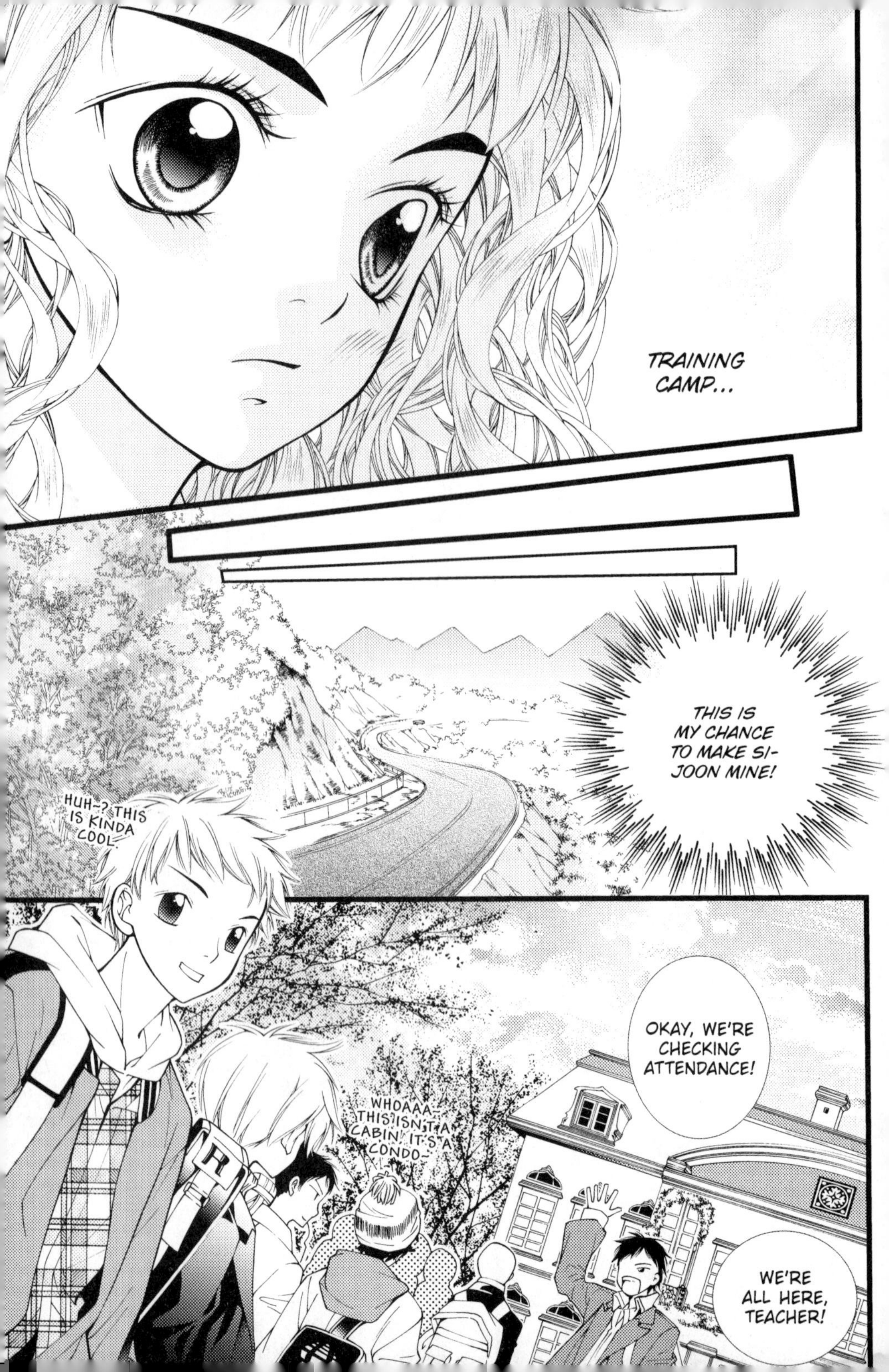
TRAINING CAMP...
HUH-? THIS IS KINDA COOL.
THIS IS MY CHANCE TO MAKE SI-JOON MINE!
WHOAAA- THIS ISN'T A CABIN, IT'S A CONDO-
OKAY, WE'RE CHECKING ATTENDANCE!
WE'RE ALL HERE, TEACHER!

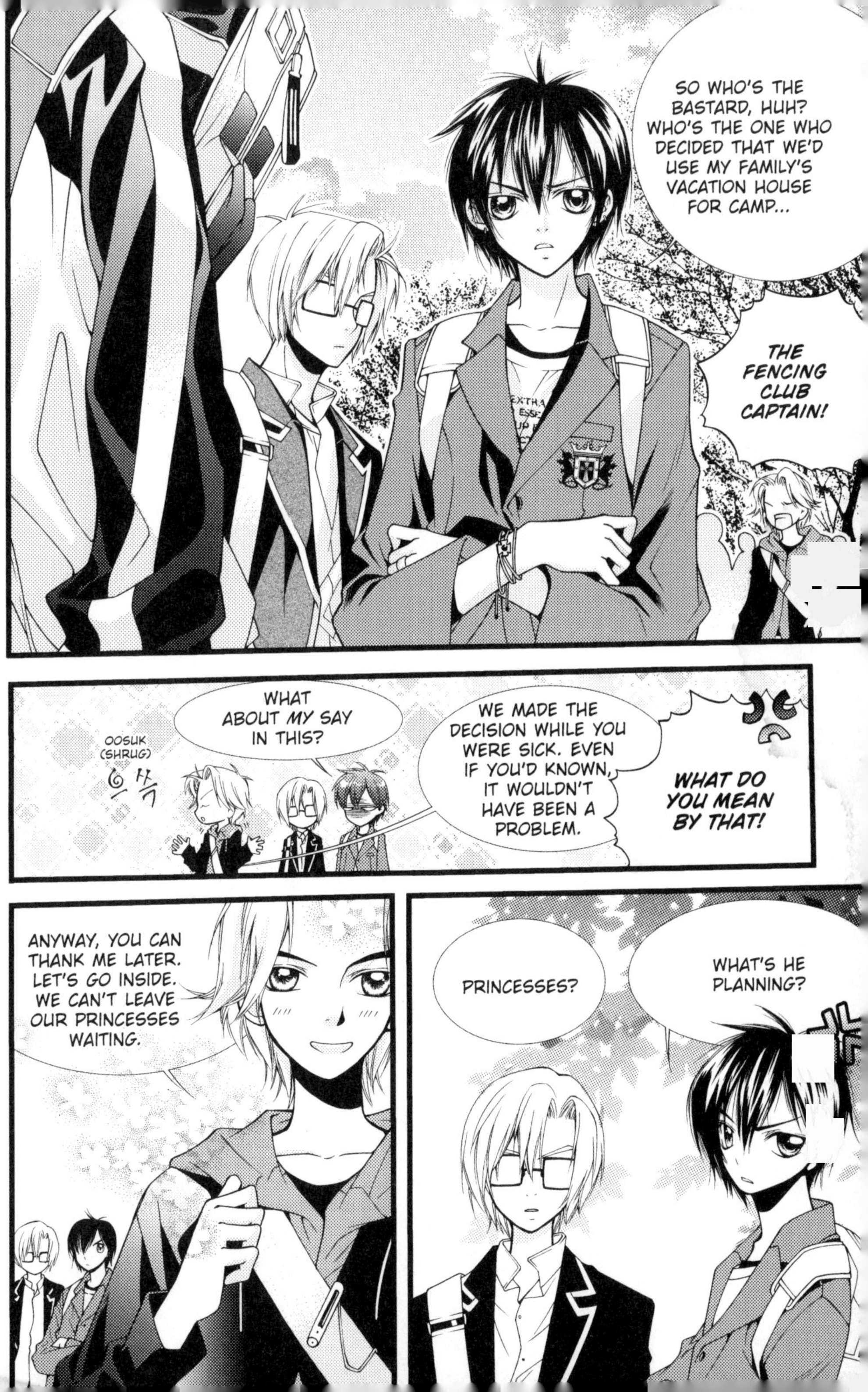
SO WHO'S THE BASTARD, HUH? WHO'S THE ONE WHO DECIDED THAT WE'D USE MY FAMILY'S VACATION HOUSE FOR CAMP...
THE FENCING CLUB CAPTAIN!
OOSUK (SHRUG)
WHAT ABOUT MY SAY IN THIS?
WE MADE THE DECISION WHILE YOU WERE SICK. EVEN IF YOU'D KNOWN, IT WOULDN'T HAVE BEEN A PROBLEM.
WHAT DO YOU MEAN BY THAT!
ANYWAY, YOU CAN THANK ME LATER. LET'S GO INSIDE. WE CAN'T LEAVE OUR PRINCESSES WAITING.
PRINCESSES?
WHAT'S HE PLANNING?

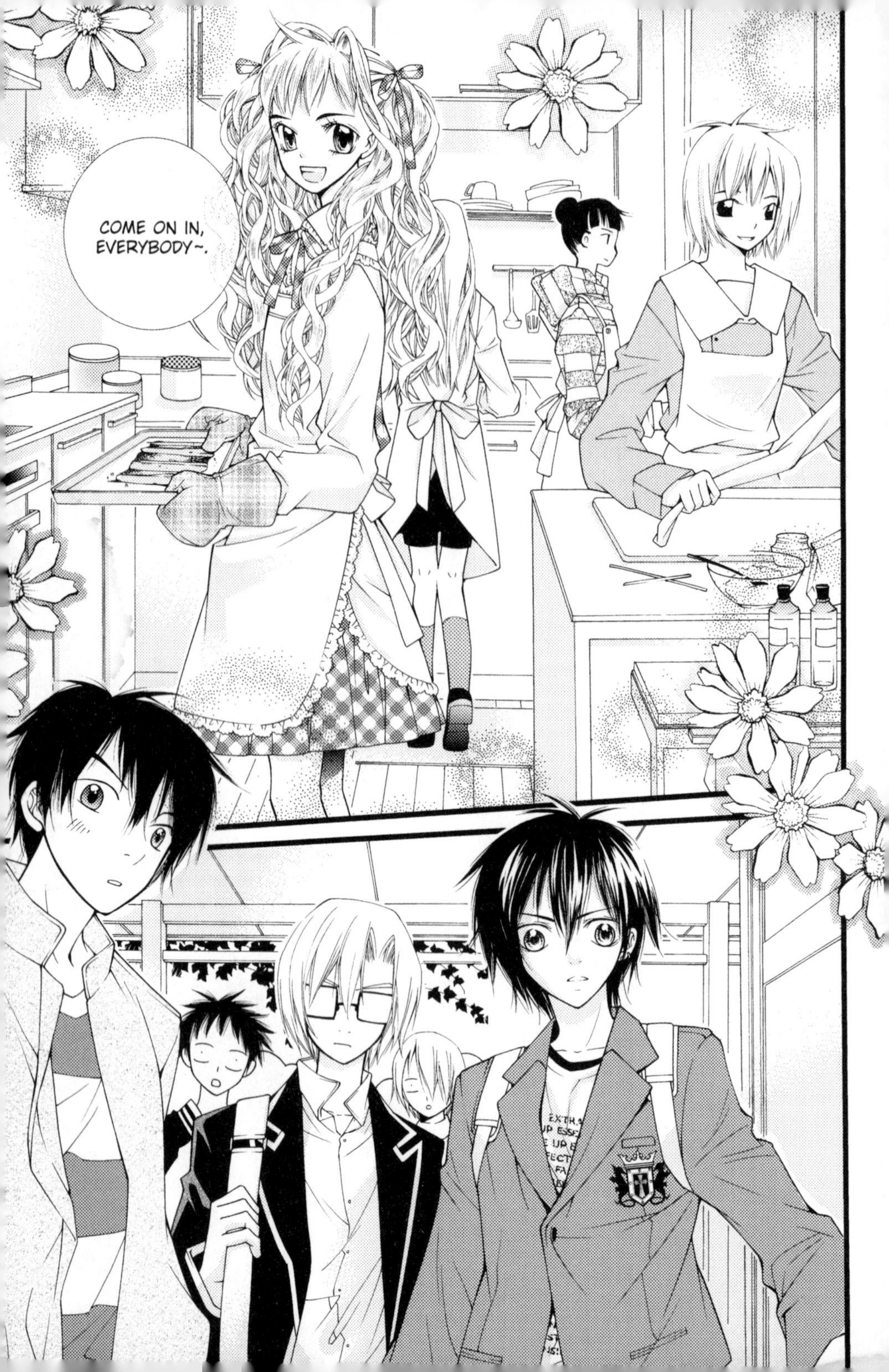
COME ON IN, EVERYBODY~.

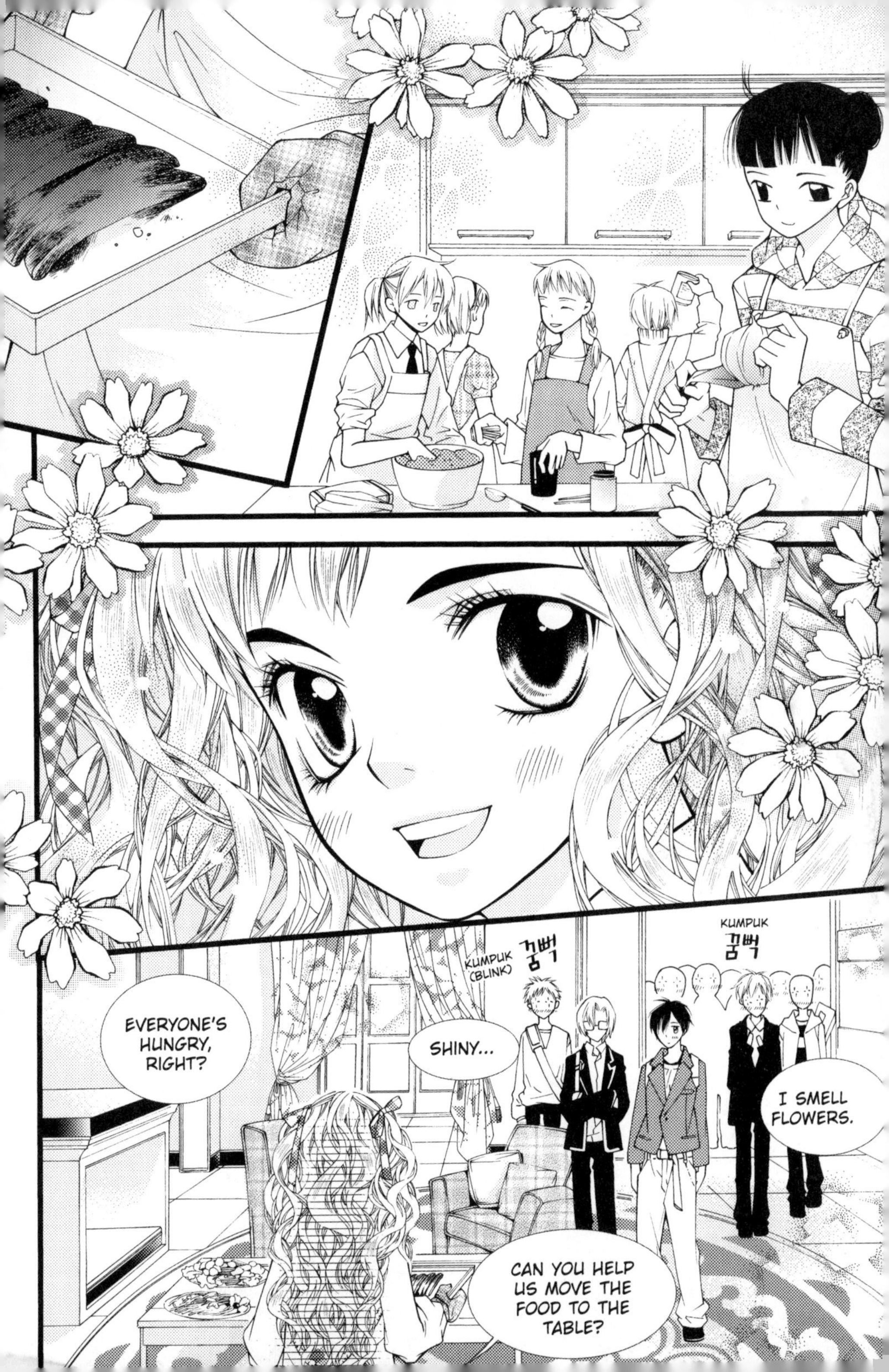
KUMPUK
(BLINK)
꿈뻑
KUMPUK
꿈뻑
EVERYONE'S HUNGRY, RIGHT?
SHINY...
I SMELL FLOWERS.
CAN YOU HELP US MOVE THE FOOD TO THE TABLE?

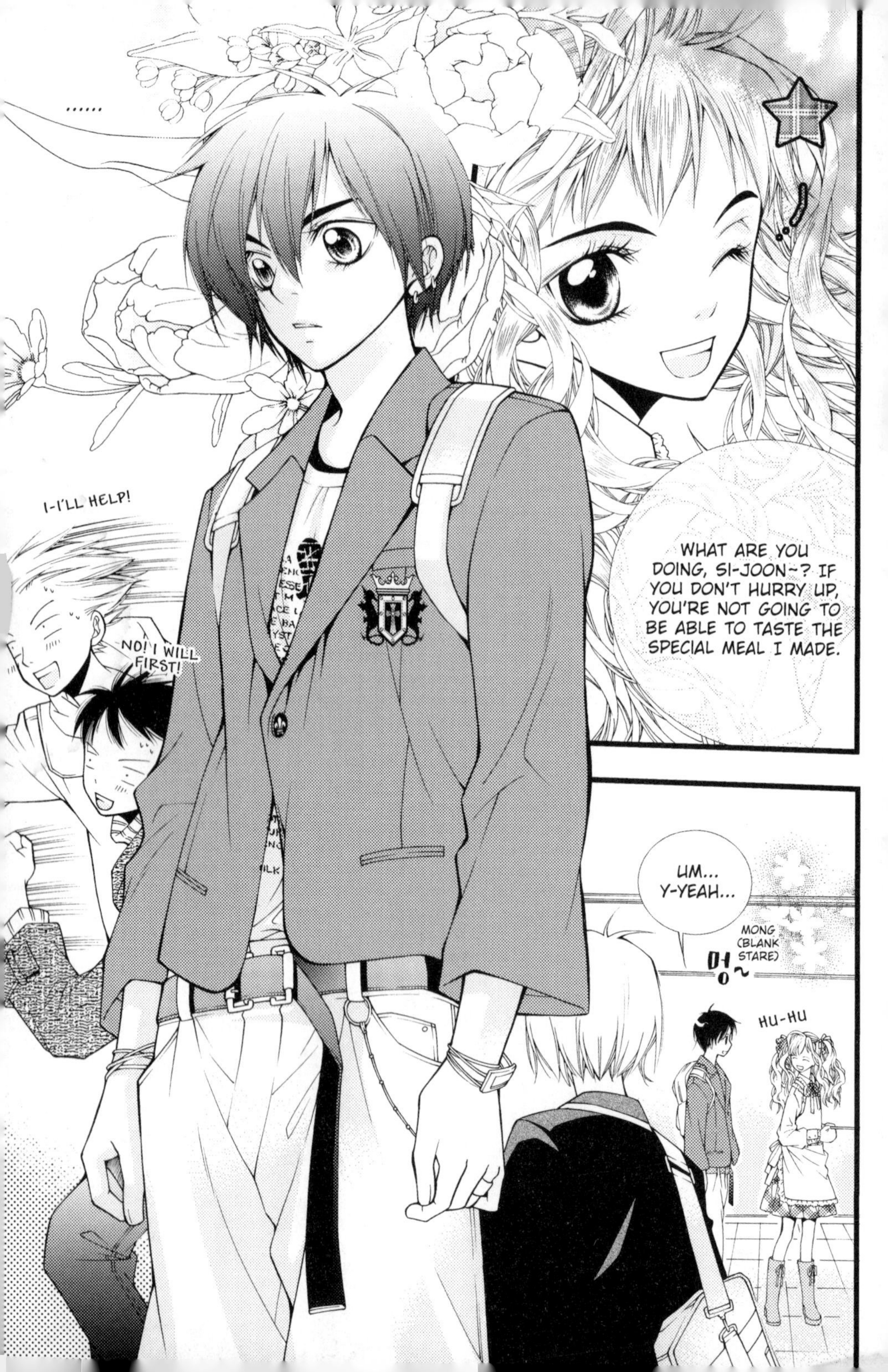
......
I-I'LL HELP!
NO! I WILL FIRST!
WHAT ARE YOU DOING, SI-JOON~? IF YOU DON'T HURRY UP, YOU'RE NOT GOING TO BE ABLE TO TASTE THE SPECIAL MEAL I MADE.
UM... Y-YEAH...
멍~
MONG (BLANK STARE)
HU-HU

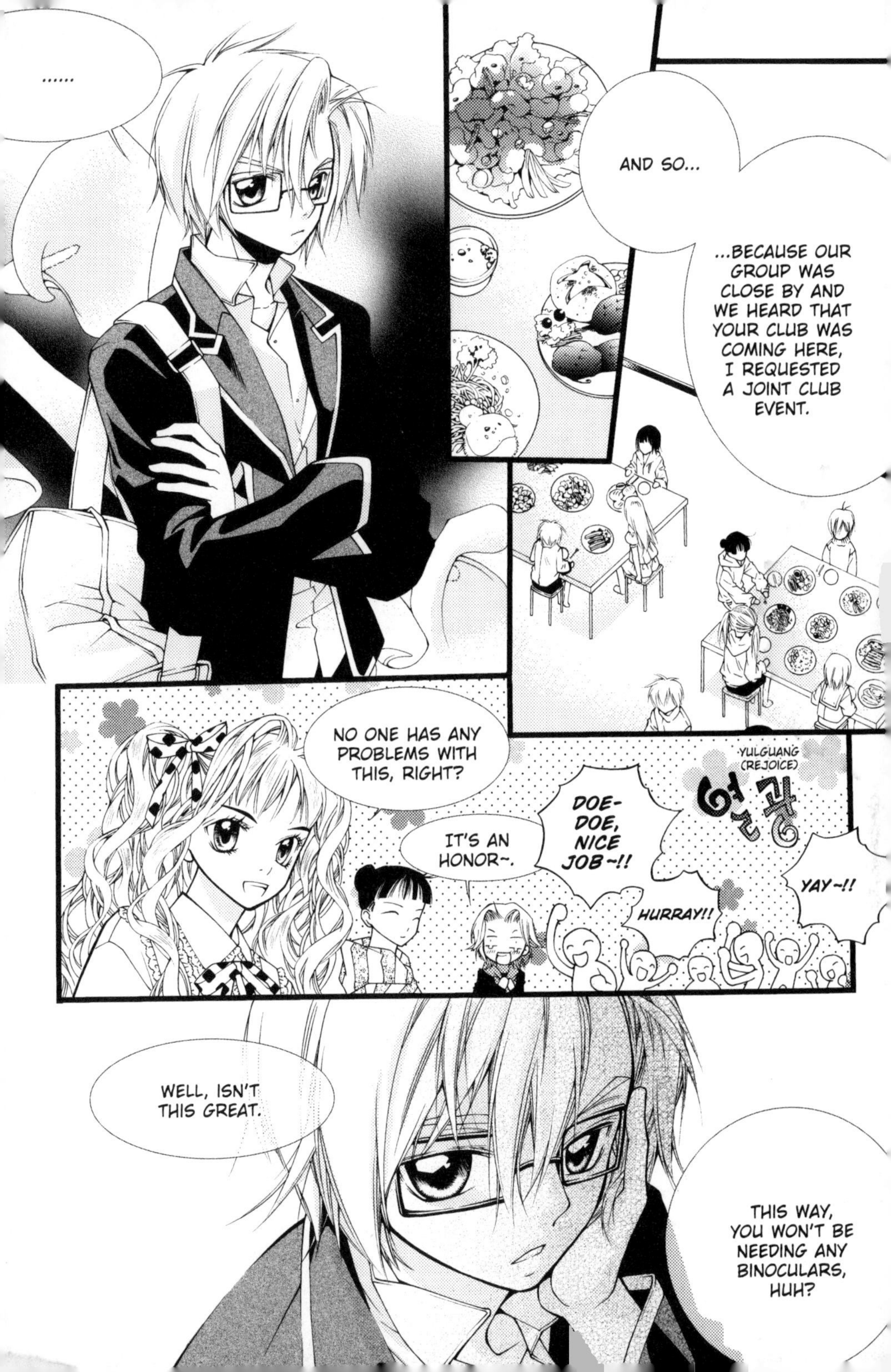
......
AND SO...
...BECAUSE OUR GROUP WAS CLOSE BY AND WE HEARD THAT YOUR CLUB WAS COMING HERE, I REQUESTED A JOINT CLUB EVENT.
NO ONE HAS ANY PROBLEMS WITH THIS, RIGHT?
IT'S AN HONOR~.
DOE-DOE, NICE JOB~!!
YULGUANG (REJOICE)
열광
HURRAY!!
YAY~!!
WELL, ISN'T THIS GREAT.
THIS WAY, YOU WON'T BE NEEDING ANY BINOCULARS, HUH?

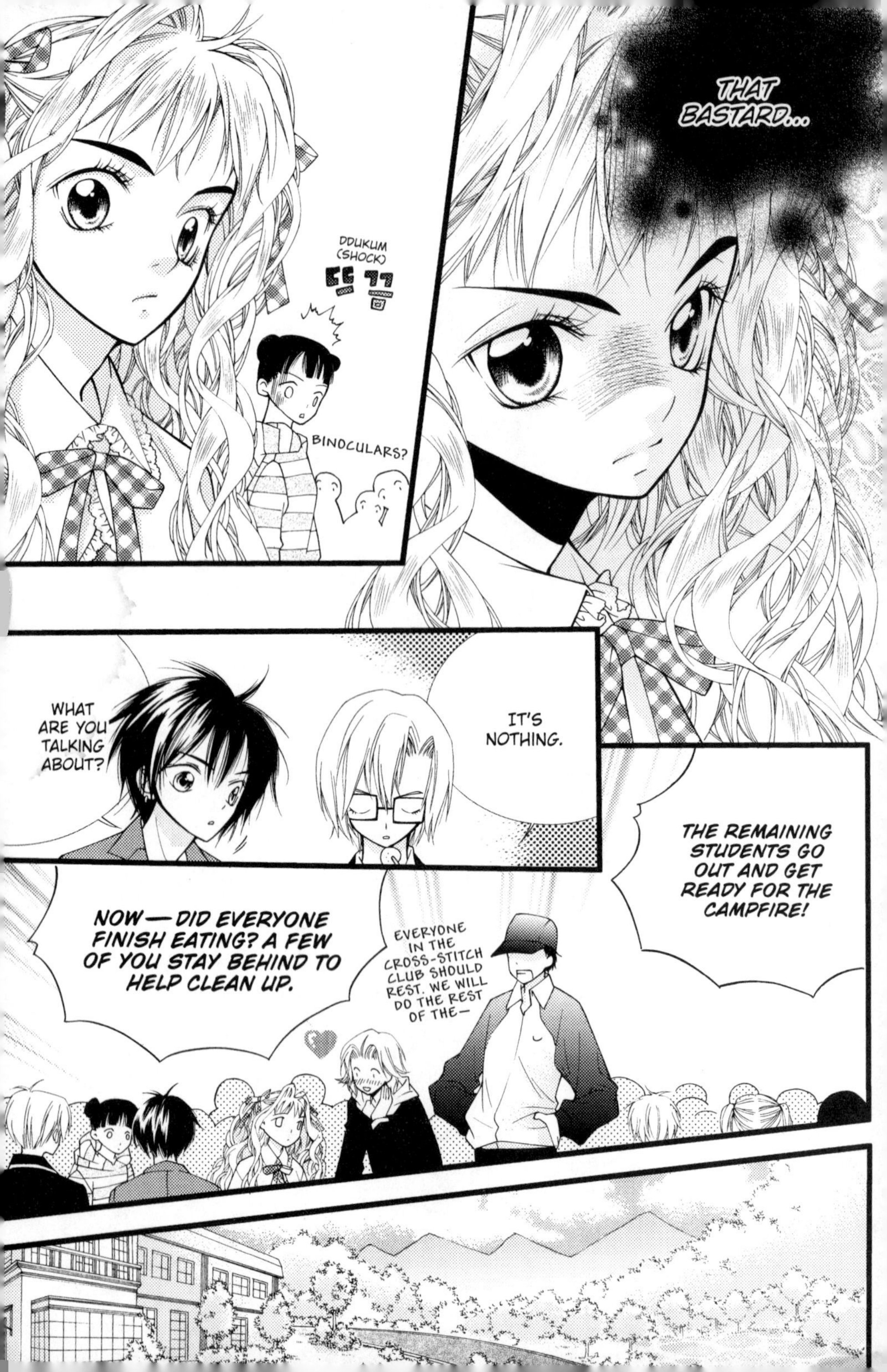
DDUKUM (SHOCK)
뜨끔
BINOCULARS?
THAT BASTARD...
WHAT ARE YOU TALKING ABOUT?
IT'S NOTHING.
THE REMAINING STUDENTS GO OUT AND GET READY FOR THE CAMPFIRE!
NOW— DID EVERYONE FINISH EATING? A FEW OF YOU STAY BEHIND TO HELP CLEAN UP.
EVERYONE IN THE CROSS-STITCH CLUB SHOULD REST. WE WILL DO THE REST OF THE—

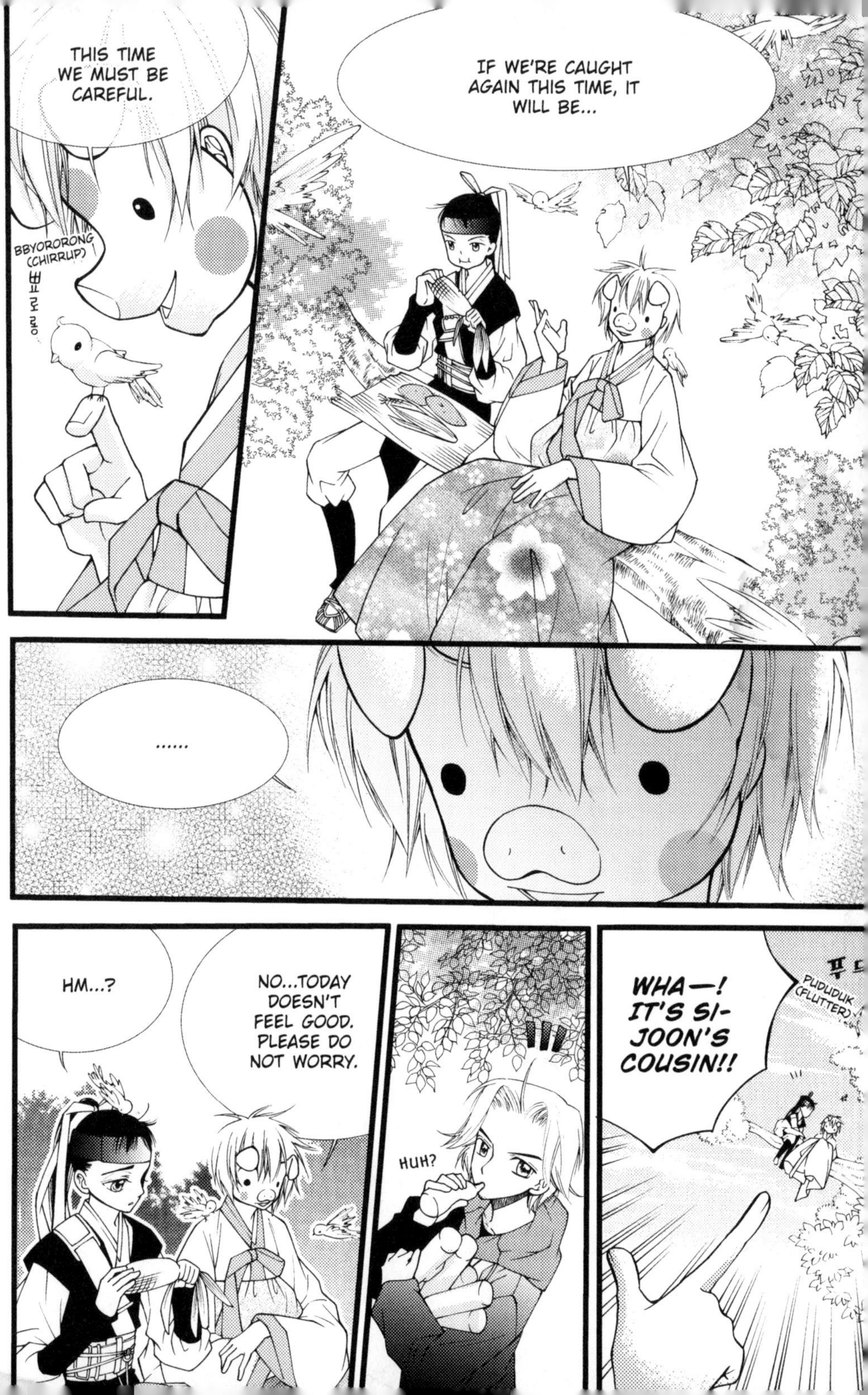
THIS TIME WE MUST BE CAREFUL.
BBYORORONG (CHIRRUP)
IF WE'RE CAUGHT AGAIN THIS TIME, IT WILL BE...
......
HM...?
NO...TODAY DOESN'T FEEL GOOD. PLEASE DO NOT WORRY.
HUH?
WHA—! IT'S SI-JOON'S COUSIN!!
PUDUDUK (FLUTTER)

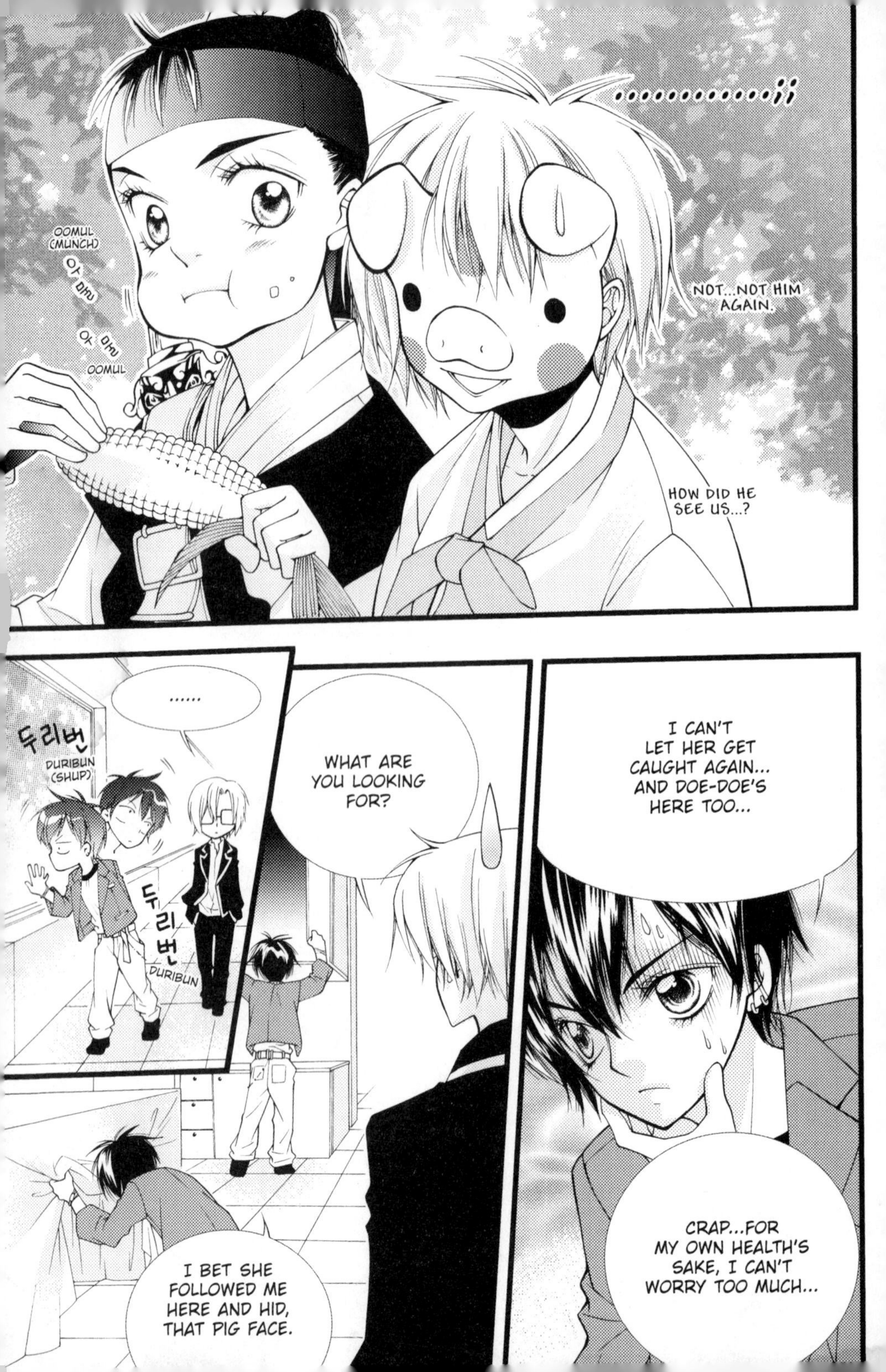
OOMUL (MUNCH)
아 물
아 물
OOMUL
............;;
NOT...NOT HIM AGAIN.
HOW DID HE SEE US...?
......
두리번
DURIBUN (SHUP)
두리번
DURIBUN
WHAT ARE YOU LOOKING FOR?
I BET SHE FOLLOWED ME HERE AND HID, THAT PIG FACE.
I CAN'T LET HER GET CAUGHT AGAIN... AND DOE-DOE'S HERE TOO...
CRAP...FOR MY OWN HEALTH'S SAKE, I CAN'T WORRY TOO MUCH...

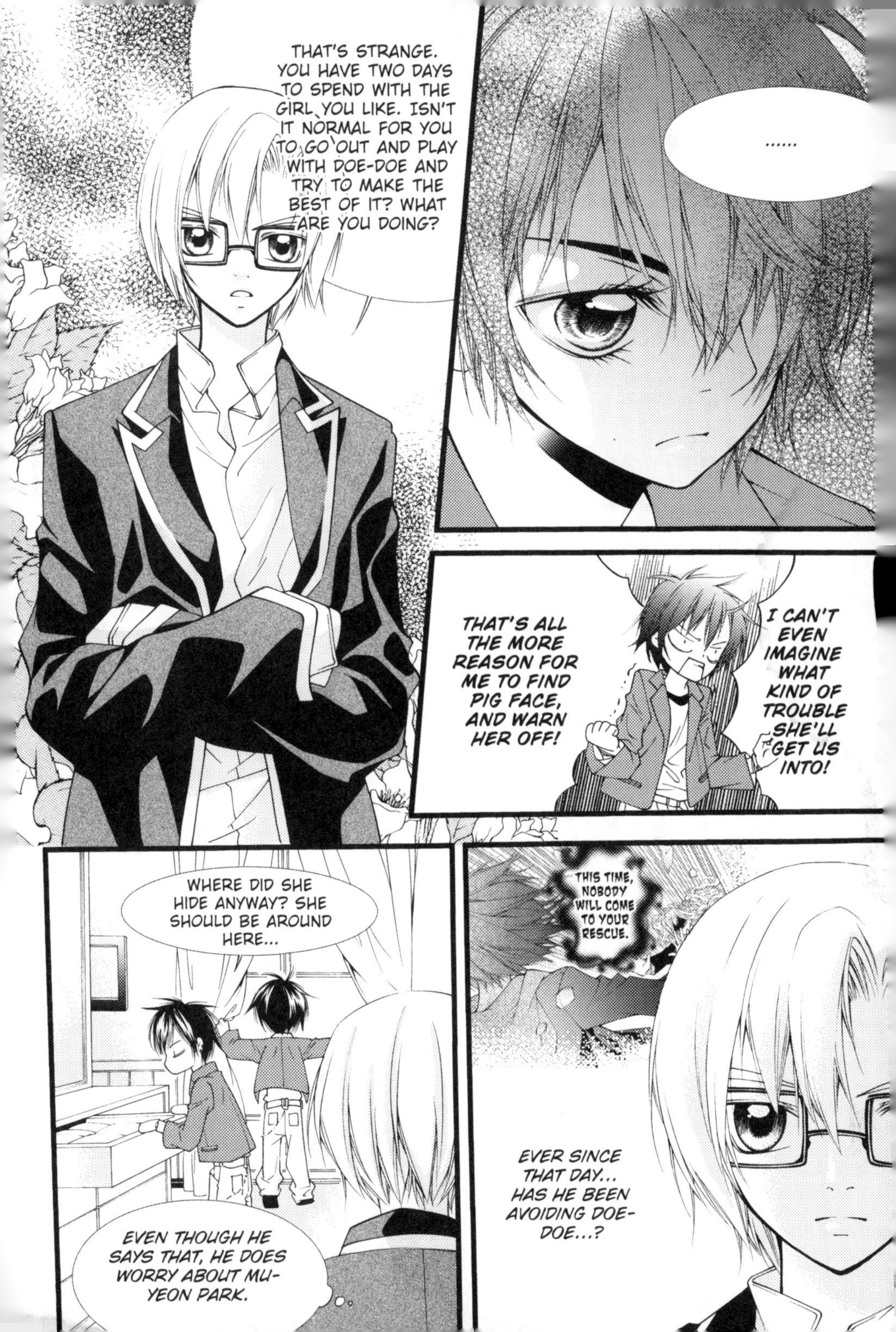
THAT'S STRANGE. YOU HAVE TWO DAYS TO SPEND WITH THE GIRL YOU LIKE. ISN'T IT NORMAL FOR YOU TO GO OUT AND PLAY WITH DOE-DOE AND TRY TO MAKE THE BEST OF IT? WHAT ARE YOU DOING?
......
THAT'S ALL THE MORE REASON FOR ME TO FIND PIG FACE, AND WARN HER OFF!
I CAN'T EVEN IMAGINE WHAT KIND OF TROUBLE SHE'LL GET US INTO!
WHERE DID SHE HIDE ANYWAY? SHE SHOULD BE AROUND HERE...
EVEN THOUGH HE SAYS THAT, HE DOES WORRY ABOUT MU-YEON PARK.
THIS TIME, NOBODY WILL COME TO YOUR RESCUE.
EVER SINCE THAT DAY... HAS HE BEEN AVOIDING DOE-DOE...?

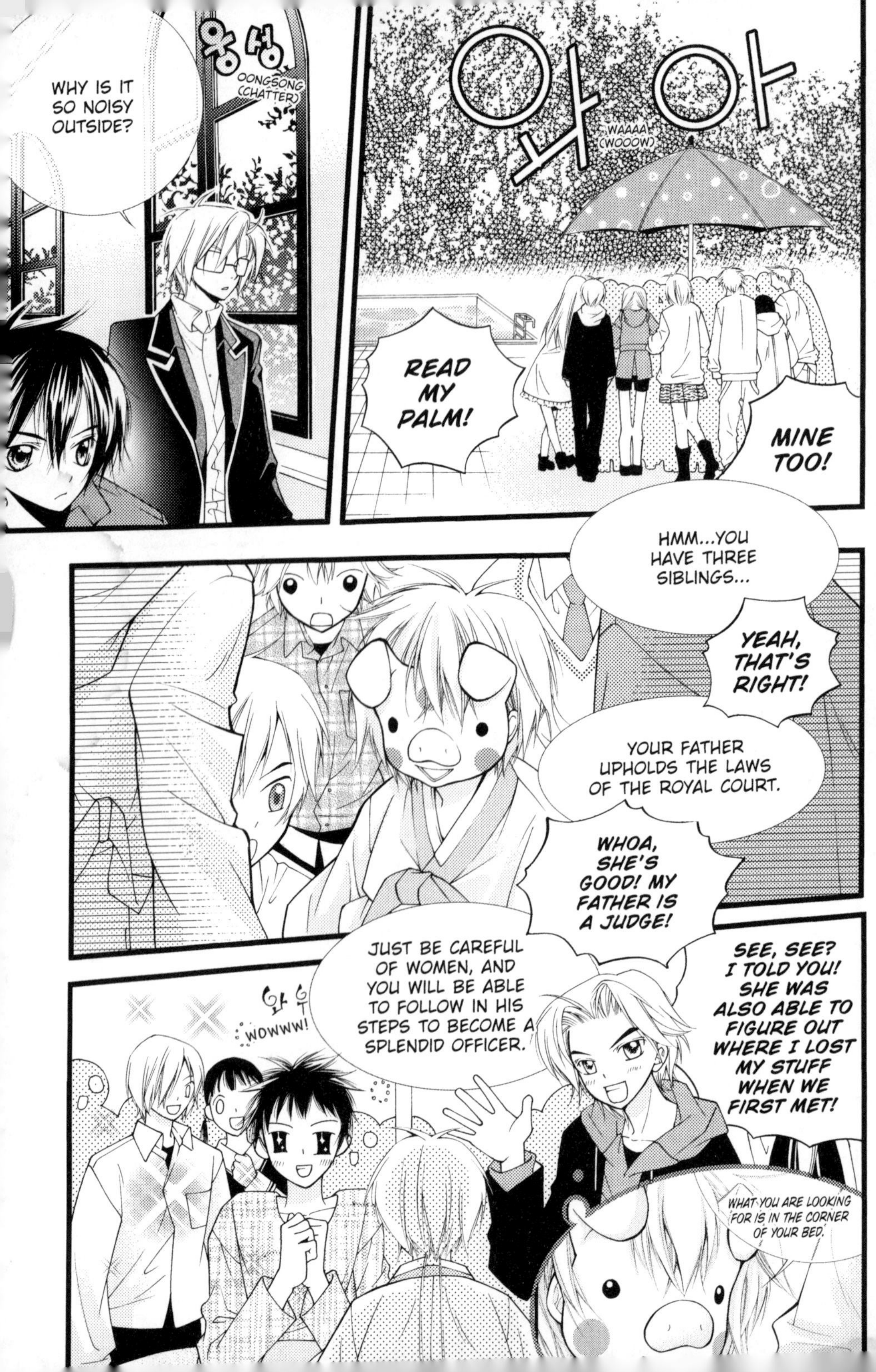
WHY IS IT SO NOISY OUTSIDE?
웅성
OONGSONG (CHATTER)
와아
WAAAA (WOOOW)
READ MY PALM!
MINE TOO!
HMM...YOU HAVE THREE SIBLINGS...
YEAH, THAT'S RIGHT!
YOUR FATHER UPHOLDS THE LAWS OF THE ROYAL COURT.
WHOA, SHE'S GOOD! MY FATHER IS A JUDGE!
와우
WOWWW!
JUST BE CAREFUL OF WOMEN, AND YOU WILL BE ABLE TO FOLLOW IN HIS STEPS TO BECOME A SPLENDID OFFICER.
SEE, SEE? I TOLD YOU! SHE WAS ALSO ABLE TO FIGURE OUT WHERE I LOST MY STUFF WHEN WE FIRST MET!
WHAT YOU ARE LOOKING FOR IS IN THE CORNER OF YOUR BED.

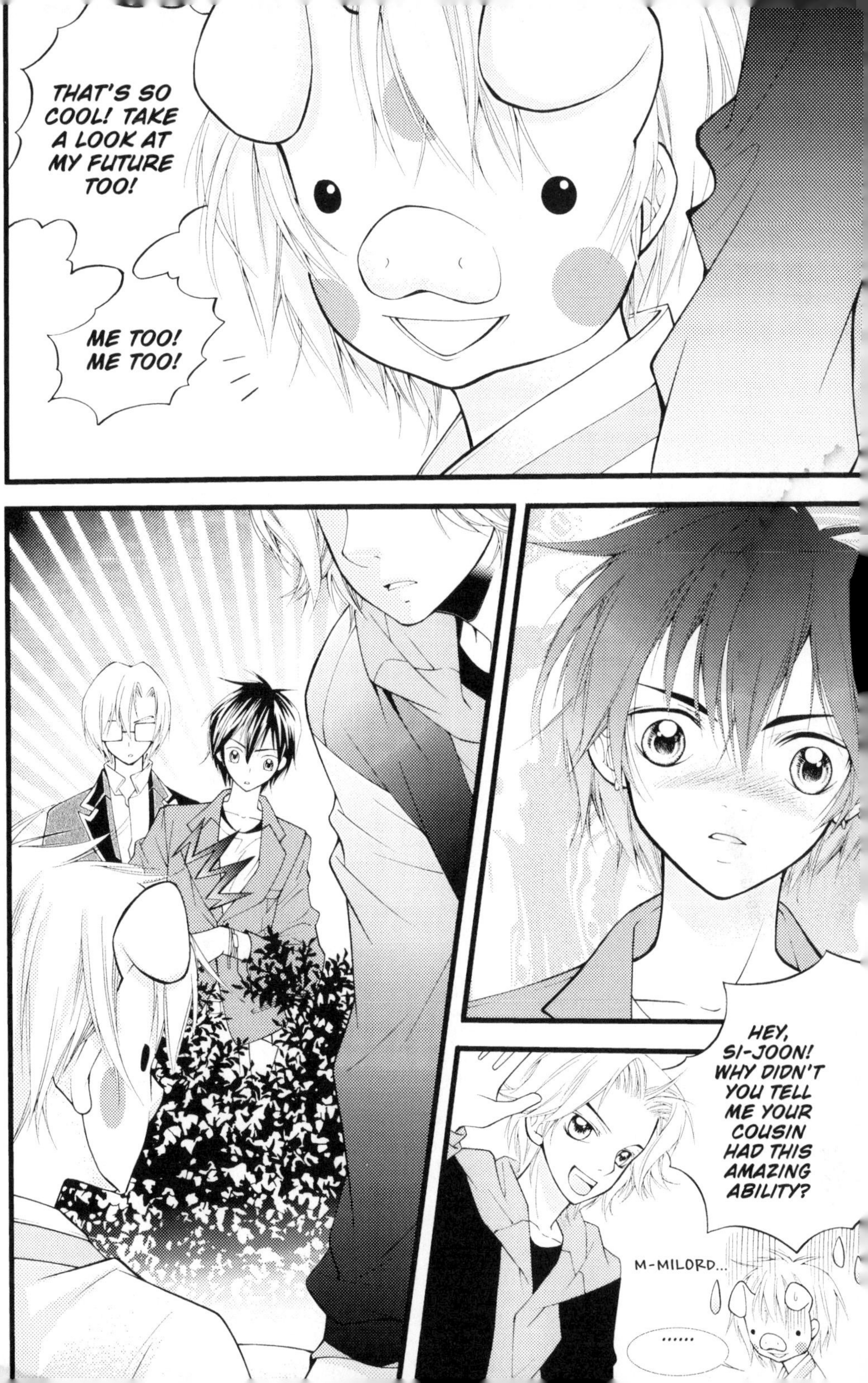
THAT'S SO COOL! TAKE A LOOK AT MY FUTURE TOO!
ME TOO! ME TOO!
HEY, SI-JOON! WHY DIDN'T YOU TELL ME YOUR COUSIN HAD THIS AMAZING ABILITY?
M-MILORD...
......

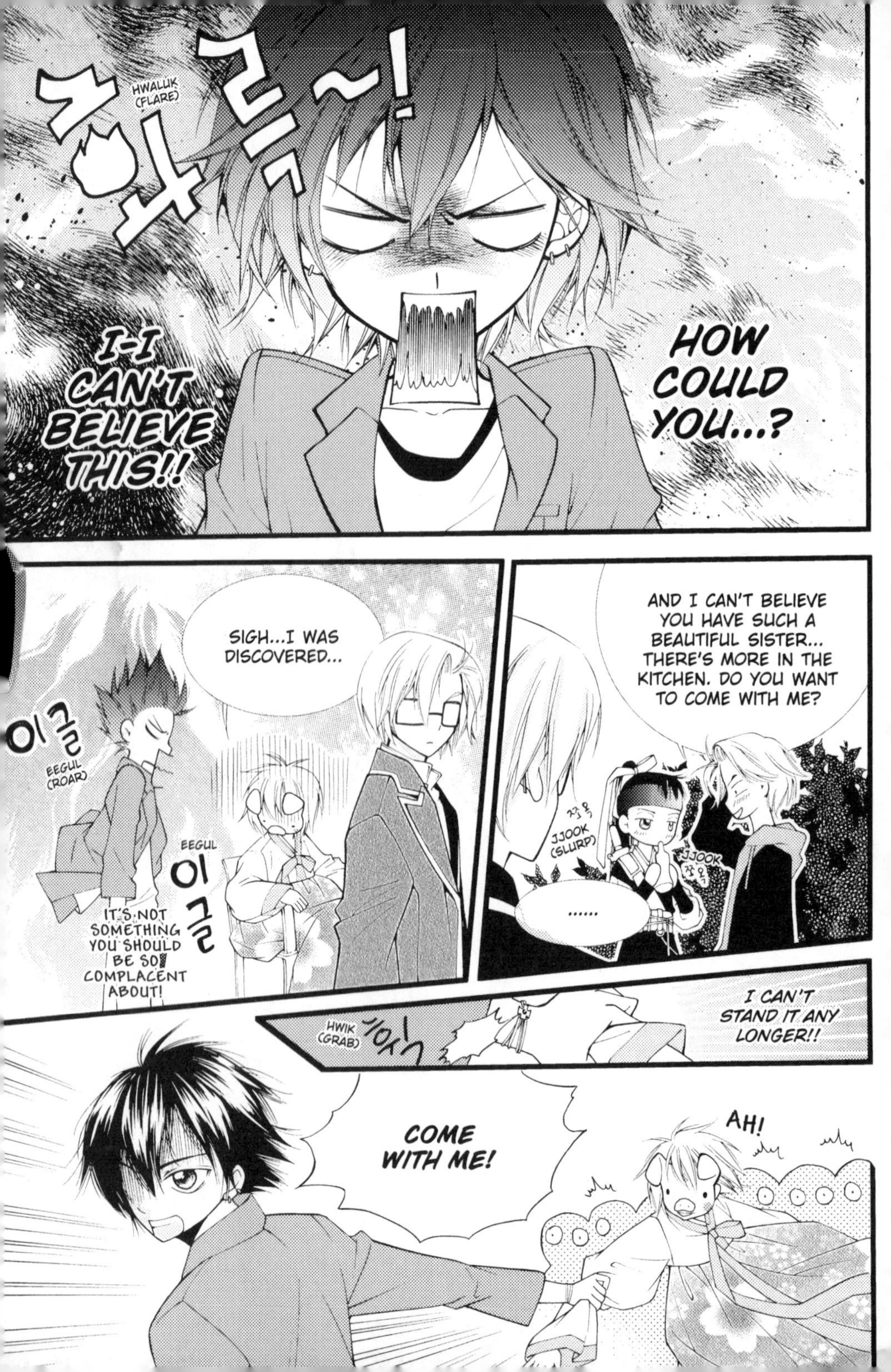
HWALUK (FLARE)
I-I CAN'T BELIEVE THIS!!
HOW COULD YOU...?
이글
EEGUL (ROAR)
SIGH...I WAS DISCOVERED...
EEGUL
이글
IT'S NOT SOMETHING YOU SHOULD BE SO COMPLACENT ABOUT!
AND I CAN'T BELIEVE YOU HAVE SUCH A BEAUTIFUL SISTER... THERE'S MORE IN THE KITCHEN. DO YOU WANT TO COME WITH ME?
JJOOK (SLURP)
JJOOK
......
HWIK (GRAB)
I CAN'T STAND IT ANY LONGER!!
COME WITH ME!
AH!

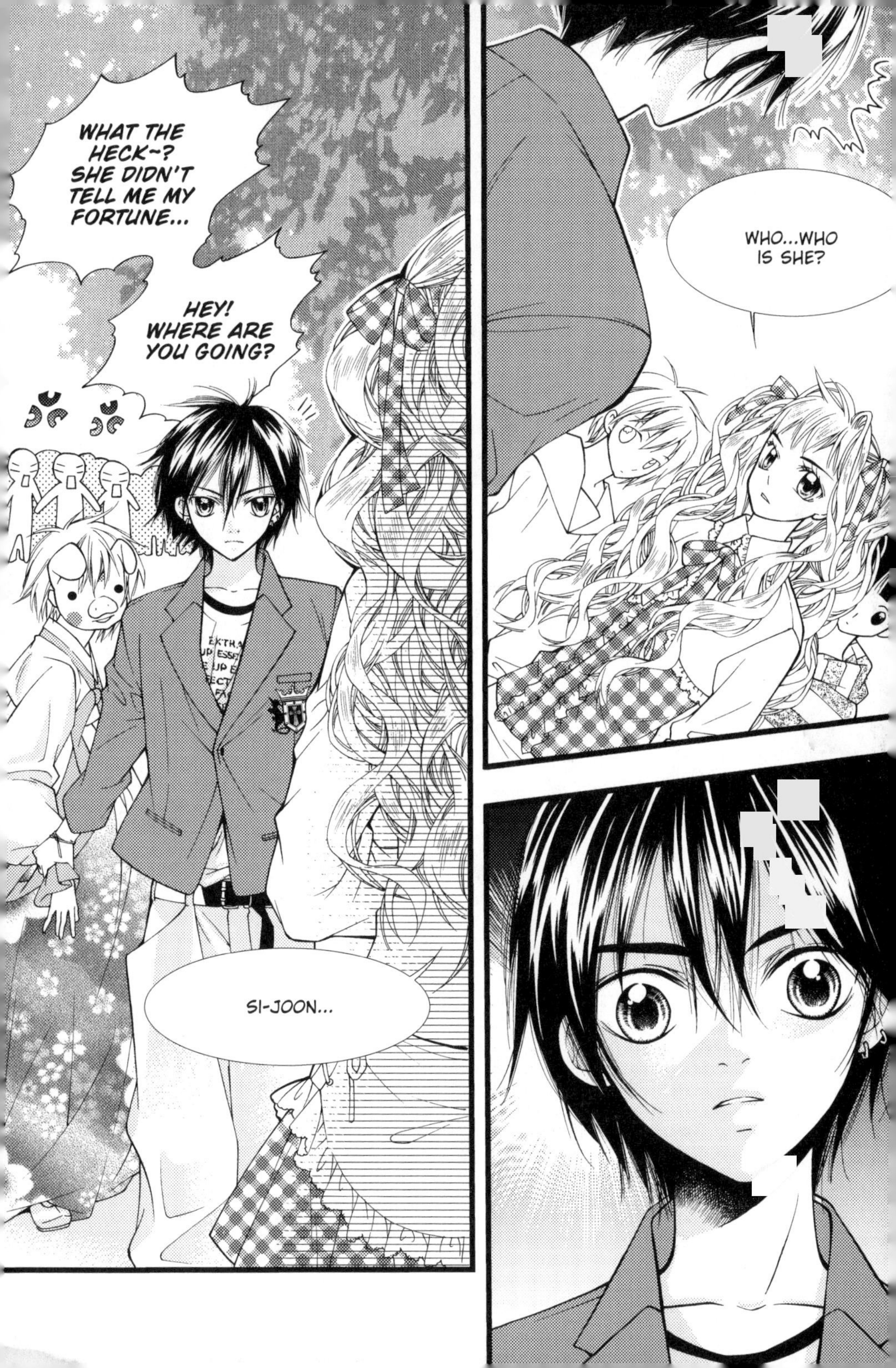
WHAT THE HECK~? SHE DIDN'T TELL ME MY FORTUNE...
HEY! WHERE ARE YOU GOING?
SI-JOON...
WHO...WHO IS SHE?

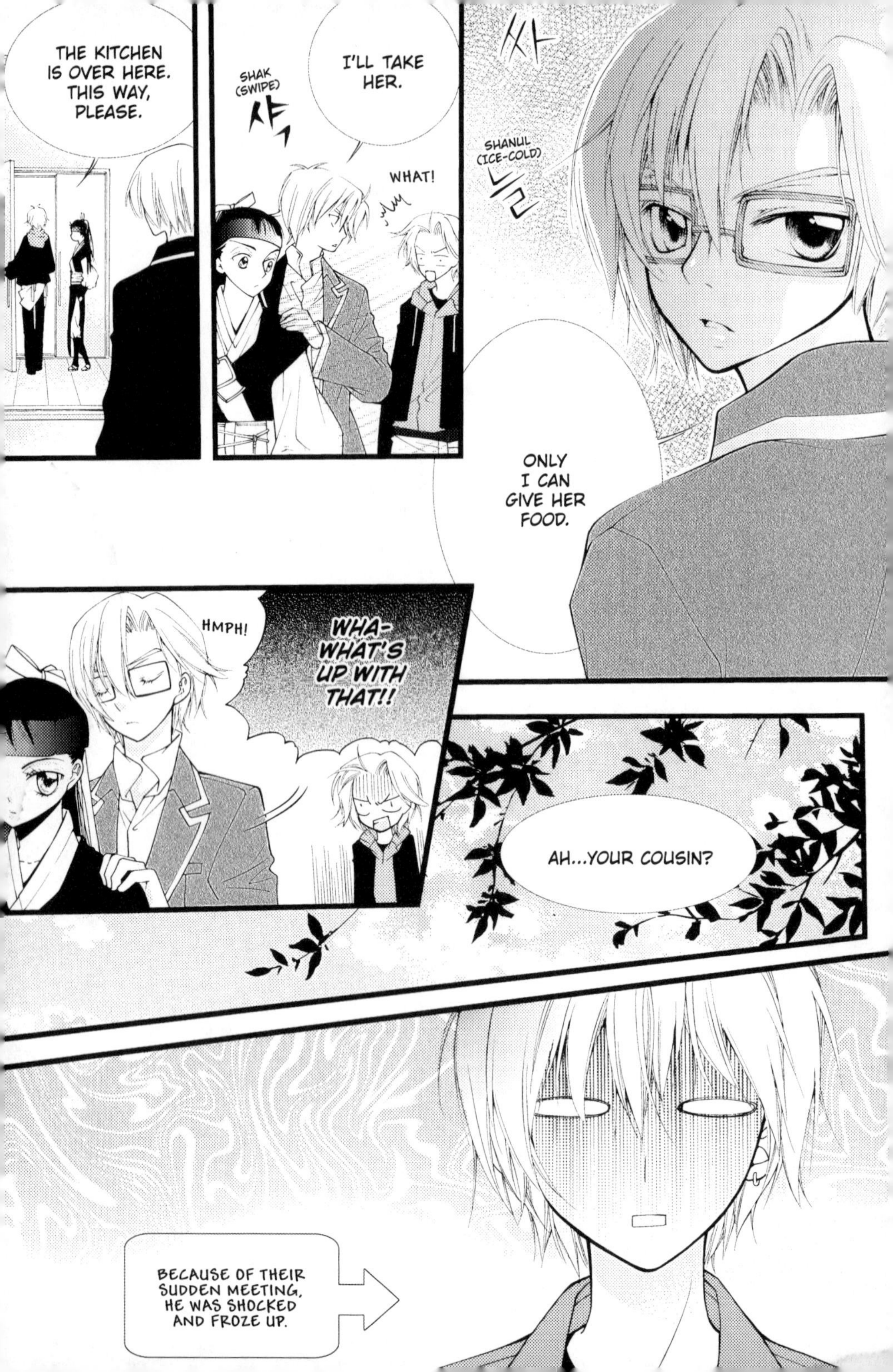
THE KITCHEN IS OVER HERE. THIS WAY, PLEASE.
SHAK (SWIPE)
I'LL TAKE HER.
WHAT!
SHANUL (ICE-COLD)
ONLY I CAN GIVE HER FOOD.
HMPH!
WHA- WHAT'S UP WITH THAT!!
AH...YOUR COUSIN?
BECAUSE OF THEIR SUDDEN MEETING, HE WAS SHOCKED AND FROZE UP.

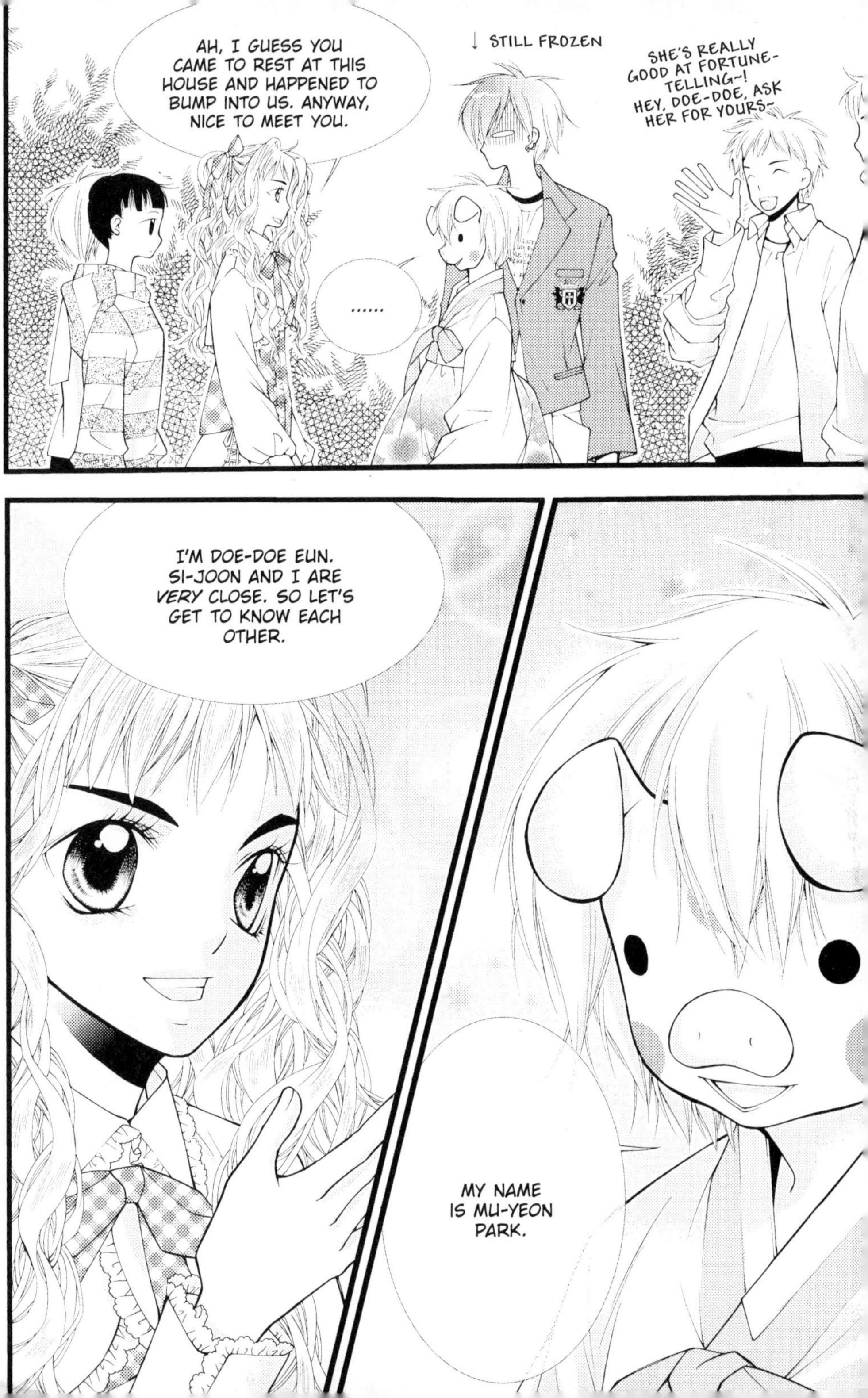
AH, I GUESS YOU CAME TO REST AT THIS HOUSE AND HAPPENED TO BUMP INTO US. ANYWAY, NICE TO MEET YOU.
......
↓ STILL FROZEN
SHE'S REALLY GOOD AT FORTUNE-TELLING~! HEY, DOE-DOE, ASK HER FOR YOURS~
I'M DOE-DOE EUN. SI-JOON AND I ARE VERY CLOSE. SO LET'S GET TO KNOW EACH OTHER.
MY NAME IS MU-YEON PARK.

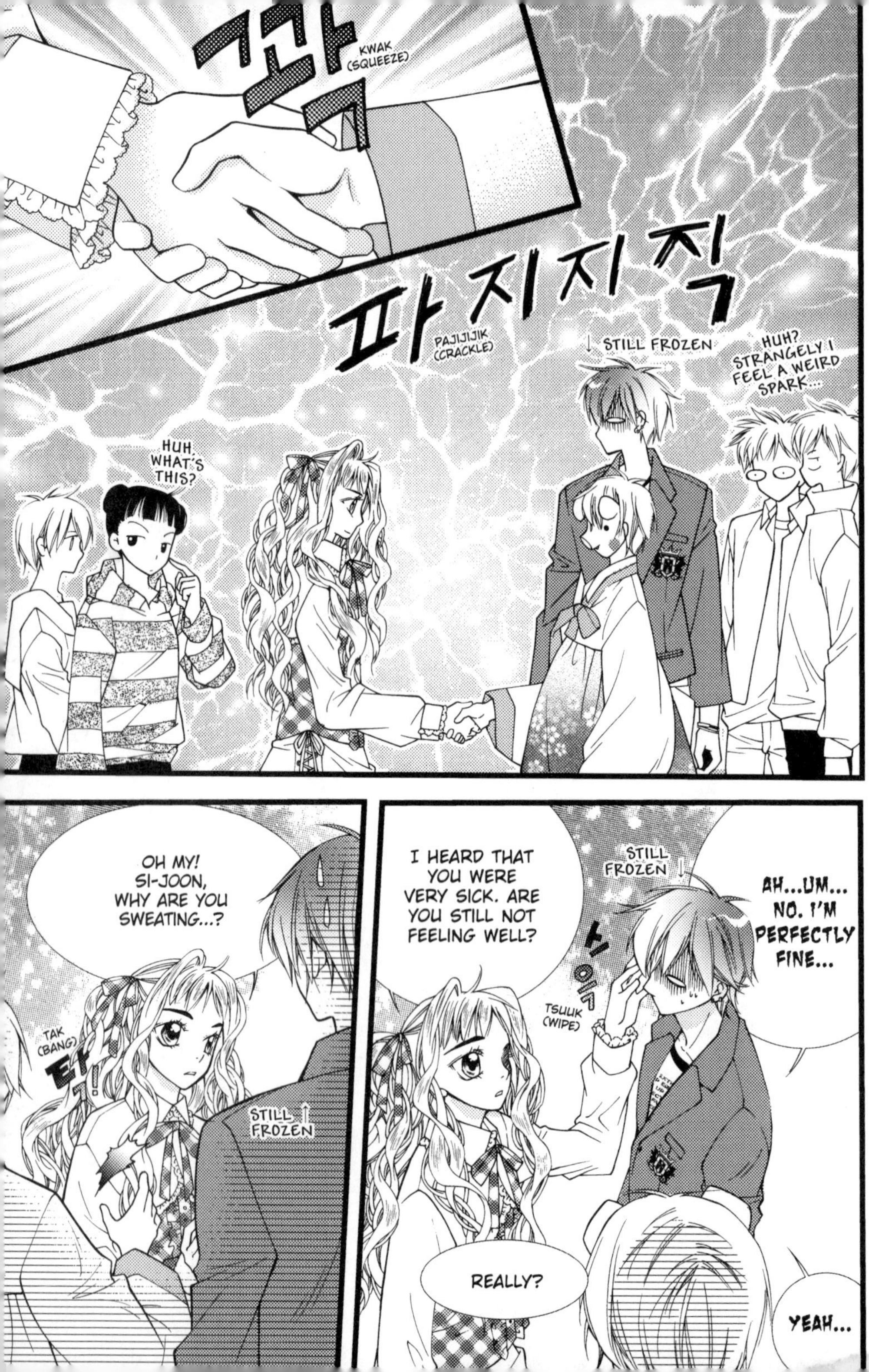

꽉
KWAK (SQUEEZE)
파지지직
PAJIJIJIK (CRACKLE)
HUH WHAT'S THIS?
↓ STILL FROZEN
HUH? STRANGELY I FEEL A WEIRD SPARK...
OH MY! SI-JOON, WHY ARE YOU SWEATING...?
TAK (BANG)
탁
STILL ↑ FROZEN
I HEARD THAT YOU WERE VERY SICK. ARE YOU STILL NOT FEELING WELL?
STILL FROZEN ↓
스윽
TSUUK (WIPE)
AH...UM... NO. I'M PERFECTLY FINE...
REALLY?
YEAH...

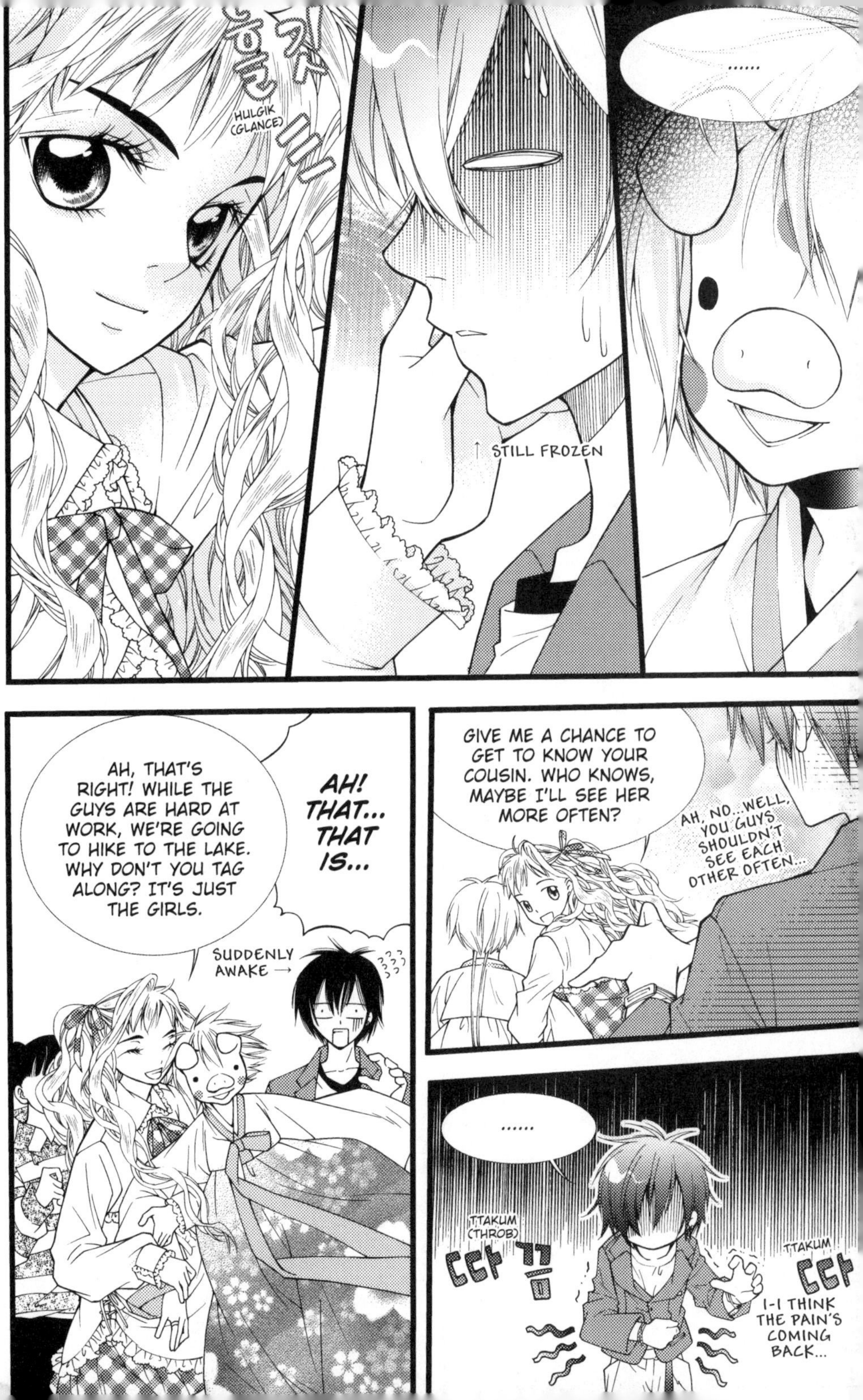
흘깃
HULGIK (GLANCE)
↑ STILL FROZEN
......
AH, THAT'S RIGHT! WHILE THE GUYS ARE HARD AT WORK, WE'RE GOING TO HIKE TO THE LAKE. WHY DON'T YOU TAG ALONG? IT'S JUST THE GIRLS.
AH! THAT... THAT IS...
SUDDENLY AWAKE →
GIVE ME A CHANCE TO GET TO KNOW YOUR COUSIN. WHO KNOWS, MAYBE I'LL SEE HER MORE OFTEN?
AH, NO...WELL, YOU GUYS SHOULDN'T SEE EACH OTHER OFTEN...
......
TTAKUM (THROB)
따끔
TTAKUM
따
I-I THINK THE PAIN'S COMING BACK...

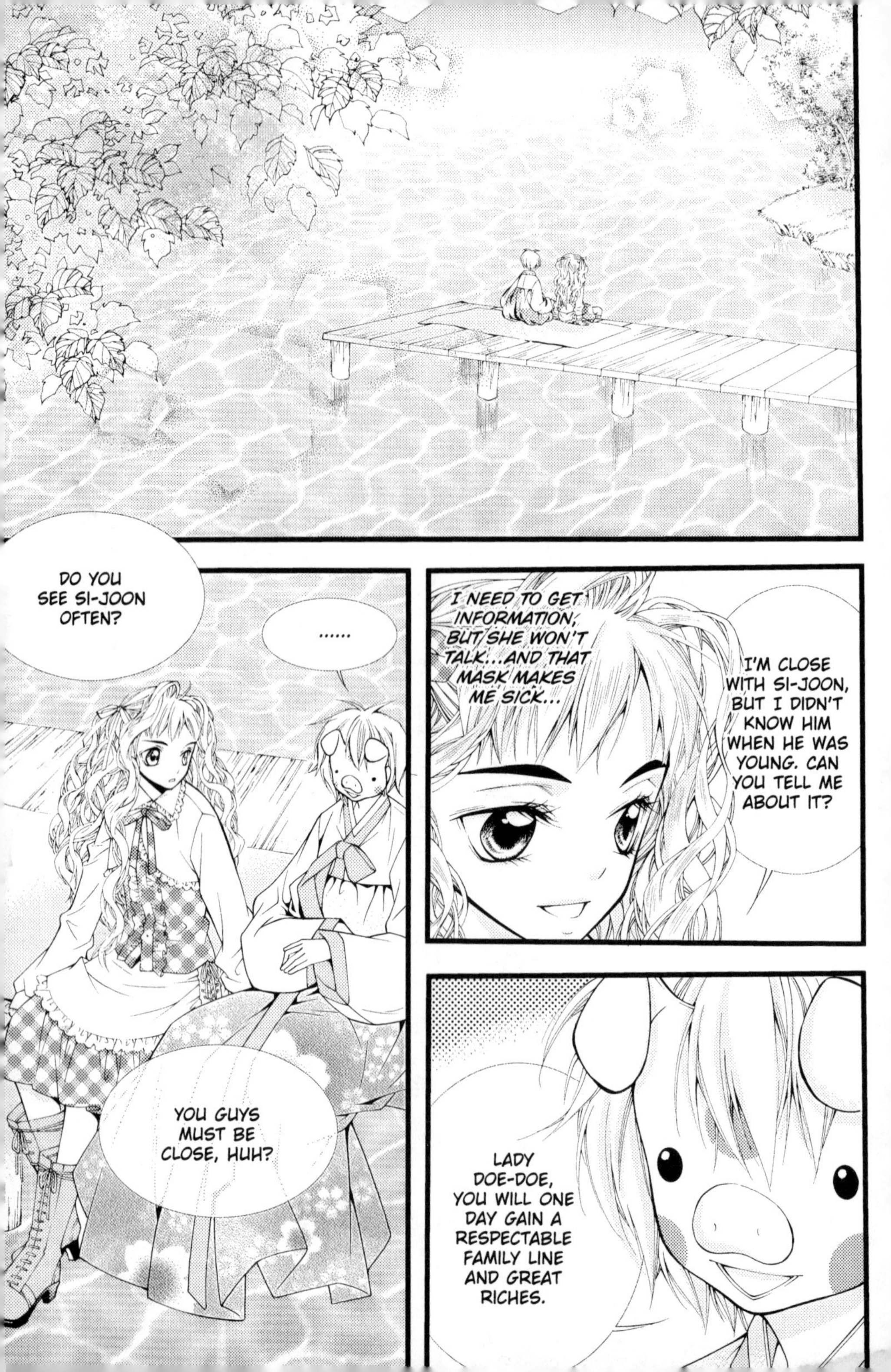
DO YOU SEE SI-JOON OFTEN?
......
YOU GUYS MUST BE CLOSE, HUH?
I NEED TO GET INFORMATION, BUT SHE WON'T TALK...AND THAT MASK MAKES ME SICK...
I'M CLOSE WITH SI-JOON, BUT I DIDN'T KNOW HIM WHEN HE WAS YOUNG. CAN YOU TELL ME ABOUT IT?
LADY DOE-DOE, YOU WILL ONE DAY GAIN A RESPECTABLE FAMILY LINE AND GREAT RICHES.

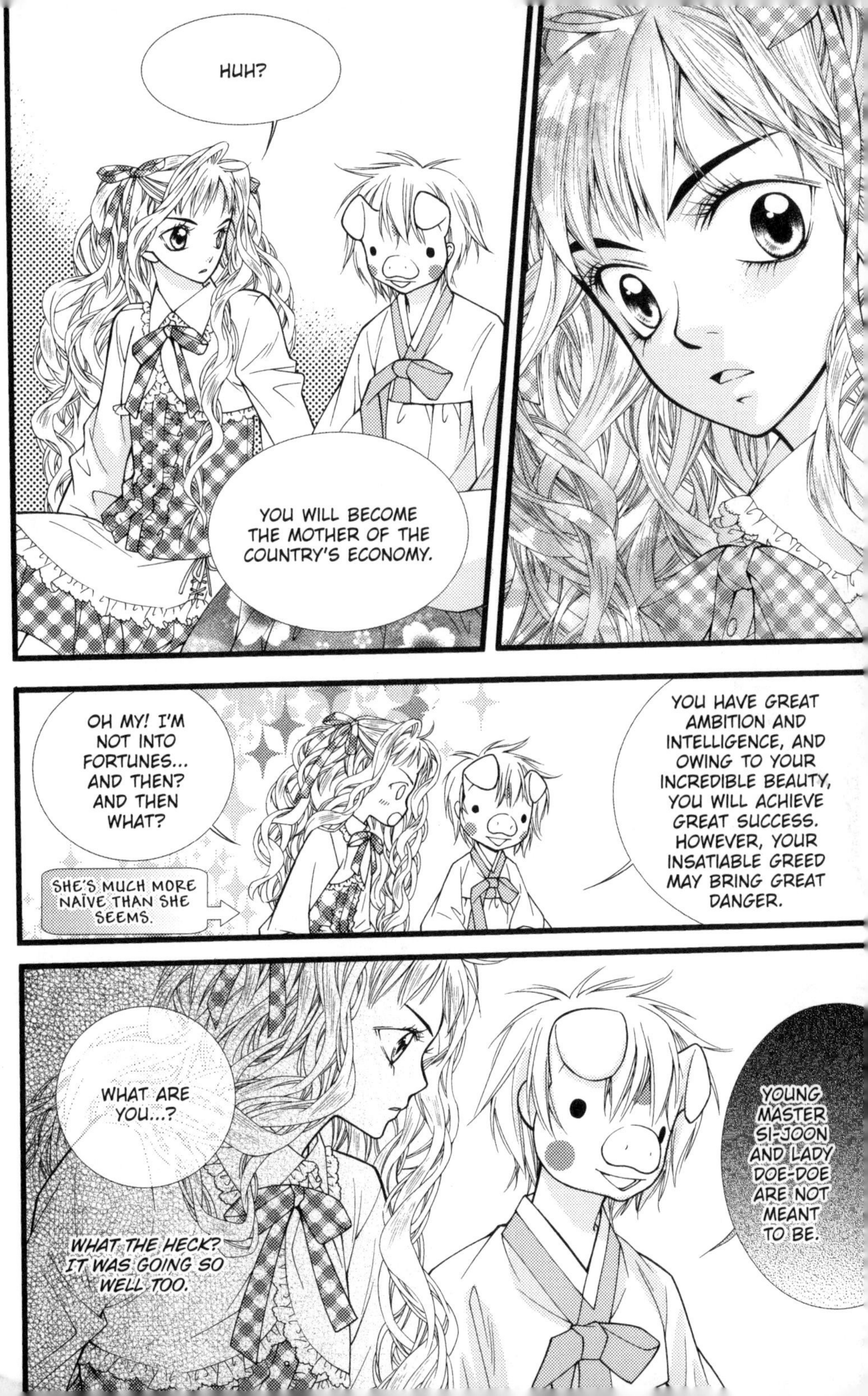
HUH?
YOU WILL BECOME THE MOTHER OF THE COUNTRY'S ECONOMY.
OH MY! I'M NOT INTO FORTUNES... AND THEN? AND THEN WHAT?
SHE'S MUCH MORE NAÏVE THAN SHE SEEMS.
YOU HAVE GREAT AMBITION AND INTELLIGENCE, AND OWING TO YOUR INCREDIBLE BEAUTY, YOU WILL ACHIEVE GREAT SUCCESS. HOWEVER, YOUR INSATIABLE GREED MAY BRING GREAT DANGER.
WHAT ARE YOU...?
WHAT THE HECK? IT WAS GOING SO WELL TOO.
YOUNG MASTER SI-JOON AND LADY DOE-DOE ARE NOT MEANT TO BE.

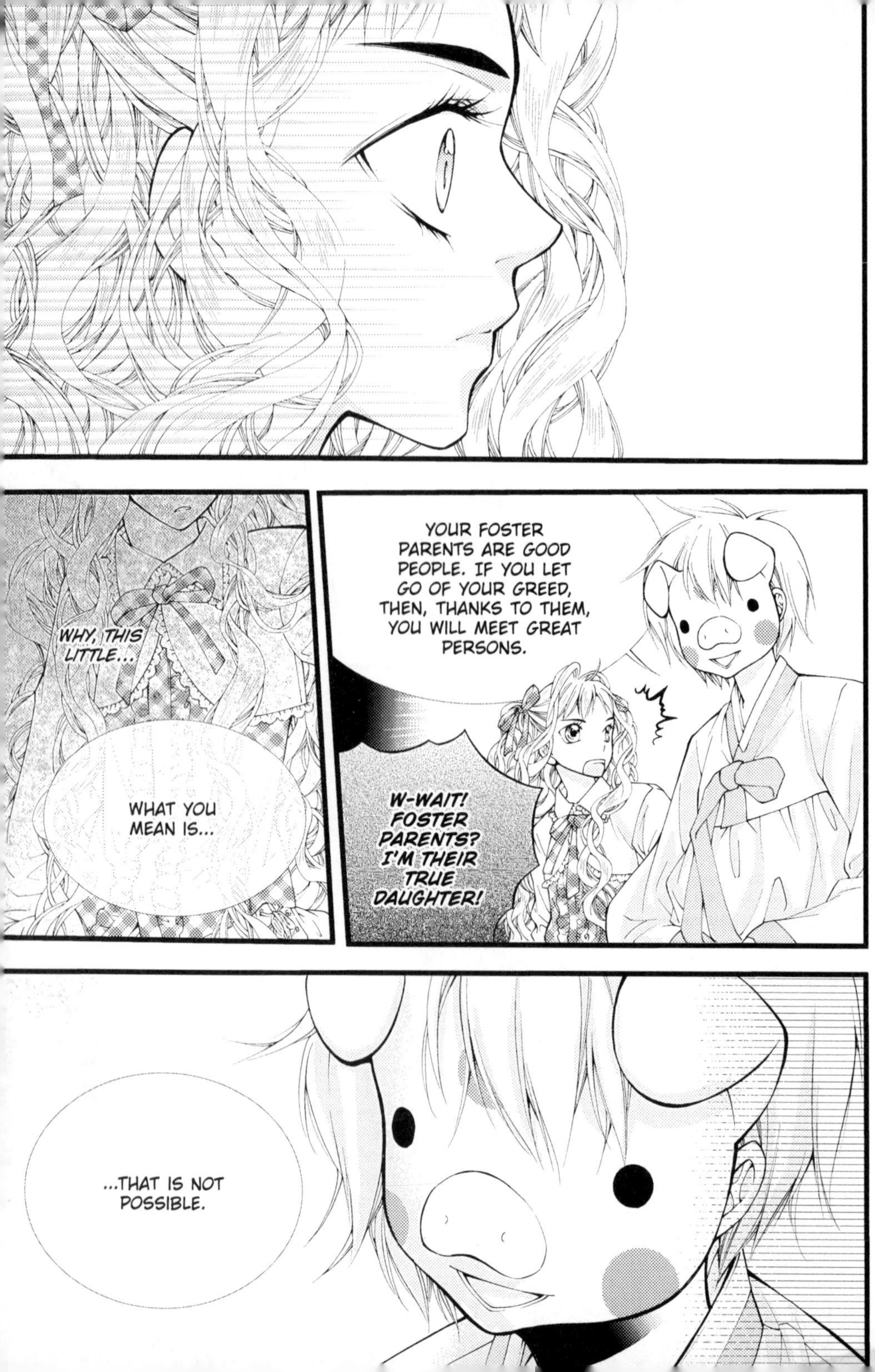
WHY, THIS LITTLE...
WHAT YOU MEAN IS...
YOUR FOSTER PARENTS ARE GOOD PEOPLE. IF YOU LET GO OF YOUR GREED, THEN, THANKS TO THEM, YOU WILL MEET GREAT PERSONS.
W-WAIT! FOSTER PARENTS? I'M THEIR TRUE DAUGHTER!
...THAT IS NOT POSSIBLE.

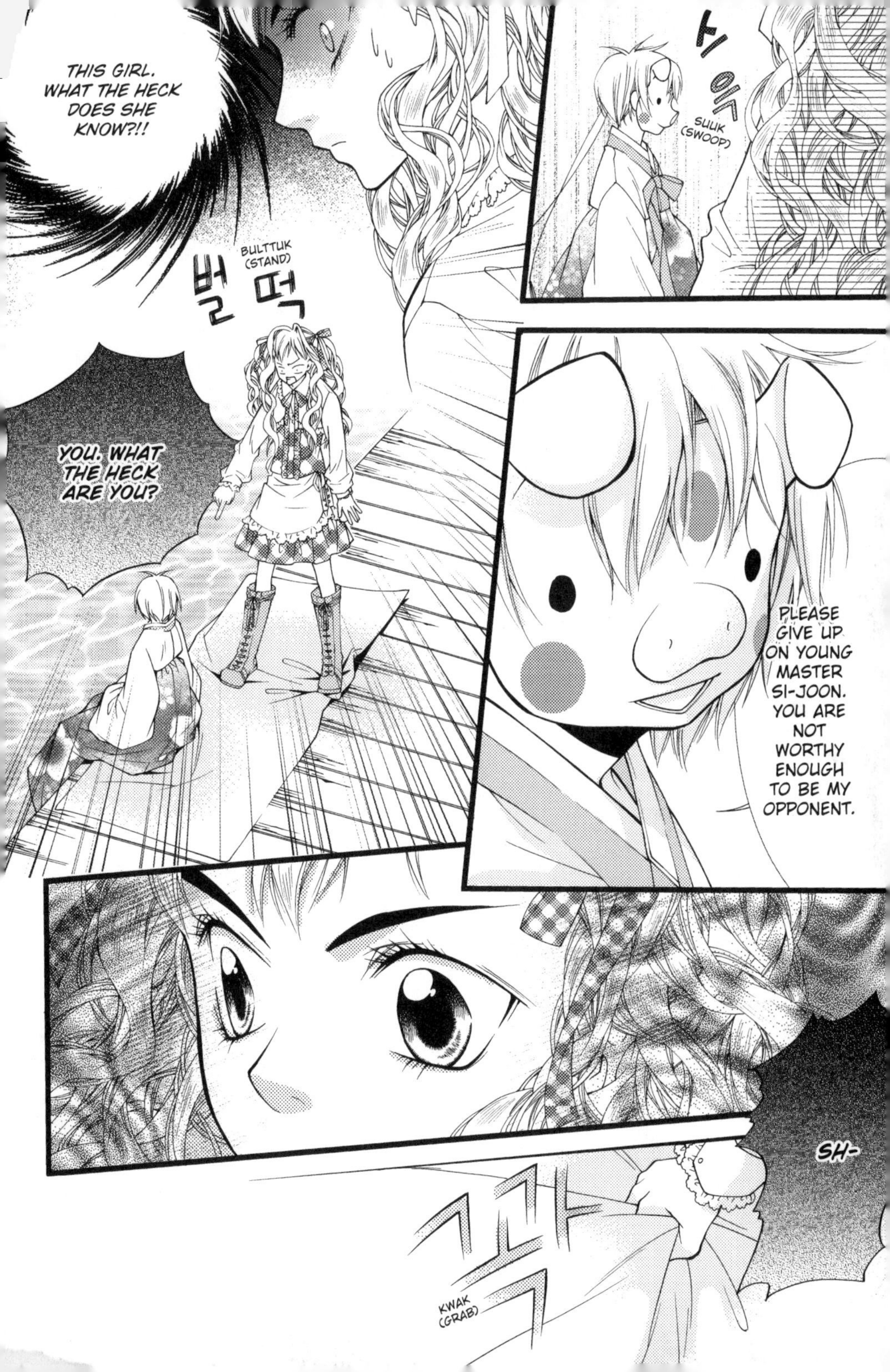

THIS GIRL. WHAT THE HECK DOES SHE KNOW?!!
SUUK (SWOOP)
벌떡
BULTTUK (STAND)
YOU. WHAT THE HECK ARE YOU?
PLEASE GIVE UP ON YOUNG MASTER SI-JOON. YOU ARE NOT WORTHY ENOUGH TO BE MY OPPONENT.
SH-
꽉
KWAK (GRAB)

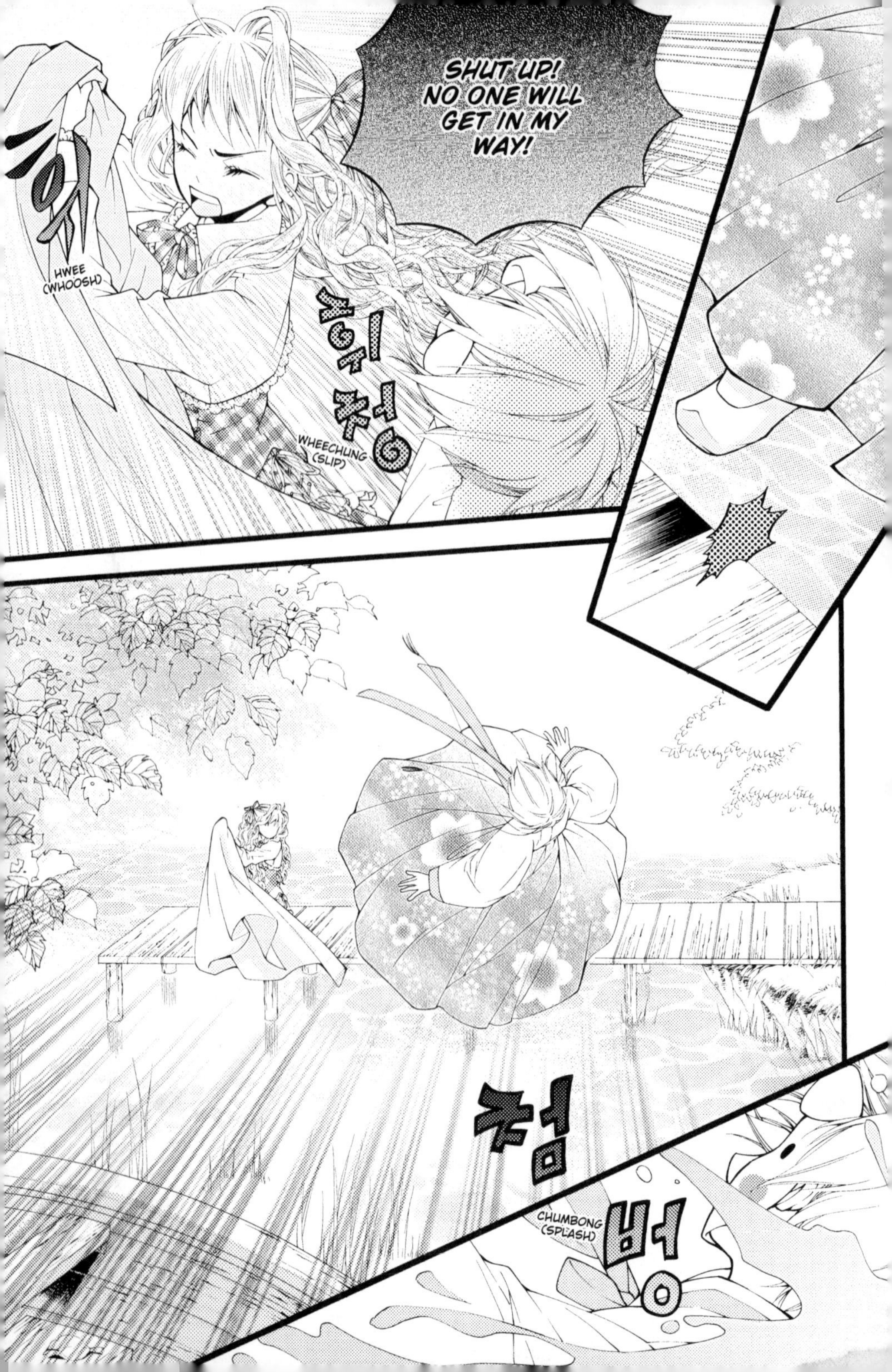

휘
HWEE (WHOOSH)
SHUT UP! NO ONE WILL GET IN MY WAY!
휘청
WHEECHUNG (SLIP)
첨벙
CHUMBONG (SPLASH)

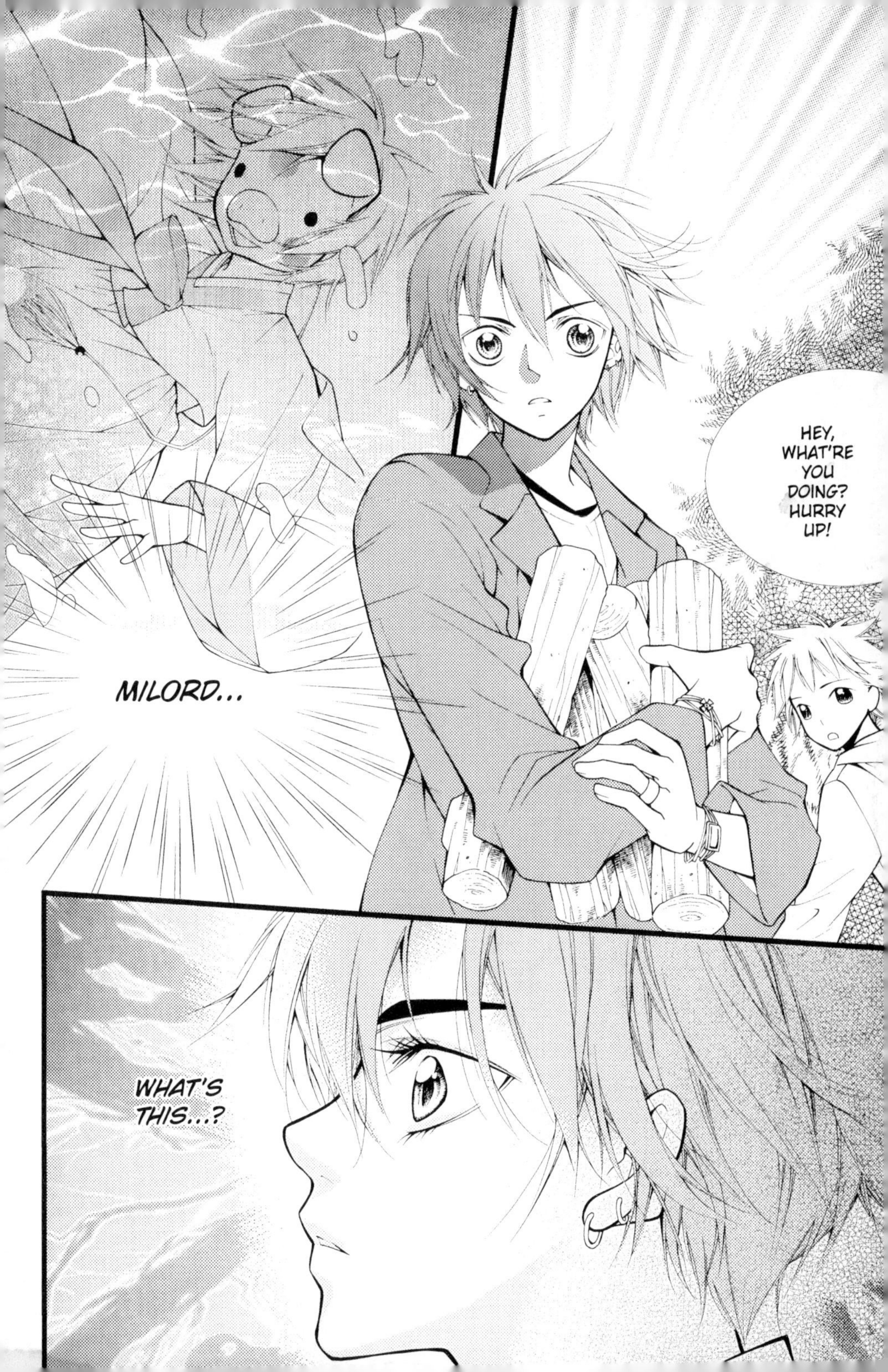
MILORD...
HEY, WHAT'RE YOU DOING? HURRY UP!
WHAT'S THIS...?

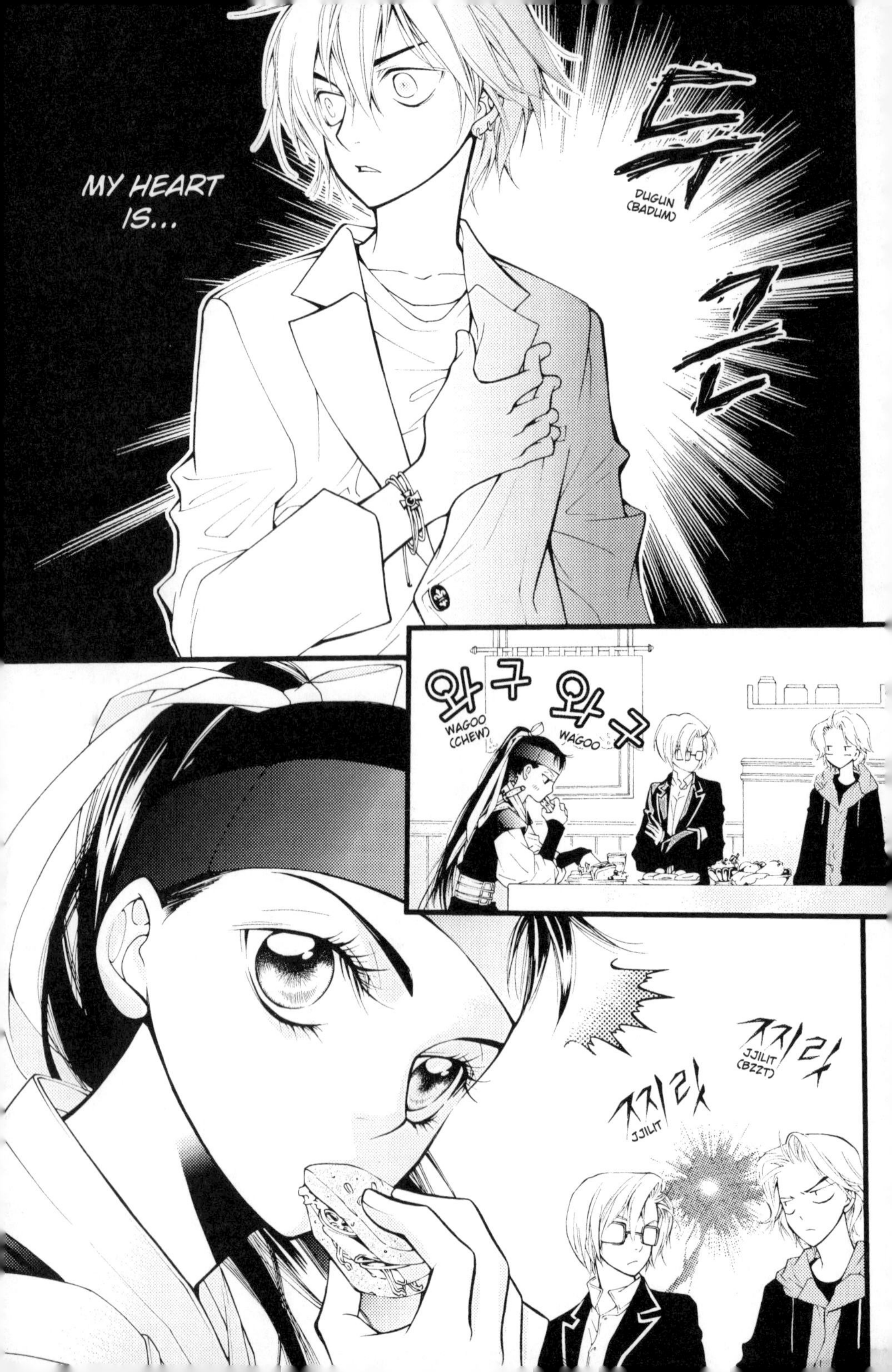
MY HEART IS...
DUGUN (BADUM)
JJILIT (BZZT)
JJILIT
와구
WAGOO (CHEW)
와구
WAGOO

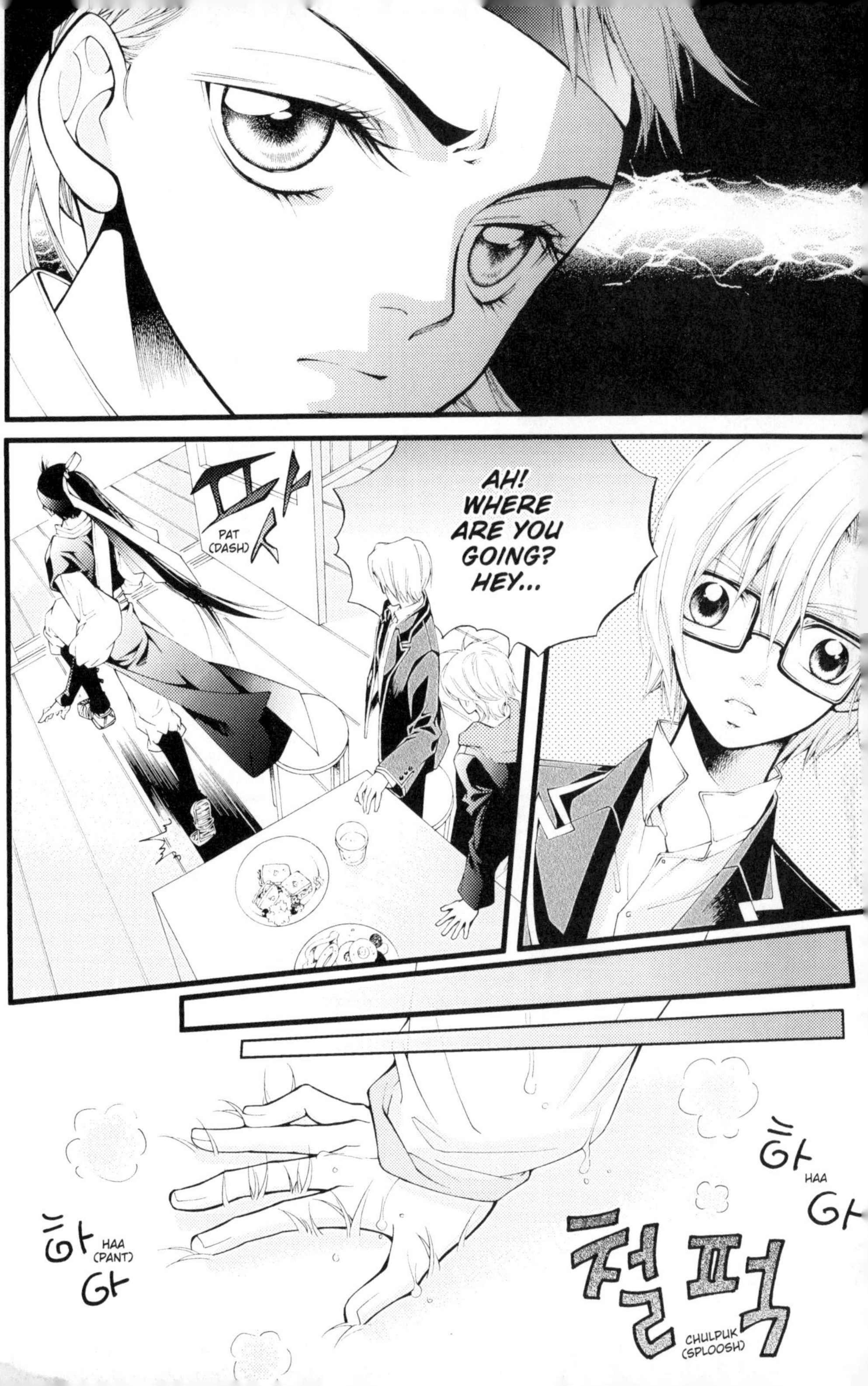
파닥
PAT (DASH)
AH! WHERE ARE YOU GOING? HEY...
하아
HAA (PANT)
하아
HAA
철퍽
CHULPUK (SPLOOSH)

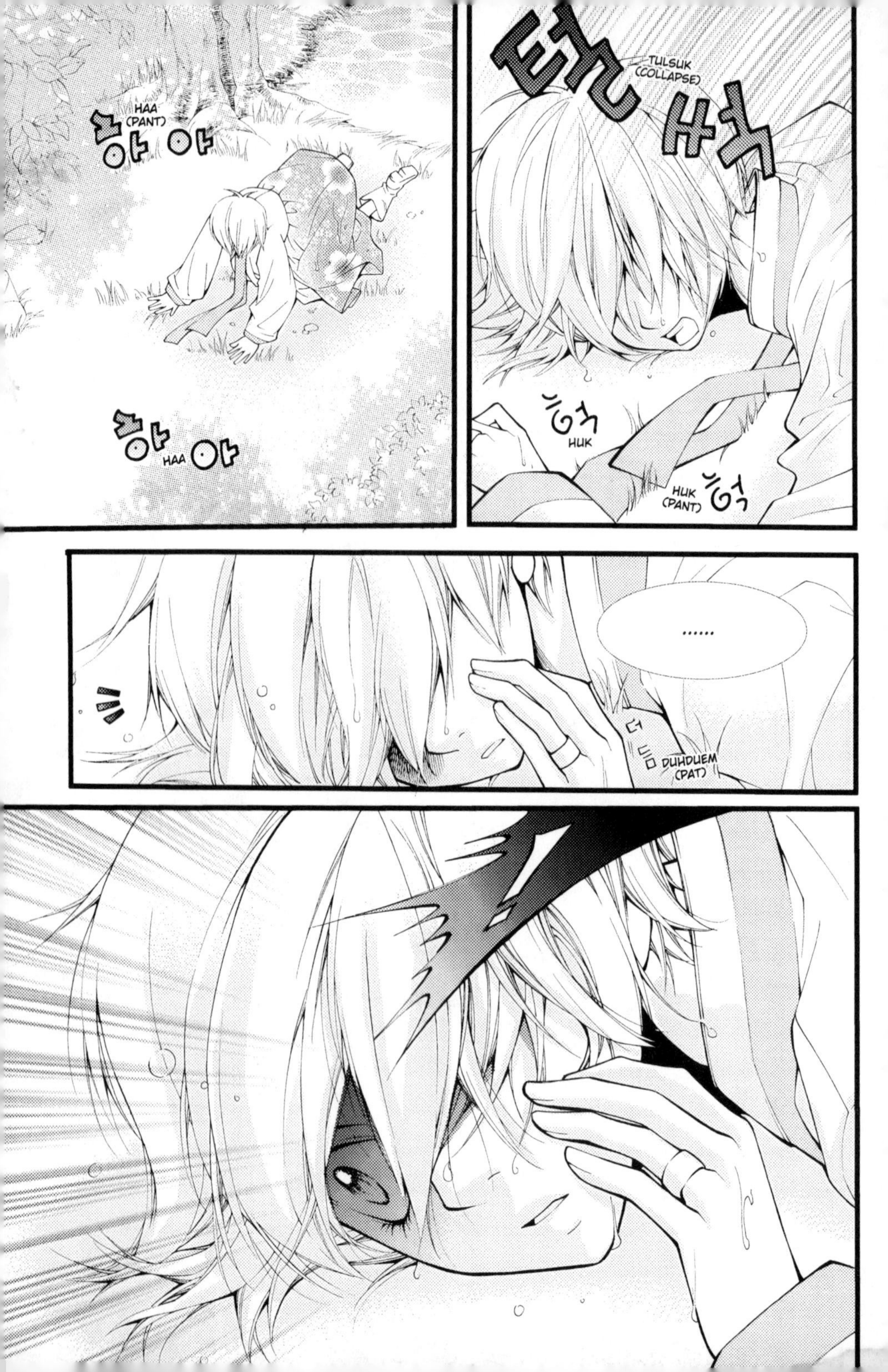

하아
HAA (PANT)
하아
HAA
털썩
TULSUK (COLLAPSE)
헉
HUK
헉
HUK (PANT)
......
더듬
DUHDUEM (PAT)

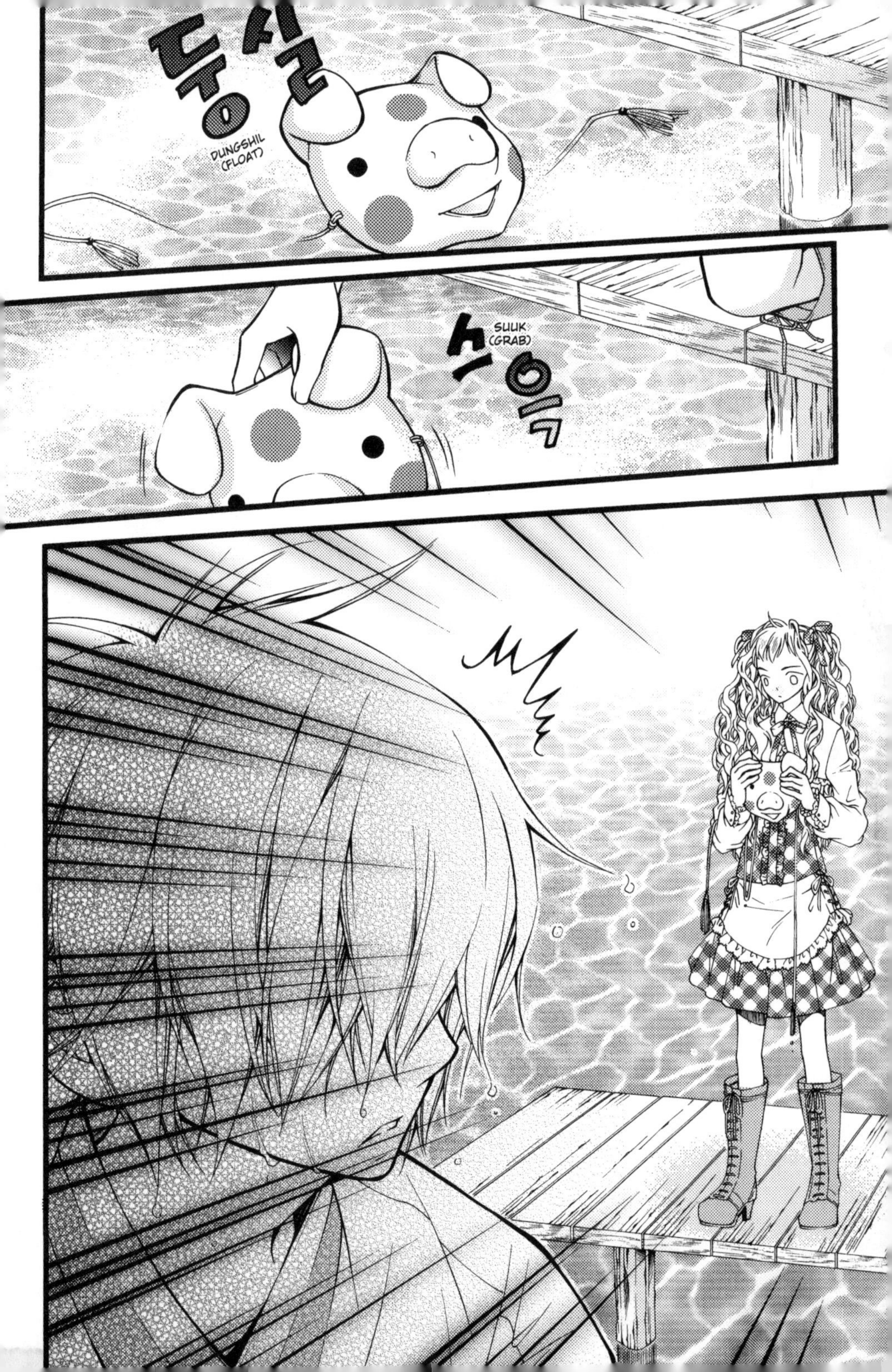

둥실
DUNGSHIL
(FLOAT)
SUUK
(GRAB)

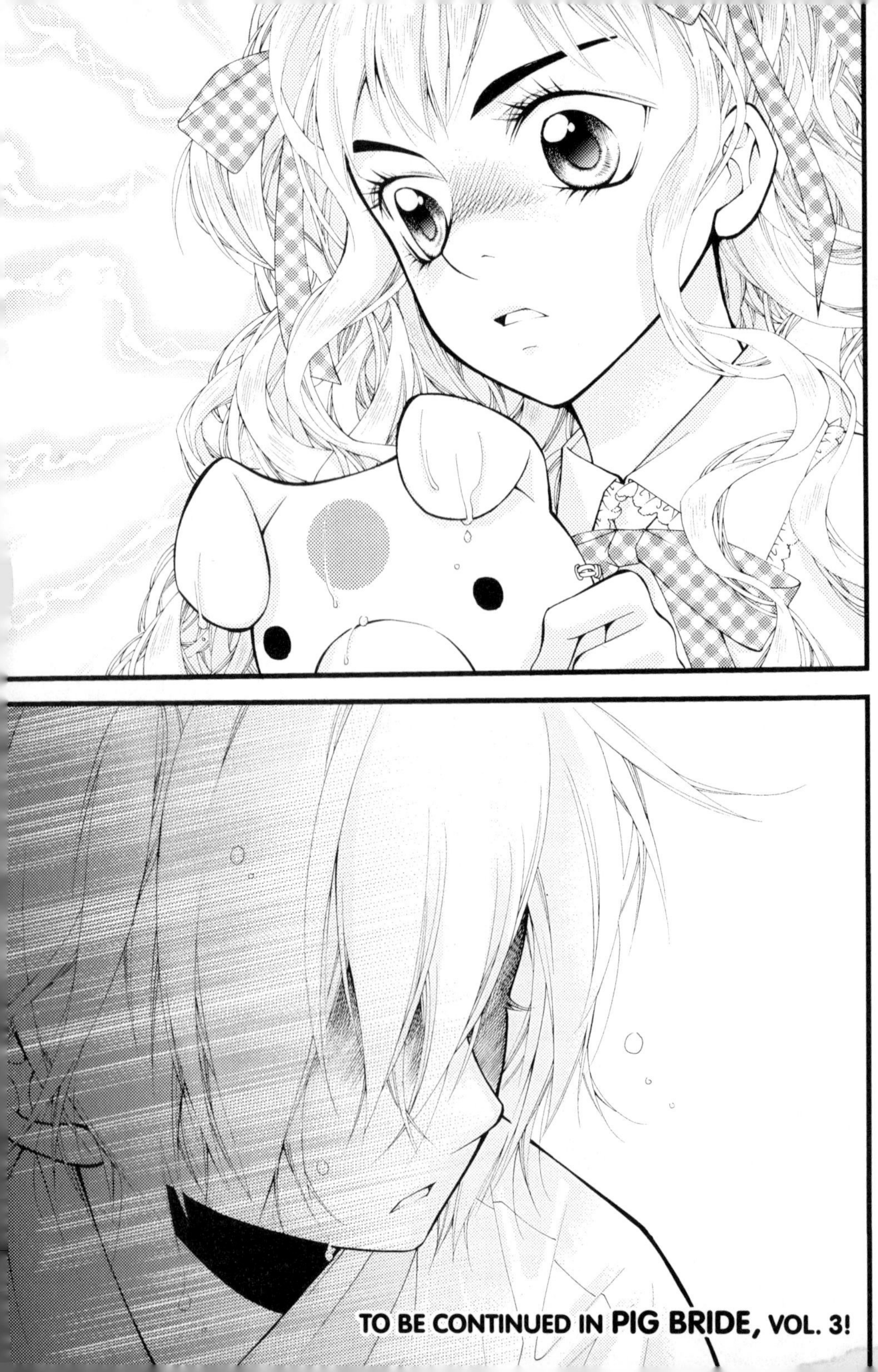
TO BE CONTINUED IN PIG BRIDE, VOL. 3!

TRANSLATION NOTES

Page 25
Bang-Ge is a common servant's name.

Page 49
Board Jumping:
One of many traditional games played by women during New Years.

Page 56
Hang-Ma:
Literally means "Conquest of Devil"

Page 86
Hanbok:
The traditional Korean clothes that Mu-Yeon wears.

Page 92
"I know that pigs and snakes are mortal enemies..."
Si-Joon is referring to those two signs in the Chinese Zodiac, which are opposite one another.

Page 128
Cho-yeong-dam:
Autumn Bellflower (Gentiana scabra var. buergeri). The root is often used as medicine in Asia.

LOOK FOR MORE *PIG BRIDE* IN

A MONTHLY MANGA ANTHOLOGY
FROM YEN PRESS!

SEE
YOU NEXT
TIME! ♥

SNEAK PREVIEW
Volume 3

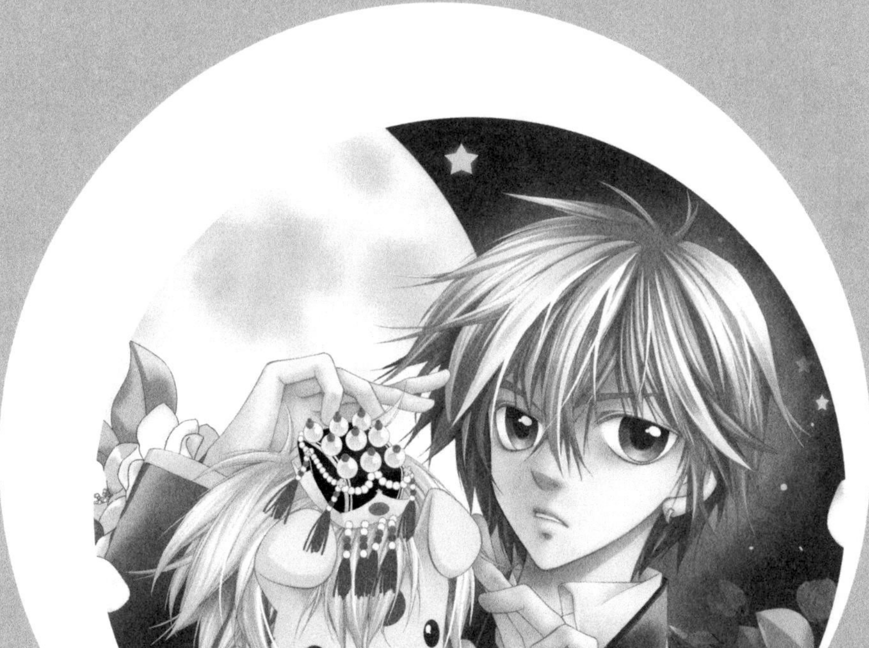

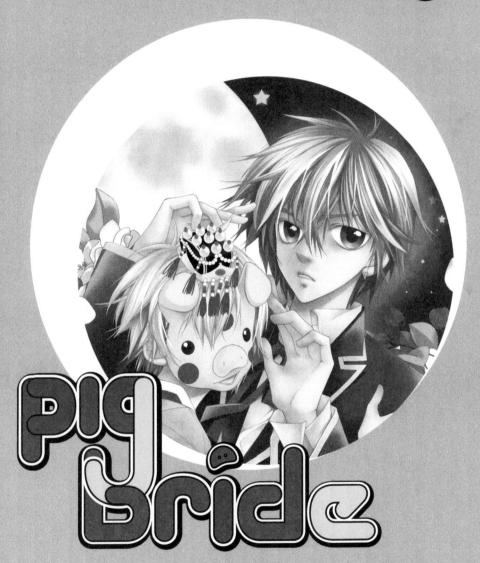

Pig Bride

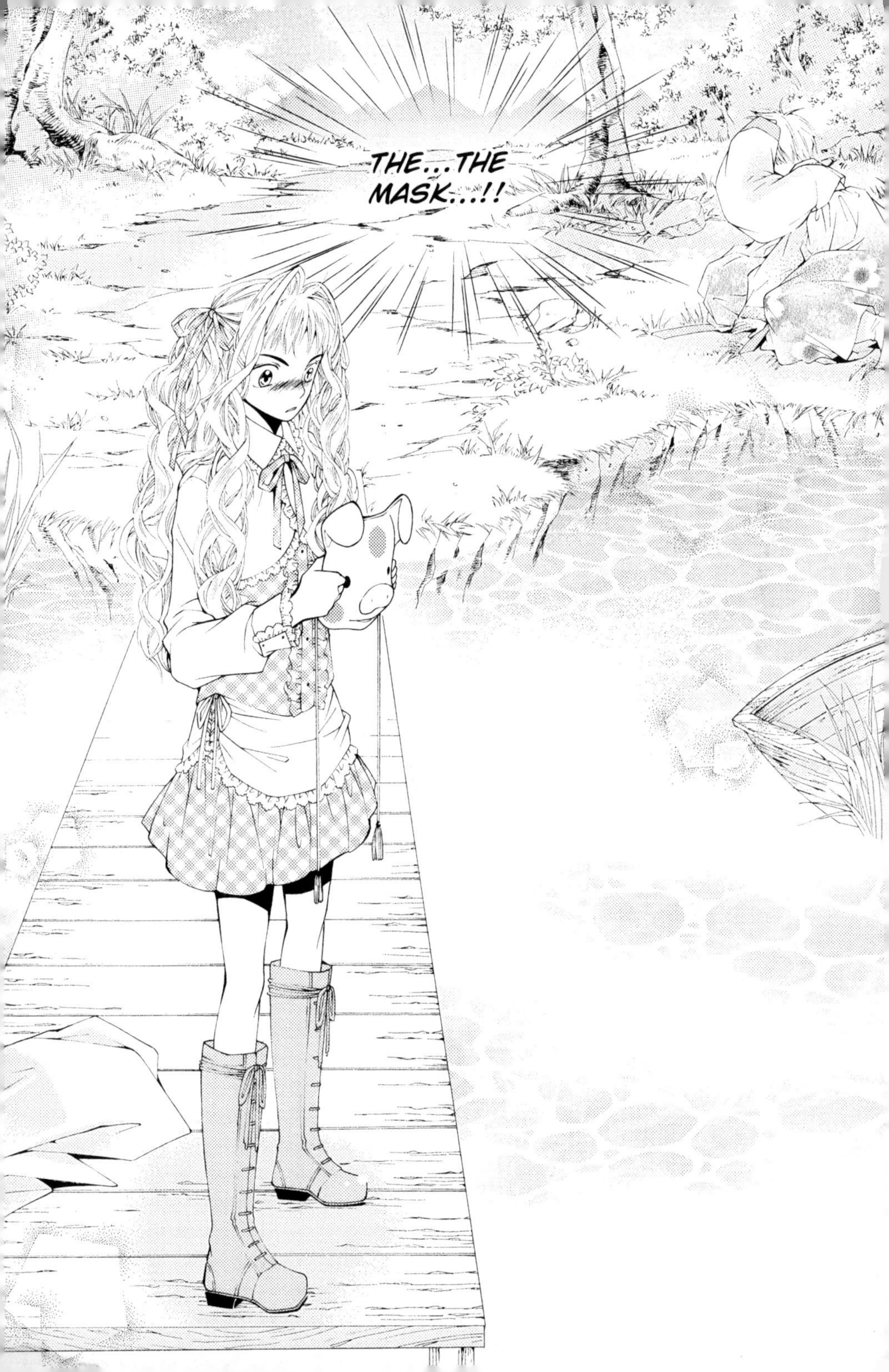
THE...THE MASK...!!

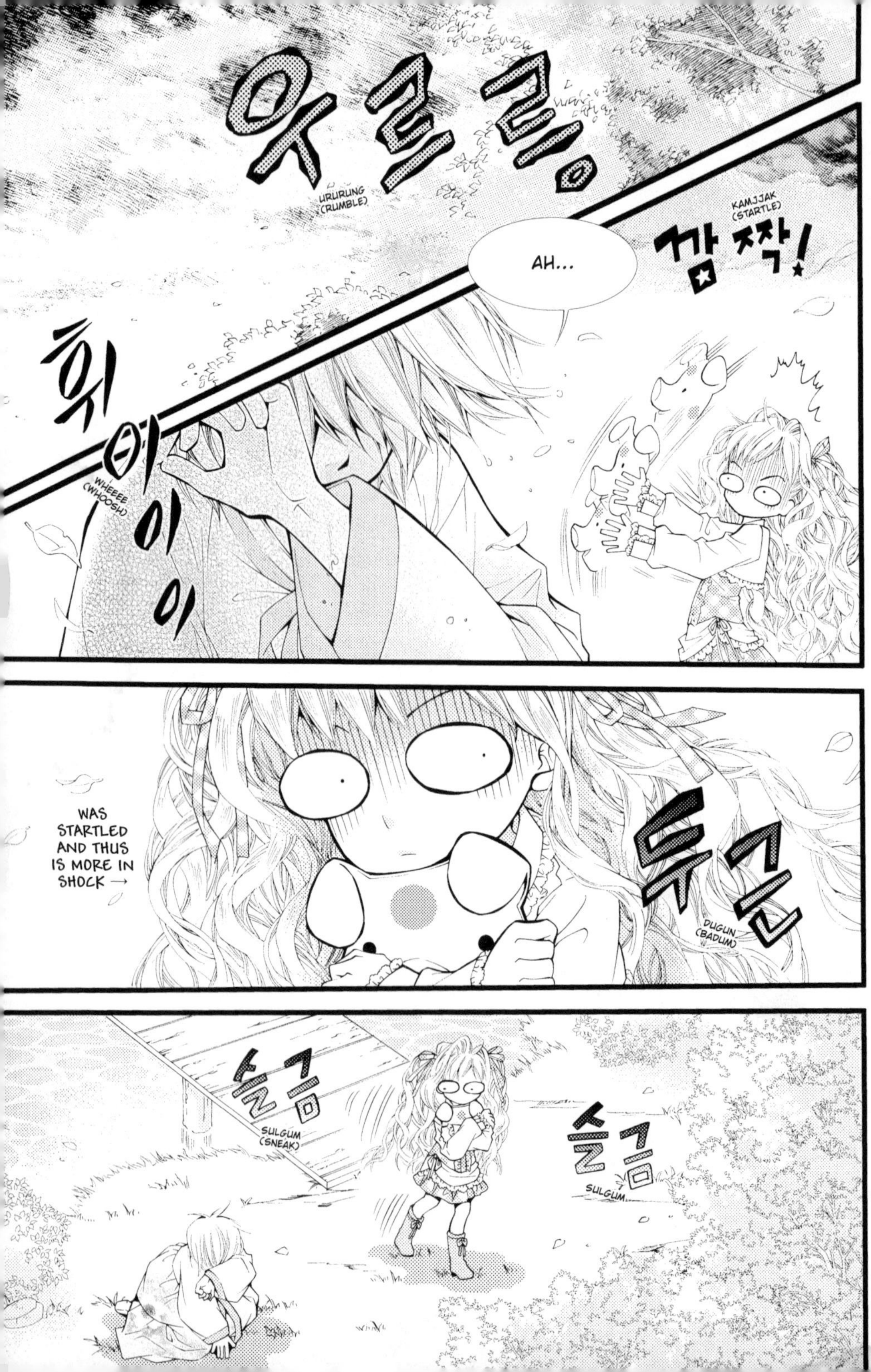

우르릉
URURUNG (RUMBLE)
WHEEEE (WHOOSH)
AH...
깜짝!
KAMJJAK (STARTLE)
WAS STARTLED AND THUS IS MORE IN SHOCK →
두근
DUGUN (BADUM)
슬금
SULGUM (SNEAK)
슬금
SULGUM

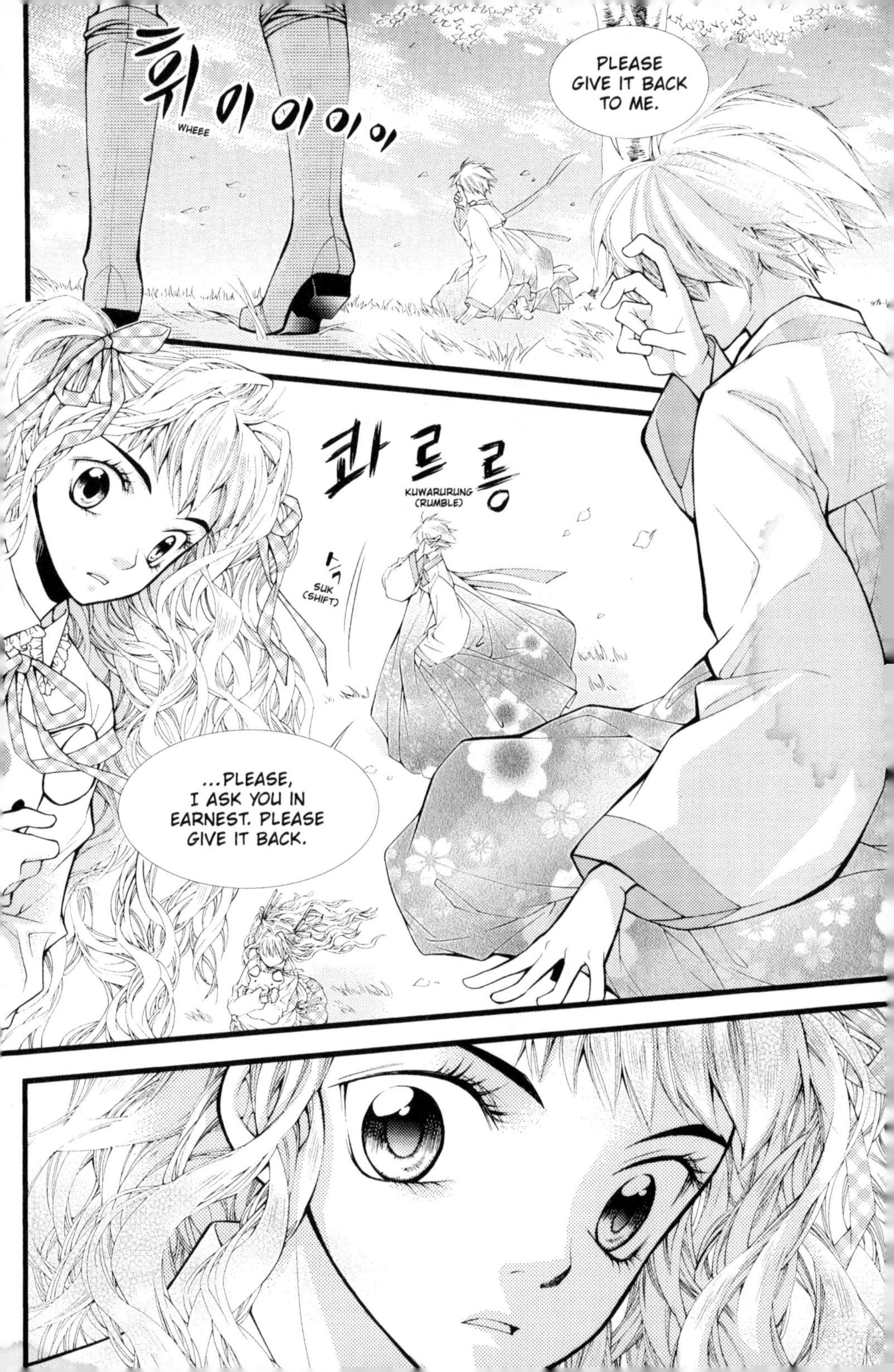
휘이이이이
WHEEE
PLEASE GIVE IT BACK TO ME.
콰르릉
KUWARURUNG (RUMBLE)
슥
SUK (SHIFT)
...PLEASE, I ASK YOU IN EARNEST. PLEASE GIVE IT BACK.

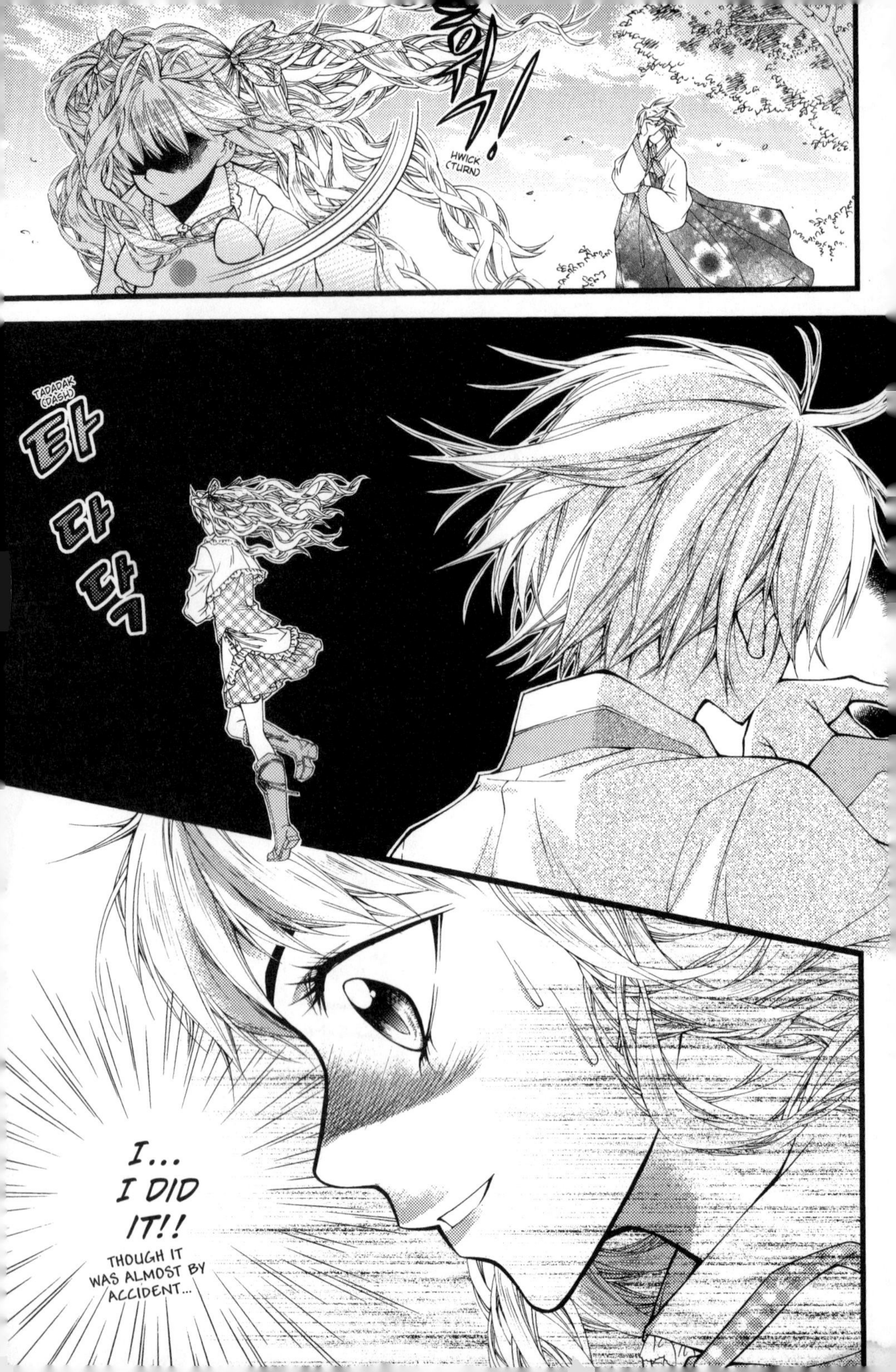
HWICK (TURN)
TADADAK (DASH)
타다닥
I... I DID IT!!
THOUGH IT WAS ALMOST BY ACCIDENT...

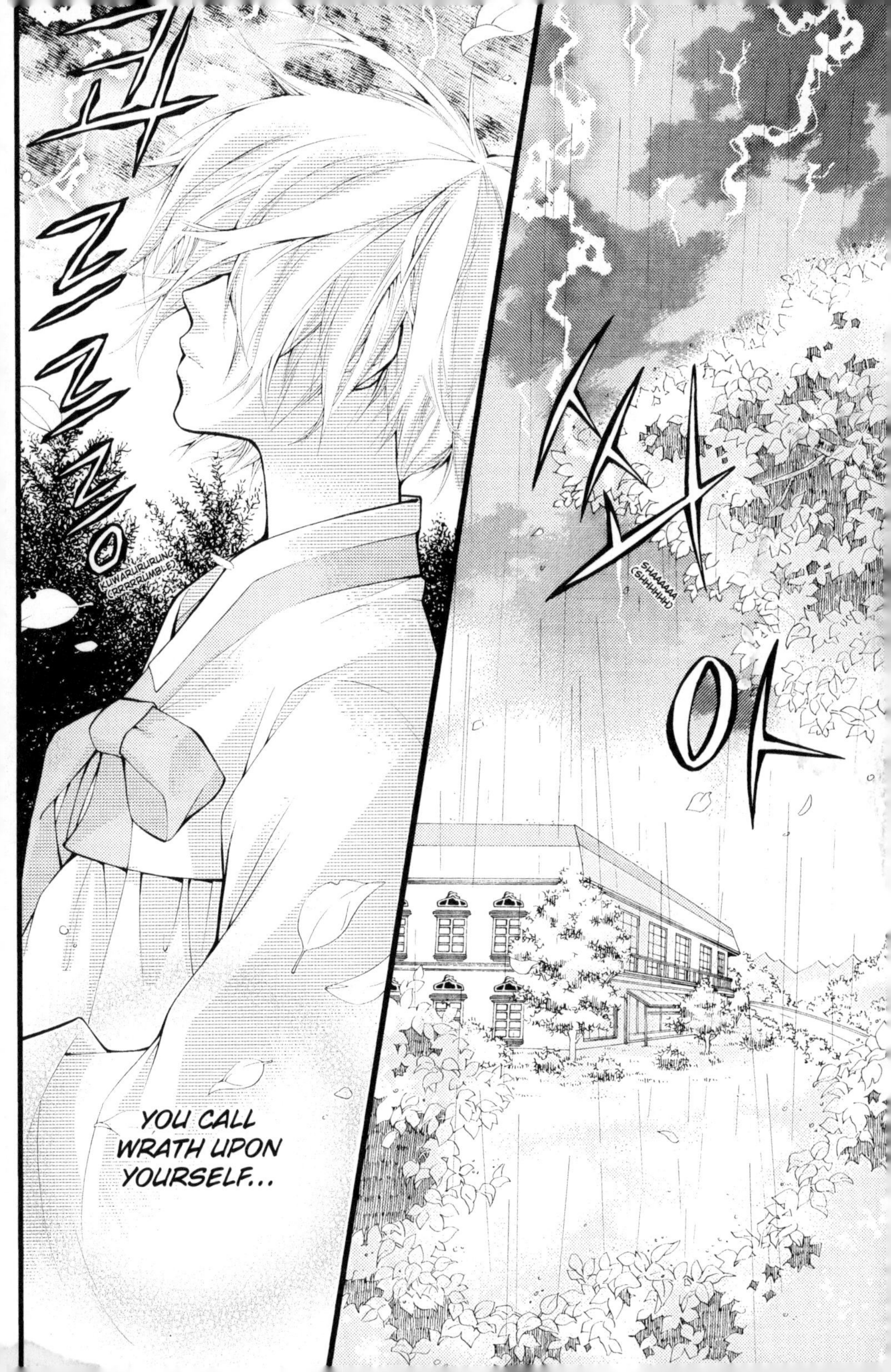
KUWARURURURUNG
(RRRRRRUMBLE)
YOU CALL WRATH UPON YOURSELF...
SHAAAAAAA
(SHHHHHH)

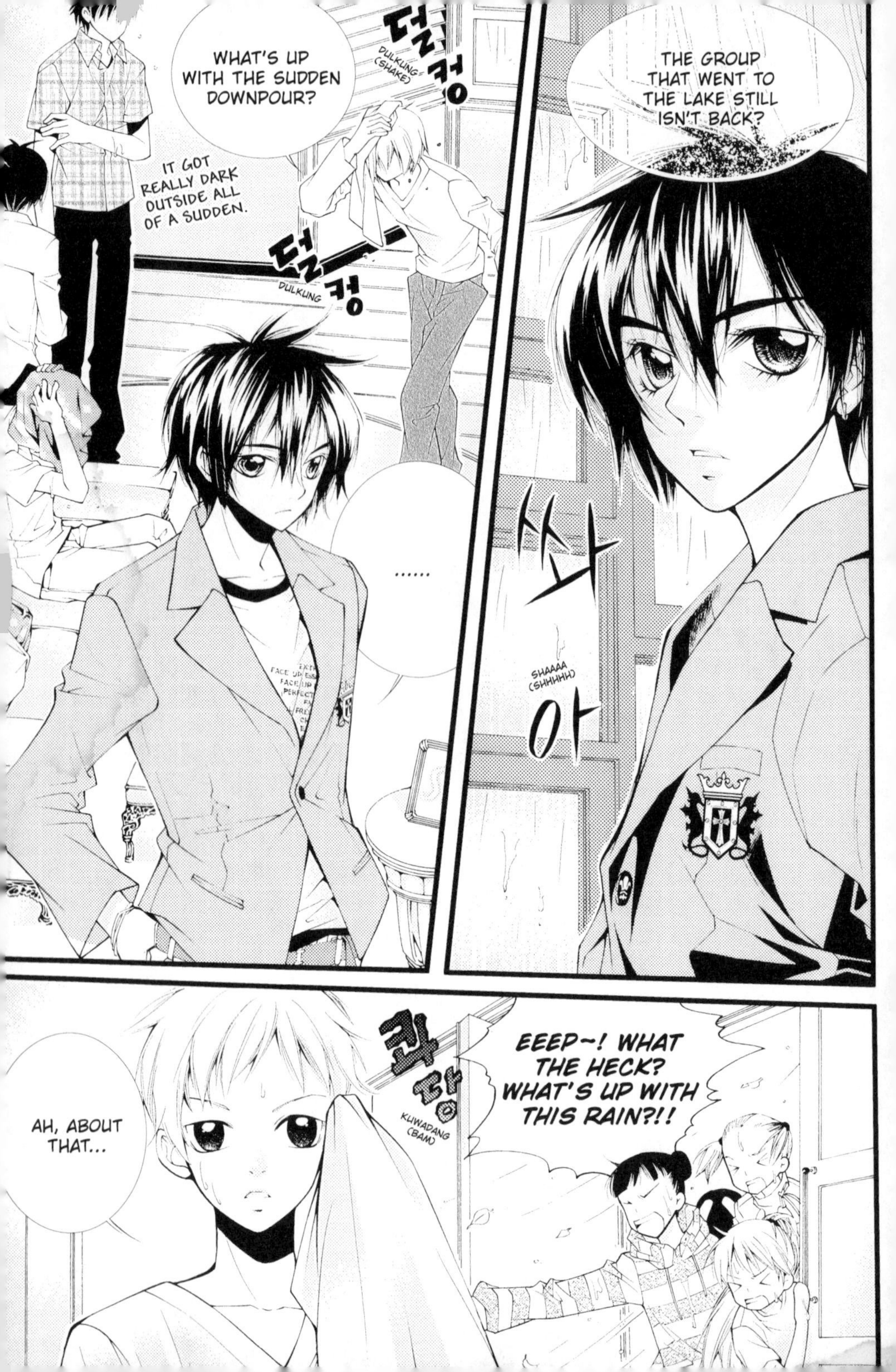
WHAT'S UP WITH THE SUDDEN DOWNPOUR?
덜컹
DULKUNG (SHAKE)
IT GOT REALLY DARK OUTSIDE ALL OF A SUDDEN.
덜컹
DULKUNG
......
THE GROUP THAT WENT TO THE LAKE STILL ISN'T BACK?
쏴아
SHAAAA (SHHHHH)
AH, ABOUT THAT...
콰당
KUWADANG (BAM)
EEEP~! WHAT THE HECK? WHAT'S UP WITH THIS RAIN?!!

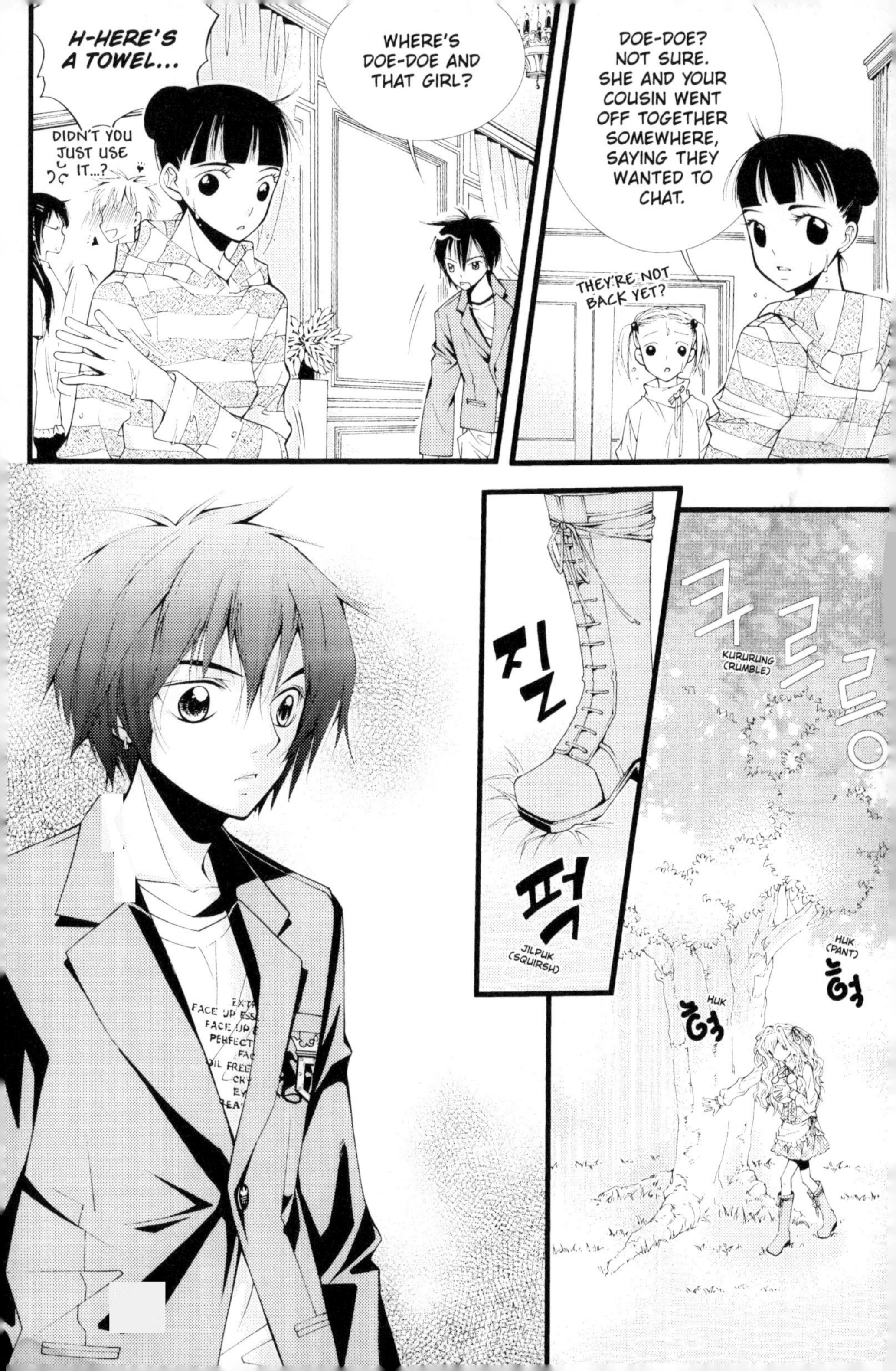
H-HERE'S A TOWEL...
DIDN'T YOU JUST USE IT...?
WHERE'S DOE-DOE AND THAT GIRL?
DOE-DOE? NOT SURE. SHE AND YOUR COUSIN WENT OFF TOGETHER SOMEWHERE, SAYING THEY WANTED TO CHAT.
THEY'RE NOT BACK YET?
질퍽
JILPUK (SQUIRSH)
쿠르릉
KURURUNG (RUMBLE)
헉
HUK
헉
HUK (PANT)

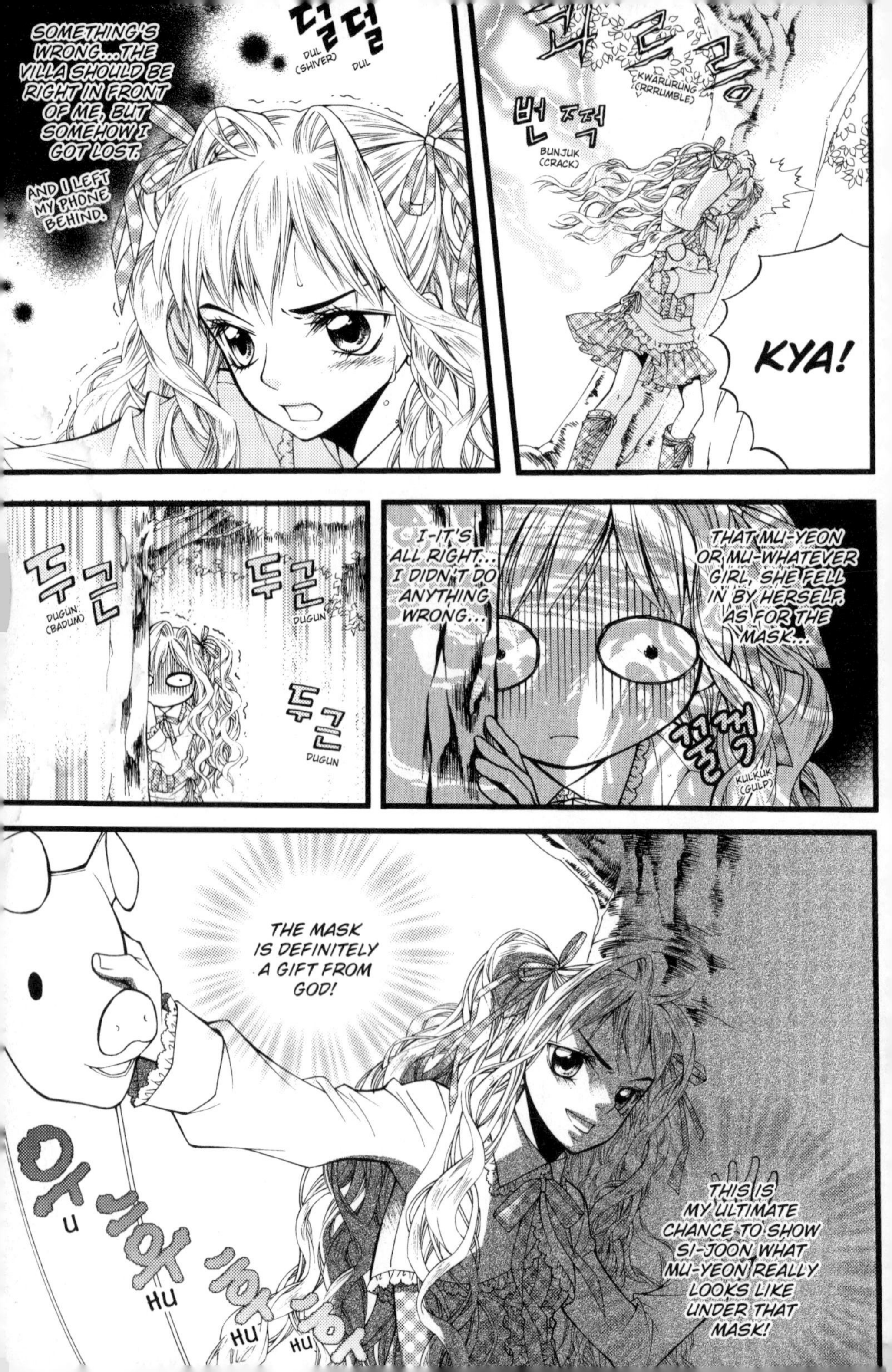

SOMETHING'S WRONG... THE VILLA SHOULD BE RIGHT IN FRONT OF ME, BUT SOMEHOW I GOT LOST.
AND I LEFT MY PHONE BEHIND.
덜덜
DUL (SHIVER) DUL
콰르릉
KWARURUNG (RRRUMBLE)
번쩍
BUNJUK (CRACK)
KYA!
두근
DUGUN (BADUM)
두근
DUGUN
두근
DUGUN
I-IT'S ALL RIGHT... I DIDN'T DO ANYTHING WRONG...
THAT MU-YEON OR MU-WHATEVER GIRL, SHE FELL IN BY HERSELF. AS FOR THE MASK...
꿀꺽
KULKUK (GULP)
THE MASK IS DEFINITELY A GIFT FROM GOD!
U
HU
HU
HU
THIS IS MY ULTIMATE CHANCE TO SHOW SI-JOON WHAT MU-YEON REALLY LOOKS LIKE UNDER THAT MASK!

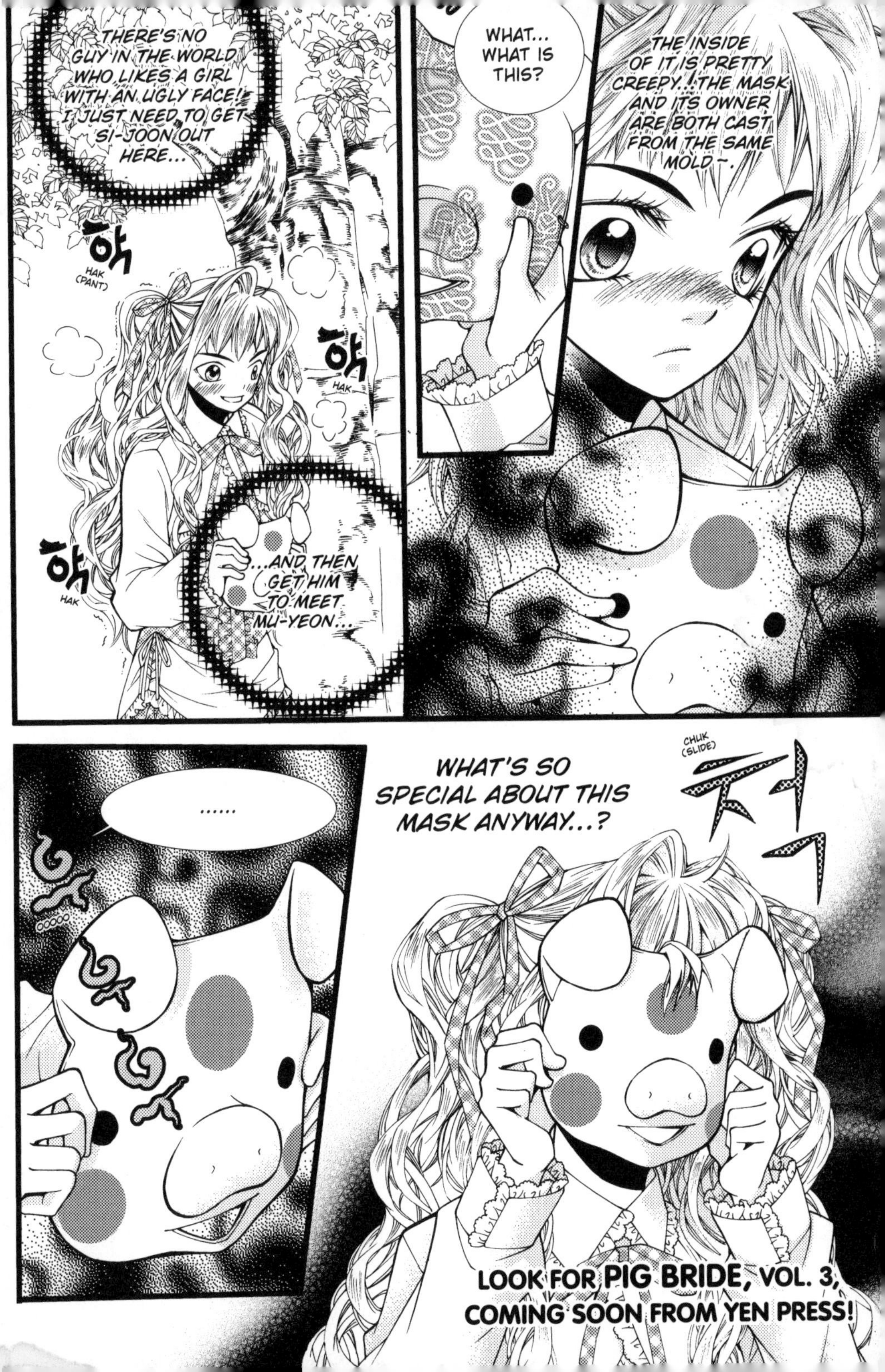
THERE'S NO GUY IN THE WORLD WHO LIKES A GIRL WITH AN UGLY FACE! I JUST NEED TO GET SI-JOON OUT HERE...
학
HAK (PANT)
학
HAK
학
HAK
...AND THEN GET HIM TO MEET MU-YEON...
WHAT... WHAT IS THIS?
THE INSIDE OF IT IS PRETTY CREEPY...! THE MASK AND ITS OWNER ARE BOTH CAST FROM THE SAME MOLD~.
......
OOOOO
WHAT'S SO SPECIAL ABOUT THIS MASK ANYWAY...?
CHUK (SLIDE)
LOOK FOR PIG BRIDE, VOL. 3, COMING SOON FROM YEN PRESS!

PIG BRIDE ②

KOOKHWA HUH
SUJIN KIM

Translation: Jackie Oh

Lettering: Erika T.

PIG BRIDE, Vol. 2 © 2007 KookHwa Huh & SuJin Kim. All rights reserved. First published in Korea in 2007 by Haksan Publishing Co., Ltd. English translation rights in U.S.A., Canada, UK, and Republic of Ireland arranged with Haksan Publishing Co., Ltd.

English translation © 2009 Hachette Book Group, Inc.

Yen Press
Hachette Book Group
237 Park Avenue, New York, NY 10017

Visit our Web sites at www.HachetteBookGroup.com and www.YenPress.com.

Yen Press is an imprint of Hachette Book Group, Inc. The Yen Press name and logo are trademarks of Hachette Book Group, Inc.

First Yen Press Edition: August 2009

ISBN: 978-0-7595-2955-7

10 9 8 7 6 5 4 3 2 1

BVG

Printed in the United States of America

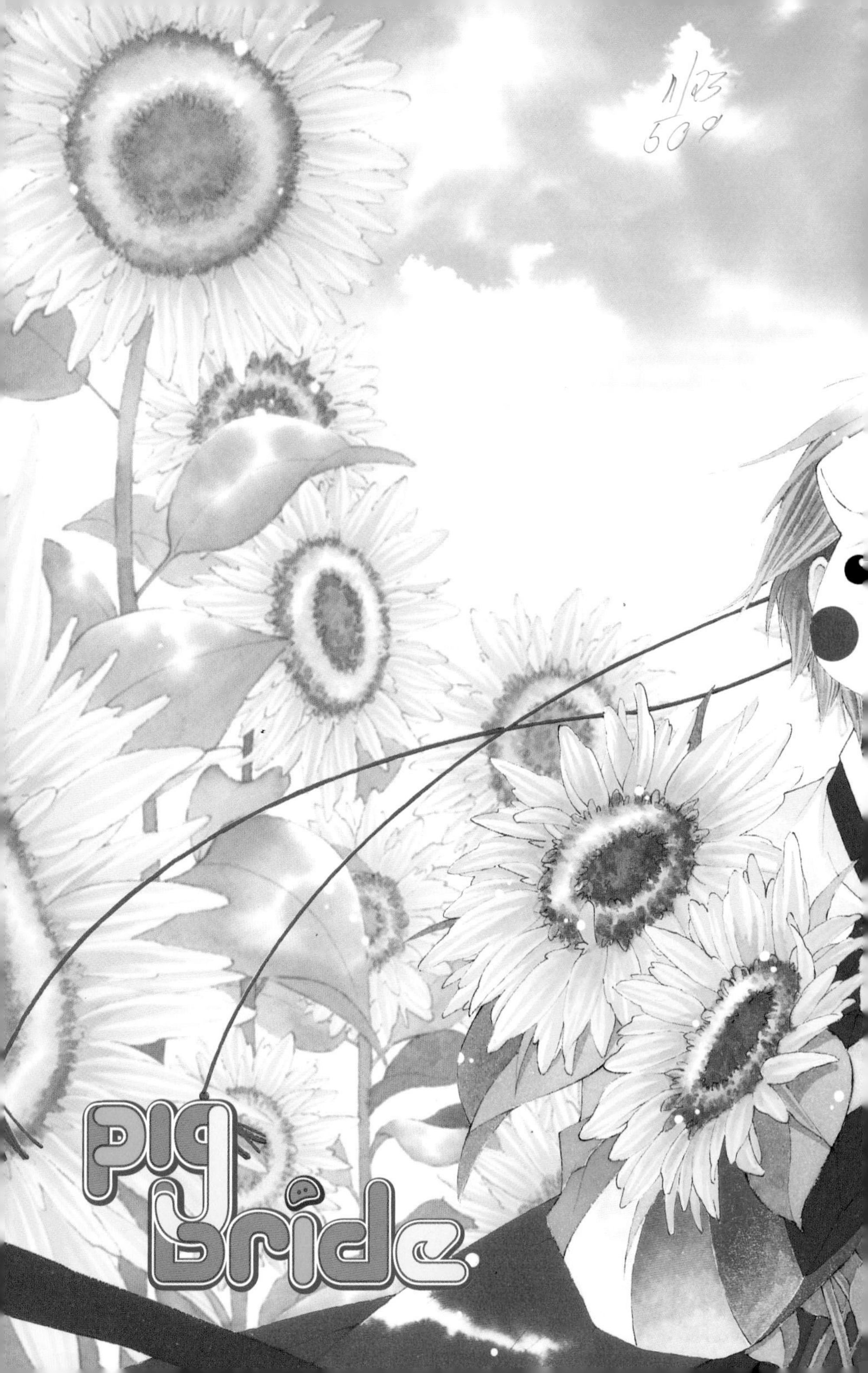
pig bride

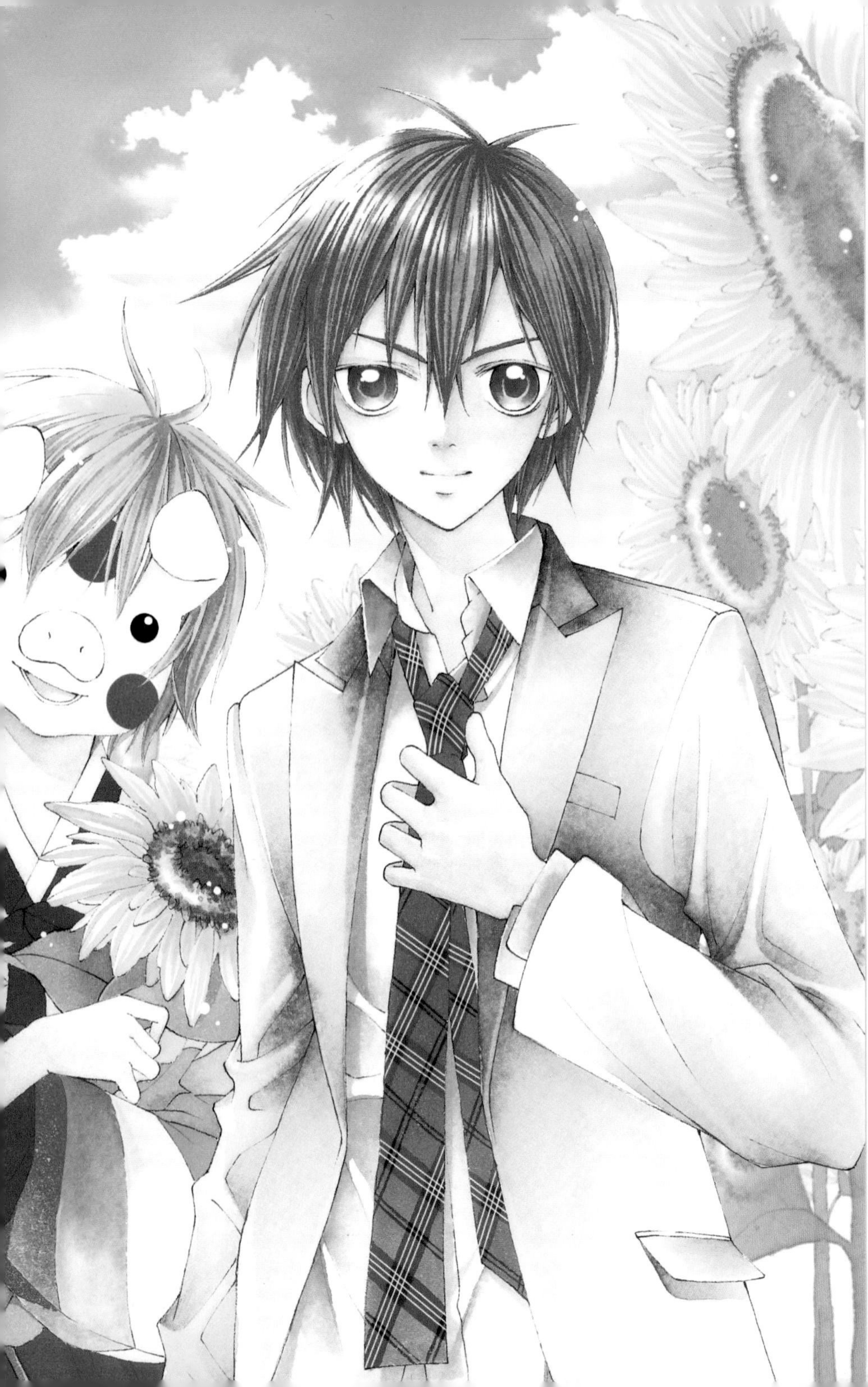